Britain Votes: The 2019 General Election

Edited by Jonathan Tonge, Stuart Wilks-Heeg and Louise Thompson

OXFORD
UNIVERSITY PRESS

in association with

HANSARD SOCIETY SERIES IN POLITICS
AND GOVERNMENT

OXFORD
UNIVERSITY PRESS

Great Clarendon Street, Oxford OX2 6DP, UK

Oxford University Press is a department of the University of Oxford.
It furthers the University's objective of excellence in research, scholarship,
and education by publishing worldwide in

Oxford New York

Athens Auckland Bangkok Bagotá Buenos Aires
Cape Town Chennai Dar es Salaam Delhi Florence Hong Kong Istanbul
Karachi Kuala Lumpur Madrid Melbourne Mexico City Mumbai
Nairobi Paris São Paulo Shanghai Singapore Taipei Tokyo Toronto Warsaw

and associated companies in
Berlin Ibadan

Oxford is a registered trade mark of Oxford University Press
in the UK and in certain other countries

Published in the United States
by Oxford University Press Inc., New York

A catalogue for this book is available from the British Library

Library of Congress Cataloging in Publication Data

ISBN 978-0-19-886983-2

Typeset by Cenveo publisher services, Bangalore, India
Printed in Great Britain by Bell & Bain Ltd, Glasgow, UK

Acknowledgements

We wish to thank many people for their help in producing *Britain Votes: the 2019 General Election*. We are extremely grateful to all the contributors for their hard work and adherence to deadlines. That the contributions of our colleagues were written amid the acute disruption of a global pandemic makes their efforts even more laudable than usual.

In addition to expressing our gratitude to the contributors, we wish to thank other individuals who offered considerable assistance. We are indebted to Dr Ruth Fox, the Director of the Hansard Society, for all her support for this and all the previous editions. Brigid Fowler and Luke Boga Mitchell have again been very helpful in checking the final manuscript.

Oxford University Press has always been a pleasure to deal with and we are particularly grateful to Alex Johnson, Dr Laura Jose, Katie Hellier, Katy Roberts, Katie Kent, Scott Healey, Jac Keron and Deepu H.R. for all their advice, hard work and patience.

Finally, we wish to thank our families for their forbearance in the time sacrifices involved in producing this volume.

Jonathan Tonge, Stuart Wilks-Heeg and Louise Thompson

Contributors and Editors

Mehmet Emin Bakir is a Research Associate in the Department of Computer Science at the University of Sheffield. He is a member of the Natural Language Processing Group and conducts research on social media, data mining and artificial intelligence.

Tim Bale is Professor of Politics at Queen Mary University of London where he specialises in British and European party politics. He is the author of numerous books and articles on both Labour and the Conservatives.

Jonathan Bradbury is Professor of Politics and Director of Research for the College of Arts and Humanities, Swansea University. He researches on statecraft, territorial politics and constitutional development, party strategies, public policy and representation. He is co-convenor of the UK Political Studies Association's Specialist Group on Territorial Politics.

Sir John Curtice is Professor of Politics at the University of Strathclyde and leads the team which analyses the exit poll at UK general elections. He is also President of the British Polling Council, Senior Research Fellow at NatCen Social Research and the UK in a Changing Europe, and Chief Commentator on the What UK Thinks: EU and What Scotland Thinks websites. His numerous publications include co-editorship of the annual British Social Attitudes report series since 1994 and journal articles on the Alternative Vote, Scottish independence, and EU membership referendums. Professor Curtice is a regular media commentator on both British and Scottish politics.

David Cutts is Professor in Political Science at the University of Birmingham. His specific areas of interest include political engagement, party and political campaigning, electoral behaviour and party politics, party competition and methods for modelling political behaviour. Professor Cutts has published numerous articles in leading journals including the *American Journal of Political Science*, *Journal of Politics*, *European Journal of Political Research* and the *British Journal of Political Science* and is co-writing a book on the Liberal Democrats, with Andrew Russell, for Manchester University Press.

James Dennison is a Researcher at the University of Stockholm, a part-time Professor at the European University Institute in Florence and a Visiting Scholar at the University of Harvard. His research interests include political attitudes and behaviour.

David Denver is Emeritus Professor of Politics at Lancaster University and the author of numerous publications on British elections and voting behaviour.

Katharine Dommett is Senior Lecturer in Politics at the University of Sheffield. Her research focuses on digital campaigning and the role of technology in democracies. She is currently serving as Special Advisor to the House of Lords Select Committee on Democracy and Digital Technologies and has recently been awarded the Political Studies Association's Richard Rose Prize for an early-career scholar who has made a distinctive contribution to British politics. In 2020 she published her book, *The Reimagined Party* and is the author of over 30 academic journal articles.

Jocelyn Evans is Professor of Politics at the University of Leeds. He has written widely on aspects of voting behaviour and political parties. He is editor, with Kai Arzheimer and Michael Lewis-Beck, of the *Handbook of Electoral Behaviour* (2 vols) Sage, 2017, and the author, with Gilles Ivaldi, of *The 2012 French Presidential Elections: The Inevitable Alternation* and *The 2017 French Presidential Elections: A Political Reformation?* Palgrave, 2018.

Justin Fisher is Professor of Political Science and Head of the Department of Social and Political Sciences at Brunel University London. He has been Principal Investigator of Economic and Social Research Council-funded studies of constituency campaigning at the 2010, 2015, 2017 and 2019 British general elections, and has published widely on party finance and elections more generally.

Matthew Flinders is Founding Director of the Sir Bernard Crick Centre and Professor of Politics at the University of Sheffield. He has worked as a special adviser in both the House of Commons and House of Lords, and his research focuses on governance, public policy, populism and political disaffection.

Eunice Goes is Professor of Politics at Richmond University and Visiting Research Fellow at the Portuguese Institute of International Relations. She is the, author of *The Labour Party Under Ed Miliband: Trying but Failing to Renew Social Democracy*, Manchester University Press, 2016.

Emily Harmer is Lecturer in Media at the University of Liverpool. Her research analyses the relationship between media and politics, with a specific interest in gendered political communication. Emily is co-convener of the UK Political Studies Association's Media and Politics Specialist Group and Assistant Editor of the *European Journal of Communication*.

Sarah Harrison is the Deputy Director of the Electoral Psychology Observatory. She is an Assistant Professorial Research Fellow in the Department of Government at the LSE and is a specialist in the field of electoral psychology, extreme right politics, and youth political behaviour. Her recent publications include *Inside the Mind of a Voter* (Princeton University Press, with Michael Bruter) and her research has been recognised by prestigious awards and honourable mentions from the Economic and Social Research Council, the Michael Young Award, and the political psychology section of the American Political Science Association.

Ailsa Henderson is Professor of Political Science at the University of Edinburgh and Principal Investigator of the Scottish Election Study.

James Mitchell holds the Chair in Public Policy at the University of Edinburgh and is the author of numerous publications on Scottish politics.

Sam Power is Lecturer at the University of Sussex. His research focuses on political parties, political financing, online campaigns and corruption. He is the author of *Party Funding and Corruption*, Palgrave, 2020.

Andrew Russell is Professor and Head of Politics at the University of Liverpool. He is best known for writing about political parties and marginalized communities – which he sometimes combines by writing about the British Liberal Democrats. During the 2019 general election he was a featured expert on The North Poll election podcast and he continued to work on BBC Radio 5 Live's *Political Ideas Phone-in* - the political broadcasting flagship of the prestigious 01:30 to 3:00am Monday morning slot.

Rosalynd Southern is a Lecturer in Political Communication at the University of Liverpool. Her research focuses on political communication during election campaigns, particularly online. More recently she has studied how voters use social media to communicate politically via her work on the iBES module of the British Election Study. In addition to this, she has conducted research on female politicians and their use of, and treatment by, various media.

Louise Thompson is Senior Lecturer in Politics at the University of Manchester. Her research focuses on the UK Parliament, particularly the legislative process and the role of political parties. Her publications include *Exploring Parliament* Oxford University Press 2018, with Cristina Leston-Bandeira and *The End of the Small Party?* Manchester University Press, 2020.

Jonathan Tonge is Professor of Politics at the University of Liverpool. He was Principal Investigator of the 2010, 2015, 2017 and 2019 Economic and Social Research Council Northern Ireland general election surveys and co-author of books on the DUP and UUP, with Oxford University Press, and on Sinn Féin and the SDLP, with Hurst. He has co-edited volumes on each UK general election since 1997.

Stephen Ward is a Reader in Politics at the University of Salford. His research focuses on the role of the internet and social media in parties, election campaigning and political participation.

Paul Webb is Professor of Politics at the University of Sussex and editor of the journal *Party Politics*.

Stuart Wilks-Heeg is Reader in Politics at the University of Liverpool. His research focuses primarily on British politics and he was also co-editor of Britain Votes 2017. He is particularly known for his work on electoral administration and electoral integrity and, during 2019-20, he served as a specialist adviser to the House of Lords Select Committee on the Electoral Registration and Administration Act 2011. Stuart is also a trustee of the Political Studies Association.

Dominic Wring is Professor of Political Communication at Loughborough University where he co-directed the 2019 general election media analysis project (https://blog.lboro.ac.uk/crcc/general-election/). He was lead editor of *Political Communication in Britain: Campaigning, Media and Polling in the 2017 General Election* (Palgrave, 2019) and is working on another volume in this series devoted to the 2019 campaign.

CONTENTS

List of figures and tables

Figures

Tables

Britain Votes (2019) 1–6

JONATHAN TONGE, STUART WILKS-HEEG AND LOUISE THOMPSON[*]

Introduction: A Conservative Victory Like No Other?

The 2019 general election was another extraordinary chapter in a series of dramatic recent contests. Yet, given the consistent story from opinion pollsters (who had a good election) the extent of apparent wonderment at the broadcasters' exit poll (enjoying another outstanding election) on election night was itself remarkable. A resounding Conservative majority was always a strong possibility. This was a mini-landslide forewarned—and in considerable detail. YouGov's multi-level regression with post-stratification forecasts had catalogued the likely geography of Labour's disaster.[1] Nonetheless, the shock of the 2017 mislaying of the Conservatives' majority by Theresa May loomed large over the election 30 months later, until that exit poll moment when the scale of the rout of Labour was revealed. Few had seriously doubted that the Conservatives under Boris Johnson would win the most seats; just not that many. In the weeks before the

---

[*]Jonathan Tonge, Department of Politics, University of Liverpool, j.tonge@liverpool.ac.uk; Stuart Wilks-Heeg, Department of Politics, University of Liverpool, swilks@liverpool.ac.uk; Louise Thompson, Politics, School of Social Sciences, University of Manchester, louise.thompson-4@manchester.ac.uk

[1]In 2017, YouGov pioneered the use of multi-level regression with post-stratification (MRP) to forecast a UK general election outcome, correctly predicting a hung parliament when virtually all conventional opinion polls pointed to a large Conservative majority. In contrast to opinion polls that estimate party shares of the vote from a representative sample of around 1,000 people, MRP forecasts use samples of tens of thousands of electors in combination with other data sources to estimate the number of seats each party will win. Under MRP, polling data are first modelled using numerous individual-level socio-demographic characteristics to estimate the probability of different groups of people voting for a party (multi-level regression). These probabilities are then applied to the socio-demographic make-ups of each individual constituency and weighted for other factors such as past voting patterns in that locality (post-stratification). In 2019,' MRP' entered the mainstream of the general election lexicon. The publication of YouGov's MRP forecast, in late November, was eagerly awaited and its central forecast was a Conservative majority of 68 (a subsequent iteration closer to the election revised this down to 28). In a notable development, political parties also produced their own MRP forecasts to inform their campaign strategies – see Fisher, this volume.

doi:10.1093/pa/gsaa020

election, some commentators even speculated on the possibility of Jeremy Corbyn as Prime Minister, leading a minority rainbow government backed by virtually all the non-Conservative parliamentary forces (Finkelstein, 2019). The election night pre-exit poll forecasts of Boris Johnson and his team, while reflecting confidence in victory, all anticipated triumph by a smaller margin (Shipman, 2019).

The scale of the Conservative victory, producing the UK's first majority government for almost a decade, was quite something. For Labour, suffering a fall in vote share not far shy of 8%, the scale of the catastrophe is apparent when one remembers that 14 of the party's seat losses occurred in constituencies held at every election since 1945—part of the collapse of the fabled 'red wall' of Labour strongholds, in which a majority had voted to leave the EU in 2016. The geographical parameters of this 'red wall' were imprecise. The term tended to be used most often in respect of seats in northern England which had been held by Labour for decades but was readily extended to similarly hitherto loyal Labour seats in the Midlands. Here, the scale of the move against Labour in long-time loyal seats such as Bassetlaw, which saw an 18% swing to the Conservatives, was remarkable. Yet, there was also a reasonable case for including solid Labour seats in north Wales as part of the 'red wall', as Jonathan Bradbury suggests in this volume.

The Conservatives increased their vote share and seats, unprecedented for a party seeking a fourth consecutive term in office. In most of the constituencies captured it was a case of the Labour vote share plummeting, rather than the Conservatives' vote share increasing by much. That, if anything, highlights the problems which confronted Labour more than it demonstrates hollowness in the Conservative victory.

Following Johnson's election as party leader in July 2019, the Conservatives had much sharper definition as the party of Brexit than under Theresa May. This is ironic given that May voted consistently in the Commons for Brexit, whereas Johnson did so only once. Johnson's repeated assertions that May's 'Brexit with a Backstop' (to keep Northern Ireland's land border seamless) was the wrong type of EU departure were tactical. They looked hollow when he, upon elevation to the top job, quickly accepted what May had endorsed, dumping her awkward allies, the Democratic Unionist Party (DUP) in the process. The course was now set for Brexit to be delivered. If parliament continued to stall such a move, an election would be called, based upon Brexit delivery.

Polling evidence suggested two key things. First, most voters had not changed their mind on Brexit (Curtice, 2020). Secondly, the Conservatives would win an election. Although Johnson's election gambit initially met with hesitation from Labour, Corbyn's party could hardly be seen to be ever running away from a contest. As such, they acquiesced. A more sensible electoral strategy for Labour might possibly—it's difficult to argue more strongly—have been to let Johnson struggle on, in office but barely in power in respect of Brexit and with the goodwill of a honeymoon period likely to fade.

Given Johnson's Brexiteer credentials and the likelihood of him delivering the 2016 referendum verdict, the Conservatives unsurprisingly monopolised the Leave vote. The only other major player in that field, Nigel Farage's Brexit Party, an easy winner of the 2019 European elections, stood aside in Conservative-held seats at the general election. Given the scale of the winning margin, it was clearly not a case of Farage acting as midwife to the delivery of Conservative election success. Nonetheless, there is evidence that Nigel Farage's Brexit outriders offered a very modest boost. Where the Brexit Party stood, Labour's vote fell by 8.6%, compared to 7.3% with the Brexiteers absent. The rise in the Conservatives' vote averaged only 1.7% in constituencies with the Brexit Party present, compared to 2.5% elsewhere (Norris, 2019). Thus, Labour's average percentage vote share was harmed nearly twice as much as was the Conservatives' by the presence of Farage's party.

For the Prime Minister, his chief adviser, Dominic Cummings and election campaign manager, Isaac Levido, the outcome vindicated offering only a small core set of promises, dominated by the pithy appeal to 'Get Brexit Done'. The slogan appeared to offer closure—of a sort—to a saga which had bedevilled UK politics since the June 2016 referendum. Having seen the fate of his predecessors, David Cameron and Theresa May, Johnson's approach was simple; cut through the confusion; cast aside erstwhile allies; deliver on the instruction from voters; and leave the EU. The details of a trade deal seemingly unlikely to be advantageous to the UK could be sorted later. How a trading bloc of 66 million would achieve better terms by quitting one of over 500 million remained unexplained. Johnson calculated, correctly, that a combination of the satisfaction of the pro-Brexit demands of the committed; the end of the affair for the weary; the lack of desire for the second referendum offered by Labour and the split in the Remain vote, would allow the Conservatives to chart a course for victory. It came to pass. The Conservatives gained 56 seats that had voted to leave the EU in 2016. Labour lost 53 such constituencies.

Johnson's shrewd political judgement was, however, greatly abetted in its success, by the shortcomings of the leader of the Labour Party. Jeremy Corbyn entered the 2019 election with the worst ratings of any party leader in British political history. Having trailed Theresa May on the 'who would make the best Prime Minister?' question throughout her period in office, Corbyn found himself even further behind Johnson, despite the new Prime Minister's ratings being only modest. Corbyn's mandate from his party was manifestly large and had been confirmed twice but it had not eased the concerns of many within Labour's parliamentary ranks that their leader could not win an election. Meanwhile, Johnson, although confronted by a difficult political in-tray on assuming the top job - one soon to become much worse - had a clear mandate from his parliamentarians and his party membership in his elevation. His internal control of his party appeared even more assured after the election. The Conservative parliamentary ranks were infused by new blood: 30% of its 2019 intake were Commons freshers. Johnson was entitled to take the view that many would not have arrived had it not been for him— although one might reasonably assert that Jeremy Corbyn also assisted their passage.

The plan of the volume

This volume analyses the 2019 general election by dissecting its context, results, parties, finances, geography and media. The analysis is divided into four sections: results and context, political parties, territorial dimensions and election themes.

To begin the first section, David Denver outlines the election results and discusses how the opinion polls consistently pointed to a denouement involving a clear Conservative victory. That outcome is considered by Sir John Curtice in the broader context of whether a large overall majority represented a return to normality within our electoral system, after a decade of hung parliaments or narrow majorities. Does the outcome indicate that overall majorities are likely to be the norm once more or was this in some sense an exceptional result? That overall majority was a response to frustration with political stalemate and Louise Thompson contextualises the election in examining the parliamentary impasse that yielded such a decisive election result.

Section two's examination of the campaigns of the political parties begins with Sam Power, Tim Bale and Paul Webb exploring the Conservatives' approach. They note how a tight campaign swerved potential dangers. Although Boris Johnson could be regarded as a potential asset, he was also high risk and it was decided to run a carefully controlled campaign, averting dangerous confrontations. The journalist, Andrew Neil, was left without a BBC interview with the Conservative leader. Beyond the endless insistence upon getting Brexit done, the Conservatives emphasised that the age of austerity and its attendant fiscal rules were in the rear-view mirror. Borrowing was permissible.

Eunice Goes examines Labour's campaign, which lacked the verve and mobilisation of 2017 as it charted a course towards a record-equalling fourth consecutive defeat. The lack of confidence within Labour's ranks was displayed on Jeremy Corbyn's campaign trail. Many of the seats visited by the Labour leader were already held by his party. The concern for the 76 Labour-held seats with a majority of less than 8,000 over the Conservatives was apparent. Goes analyses the impacts of Brexit, Corbyn and anti-Semitism, a negative triple whammy, upon Labour's performance.

David Cutts and Andrew Russell assess the performance of another party which, from a very different perspective from the Conservatives, at least offered clarity on Brexit. The Liberal Democrats' 2019 decision to simply revoke Article 50 and cancel EU withdrawal drew accolades among the fellow-travellers at the party conference three months before the election. It also contributed to the Liberal Democrats becoming more exclusively a party backed by 2016 Remain voters—but not many of them and very few beyond. More broadly, the public had little knowledge of what else the Liberal Democrats stood for (see also Curtice 2019). This inability to harness the Remain vote placed the prospect of 'Jo Swinson – our next Prime Minister', as trumpeted on party leaflets, look on the implausible, even ludicrous, side of optimism.

James Dennison examines the smaller parties, assessing the significance of the decision by Nigel Farage's Brexit Party not to contest any of the 317 seats won by the Conservatives at the 2017 election. The Brexit Party offered a possible electoral repository for Labour Leave voters who could neither bring themselves to vote Conservative nor back a Labour Party led by Jeremy Corbyn. Dennison also examines the modest progress, in vote share at least, of the Greens, under their Remain Alliance with the Liberal Democrats and Plaid Cymru, noting that a sizeable minority of the Green vote had previously voted Labour. This section also considers the brief life of Change UK, the main changes wrought by its defectors from the Labour and Conservative parties being the regular ones to the new party's name.

Section three's consideration of the election in the devolved nations begins with the analysis of Scotland by James Mitchell and Ailsa Henderson. As a pro-Remain party with a monopoly of a large pro-independence vote, the SNP was always likely to do well and so it transpired. The Conservatives' attempt to harness the anti-independence majority was ranged against their minority status as a pro-Leave party, toned down where possible for Scottish consumption but unhelpful. Meanwhile, Labour struggled to define itself via either constitutional question. In Leave-voting Wales, Jonathan Bradbury analyses how and why Labour struggled to hold part of its 'natural' territory, conceding long-held seats in the north of the country and suffering losses in vote shares throughout. Northern Ireland's concerns over Brexit led to election pacts which also took on a nationalist (anti-Brexit) versus unionist (pro-Brexit, albeit not on British Johnson's terms) flavour. As Jonathan Tonge and Jocelyn Evans note, however, detachment from unionism and nationalism helped the Alliance Party, also anti-Brexit but opposed to Remain pacts, to make strides. The DUP and Sinn Féin were punished for the failure to restore the power-sharing Northern Ireland Assembly, a problem rectified within one month of the election.

The fourth section covers various important aspects of the campaign, analysing some of its target recipients. In *Britain Votes 2017*, Justin Fisher noted how, despite being the party of government calling the snap election, the Conservative party machine was under-prepared. He outlines how this was not the case in 2019, with the Conservatives much better prepared for an early election, organisationally and financially. Katharine Dommett and Mehmet Emin Bakir examine how that preparation played out online, noting how both the Conservative and Labour parties invested heavily in Facebook advertising. Matthew Flinders' analysis of the campaign notes how *all* political leaders were trying to overcome a lack of trust in them among the electorate. In that respect, Corbyn's problems were acute but not isolated. Sarah Harrison considers these democratic frustrations among young voters and, notwithstanding a propensity to vote for alternatives to the prevailing Conservative government, does not find an exceptional level of disillusionment. Her findings highlight concerns that the problem is the democratic journey. The targeting of the campaign at women is assessed by Emily Harmer and Rosalynd Southern. Party manifestos concentrated their gendered concerns in familiar areas. The authors note, however, significant improvements in representation, with Labour and the Liberal Democrats now having more female MPs than male. Finally, Dominic Wring and Stephen Ward assess the role of the traditional media, noting that the press still matters as its older readership are likely to vote. They also observe how the backing of many newspapers for the Conservatives was the most gung-ho for some time.

Our concluding analysis assesses the relative importance of the key aspects of the election; Johnson's elevation to the Conservative leadership in the summer; the promise to 'Get Brexit Done', the failures of the Labour opposition under Corbyn and the apparent hubris of the Liberal Democrats. The sum of the parts was a victory which surprised in terms of its scale but not its victor.

References

Curtice, J. (2019) 'After "Stop Brexit", the Public Draws a Blank on Lib Dem Policies', *The Times*, 6 December.

Curtice, J. (2020) 'Brave New World: Understanding the 2019 General Election', *Political Insight*, **11**, 8–12.

Finkelstein, D. (2019) 'Corbyn Doesn't Need to Win to Become PM', *The Times*, 6 November.

Norris, P. (2019) 'Divided we Fall: Was Nigel Farage the Kingmaker of the Johnson Victory?'. In Jackson, D., Thorsen, E., Lilleker, D. and Weidhase, N. (eds.) *UK Election Analysis 2019: Media, Voters and the Campaign*, Bournemouth, Centre for Comparative Politics and Media Research, pp. 38–39.

Shipman, T. (2019) 'Sedgefield Fell and They Erupted into Song – Things Can Only Get Better', *Sunday Times*, 15 December.

DAVID DENVER[*]

The Results: How Britain Voted

Unlike the situation in 2017, the calling of the 2019 general election did not take the country by surprise. Boris Johnson had succeeded Theresa May as Prime Minister in July and formed a government avowedly committed to exiting the European Union (EU) as soon as possible. However, parliament had repeatedly frustrated all previous attempts to do so and the chances of MPs passing an act to implement a withdrawal agreement were slim. When parliament reconvened in September, therefore, the government twice introduced motions to allow an early general election to be held under the terms of the Fixed-term Parliaments Act. This required the support of two-thirds of MPs but on both occasions the numbers voting for an election fell well short of this.

By mid-October, Johnson had successfully negotiated a new—if not dramatically different—Brexit deal with the EU and the relevant withdrawal agreement bill passed its second reading on the 22nd of the month. Any hopes that this meant that the end to the Brexit saga was in sight were quickly dispelled, however, as the House immediately rejected the proposed timetable for further consideration of the bill. Another attempt to force a general election was made on Monday 28 October but once again failed to obtain the votes necessary. Next day, however, the government sought to circumvent the Fixed-term Parliaments Act by bringing forward a short bill declaring that there would be an election on 12 December. This required only a simple majority to pass and the Liberal Democrats and Scottish National Party (SNP) indicated their support. Since this made a majority inevitable, Labour reversed its position of the day before and also voted for an election. Once again, the Fixed-term Parliaments Act had been shown to be a flawed piece of constitutional tinkering and the country embarked on its first December general election since 1923.

1. The inter-election cycle of party support

After the 2017 election, the government's agenda and the political scene generally were dominated by a single issue to an extent never before seen in peacetime—

[*]David Denver, Department of Politics, Philosophy and Religion, Lancaster University, d.denver@lancaster.ac.uk

doi:10.1093/pa/gsaa037

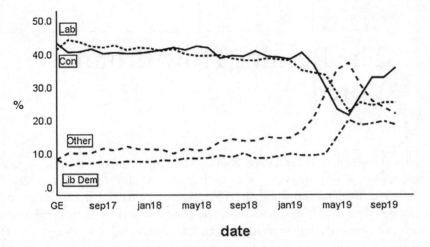

Figure 1.1 Trends in party support, July 2017–October 2019
Note: The data shown are the mean monthly voting intentions in published polls reported by Anthony Wells on his *UK Polling Report* website.

whether and how the UK should exit the EU in line with the result of the 2016 referendum (i.e. 'Brexit'). Despite failing to make much progress on this process, the Conservatives enjoyed fairly steady support for a year before dipping slightly in the second half of 2018 (Figure 1.1). However, the so-called 'Chequers meeting' in July of that year, at which Mrs May informed her cabinet of her proposed post-Brexit relationship with the EU, proved a significant turning point for the party. Having previously been encouraged by her assertion that 'no deal for Britain is better than a bad deal for Britain', Brexiteers were now appalled by her proposals. Shortly after the meeting, David Davis and Boris Johnson (respectively Brexit Secretary, and Foreign Secretary) resigned along with two junior ministers, two vice-chairs of the Conservative party and four parliamentary private secretaries. Four months later, when the final proposed withdrawal agreement was revealed, more resignations from the government followed. The rallying cry of the European Research Group (ERG) of Eurosceptic Conservative backbenchers was now 'Chuck Chequers'.

In early December, the House of Commons was due to hold a 'meaningful vote' on the agreement but at the last moment this was postponed by the Prime Minister, claiming that she would seek changes from the EU. On the next day, Conservative malcontents (led by the ERG) gathered enough support to initiate a vote of confidence in Mrs May as Conservative leader. She managed to win the ensuing vote by 200 votes to 117 but was obviously seriously weakened.

The withdrawal deal that the Prime Minister had negotiated with the EU finally came before the House of Commons in January 2019 and was defeated by a

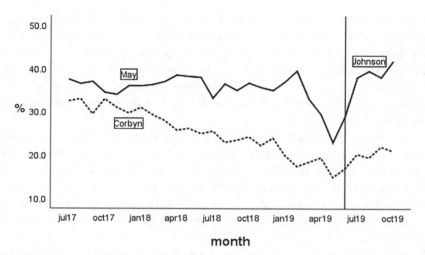

Figure 1.2 Best person for Prime Minister, July 2017–October 2019
Source: YouGov.

historic margin—432 to 202. There followed a chaotic period in parliament which included numerous further defeats for the government and the abandonment of the original date set for withdrawal from the EU (29 March). Unsurprisingly, support for the Conservatives declined sharply (Figure 1.1) and the proportion of poll respondents preferring Mrs May as Prime Minister nosedived (Figure 1.2).

Meanwhile, the Labour party had problems of its own. Following its unexpectedly good performance in 2017 support for the party drifted steadily downwards to the end of 2018. Doubts about the party leader, Jeremy Corbyn, as a potential Prime Minister re-emerged—at no point during this period did he lead Mrs May as the electorate's preferred occupant of 10 Downing Street (Figure 1.2). More specifically, there was discontent over the leadership's handling of Brexit and accusations that anti-Semitism had infected the party, with Jewish Labour MPs being subject to abuse by party members, and that these cases had not been adequately dealt with.

As a consequence of these developments, in February 2019 seven Labour MPs resigned the Labour whip and formed what they called 'The Independent Group'. They were shortly joined by another Labour MP and three Conservative Remainers. By April the 'TIGS', as they were swiftly christened, had become a registered party named 'Change UK – The Independent Group'.

More worryingly for the Conservatives, a spectre from the past also re-emerged at this time in the person of Nigel Farage and the Brexit Party he co-founded. He was joined by most of UKIP's MEPs and indicated that the party would contest the forthcoming European Parliament elections which the government was forced to hold due to its failure to leave the EU by the appointed date. The impact on the electorate was immediate and striking. As Figure 1.1 shows, support for 'others', mainly the Brexit party which drew level with the Conservatives by April, increased rapidly. Voters who had previously been inclined towards UKIP now flocked to the new party as the former staggered from one internal crisis to another.

The opinion poll results were reflected in local elections held across England in early May. Of the 248 councils involved, the Conservatives lost control of 44 and Labour of six. In the process, the former lost 1,330 seats and the latter 84. Although UKIP also lost ground, the gainers were the Liberal Democrats (+704 seats), Independents (+605) and Greens (+194). The BBC's 'projected national vote share' was 28% for both the Conservatives and Labour, 19% for the Liberal Democrats and 25% for others. The Liberal Democrats and Greens tried to claim that the elections represented a success for anti-Brexit forces but, although this may have played a part, it seems more likely that many voters were simply going for 'anyone but the big two'.

After these bad results, Conservative calls for Mrs May's resignation grew even louder and, if any further evidence that she could not carry on was needed, this was provided by the results of the European Parliament elections in late May. These shattered any notion that the 2017 general election had heralded a return to stable two-party politics in Britain as they were simply disastrous for both major parties. The Conservatives came fifth with only 9.1% of the votes in Great Britain—their worst performance in a national election since 1832; Labour managed just 14.1%—the party's worst showing since 1910. In Scotland, Labour contrived to come fifth in votes and won no seats. The Liberal Democrats (20.3%) and the Greens (12.1%) did well but it was the newly-formed Brexit party which topped the poll with 31.6%. The latter led in every English region outside London, as well as in Wales, and even managed to win a seat in Scotland where it came second (14.8%), albeit a long way behind the SNP (on 37.8%). On the other hand, the other new party that had emerged—Change UK—sank virtually without trace and six of its 11 MPs resigned from the party shortly afterwards. The Prime Minister herself announced her imminent resignation on 24 May.

In the Conservative leadership election which followed, the contestants were quickly whittled down to two—Boris Johnson and Jeremy Hunt—and in the run-off party members gave the former two-thirds of the 139,000 votes cast. Thus, in late July Johnson became the third Conservative Prime Minister in the space of three years. The change of personnel produced an immediate fillip in support for the Conservatives (Figure 1.1) although Labour also benefitted a little as the popularity of the Brexit party declined from its June peak and the Liberal Democrat advance stalled.

Despite continuing difficulties with Remainers in his party, which resulted in a number having the whip withdrawn, Johnson's Conservatives embarked on the 2019 campaign enjoying a clear lead over their rivals. He also quickly opened up a commanding lead over Jeremy Corbyn as the electorate's preferred Prime Minister (Figure 1.2) although his support in this respect never exceeded 45% and his situation did not appear as rosy as Theresa May's had been at the start of the 2017 campaign.

The surprise announcement of an early election in 2017 had contributed to a sharp fall in the number of candidates nominated across Great Britain (the situation in Northern Ireland is discussed in a separate chapter) to 3,195. There was little change in 2019, however, with 3,218 coming forward. As usual, the Conservatives and Labour contested all but the (new) Speaker's seat and the SNP all Scottish constituencies. However, the Liberal Democrats, Greens and Plaid Cymru agreed not to oppose one another in 60 seats—a tactic which had denied the Conservatives victory in the Brecon and Radnorshire by-election in August 2019—and there were, therefore, 611 Liberal Democrat candidates and 36 for Plaid. The number of Green Party candidates increased from 460 to 494 while, having eventually decided not to oppose sitting Conservatives, the Brexit party contested 275 seats. Among the assorted 'others' who, according to taste, enliven or add unnecessary clutter to the British electoral scene, by far the largest group comprised Independents (223, including six in Boris Johnson's constituency) followed by UKIP with 31 (down from 614 in 2015 and 379 in 2017). A reminder of earlier political times—and confirmation that hope springs eternal in some breasts—is provided by the fact that more than 30 years after the two parties merged there were 19 candidates representing the Liberal Party and the same number carrying the flag for the Social Democratic Party (SDP).

2. Trends in party support during the 'short' campaign

In some ways, the trends in party support during the 2019 campaign resembled those witnessed in 2017 (Figure 1.3).

In both cases, Labour's position improved steadily while the Liberal Democrats and others declined. In 2019, over the six weeks involved, the Liberal Democrats fell from the mid-to-high teens to around 12% of voting intentions while the Brexit party—the most significant of the others in the British context at the outset—slid from around 10% to about 3%, rendering it close to insignificance. The main difference between the two campaigns concerns the Conservatives. In 2017 their campaign was singularly inept. Their manifesto included controversial proposals relating to social care for the elderly and its launch produced an immediate change in the mood of the electorate. At the same time Theresa May, then Prime Minister, proved to be a poor performer on the national

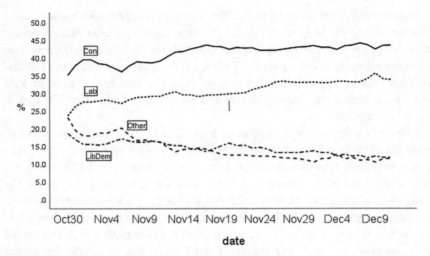

Figure 1.3 Trends in voting intentions during the 'short' campaign
Note: The data are three-day moving averages of polls reported by Mark Pack (https://www.markpack.org.uk/155623/voting-intention-opinion-poll-scorecard/).

campaign stage and was widely ridiculed as 'robotic'. On this occasion the Conservative manifesto (and, indeed, the whole campaign strategy) was ultra-cautious, while Johnson appeared affable and energetic, constantly reiterating that his aim was simply to 'Get Brexit Done' while avoiding potential 'car crash' moments such as a televised interview with the BBC's Andrew Neil. On the other side, it was apparent that Mr Corbyn was not attracting the same enthusiastic audiences that he had in 2017. The consequence was that although Labour's standing improved over the campaign so too did that of the Conservatives. On the basis of the data used to construct Figure 1.3 the latter's lead over their main opponents fell below ten points on only 13 of the 43 days involved.

Four of these cases occurred in the last week of the campaign. This, no doubt, encouraged optimists in Labour quarters hoping that the 'miracle' of 2017 could be repeated while, perhaps indicating some Conservative panic, a *Daily Telegraph* headline (11 December 2019) warned that the election was 'on a knife edge'. Unfortunately for the headline writers, of the 12 polling firms which produced fi-nal predictions, the one used by the *Telegraph* (Savanta Com Res) was the least accurate, underestimating the Conservatives' vote share by 5 points and overesti-mating that of Labour by 3. Nonetheless, the averages for all the final polls (Conservative 43.3%, Labour 33.5% and Liberal Democrats 11.6%) suggested that the Conservatives were on course for a clear victory.

In Scotland, meanwhile, five campaign polls indicated that the SNP was set to improve upon its 2017 performance (averaging 42% of voting intentions) mainly at the expense of Labour. The latter (average 18%) consistently lagged in third place, well behind the Conservatives (28%). In Wales, in contrast, two commercial polls published once the campaign was in full swing reported that Plaid Cymru was making no headway and that, although Labour was losing support, it continued to be the most popular party.

Despite the solid Conservative lead predicted by the Britain-wide polls, commentators were chary of extrapolating from voting intention figures to guessing what the election outcome might be in terms of seats in the House of Commons. In part this reflected the fact that in 2017 all the polls had seriously underestimated Labour's performance but there were also worries about the potential impact of the Brexit Party and the possible extent and nature of tactical voting, which were difficult to be sure about in advance of the results. However, the much vaunted 'Multiple Regression and Post-Stratification' model developed by YouGov, which had proved spectacularly successful in 2017, finally predicted an overall Conservative majority of 28 seats, although the relevant report was hedged about with numerous cautionary warnings. In the event, the Conservatives far out-performed expectations in this respect.

3. The national result

For the fourth successive election, the eagerly-awaited announcement of the results of the BBC/ITN/Sky exit poll, made as soon as voting was over, provoked emotions of elation, consternation and anguish among the various partisans although, on this occasion, there were few expressions of outright disbelief. The poll predicted a Conservative majority of 86 seats in the House of Commons with the party taking 368 constituencies to 191 for Labour, 55 for the SNP and 13 for the Liberal Democrats. As Table 1.1 shows, the final

Table 1.1 Share of votes and number of seats won (Great Britain) and changes from 2017

	Share of votes (%)	Change 2017–2019	Number of seats	Change 2017–2019
Conservative	44.7	+1.3	365	+48
Labour	32.9	−8.1	202	−60
Liberal Democrat	11.8	+4.2	11	−1
Green	2.8	+1.1	1	0
Brexit	2.1	—	0	—
SNP/Plaid Cymru	4.5	+0.9	52	+13
Other	1.2	−1.5	1	0

Note: The Speaker, who was not opposed by the Conservatives, Labour or Liberal Democrats, is treated as an 'Other'.

Labour total was slightly underestimated but the party nonetheless ended up with 60 seats fewer than in 2017.

The SNP performance was less dramatic than the exit poll suggested but it racked up 48 of the 59 seats in Scotland (while Plaid Cymru retained its four seats in Wales). The actual Conservative majority over all others was 80 seats—easily enough to guarantee five years in government barring some unforeseen catastrophe.

In terms of vote share, the Conservatives improved somewhat on their 2017 tally but Labour fell back sharply, giving an overall 'swing' of 4.7% from the latter to the former. This was the second largest swing between the two parties since 1997 (the largest, 5.1%, having been seen in 2010). Under their new leader, Jo Swinson, the Liberal Democrats achieved a healthy increase in vote share but the total (11.8%) was clearly a disappointment given their performances in the local and European elections only some seven months previously and the fact that in October they still averaged over 18% in the polls. It would appear that their standing declined as their key policy of simply ignoring the result of the Brexit referendum and remaining in the EU became more widely known, while their participation in the coalition government with the Conservatives from 2010 to 2015 still rankled with some Labour supporters. Despite winning more votes than in the previous election, the Liberal Democrats recorded a net loss of one seat and their losses included that of Ms Swinson herself, narrowly defeated in East Dunbartonshire.

As expected, the Greens and the Brexit party were fringe players in the election although the only Green MP, Caroline Lucas, easily retained her Brighton Pavilion seat. The apparently weak performance of Nigel Farage's party reflects in part, of course, the fact that it did not put forward candidates in Conservative-held seats. In the 275 constituencies it contested, the Brexit Party share of votes was a slightly more respectable 5.1% (the respective figure for the Greens being 3.5% in 494 seats).

3.1 Regional and urban–rural variations

Although the shift from Labour to the Conservatives was evident in every region (and in Scotland and Wales), its extent varied substantially. Table 1.2 shows the regional swing figures.

It was clearly most marked in the North East and above average in the rest of the North of England and the Midlands. In the South East and South West the Conservatives fared less well while the swing was smallest of all in London. Given that the capital also had much the largest pro-Labour swing in 2017, the 2019 outcome could add grist to the mill of those who argue that it houses a 'metropolitan liberal elite' who are out of touch with the rest of the country. Perhaps

Table 1.2 Labour-Conservative swing in regions

North East	8.3% to Con	London	2.6% to Con
North West	4.9% to Con	South East	3.3% to Con
Yorkshire/Humber	6.4% to Con	South West	3.6% to Con
East Midlands	6.4% to Con		
West Midlands	6.5% to Con	Wales	5.2% to Con
Eastern	5.4% to Con	Scotland	2.5% to Con

Note: The figure for Scotland is not very meaningful as the SNP came first or second in every constituency.

Table 1.3 Party shares of votes (%) and seats won in regions

	Con	Lab	Lib Dem	Brexit	Green	SNP/PC	Other
North East	38.3	42.6	8.8	7.9	2.4		1.9
Seats	10	19					
North West	37.5	46.5	7.9	3.9	2.5		1.8
Seats	32	41	1				1
Yorkshire/Humber	43.1	38.9	8.1	5.9	2.3		1.8
Seats	26	28					
East Midlands	54.8	31.7	7.8	1.5	2.6		1.7
Seats	38	8					
West Midlands	53.4	33.9	7.9	1.4	3.0		0.5
Seats	44	15					
Eastern	57.2	24.4	13.4	0.4	3.0		1.7
Seats	52	5	1				
London	32.0	48.1	14.9	1.4	3.1		0.5
Seats	21	49	3				
South East	54.0	22.1	18.2	0.3	3.9		1.4
Seats	74	8	1		1		
South West	52.8	23.4	18.2	0.4	3.8		1.6
Seats	48	6	1				
Wales	36.1	40.9	6.0	5.4	1.0	9.9	0.6
Seats	14	22				4	
Scotland	25.1	18.6	9.5	0.5	1.0	45.0	0.3
Seats	6	1	4			48	

Note: The Speaker is counted as 'Other'.

more plausibly, it may be the presence of large and increasing numbers of ethnic minority voters—who strongly favour Labour—which explains London's divergence from national trends. The 2019 results in the regions are shown in more detail in Table 1.3.

In Scotland, the partial recovery that Labour had achieved in 2017 fizzled out in this election as its vote share slumped by ten points, leaving Ian Murray in

Edinburgh South as once again the party's sole Scottish representative at Westminster. The Conservatives also fell back, losing seven seats, but nonetheless retained second place. The beneficiary of these developments was the SNP which lost no time in claiming that its overwhelming victory (in terms of seats, at least) was a mandate for a second independence referendum. In Wales, in contrast, nationalist support declined a little and, while Labour remained the largest party, the Conservatives were not far behind.

Across England, the more pronounced swing to the Conservatives in the North and Midlands resulted in the party gaining in spectacular fashion some seats which had long been considered very safe for Labour. In Bolsover, for example, Dennis Skinner was ousted after almost 50 years as MP, while Blyth Valley went Conservative for the first time since the creation of the seat in 1950. Nonetheless, the north–south (outside London) divide in party support remains a significant feature of election outcomes. In England as a whole, the Conservatives had a lead of 13.3 points over Labour but in the three southern regions it was 31.5 points and in the Midlands 21.5. In the three northern regions, however, Labour led by 3.6 points.

Turning to the smaller parties, the Liberal Democrats clearly had more appeal in the South than in the North and Midlands and the same is true of the Green Party. In the case of the Brexit Party the reverse is the case—the further south one travels in England, the poorer was the Brexit Party performance. In part this reflects the pattern of Brexit Party candidatures but in seats which it contested the party scored 7.5% in the North, 4.3% in the Midlands and 2.6% in the South.

Another geographical divide that has characterised British elections is that between big cities and other heavily urban areas on the one hand and smaller towns and rural areas on the other. Labour always gets much better results in the former and the Conservatives in the latter. This difference remained fairly stark in 2019 as Table 1.4 shows.

Labour won more than half of the votes (and the Conservatives made least progress) in the very urban constituencies (mainly in the cities) but was heavily outscored in those classified as 'mixed' or rural. The Liberal Democrats also had their best results in these sorts of areas.

4. Constituency variations in changes in party support

Although most media reporting tends to give the impression that modern general elections are essentially national contests between competing party leaders, the fact remains that they involve 650 separate elections in the constituencies. Consequently, local personalities, issues, events and traditions, as well as demographic changes and constituency campaigning at the grass roots, all have a part to play in affecting results. In 2019, in particular, several incumbent Remain—

Table 1.4 The urban–rural divide 2019 (England)

	Share of Votes				Change 2017–2019			
	Very	Mainly			Very	Mainly		
	Urban %	Urban %	Mixed %	Rural %	Urban	Urban	Mixed	Rural
Conservative	30.2	45.8	54.3	59.4	+0.4	+2.5	+1.5	+2.5
Labour	52.2	37.1	25.7	19.7	−7.2	−8.3	−8.5	−7.2
Lib. Democrat	10.3	10.6	13.1	16.4	+4.1	+3.7	+5.1	+5.7
Green	3.7	2.4	3.0	3.2	+1.5	+1.1	+1.1	+1.0
Other	3.6	4.2	3.9	1.3	+1.2	+1.1	+0.8	−2.0
(Constituencies)	(138)	(143)	(159)	(93)				

supporting Conservative MPs, who had resigned from the party or had the whip withdrawn, attempted to retain their seats by standing again under a variety of labels. We would expect, then, to find much greater variations in both the direction and extent of changes in party support at constituency, as opposed to regional, level.

In Britain as a whole, 29 seats swung to Labour while the size of the swing to the Conservatives varied (in England) from 0.1% (Sefton Central) to a massive 18.4% in Bassetlaw. Although they increased their support by just over four points overall, the Liberal Democrat vote share fell in 38 constituencies (and by more than 10 points in 5) but shot up by more than 20 points in 7. Finally, in Scotland, although the SNP improved its position in all but one constituency the upturn ranged from just over one percentage point to more than 14, while in Wales, in the 36 seats contested in both 2017 and 2019, Plaid fell back in 15, moved forward in 21 and was unchanged in one. Clearly, then, there were significant differences across constituencies in how the distribution of party support changed.

A first step in analysing these differences is to consider how changes in support for the various parties were inter-related and Table 1.5 reports the relevant correlation coefficients (focussing on England and Wales in order to avoid complications caused by the strength of the SNP in Scotland).

Negative coefficients indicate that where one of the parties concerned did better, the other had poorer results while positive figures mean that the two parties tended to rise and fall together. In a strictly two-party system where all constituencies had straight fights, we would find a perfect negative correlation between changes in their vote shares—an increase for one would be matched exactly by a decline for the other. The days of two-party dominance in Britain have long gone, however. This is amply illustrated by the coefficient measuring the

Table 1.5 Correlations between changes in vote shares (England and Wales)

	Change % Con	Change % Lab	Change % Lib Dem	Change % Brexit
Change % Lab	−0.22	—	—	—
Change % Lib Dem	−0.50	−0.18	—	—
Change % Brexit	−0.06*	−0.55	−0.25	—
Change % Green	−0.02*	0.03*	−0.25	−0.03*

Note: The coefficients that are not statistically significant are asterisked. The N in all cases is 571. Here and in other tables relating to changes in votes the Speaker's seats in 2017 and 2019 are excluded.

relationship between changes in support for the Conservatives and Labour. Although this is in the expected direction (−0.22) and statistically significant, it is not large (and smaller than in 2017 when it stood at −0.27), meaning that changes in vote shares for the two leading parties were not actually very strongly related. This is due to the presence of large numbers of third-, fourth- and fifth-party candidates.

Conservative vote changes were much more strongly related to Liberal Democrat performance (coefficient = −0.51). This is not surprising, perhaps, in the context of the 2019 election. The Conservatives campaigned for a swift exit from the EU while the Liberal Democrats advocated remaining a member. The relationship is consistent with the interpretation that a segment of voters with a strong preference for Remain were willing to switch their vote from the former to the latter. Also unsurprising is the fact that Liberal Democrat and Green changes are negatively related as these parties tend to appeal to the same sorts of voters. More puzzling is the fact that stronger Brexit performances were associated with smaller improvements by the Liberal Democrats.

The strongest correlation of all, however, relates to the Brexit Party and Labour (−0.55). Clearly, the better the new party's performance, the more Labour suffered. In contrast, there was no significant relationship between changes in support for the Conservatives and the 'Brexiteers'. This gives some support to the argument of Nigel Farage during and after the election that his party's presence helped the Conservatives and hurt Labour. Indeed, he suggested that the former won or came close in a number of seats which they would have had no chance of winning had not a Brexit candidate drawn votes from Labour. There is some substance to this as there were 20 seats won by the Conservatives in which their majority was smaller than the number of votes cast for the Brexit Party. Four of these were in Wales and most of the rest in the North of England and the Midlands. Bizarrely, however, they also include Kensington, and Carshalton and Wallington (both in London) although in

Table 1.6 The impact of Brexit candidates on changes in vote share 2017–2019 (England and Wales)

Brexit candidate 2019	No	Yes	Difference
Change % Con	+1.9	+1.3	−0.6
Change % Lab	−7.2	−8.7	−1.5
Change % Lib Dem	+5.7	+2.6	−3.1
Change % Green	+1.1	+1.4	+0.3
(Constituencies)	(312)	(259)	

these cases it was the tiny majorities rather than the strength of the Brexit candidates that was notable.

The impact of Brexit candidacies on support for the other parties more generally is illustrated in Table 1.6, which shows the changes in vote shares for the latter in seats with and without a Brexit candidate in 2019.

Across England and Wales, a Brexit presence made only a small difference to the Conservative performance, increased Labour's decline by 1.5 points and reduced the Liberal Democrat advance by 3.1 points as compared to places where there was no Brexit candidate. In the latter case, given that the two parties espoused diametrically opposite policies it is not easy to explain why Jo Swinson's party did significantly less well in seats where Brexit was in the field (as with the correlation noted above). This probably reflects the fact that the (Conservative-held) seats that Brexit did not contest are more inclined to the Liberal Democrats in any event although it may also be that, elsewhere, Brexit simply provided an alternative choice for voters unwilling to support either of the two main parties.

The overall impact of the Brexit Party on Labour suggested in Table 1.6 may appear modest but it was regionally concentrated. In London the fall in Labour's votes was almost identical in both categories of seat while in the rest of the south the party actually did better where there was a Brexit candidate than where none was standing. In the northern regions, on the other hand Labour fell by 3.3 points more in the 'Brexit seats' than in others while the relevant figure for Wales was 5.2 points.

In Scotland, correlating the changes in the parties' vote shares from 2017 produces a clear pattern. SNP increases were strongly related to Labour declines (coefficient = −0.70) and also, but less strongly, to changes in Conservative support (−0.21). The latter's performance was more influenced by how well the Liberal Democrats did (−0.54) and this also affected Labour (−0.32). Illustrative of the complex and changed nature of Scottish electoral politics, there was no significant relationship between changes in support for the Conservatives and Labour across the constituencies.

Table 1.7 Bivariate correlations between changes in Conservative and Labour shares of vote 2017–2019 and constituency characteristics (England and Wales)

	Con	Lab	Lib Dem		Con	Lab	Lib Dem
Manual Workers (%)	0.66	−0.38	−0.51	% Prof./ Managerial	−0.67	0.32	0.56
Owner occupiers (%)	0.14	−0.07*	0.09	% Private renters	−0.26	0.29	−0.01*
No qualifications (%)	0.62	−0.41	−0.43	% With degrees	−0.68	0.35	0.46
Aged 65+ years (%)	0.22	−0.05*	0.02*	% Aged 18-24	−0.09	0.17	−0.22
				% Students	−0.22	0.25	−0.12
				Persons per hectare	−0.23	0.15	0.02*
Leave in EU ref. (%)	0.67	−0.40	−0.27	% Ethnic minority	−0.20	0.18	0.02*

Note: N = 571. All coefficients are statistically significant except those asterisked.

Changes in support for the major parties are explored further in Table 1.7 which shows, first, the direction and strength of the relationship between changes in vote shares for the major parties in English and Welsh constituencies and a standard set of social and demographic variables. The latter are taken from the 2011 Census. Although these data are now nine years old, few constituencies will have undergone dramatic changes in their make-up in the intervening period so they can still be usefully applied in analysis.

The pattern of correlation coefficients shown for the Conservatives and Labour is very similar to the pattern found in 2017. In this election, as in the previous one, the inter-election change in support was better for the former and worse for the latter the more manual workers and people without educational qualifications there were in a constituency. In contrast, the more professional and managerial workers and people with a degree, the worse was the change in vote share for the Conservatives and the better (or less bad) the outcome for Labour. In short, working-class areas moved more from Labour to the Conservatives while middle-class areas moved less. One change from the comparable analysis of 2017 results concerns young people and students. In that election a promise to abolish university tuition fees had featured prominently in Labour's campaign and the change in its vote share correlated positively with the percentage of those aged 18–24 years and the percentage of students in a constituency (0.34 in both cases) while Conservative change was negatively related (−0.20 and −0.35 respectively). In 2019, Labour's policy on tuition fees remained the same but, as can be seen in Table 1.7, although the coefficients were in the same direction they were rather less strong than they had been previously. As far as the Liberal Democrats are concerned, their advance was clearly strongest in more middle-class constituencies and weakest in those that are more working-class. Repeating this analysis for Scotland reveals that there was no significant relationship between any of the social and demographic variables and changes in support for Labour and the SNP. Here, it was more a case of the nationalists gaining and Labour losing ground across the board.

Again, as in 2017, the kinds of places where the Conservatives did best in comparison to the previous election are strikingly similar to those which had the largest Leave majorities in the 2016 EU referendum. Unsurprisingly, then, there is a strong positive correlation (0.67) between the estimated percentage Leave vote and the change in Conservative vote share and negative relationships for Labour (−0.40) and the Liberal Democrats (−0.27). The more Leave voters there were in a constituency, the better the Conservatives did and the worse the outcome for Labour and the Liberal Democrats, as compared with the results in 2017. This pattern was reversed, of course, the more Remain voters there were.

5. Patterns of party support in 2019

Having examined the extent and nature of electoral change between 2017 and 2019, the question remains as to what extent the pattern of absolute levels of party support across constituencies continues to display long-familiar features. Table 1.8 shows correlation coefficients measuring the associations between the shares of the vote obtained by the parties and a range of social and demographic variables.

The figures relating to occupational class are striking. The level of Conservative support was not significantly related to variations in the proportion of manual workers in a constituency and very weakly related to the size of the solidly middle-class professional and managerial groups. The relevant coefficients for Labour are in the expected direction but do not indicate particularly strong relationships. In 2019, indeed, it is the Liberal Democrats whose local support was most strongly influenced by the class composition of constituencies: the more middle-class the constituency, the better they did.

The weak class-party relationships in the case of the major parties did not come out of the blue, as it were, but represent a continuation and acceleration of a longer-term trend. This is illustrated in Figure 1.4 which charts the strength of the correlations between the occupational class variables and support for the Conservatives and Labour since the 2005 election.

In Labour's case, there has been a steady decline in the strength of these relationships which have become weaker at each successive election. On the Conservative side, the influence of the size of the middle class on their vote declined only a little to 2015 but then dropped sharply in the next two elections. It

Table 1.8 Bivariate correlations between party shares of vote in 2019 and constituency characteristics (England and Wales)

	Conservative	Labour	Liberal Democrat
Prof./Managerial (%)	0.09	−0.34	0.66
Manual Workers (%)	−0.07*	0.28	−0.61
Owner occupiers (%)	0.70	−0.68	0.14
Social renters (%)	−0.63	0.66	−0.29
Private renters (%)	−0.52	0.46	0.07*
Aged 18–24 years (%)	−0.53	0.51	−0.13
Aged 65+ years (%)	0.63	−0.66	0.16
In agriculture (%)	0.39	−0.45	0.18
Persons per hectare	−0.62	0.61	−0.05*
With degrees (%)	0.16	−0.10	0.61
No qualifications (%)	−0.04*	0.25	−0.61
Students (%)	−0.56	0.50	0.01*
With no car (%)	−0.76	0.77	−0.26
Ethnic minority (%)	−0.54	0.59	−0.11

Note: N = 572 for Conservatives and Labour and 552 for the Liberal Democrats. All coefficients are statistically significant except those asterisked.

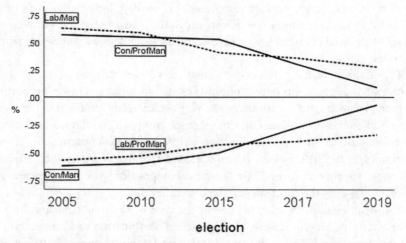

Figure 1.4 Correlations between occupational class and constituency vote shares for major parties, 2005–2019

was in the 2015 election, however, that the weakening (negative) influence of the proportion of manual workers on variations in Conservative support became more apparent and this trend continued apace in 2017 and 2019.

It should be emphasised that this sort of analysis of aggregate data does not, of itself, tell us anything about the extent of class voting among the electorate. It concerns variations among places (constituencies) not people. Nonetheless, opinion poll data relating to the 2019 election confirm the impression that class was not a major influence on party choice. An 'on the day poll' conducted on behalf of Lord Ashcroft reported that non-manual workers divided 44% Conservative to 32% Labour while for manual workers the respective figures were 46% and 34% (see https://lordashcroftpolls.com/2019/12/how-britain-voted-and-why-my-2019-general-election-post-vote-poll/).

Returning to the data in Table 1.8, the type of housing prevalent in constituencies continued to influence election outcomes with those having more owner occupiers being more inclined to the Conservatives. Two elections ago it would have been surprising to find no Conservative benefit in seats where people with degrees were thicker on the ground but Brexit has changed that relationship. In 2019, however, larger proportions of graduates made for happier hunting grounds for the Liberal Democrats. University towns (and university areas in the cities) also proved more difficult for the Conservatives but provided a boost for Labour, as indicated by the coefficients for the percentage of students aged over 18 years in the constituencies. The remaining variables—age, % in agriculture, persons per hectare, those with no car and the proportion of ethnic minority residents—are all inter-related to a degree. The latter two, as well as younger people, are more numerous in cities while population density is a direct measure of urbanisation. As noted above, Labour remains especially strong in cities and it is unsurprising that the correlations involving these variables are all in the expected direction. The strength of the associations between levels of party support and the age structure of the relevant electorates is worth noting but the best single predictor of the share of votes obtained by the Conservatives and Labour is the percentage of household without a car (-0.76 for the former and $+0.77$ for the latter). Although it might be tempting to interpret this as indicating widespread dissatisfaction with the abysmal performance of some privatised railway companies in the years and months before the election, the likelihood is that it reflects levels of deprivation as well as the fact that car-owning is less necessary in city locations.

In Scotland, the 2017 election appeared to confirm the view that the SNP had successfully taken over what were formerly the bases of Labour dominance there and, in general, this remained the case in 2019. Although the party advanced almost everywhere and the correlations are weaker, the size of the SNP vote in constituencies was positively and significantly associated with % social renters (0.45), % with no car (0.37) and % with no educational qualifications (0.23) while there were negative effects for % owner occupiers (-0.40), % professional and managerial (-0.39), % in agriculture (-0.34) and % aged 65 and over (-0.30).

6. Turnout

Measuring turnout in Britain is not as straightforward as it may seem. It is defined as the percentage of those on the electoral register who cast a ballot. Unfortunately, the media (and even the House of Commons Library) generally base the calculation on the sum of votes cast for all parties and candidates that is the number of *valid* votes. However, this excludes those who voted but whose ballots were rejected for one reason or another—people who deliberately spoiled their paper, for example. In most cases, of course, the difference between valid votes and total ballots is small but in the Chorley constituency of the Speaker in 2019 there were 1,303 rejected ballots and including these clearly makes a difference to the turnout calculation. Across Britain, almost 113,000 ballots were rejected—about 42,000 more than in 2017.

A more recent problem in calculating turnout relates to postal voting. Following the introduction of 'on demand' postal voting just before the 2001 general election, the proportion of votes cast in this way has risen steadily—from 2.4% of those included in the count in 1997 to 21.6% in 2017. Voting by post is more complicated than voting in person, however, and, as a consequence, a large number of postal ballots—in 2017, more than 140,000 (2.4% of all postal votes)—are disqualified on technical grounds. Whether these (attempted) votes should be included in the turnout calculation is a moot point. Some may be genuine attempts which involved a minor slip; others may be fraudulent.

Measuring the 'eligible electorate' also raises issues. Electoral registers obviously exclude those who, for one reason or another, have never got round to (the relatively simple task of) adding their names. On the other hand, it is possible to be registered (but not, legally, to vote) in more than one place. Students, for example, may be registered at home and at their university. Since electoral registration is the responsibility of local authorities, however, there is no central register and hence no way of knowing the number of names entered more than once. Despite these niggling difficulties, the turnout figures given here refer to total votes cast (including those rejected at the count) as a percentage of the registered electorate.

In advance of polling day, there were fears that an election held in the depths of winter would result in a significant drop in turnout but, although the weather was indeed wet and windy across much of the country, the Britain-wide figure of 67.7% was only slightly down on 2017. Table 1.9 shows that participation by the electorate was little changed in the South East and South West and increased in Scotland. Elsewhere, the largest decline (−2.7 points) was recorded in London (which had had the largest rise in 2017) with most of the others being close to a two point drop. In absolute terms, the southern regions outside London continue to have a somewhat higher turnout (70.4% taken together) than the three northern regions (65.1%).

Table 1.9 Turnout in 2019 (%)

	Turnout 2019	Change 2017–2019
North East	64.3	−1.9
North West	65.8	−2.2
Yorkshire/Humber	64.6	−1.9
East Midlands	67.4	−1.9
West Midlands	64.9	−2.0
Eastern	68.6	−1.4
London	67.6	−2.7
South East	70.5	−0.8
South West	72.3	+0.3
Wales	66.8	−1.9
Scotland	68.2	+1.7
Great Britain	67.7	−1.3

At constituency level, of course, there was much greater variation in turnout. At the bottom end, 15 constituencies failed to reach 55%, Hull East coming bottom of the pile with a turnout of 49.5%. At the other extreme, the figure was 75% or greater in 61 constituencies with the highest figure of all (80.4%) being recorded in East Dunbartonshire where the Liberal Democrat leader, Jo Swinson, lost her seat by 149 votes. Across England and Wales, the correlations between the change in constituency turnouts and changes in the parties' vote shares are relatively weak, being −0.21 for the Conservatives, +0.20 for Labour and +0.23 for the Liberal Democrats. There was, then, a slight tendency for the latter two parties to have better results and the former to do less well where turnout declined least.

In examining the sources of turnout variations across constituencies we encounter a familiar pattern. Table 1.10 shows correlations between the level of turnout in 2019 and variables indicating the socio-economic characteristics of constituencies.

If the occupational class structure has ceased to be a reliable indicator of support for the major parties it nonetheless remains strongly associated with turnout levels. The more middle-class a constituency, the higher the turnout; the more working class, the lower the turnout. Other class-related variables—housing tenure, education and car ownership—show a similar pattern. Turnout is also lower the more urban a constituency and the more young people and ethnic minority citizens there are but the effect of the size of the student population is slight. It is worth mentioning again the point that this analysis does not tell us the extent to which people in the various groups listed turned out to vote. Rather, it tells us that the more professionals, owner occupiers, people with degrees, people

Table 1.10 Bivariate correlations between turnout in 2019 and constituency characteristics (Great Britain)

Professional & Managerial (%)	0.73	**% Manual Workers**	**−0.70**
Owner occupiers (%)	0.47	% Social renters	−0.59
		% Private renters	−0.13
In agriculture (%)	0.31	Persons per hectare	−0.27
With degrees (%)	0.63	% No qualifications	−0.69
Aged 65+ years (%)	0.37	% Aged 18–24	−0.29
		% Students	−0.16
		% Ethnic minority	−0.28
		% With no car	−0.53
Constituency marginality 2017	0.13		

Note: For all variables except marginality N = 631 (Chorley excluded) and for marginality N = 630 (Buckingham also excluded). All coefficients are statistically significant.

employed in agriculture and older people there are in a constituency, the higher was its turnout.

In the two previous elections, for reasons that no-one has been able to explain satisfactorily, the formerly strong relationship between marginality—the closeness of the contest in the preceding election—and turnout, which persisted over many years, disappeared. In 2019, however, there was something of a return to normality—the more marginal the seat the higher the turnout—but the relationship was very weak so that there remains a puzzle for electoral analysts given that the parties campaign harder than ever in more marginal seats while expending less effort in those that are hopeless prospects or very safe for them.

7. Explaining the outcome

Although the size of the majority won by the Conservatives surprised many observers, the 2019 outcome could not have astonished them in the way that the 2017 contest had. After all, as has been seen, Labour lagged well behind in voting intentions throughout the campaign, the Conservatives avoided the gaffes that had derailed them in 2017 and the decline of the Brexit Party and the Liberal Democrats as the campaign progressed had been clearly charted. In Scotland, too, the progress made by the SNP was not unexpected (although Labour's decline was probably greater than anticipated).

The various factors which explain what happened in 2019 are explored elsewhere in this volume and will, no doubt, be thoroughly examined in future publications. As soon as the results of the exit poll were announced, however, and in the immediate aftermath of the election, attention focussed on Labour's dismal performance and three topics dominated the discussion—Brexit, 'Corbynism' and Jeremy Corbyn himself.

As far as Brexit is concerned, there was a widespread belief—certainly among Leave supporters—that Labour had helped to stymie the process by voting against withdrawal bills in the Commons, supporting extensions to the dates set for departing from the EU and shilly-shallying about whether a second referendum should be held. In addition, its own policy on the issue was unclear—at least as compared with those of its rivals. There seems little doubt that this hurt the party in the election. As has been seen, Labour lost votes to the Brexit Party and did worse than average in Leave-supporting areas. The Ashcroft poll referred to earlier found that among 2016 Leave voters 73% voted Conservative in 2019 while only 26% voted Labour. Among Remainers, the figures were 20% Conservative, 47% Labour and 21% Liberal Democrat. It is worth noting also— although it is largely irrelevant to Labour's performance—that none of the Remain-supporting ex-Conservative MPs who sought re-election mentioned above came anywhere near success. Dominic Grieve, for example, who was perhaps the most prominent, lost by more than 15,000 votes in his constituency. If the 2017 election result could be characterised as 'the revenge of the Remainers', then it would appear that Leavers got some of their own back in 2019.

By 'Corbynism' is meant the generally left-wing policies espoused by Labour under Corbyn's leadership. Whether this contributed to Labour's poor showing is rather more debatable. Certainly, some of the individual policies put forward in Labour's manifesto—the proposal to renationalise the railways, for example, or to greatly increase spending on the National Health Service—commanded wide support. It may be, however, that voters were sceptical about the sheer scale of the spending commitments undertaken by the party and worried about where the money would come from to finance them. Reliable survey data will be required to throw more light on these issues.

There is rather less room for doubt about the electoral impact of the Labour leader himself. As described above, he lagged well behind Theresa May as the electorate's preferred Prime Minister for most of the inter-election period and the gap widened when Boris Johnson took over the top job. On another long-standing measure of leader popularity—Ipsos MORI's satisfaction ratings—the news for Corbyn supporters was equally bleak. From February to June 2019 his average net score (% satisfied minus % dissatisfied with his performance) was −57 (compared with −37 for Mrs May) while in September and October, during Johnson's brief 'honeymoon' period he plumbed new depths for an Opposition leader recording scores of −60 in both months.

Corbyn's ratings improved somewhat during the election campaign—in Ipsos MORI's December figures he stood at −44 compared with −20 for Johnson— but there was no miraculous comeback such as had occurred in 2017. A plethora of polls confirmed Johnson's lead as the preferred Prime Minister and just a week before the election Opinium asked respondents whether they could imagine Jeremy Corbyn holding the office. Only 29% said 'Yes' while 59% gave a negative response. Even among intending Labour voters 24% said that they could not imagine him as PM. These people had company in the Labour party. In what was surely an unprecedented development, 15 former Labour MPs placed advertisements in local newspapers on the eve of the election arguing that Corbyn was unfit to be Prime Minister. Whatever it was that made people warm to the Labour leader during the previous election campaign was patently absent on this occasion.

Not long after the election, Brexit was finally achieved and Jeremy Corbyn announced that he would resign as Labour leader. Whether 'Corbynism' will continue to dominate Labour thinking remains to be seen. By the time the next general election comes round, however, it is certain that new issues, new personalities and simple 'events'—including the still uncertain consequences of Brexit—will provide a new context and new questions on which a fickle and volatile electorate will be asked to pass judgement.

Acknowledgements

I am grateful to Mark Garnett and Rob Johns for comments on a draft of this chapter.

Reference

Daily Telegraph, 'Wednesday Morning News Briefing: General Election on a Knife Edge', accessed at https://www.telegraph.co.uk/news/2019/12/11/wednesday-morning-news-briefing-general-election-knife-edge/ on 31 March 2020.

Britain Votes (2019) 29–47

JOHN CURTICE*

A Return to 'Normality' at Last? How the Electoral System Worked in 2019

1. Introduction

Recently, Britain's single-member plurality electoral system has not been living up to its traditional billing. Its advocates argue that because it is more or less guaranteed to give the winning party an overall majority of seats even though that party may win considerably less than 50% of the vote, the system helps facilitate alternating single-party majority government and ensures governments are directly accountable to voters (Norton, 1997; Bingham Powell, 2000; Renwick, 2011). Yet in both 2010 and 2017, the election produced a hung parliament that in one instance resulted in a coalition government and, in the other, a minority administration underpinned by a 'confidence and supply' arrangement with a small party. Meanwhile, although the 2015 contest did produce an overall majority, at 12 it was relatively small and indeed was deemed to be too small when the then Prime Minister, Theresa May, triggered the 2017 election in the hope that she would win a larger majority.

But in the 2019 election, 'normality' was seemingly restored. The Conservatives were elected with an overall majority of 80. As a result, what had been a long-running impasse in the House of Commons about what should be done about Brexit was swiftly resolved, and less than two months after polling day, the UK left the EU. There could, it seemed, be no clearer demonstration of the claim that single-party majority administrations deliver 'strong government'—in contrast to the weakness and immobilisme that are often thought to characterize coalitions and minority government and which appeared to be exemplified by the impasse over Brexit that had gripped the Commons between 2017 and 2019.

*Sir John Curtice, School of Government and Public Policy, University of Strathclyde, j.curtice@strath.ac.uk

doi:10.1093/pa/gsaa021

In this article, we look more closely at how the electoral system operated in 2019. To what extent did it represent a return to normality—and the result indicate that overall majorities are likely to be the norm once more? Or was this in some sense an exceptional result that provides little indication as to what might happen in future? Why did the system work as it did in the 2019 contest—and how important was its use in determining the fate of Brexit?

2. Three comparisons

In the election, the Conservatives secured a lead in votes of nearly 12 percentage points over Labour. It was the largest lead to be won by either party since 1997 when Labour was nearly 13 points ahead of the Conservatives. As Table 2.1 shows, since 1979, only one other contest—Mrs Thatcher's landslide success in 1983—witnessed a significantly bigger lead for the winning party than the one that was in evidence in 2019. Against that backdrop, it would have been very surprising indeed if the 2019 contest had not resulted in anything other than a substantial majority for the winning party.

Yet, while there have only been two elections during the last 40 years in which the winning party had a markedly bigger lead in votes than transpired in 2019, there were as many as four elections in which the winning party's majority was bigger than the 80-seat one the Conservatives secured in 2019. Of particular note is the outcome of the 1987 election, in which the Conservative lead over Labour (11.7 points) was almost exactly the same as that in 2019, but the outcome was a majority of 102 rather than 80. Meanwhile, what was no more than a 9.3-point

Table 2.1 Winning party's lead in votes and size of overall majority, 1979–2019

Election	% Lead in votes	Overall majority (seats)
1979	7.0	43
1983	15.2	144
1987	11.8	102
1992	7.6	21
1997	12.8	179
2001	9.3	167
2005	2.9	66
2010	7.2	None
2015	6.6	12
2017	2.5	None
2019	11.7	80

Source: Calculated from Rallings and Thrasher (2012), Cowley and Kavanagh (2016, 2018) and Baker *et al.* (2019).

lead in 2001 resulted in a Labour majority of as many as 167 seats. It seems that the past record might have led us to expect a rather larger overall majority for the Conservatives than the one of 80 that they obtained.

However, perhaps some inconsistency between the lead a party secures in votes and the outcome in seats should not surprise us. After all, under the single-member plurality electoral system, there is no formal mechanism that ensures that a party that wins any particular share of the vote across the country as a whole secures any particular proportion of the seats in the House of Commons. A general election simply consists of 650 separate constituency contests in which the (sole) winner in each case is the candidate with most votes. Nevertheless, it was observed in the immediate post-war period that in practice the electoral system appeared to produce results that were consistent with a 'cube law' (Butler, 1951; Gudgin and Taylor, 1979; Taagerpera and Shugart, 1989). This states that if the votes cast for the two largest parties are shared in the proportion A: B, the seats they win are shared in the proportion $A^3: B^3$—a ratio that exaggerates the lead of the largest party over its principal rival and—assuming few seats are won by any other parties—should ensure that in all but the narrowest of outcomes the party with most votes obtains a substantial overall majority.

However, large though it might seem, the Conservatives' majority in 2019 falls well short of the expectations of the cube law. In the election, the Conservatives won 57.6% of the votes cast for Conservative and Labour alone (otherwise known as the 'two-party vote'). According to the law, that should have reaped a dividend of 71.4% of the seats—or 406, well above the Conservatives' actual tally of 365.[1] So, by this criterion too, it looks as though the Conservatives' majority was rather less than we might have anticipated.

The expectation that the electoral system should usually deliver the winner a substantial majority, even if that party secures much less than half of all votes cast, rests not only on its supposed tendency to operate in conformity to the cube law, but also on the expectation that few MPs from parties other than the Conservatives or Labour will be elected to the House of Commons. Even if some voters do vote for smaller parties, the winner take all nature of the system in every constituency is expected to make it difficult for those parties to win any seats—a feature that in turn is thought to discourage voters from voting for smaller parties in the first place (Duverger, 1954; Blais and Carty, 1991).

Yet plenty of third-party MPs were elected in 2019—a grand total of not less than 82. In this respect, the outcome did not look anything like 'normality' at all. True, this tally was a little lower than in the three elections between 2005 and

---

[1]The result is the same if we undertake the calculation on the basis of only those votes cast in seats won by either the Conservatives or Labour, where, at 57.54% the Conservative share of the two-party vote was almost exactly the same as the 57.56% figure for the country as a whole.

2015, but it was still well above anything that was recorded before 1997. What has seemingly become a persistent 'failure' of the system at recent elections to exclude third parties from the Commons was once again in evidence.

So, while the electoral system did deliver a substantial majority for the largest party in 2019, once we look underneath the surface there is reason to question whether the outcome did represent a return to 'normality'. Whether judged by historical precedent or the expectations of the 'cube law', the Conservatives' over-all majority was rather less than might have been expected given the extent of their lead over Labour. Meanwhile, there were still many more third-party MPs elected than would once have seemed imaginable. There is evidently a need to ex-amine further how the electoral system worked in 2019.

3.   Marginal seats

The early post-war literature that originally identified the 'cube law' did not indi-cate that it was an inevitable feature of how the system operated. Rather, it dem-onstrated that the way the single member plurality system translates votes into seats depends on the geography of party support—and in particular on how many seats are closely contested between the Conservatives and Labour (Kendall and Stuart, 1950). Formally, it indicated that the frequency distribution of the Conservative share of the two-party vote across all constituencies should be simi-lar to that of a normal curve with a standard deviation (a measure of spread) of 13.7. In practice, what this means is that in a 600-seat legislature, 180 (or 30%) of the seats should be ones where—if the two largest parties enjoy the same share of the vote across the country as a whole—the share of the two-party vote secured by the winning party should be between 50% and 55%. In short, the cube law works so long as there are sufficient marginal seats.

Table 2.2 assesses the geographical distribution of the two-party vote against these criteria at each election since 1955. In the first pair of columns, it shows the number of seats that satisfy our definition of a 'marginal' seat, and the proportion of the seats won by Conservative and Labour that this figure represents. In the second pair of columns, we give an indication of how the distribution of party support across all constituencies measures up against the more formal require-ments that need to be satisfied for the law to operate. We show, first, the standard deviation of the distribution and secondly, the kurtosis, a measure of the extent to which there are more or fewer seats in the middle of the distribution than would be expected from a normal curve.

The table shows that there has been a marked change in the geography of the two-party vote during the post-war period. In the 1950s and 1960s that geogra-phy more or less satisfied the requirements of the cube law (Curtice and Steed, 1982). The standard deviation was around 13.7. The kurtosis was a little less than

Table 2.2 Distribution of the two-party vote, 1955–2019

Party	Marginals		Two-party vote	
	No.	**%**	**Standard deviation**	**Kurtosis**
1955	166	27.2	13.5	−0.25
1959	157	25.7	13.8	−0.29
1964	166	27.3	14.1	−0.45
1966	155	25.6	13.8	−0.46
1970	149	24.5	14.3	−0.27
1974 (Feb)	119	19.9	16.1	−0.68
1974 (Oct)	98	16.4	16.8	−0.82
1979	108	17.8	16.9	−0.87
1983	80	13.2	20.0	−1.05
1987	87	14.4	21.4	−1.03
1992	98	16.1	20.2	−1.03
1997	114	19.6	18.1	−0.85
2001	114	19.7	18.3	−0.82
2005	104	18.8	19.7	−0.96
2010	85	15.0	22.2	−1.08
2015	74	13.1	21.7	−1.19
2017	89	15.3	18.6	−0.89
2019	88	15.5	20.3	−0.69

Marginal Seat: Seat where Conservative share of two-party vote − (overall Conservative share of two-party vote - 50%) lies within the range 45–55%.
Two-party vote: Votes cast for Conservative and Labour combined.
Table based only on seats won by Conservative or Labour at that election and contested by both parties.
Source: Curtice (2017a) and author's calculations.

that of a normal curve—and thus the proportion of seats that were marginal a little less than 30%—but it can be seen that overall the electoral system could be expected to produce an outcome that would more or less satisfy the expectations of the cube law. However, at the two elections in 1974, there was a marked drop in the number of marginal seats, and it fell yet further thereafter. Although thanks to her large lead in votes Mrs Thatcher still won a hefty three-figure majority in 1983, by this stage, the number of marginal seats had halved and the standard deviation of the two-party vote increased to 20. If the elections held in the 1980s had resulted in a narrower outcome in terms of votes, then they could well have resulted in hung parliaments. Meanwhile, although there was subsequently some variation in the number of marginal seats, the long-term decline that set in during the 1970s has never been reversed.

The decline in the number of marginal seats has been attributed to the tendency from the 1950s onwards for northern and more urban Britain to become more strongly Labour, while southern and more rural parts of the country became more favourable to the Conservatives (Curtice and Steed, 1982, 1986). The result was a country whose political geography became much more polarised. However, the outcome of the 2019 election appears to have disrupted this pattern—the Conservatives captured from Labour for the first time ever a number of seats in Leave-voting areas in the North of England and the Midlands (see Power *et al.*, and Goes, both this volume). Nevertheless, our table suggests this did little to change the overall geography of the two-party vote or the number of marginal seats, which, at 88, is much the same as it was in 2017.

Labour's loss of seats in Leave-voting constituencies that had once been bastions for the party was highly visible. However, in practice, the tendency for the Conservatives to perform more strongly in Leave-voting areas was far from confined to seats that were being defended by Labour. It was also clearly in evidence in Leave-voting areas that were being defended by the Conservatives. On average, there was a 7.5% swing from Labour to Conservative in Conservative-held seats where more than 60% voted Leave in 2016. Although this was somewhat lower than the equivalent figure among heavily Leave-inclined seats that Labour was defending (9.3%), it was still well above the GB-wide average of 4.7 points. Moreover, the proportion of Conservative-held seats (as of 2017) in which more than 60% voted Leave was, at 29%, just as big as (indeed, it was slightly higher than) the proportion of Labour seats that fell into that category (26%). In short, as well as turning some Labour seats blue, the tendency for Leave-voting Britain to swing more strongly to the Conservatives also resulted in many a Conservative-held seat becoming more strongly Conservative. As a result, the overall character of the distribution of the two-party vote was not radically changed.

A look at what happened in the seats that on our definition were marginal in 2017 also helps explain why there was no marked change in the overall distribution of the two-party vote. On average, at 5.2%, the swing from Labour to Conservative in these seats was not very different from that across the country as a whole. Consequently, most of these remained marginal (indeed 62 of the 89 did so). At the same time, the swing from Conservative to Labour in those seats that can be defined as near-marginal for Labour in 2017[2] was, at 6.1%, sufficiently above the national swing to turn some of these seats into marginals, but only at a level that resulted in the replacement of those seats that ceased being so.[3]

---

[2]These are seats where Labour would have won between 55% and 60% of the two-party vote in 2017 if, as a result of a uniform swing, the Conservatives and Labour had won the same share of the overall national vote.

[3]Strictly speaking, the swing that matters here is that based on the change in the share of the two-party vote rather than that based (as quoted here) on the change in the overall share of the vote. However, the point still stands. The mean swing in the Conservative share of the two-party vote was 5.8%, little

So, the 2019 election did not result in any marked change in the overall distribution of the two-party vote. There continued to be many fewer seats that were marginal between the Conservatives and Labour than was required for the cube law to operate, and this helped ensure that the Conservatives' overall majority was, indeed, rather less than we might have anticipated. But securing a large overall majority is also likely to be more difficult if more seats are won by parties other than the Conservatives and Labour, so it is to the continued high prevalence of third-party successes to which we turn next.

4. Third-party MPs

Just as whether the electoral system conforms to the expectations of the cube law depends on the geography of party support, so also does the extent to which the system discriminates against smaller parties (Gudgin and Taylor, 1979). A small party whose vote is much the same from one constituency to another will, inevitably, tend to be a loser more or less everywhere. That is the fate that befell UKIP in 2015 when, even though the party won as much as 13% of the vote, it still only secured one seat. On the other hand, a small party whose vote is geographically concentrated may be relatively strong in—and thus capable of winning—some seats. One particularly striking example is Plaid Cymru who in both 2017 and 2019 won just 0.5% of the UK-wide vote but 0.6% (four) of the seats.

The 1997 election witnessed a sharp increase in the number of third-party MPs (from 44 to 75), even though, at 26.1%, the share of the vote won by smaller parties was little different from that recorded at the three previous elections. It is an increase that has never been reversed. Most of it was accounted for by a change in the geography of the Liberal Democrat vote, which traditionally had been relatively evenly spread but now became somewhat more geographically concentrated, such that between 1997 and 2010 the party won between 46 and 62 seats (Russell and Fieldhouse, 2005; Curtice, 2009). However, a collapse in the party's vote in 2015, after being in coalition with the Conservatives for five years, saw its representation fall to just eight seats. And although there was some recovery in its electoral support in 2019 (see Cutts and Russell, this volume), the party still won only 11 seats, one less than in 2017.

However, the 2015 election also witnessed a dramatic increase in the number of SNP MPs. Scotland's nationalist party only contests seats north of the border—but there it now stopped being a small party (Curtice, 2017b). Indeed, with as much as 50% of the Scottish vote, the single-member plurality electoral system worked in the party's favour, crediting it with all but three of Scotland's 59

different from the overall national figure of 6.1%. The mean swing in Labour's 'near-marginals' was 6.6%.

constituencies. Although a dip in support in 2017 to 37% saw its number of MPs fall to 35, in 2019, the party's vote rose once more and its representation increased to 48 (see Denver, this volume)—an increase of 13 seats that (bearing in mind the Liberal Democrats' loss of one seat) wholly accounts for the overall increase of 12 third-party MPs compared with 2017.

The 2019 election proved to be the third in a row in which the outcome in Scotland departed radically from that in the rest of Britain, with its representation dominated by a party other than the Conservatives or Labour. In that respect, Scotland is now much like Northern Ireland, where parliamentary representation has been dominated by small parties ever since the early 1970s. Britain's electoral system cannot be expected to deliver normal service for as long as that proves to be the case.

5.   Electoral bias

So far, in assessing how the electoral system treats the Conservatives and Labour, we have examined the extent to which it exaggerates the lead of the largest party over the second party irrespective of which of those parties is in the lead. However, we cannot assume that the system treats the two parties in the same way. In particular, we might wonder what would have happened if it had been Labour rather than the Conservatives that had been 12 points ahead of their principal rivals in 2019?

This question is addressed in Table 2.3. It shows what the outcome would be in seats for various possible outcomes in votes assuming that the geographical distribution of party support remained as it was in 2019. This is done by assuming that any change in the share of the vote won by Conservatives and Labour across the country as a whole is replicated in each and every constituency, while the level of support for all other parties (and the level of turnout) is unchanged. Thus, for example, in the second row of the table, we show what the outcome would be if the Conservative share of the vote fell by one point and the Labour share increased by one point in each and every seat, an outcome that would reduce the overall Conservative lead over Labour by two points—and reduce the Conservative tally of seats by eight.

One point immediately stands out. Under these assumptions, Labour would need to be as much as 19 points ahead of the Conservatives in order to win an overall majority of 80. Other yardsticks also indicate that, for any given performance, the electoral system was inclined to reward the Conservatives more richly than Labour. If the two parties were to win the same share of the vote, the Conservatives, with 290 seats, would still be 23 seats ahead of Labour on 267 seats. If Labour had obtained the lead of 11.7 points that the Conservatives enjoyed, the party would have failed, albeit narrowly, to secure an overall

Table 2.3 Relationship between votes and seats following the 2019 general election

Swing to Con from 2019 result	% Vote (GB)			Seats (UK)			
	Con	Lab	Con lead	Con	Lab	Others	Majority
0.0	44.7	33.0	11.7	365	203	82	Con 80
−1.0	43.7	34.0	9.7	357	211	82	Con 64
−2.0	42.7	35.0	7.7	340	222	88	Con 30
−3.0	41.7	36.0	5.7	331	232	88	Con 12
−3.5	41.2	36.5	4.7	325	238	88	None
−4.0	40.7	37.0	3.7	316	246	88	None
−5.0	39.7	38.0	1.7	304	254	92	None
−5.85	38.85	38.85	0.0	290	267	93	None
−6.0	38.7	39.0	−0.3	288	269	93	None
−7.0	37.7	40.0	−2.3	278	280	92	None
−8.0	36.7	41.0	−4.3	269	288	93	None
−9.0	35.7	42.0	−6.3	256	300	94	None
−10.0	34.7	43.0	−8.3	244	311	95	None
−11.0	33.7	44.0	−10.3	237	318	95	None
−12.0	32.7	45.0	−12.3	229	326	95	Lab 2
−13.0	31.7	46.0	−14.3	224	331	95	Lab 12
−14.0	30.7	47.0	−16.3	216	342	92	Lab 34
−15.0	29.7	48.0	−18.3	201	358	91	Lab 66
−15.5	29.2	48.5	−19.3	194	366	90	Lab 82

Source: Author's calculations.

majority at all. To win a minimal overall majority Labour would need a lead of just over 12 points, whereas the Conservatives only require to be 5 points ahead to win the 326 seats required for the barest possible overall majority.

These figures further underline our argument that the outcome of the 2019 election did not represent a return to 'normality'. Under our assumptions, even the relatively modest 80-seat majority that the Conservatives obtained would not have been achieved if Labour had enjoyed a near 12-point lead. Moreover, it should be noted that if the current electoral geography remains in place—and support for third parties remains as it was in 2019—a very wide range of results—anything from a Conservative lead of 5 points to a Labour one of 12— would result in a hung parliament. In short, the single-member plurality electoral system still cannot be relied upon to facilitate alternating single-party government by being more or less guaranteed to deliver an overall majority to one or other of the two largest parties.

But why is the system inclined to reward the Conservatives more richly than Labour? Electoral bias of this kind can arise for two principal reasons (Gudgin and Taylor, 1979; Johnston, 1979). The first is that the seats won by one of the parties are on average smaller in size than those won by the other—either because fewer people are registered to vote or because the level of turnout is lower. The second is that the vote cast for one of the parties is more efficiently distributed than those won by the other. A party's vote will be more efficiently distributed if more of its votes contribute to it winning seats narrowly—and less so if much of its support is either piled up in large majorities in safe seats or losing narrowly in lots of marginal seats.

An indication of the extent to which the Conservatives and Labour are affected by these two patterns—and how this has varied over time—is given in Table 2.4 (Soper and Rydon, 1958). In the first column, we show the difference between the average (mean) share of the two-party vote won by the Conservatives across all constituencies and that party's overall share of the votes cast in the country as a whole. If a party tends to perform more strongly in seats where fewer votes are cast, its average share of the vote across constituencies will be higher than its over-all share of the vote—and thus a positive sign in the first column of the table is an indication of an advantage to the Conservatives while a negative sign points to one for Labour. In the second column, meanwhile, we show the difference be-tween the share of the two-party vote won by the Conservatives in the median constituency and the party's mean share across all constituencies. The share in the median constituency represents the tally that divides a party's constituency performances into two equal groups, half being ones where the party does better than the median and half those where it does less well. If a party is to win more seats than its principal rivals, it will need to have won more than 50% of the two-party vote in the median constituency. Thus, if a party's median share is more than its mean share, that is an indication that its vote is likely to be more effi-ciently distributed.

One of the striking, but little remarked features of the 2019 election is that the contest was fought on the same constituency boundaries as every other election since and including 2010. This is despite the fact that the four Boundary Commissions (one for each part of the UK) presented recommendations for new, more equal constituencies to parliament in the autumn of 2018. These, though, were not put to MPs for their approval (Johnston *et al.*, 2019)—most likely be-cause of concern that, against the backdrop of severe internal party divisions over Brexit, some Conservative MPs whose political careers would be put at risk by proposals that also involved reducing the number of MPs from 650 to 600 would join the opposition in voting them down.

Table 2.4 indicates why the Conservatives would be thought to have an interest in constituencies being made more equal in size. At every election since 1966, the mean Conservative share of the two-party vote has been less than the party's overall share. Moreover, until 2017 at least, the gap has gradually widened over time, only to be reduced again after a boundary review. This is in part because the

Table 2.4 Measures of two-party bias, 1955–2019

Party	Conservative percentage of two-party vote		
	Mean −overall	Median −Mean	Median −overall
1955	+ 0.3	+ 0.6	+ 0.9
1959	+ 0.4	+ 0.8	+ 1.2
1964	+ 0.1	+ 0.4	+ 0.5
1966	−0.3	+ 0.2	−0.1
1970	−0.9	+ 0.8	−0.1
1970 (NT)	−0.1	+ 0.5	+ 0.4
1974 (Feb)	−0.1	− 0.5	−0.5
1974 (Oct)	−0.3	+ 1.4	+ 1.1
1979	−0.7	− 0.5	−1.2
1979 (NT)	−0.1	+ 0.9	+ 0.9
1983	−0.5	+ 1.7	+ 1.2
1987	−0.8	+ 1.4	+ 0.6
1992	−1.2	−0.0	−1.2
1992 (NT)	−0.2	−0.7	−0.9
1997	−0.4	−1.6	−2.0
2001	−1.4	−1.5	−2.9
2001 (NT)	−1.1	−1.4	−2.5
2005	−2.1	−1.1	−3.2
2005 (NT)	−1.5	−1.0	−2.5
2010	−1.3	−0.8	−2.1
2015	−1.6	+2.1	+0.5
2017	−0.4	+0.6	+0.2
2019	−0.5	+2.0	+1.5

NT, Notional results based on estimates of what the outcome would have been if that election had been fought on the new constituency boundaries that were introduced at the subsequent election. The 2001 redistribution (together with a reduction in the number of seats) was confined to Scotland, while the 2005 one only occurred in England and Wales.
Two-party vote: Votes cast for Conservative and Labour combined.
Figures based on all seats in Great Britain. Northern Ireland excluded.
Source: Author's calculations.

rules for drawing up constituency boundaries have hitherto resulted in smaller constituencies in Scotland and (more recently at least, especially in) Wales, where the Conservatives have performed less well, while for much of the post-war period, the pattern of population movement has seen people move away from (Labour-voting) inner cities towards (more Conservative-inclined) suburbs and rural areas (Champion, 2005; Rossiter *et al.*, 2009). Meanwhile, turnout also tends to be lower in Labour-held seats.

However, the 2017 election was the first at which the difference between the Conservatives' mean share of the two-party vote and their overall share fell even though there had not been a boundary review. This was because (i) turnout increased more in Labour-held seats than in Conservative ones and (ii) there was a tendency for the Conservatives to perform more strongly in areas that voted Leave, a pattern that resulted in more of the party's vote being garnered in smaller constituencies (Curtice, 2017a).

The first of these patterns was not repeated in 2019. Rather, on average, turn-out fell much more (by 2.6 points) in seats that Labour was defending than it did in those where the Conservatives were the incumbents (0.8 points). This pattern more or less wholly reversed the narrowing of the gap in turnout that was in evi-dence in 2015.[4]

On the other hand, the tendency in 2017 for the Conservatives to advance more strongly in areas that voted Leave—many of them places with smaller elec-torates—was repeated. The average electorate in the 54 seats the Conservatives gained from Labour was just 69,223. Not only is this lower than the GB-wide av-erage of 73,245, but also than the figure of 72,242 in those seats that Labour defended successfully. In short, the Conservatives' headline-grabbing gains oc-curred disproportionately in relatively small seats. Meanwhile, the swing to the Conservatives was also higher in seats with a lower turnout; in seats where less than 62% turned out to vote the average swing was 7.4 points, whereas in those where more than 72% turned out it was just 2.3 points.

At the same time, the hitherto persistent tendency for the difference between the size of the registered electorate in Conservative and Labour-held seats to widen came to a halt. It has been evident for some time that the pattern of popu-lation movement out of the inner city into the suburbs and rural areas was slow-ing down (Champion, 2016). Meanwhile, the Electoral Commission estimated that in 2018 only 85% of those who should be on the electoral register (for parlia-mentary elections) in 2018 were actually registered, so there was plenty of room for improvement in the quality of the register—and especially so in more Labour-inclined urban areas (Electoral Commission, 2019). In any event, the level of registration increased just as much between 2017 and 2019 in seats that Labour was defending (by 1,134) as it did in those where the Conservatives were first (1,101). Although there was still a difference of 3,889 between the average electorate in seats Labour were defending (71,644) and that in those where the Conservatives were the incumbents (75,533), the fact the gap did not widen fur-ther stands in sharp contrast to previous experience.[5]

Fighting the 2019 election on constituency boundaries that were nearly 20 years out of date was not then as disadvantageous to the Conservatives as might have been anticipated. The difference in the average size of Conservative and Labour-

---

[4]In 2019, turnout in seats that the Conservatives won in 2017 was 5.2 points higher than in seats Labour were defending; the equivalent gap in 2015 was 5.4 points.

[5]Indeed, if we classify seats according to who won in 2019, we find that on this basis, the gap fell some-what from 2,651 in 2017 to 2,470 in 2019.

Table 2.5 Distribution of the two-party vote, 2017 and 2019

Winning party share of two-party vote	Winning party: 2017		Winning party: 2019	
	Conservative	Labour	Conservative	Labour
50–55	42	47	39	49
55–60	45	42	35	31
60–65	64	40	50	43
65–70	66	51	72	37
70–80	72	64	79	49
80–100	10	36	18	56

Winning party share of two-party vote: Share of the two-party vote for the winning party assuming a 50:50 division of the overall two-party vote nationally, but an unchanged electoral geography.
Two-party vote: Votes cast for Conservative and Labour combined.
Table based only on seats won by Conservative or Labour at that election and contested by both parties.
Source: Author's calculations.

held seats did not widen. Meanwhile, as in 2017, the Conservative vote tilted further towards seats with smaller electorates and lower turnouts. Only a larger drop in turnout in Labour-held seats worked in the opposite direction—and even here the resulting gap in turnout simply resulted in a return to the status quo ante.

Still, while the Conservatives may not have been significantly further disadvantaged by differences in constituency sizes, they were hardly advantaged by them. To understand why the electoral system was inclined to treat the Conservatives more favourably than Labour, we need to look at the relative efficiency of the geographical distribution of the two parties' votes. Indeed, Table 2.4 suggests that the Conservatives were advantaged on this score by as much as they have been at any election since 1955.

Why this is the case is illustrated in Table 2.5, which provides fuller information on the distribution of the two-party vote in 2017 and 2019. As in Table 2.2, we assume that the two largest parties have an identical share of the vote nationally but that the geography of party support is as it actually was at the election in question. Thus, in 2019, for example, we assume that the Conservative share of the two-party vote is 7.6 points less than it actually was (and, in 2017, 1.5 points less), and that this reduction takes place everywhere. The table states the number of seats that on that basis each party would win with various shares of the two-party vote locally.

The figures in the first row of the table, which encompass the seats we have already defined as marginal, are perhaps rather surprising. It is Labour, not the Conservatives, who tend to win more seats with small majorities; the party has 49 such seats as compared with the Conservatives' 39. Moreover, the gap between the two parties in this respect widened between 2017 and 2019. However, if we turn our attention to the other end of the table, where we show the number of seats that each party wins with more than 80% of the two-party vote, we can see both that there are many more such seats in the Labour column (56) than the Conservative one (18), and that this gap is much wider than it was in 2017. In short, in 2019, Labour was 'wasting' many more votes than the Conservatives in piling up large majorities. This arose because, in seats where Labour had (on the basis of our calculation) more than 80% of the two-party vote in 2017, the Conservative share of the two-party vote increased on average by just 0.9 of a point. Meanwhile, in those seats where Labour's share of the two-party vote had been between 70% and 80%, the average increase was, at 4.1 points, also relatively low.

The headlines in the 2019 election focussed on Labour's loss of some of its traditional strongholds to the Conservatives, but in practice, Labour was also disadvantaged because it was performing best of all in seats that were already relatively safe for the party.[6] The resulting inefficiency in the distribution of its vote put it at a substantial disadvantage in its attempts to secure parliamentary representation—and unless reversed will leave the party at a disadvantage at future elections. In the meantime, it means that even though the Conservatives' 80-seat majority can be regarded by some yardsticks as relatively low, it actually exaggerates the overall propensity of the system to deliver safe overall majorities irrespective of who is in the lead. The outcome was also a reflection of a system that was treating the Conservatives markedly more favourably than Labour.

6.   An alternative system

We have demonstrated that, despite appearances, the outcome of the 2019 election did not signal that the operation of the single-member plurality electoral system has returned to a 'normality' in which most of the time either the Conservatives or Labour will win an overall majority. Yet that does not mean that the way it operated in 2019 was anything other than decisive so far as the issue that precipitated the election was concerned—Britain's future relationship with the EU. The result ensured that the UK left the EU at the end of January 2020.

---

[6]We should note that another source of electoral bias that is not captured by the statistics in Table 4 is now working to the Conservatives' disadvantage once more, after having disappeared in 2015 and 2017. The Conservatives waste more votes losing in seats that are won by third parties. On average the party won 23.9% of the vote in seats won by parties other than the Conservatives or Labour, while Labour won only 18.8%. In 2017, the two figures were virtually identical, while in 2015 it was actually Labour that 'wasted' more votes in this way. The explanation lies in the outcome in the 11 seats won by the Liberal Democrats, in which the Conservatives on average won 29.0% of the vote, whereas Labour secured only 7.5%.

Table 2.6 Projected outcome of the 2019 general election under regional proportional representation

	Projected seats	% share of seats	% seats − % votes
Conservatives	302	46.5	+2.9
Labour	221	34.0	+1.8
Liberal Democrats	74	11.4	−0.2
SNP	26	4.0	+0.1
Brexit	6	0.9	−1.1
PC	3	0.5	0.0
Green	0	0.0	−2.7
Others (NI)	18	2.6	—

Seats allocated by government region. Total number of seats in each region proportional to current electorate using St Laguë divisor. Division of seats within each region determined by D'Hondt divisor but confined in each region to those parties that won at least 5% of the vote.
Source: Author's calculations.

This is not necessarily what would have happened if a different, more proportional system had been in place.

In Table 2.6 we show what the outcome would have been if everyone had voted the same way as they did under the single-member plurality system, but seats had been allocated using a regional party list system similar to that used in European elections in the UK. Even though we assume that a party would have to win 5% of the vote in a region before it was allocated any seats (in line with the rules for the allocation of list seats on the Greater London Assembly) and the use of a rule for allocating seats that is more generous to larger parties, the Conservatives would not have won an overall majority—and, crucially, neither would they have done so in combination with the Brexit Party. The two parties' combined tally of 308 seats would have been insufficient to secure parliamentary approval for the revised Brexit deal that had been negotiated by the Prime Minister in October. Meanwhile, the parties in Great Britain that were willing to back a second EU referendum would have had 324 seats between them, which, to-gether with the half-dozen seats that would have been won by parties in Northern Ireland that were opposed to Brexit (and were willing, unlike Sinn Féin, to take their seats), would have constituted a potential parliamentary majority for a very different course of action.

Of course, in practice faced with a different system, some voters would have voted differently, and in particular, all of them would have had the opportunity to vote for one of the smaller parties such as the Brexit Party and the Greens— and not just those living in constituencies that those parties contested. This latter point, in particular, might well have resulted in a higher level of Brexit Party representation—the party's average share of the vote in the seats it contested was above 5% in five regions, whereas it won over 5% of the overall vote (and thus has been allocated seats under our scenario) in just two. Even so, bearing in mind that some of the seats the Brexit Party might otherwise have won would have been secured at the expense of the Conservatives, it is still unlikely that there would have been a pro-Brexit majority in a House of Commons elected by a regional party-list system.[7]

We should, of course, be careful of drawing the conclusion that the UK would not have left the EU if it was using a more proportional electoral system to elect its MPs. After all, if a regional party-list system of the kind examined here had been in place in 2015, the Conservatives and the United Kingdom Independence Party (UKIP) would have had a majority between them (Curtice, 2015) and perhaps a coalition of the two parties would have delivered Brexit by 2019. Equally, there is no guarantee that any second referendum would have resulted in a majority vote for Remain. But it is certainly difficult to avoid the conclusion that, in 2019 at least, the use of the single-member plurality system played a crucial role in enabling the Prime Minister to implement Brexit.[8]

7. Conclusion

After three elections in a row in which it failed to deliver a decisive overall majority for one party, the single-member plurality electoral system delivered a substantial majority that ended the impasse over Brexit that had dominated the business of the hung parliament that was elected in 2017. It appeared that 'normal' service had resumed so far as the electoral system is concerned. Yet in practice, the size of the Conservative majority reflected the large lead over Labour that the party enjoyed in votes and the fact that the system was treating it more

---

[7]This would also be the case if the Brexit Party did not stand at all, and all those who voted for the party backed the Conservatives instead. In those circumstances the Conservatives would have 313 seats, while 325 would have been won by British parties in favour of a second referendum and Northern Irish parties who oppose Brexit. With Sinn Féin winning but not taking up four seats, the latter figure would have constituted a majority irrespective of what the eight unionist MPs (who supported Brexit but not the Prime Minister's deal) opted to do.

[8]True, we should be careful about assuming that any alternative more proportional system would have resulted in a majority for another referendum. One instance where the position is less clear cut is the Single Transferable Vote system favoured by the Electoral Reform Society. According to a projection undertaken by the society itself, 315 Conservative and Brexit Party MPs would have been elected, just slightly less than the 317 representatives of British parties that were willing to back a second referendum (Garland *et al.*, 2020). In this instance, the fate of Brexit would lie in the hands of the various parties in Northern Ireland.

favourably than its principal opponents. Even then, it can be argued that the majority was smaller than might have been anticipated. Meanwhile, if the positions of the two largest parties had been reversed Labour could well have failed to secure an overall majority, and there remains a high probability that future elections will result in more hung parliaments.

There are two reasons why this is the case. First, despite the apparent dramatic changes in the geography of party support in 2019, there are still too few seats that are marginal between Labour and the Conservatives for the system to exaggerate the lead of the largest party over the second party to the extent it once did. Secondly, the system is still proving to be relatively poor at excluding third parties from the House of Commons, not least because of the collapse of the traditional two-party system in Scotland. These features may be hidden from view at present—but, unless they change, hung parliaments could well still prove to be a regular feature of British politics, a prospect that almost undoubtedly ensures that the debate about the merits of electoral reform is likely to continue.

References

Baker, C., Cracknell, R. and Uberoi, E. (2019) *General Election 2019: Results and Analysis*, London, House of Commons Library Briefing Paper CBP 8749, accessed at https://commonslibrary.parliament.uk/research-briefings/cbp-8749/ on 26 March 2020.

Bingham Powell, G., Jr. (2000) *Elections as Instruments of Democracy: Majoritarian and Proportional Visions*, New Haven, CT, Yale University Press.

Blais, A. and Carty, R. (1991) 'The Psychological Impact of Electoral Laws: Measuring Duverger's Elusive Factor', *British Journal of Political Science*, **21**, 79–93.

Butler, D. (1951) 'An Examination of the Results'. In Nicholas, H. (ed), *The British General Election of 1950*, Basingstoke, England, Macmillan, pp. 306–333.

Champion, A. (2005) 'Population Movement within the UK'. In Chappell, R. (ed) *Focus on People and Migration*, London, Palgrave Macmillan, pp. 91–114.

Champion, A. (2016) 'Internal Migration and the Spatial Distribution of the Population'. In Champion, A. and Falkingham, J. (eds.), *Population Change in the United Kingdom*, London, Rowman and Littlefield, pp. 125–141.

Cowley, P. and Kavanagh, D. (2016) *The British General Election of 2015*, London, Palgrave Macmillan.

Cowley, P. and Kavanagh, D. (2018) *The British General Election of 2017*, London, Palgrave Macmillan.

Curtice, J. and Steed, M. (1982) 'Electoral Choice and the Production of Government: The Changing Operation of the Electoral System in the UK Since 1955', *British Journal of Political Science*, **12**, 249–298.

Curtice, J. and Steed, M. (1986) 'Proportionality and Exaggeration in the British Electoral System', *Electoral Studies*, **5**, 209–228.

Curtice, J. (2009) 'Neither Representative nor Accountable: First past the Post in Britain'. In Grofman, B., Blais, A. and Bowler, S. (eds.), *Duverger's Law of Plurality Voting*, New York, NY, Springer, pp. 27–46.

Curtice, J. (2015) 'A Return to Normality? How the Electoral System Operated', *Parliamentary Affairs*, **68**, 25–40.

Curtice, J. (2017a) 'How the Electoral System Failed to Deliver – Again', *Parliamentary Affairs*, **71**, 29–45.

Curtice, J. (2017b) 'The Party and the Electorate'. In Hassan, G. and Barrow, S. (eds.), *A Nation Changed? the SNP and Scotland Ten Years On*, Edinburgh, Luath Press, pp. 32–39.

Duverger, M. (1954) *Political Parties: Their Organisation and Activity in the Modern State*, London, Methuen.

Electoral Commission (2019) *2019 Report: Accuracy and Completeness of the 2018 Electoral Registers in Great Britain*, accessed at https://www.electoralcommission.org.uk/who-we-are-and-what-we-do/our-views-and-research/our-research/accuracy-and-complete ness-electoral-registers/2019-report-accuracy-and-completeness-2018-electoral-regis ters-great-britain on 26 March 2020.

Garland, J., Palese, M. and Simpson, I. (2020) *Voters Left Voiceless: The 2019 General Election*, London, Electoral Reform Society. accessed at https://www.electoral-reform. org.uk/latest-news-and-research/publications/the-2019-general-election-voters-left-voiceless/ on 26 March 2020.

Gudgin, G. and Taylor, P. (1979), *Seats, Votes and the Spatial Organisation of Elections*, London, Pion.

Johnston, R. (1979) *Political, Electoral and Spatial Systems*, Oxford, Clarendon Press.

Johnston, R., Pattie, C. and Rossiter, D. (2019) *Boundaries in Limbo: Why the Government Cannot Decide How Many MPs there should be*, accessed at https://blogs.lse.ac.uk/politic sandpolicy/boundaries-in-limbo/ on 26 March 2020.

Kendall, M. and Stuart, A. (1950) 'The Law of Cubic Proportions in Election Results', *The British Journal of Sociology*, **1**, 183–197.

Norton, P. (1997) 'The Case for First past the Post', *Representation*, **34**, 84–88.

Rallings, C. and Thrasher, M. (2012) *British Electoral Facts 1832–2012*, London, Biteback.

Renwick, A. (2011) *A Citizens' Guide to Electoral Reform*, London, Biteback.

Rossiter, D., Johnston, R. and Pattie, C. (2009), *The Boundary Commissions: Redrawing UK's Map of Parliamentary Constituencies*, Manchester, England, Manchester University Press.

Russell, A. and Fieldhouse, E. (2005) *Neither Left nor Right? The Liberal Democrats and the Electorate*, Manchester, England, Manchester University Press.

Soper, C. and Rydon, J. (1958) 'Under-Representation and Electoral Prediction', *Australian Journal of Politics & History*, **4**, 94–106.

Taagerpera, R. and Shugart, M. (1989) *Seats and Votes: The Effects and Determinants of Electoral Systems*, New Haven, CT, Yale University Press.

Britain Votes (2019) 48–64

LOUISE THOMPSON*

From Minority Government to Parliamentary Stalemate: Why Election 2019 was Needed to Break the Brexit Logjam

It was clear from the outcome of the 2017 general election that the subsequent parliamentary term would be unusual. Theresa May had gone to the polls hoping for a clear mandate but instead found herself as a minority Prime Minister, relying on the support of the Democratic Unionist Party (DUP) to pass key pieces of legislation. May (2017) claimed that the election had brought certainty and clarity to Britain's withdrawal from the EU but any semblance of this would quickly fade away. Instead, a set of unusual circumstances would take over and make the 2017–2019 parliament stand out as nothing less than extraordinary. Government defeats in the Commons of a scale never before recorded, the centrality of an activist Speaker and an unusual degree of cross-party cooperation from MPs on opposing sides of the chamber, facilitated a stalemate between parliament and government which stymied any progress towards Brexit.

This contribution explores this state of brinkmanship between government and parliament from December 2018. It highlights the stubbornness of the government in its continued presentation of the same Brexit deal to parliament, assesses the significance of decisions made by the Speaker and examines the gradually emboldened cross-party group of MPs who would take advantage of procedural rules to put alternatives on the table. The combination of a government which failed to listen to parliament until it was too late and a parliament in which no single Brexit proposal could achieve a majority, left the UK's withdrawal from the EU stuck on a merry-go-round of meaningful votes, indicative votes and general election votes from which the bypassing of the Fixed-term Parliaments Act (FTPA) and a general election was the only escape.

*Louise Thompson, Politics, School of Social Sciences, University of Manchester, louise.thompson-4@manchester.ac.uk

© *The Author(s) 2020. Published by Oxford University Press on behalf of the Hansard Society; all rights reserved. For permissions, please e-mail: journals.permissions@oup.com*
doi:10.1093/pa/gsaa038

1. From a manageable to an unmanageable House of Commons

With the Conservative Party falling eight seats short of a majority at the start of the 2017 parliament, it was unclear whether the government's legislative programme was going to be manageable. A confidence and supply agreement negotiated with the DUP committed their Northern Irish MPs in supporting the government on key votes, including the necessary EU withdrawal legislation (Cabinet Office, 2017). Thus, in September 2017, MPs passed the second reading of the government's European Union (Withdrawal) Bill in what the Prime Minister called a 'historic decision', by a fairly comfortable majority of 326 votes to 290 (May, 2017). There were no Conservative rebels and all the DUP's MPs voted with the government, as agreed. Confident in its small parliamentary majority, the government took the bill into its committee stage in November.

There was an expectation that a considerable amount of parliamentary time over the next 18 months would be spent scrutinising further withdrawal legislation and in making post-Brexit arrangements. After all, the government had promised that MPs would be 'intimately' involved at every stage (HC Debates, 13 November 2017, c.37). May faced her first defeat at the bill's committee stage, when MPs narrowly passed an amendment by Dominic Grieve to give parliament a vote on the final Brexit deal (BBC, 2017). This 'meaningful' vote that Grieve and ten other Conservative rebels had forced on the government would go on to underpin the need for a 2019 general election. As just one of over 400 amendments tabled by MPs though, the government was not unduly fazed by the defeat, sacking one of the party's Vice-Chairs, Stephen Hammond, for joining the rebellion (Sharman, 2017). Although they faced a tough time as the bill continued its scrutiny journey, particularly in the Lords, ministers successfully brought the EU Withdrawal Bill to its conclusion the following year and it received Royal Assent at the end of June 2018.

By December 2018, however, the interaction between government and parliament became more hostile than it had been for several parliamentary sessions and the government's parliamentary majority appeared much more unstable. May suffered three significant defeats in the Commons in December 2018, including on a motion holding the government in contempt of parliament for failing to release crucial Brexit documents (BBC, 2018). The BBC's Laura Kuenssberg described it as an 'excruciating' day for May, with a record-breaking succession of defeats not seen since the 1970s (*ibid*).

The Prime Minister also faced an additional internal party battle with her own backbenchers. On 12 December, Sir Graham Brady, the Chair of the Conservative Party's 1922 Committee, announced that he had received 48 letters from Conservative MPs, triggering the 15% threshold for a vote of no-confidence in the party leader. Although a victory for May, one-third of Conservative MPs voted against her, an uncomfortably close result which would make delivering Brexit even more challenging. Over the next few months, this lack of confidence in the Prime Minister would underpin a succession of rebellions by Conservative MPs and see previously loyal backbenchers join opposition MPs in the 'no' lobby.

1.1 The balance between government and parliament begins to change

To properly understand the changing relationship between government and parliament, we must take a closer look at the parliamentary business over the weeks surrounding the Conservative Party's no-confidence vote in Theresa May. At the start of December, the government had put the negotiated withdrawal agreement before MPs for three days of debate. There was much unease about provisions for the Northern Ireland border, or 'backstop', across the House, including from the DUP. Recognising this concern, the Prime Minister delayed giving MPs the meaningful vote on the deal. In a rare admission from a Prime Minister, May admitted that if the vote had gone ahead as planned, the government would have lost 'by a significant margin' (HC Debates, 10 December 2018, c.23). The opposition parties were united in their frustration with this decision. The Scottish National Party (SNP) described it as a 'stunning display of pathetic cowardice' (Kirsty Blackman, HC Debates, 10 December 2018, c.28), while the DUP's Westminster leader, Nigel Dodds, announced that the decision was 'not credible' (HC Debates, 10 December 2018, c.31). During three hours at the despatch box answering questions from MPs, May reaffirmed to the House that the choice before them would be the choice between 'a deal, no deal and no Brexit', with no majority among MPs for any alternative (HC Debates, 10 December 2018, c.64). She would not be pressed though on precisely when the vote would now happen.

The views held by MPs on the type of Brexit which should be sought by the government and on the process by which it should be pursued and agreed by the House had long cut across party lines. But the degree of the divisions within and between parties on Brexit was becoming increasingly important. Father of the House Ken Clarke summarised the situation nicely when he observed:

> this House is divided not just into parties; it is divided into factions. It becomes clear that, at the moment, there is no predictable majority for any single course of action going forward (Ken Clarke, HC Debates, 10 December 2018, c.28).

Some MPs began to believe that the Prime Minister had been 'captured' by the group of hard Brexiteer Conservative backbenchers who formed the party's European Research Group (see HC Debates, 10 December 2018, c.40).

This was also a period during which the Commons Speaker began to play a role in providing a platform for backbenchers to cause trouble for the government. One of the principal ways in which he would do this was through urgent questions (UQs), emergency questions that require a government minister to attend the House of Commons that day, making a statement and answering questions from backbenchers. This procedure was already a marked feature of Bercow's speakership, but UQs relating to the Brexit process dominated UQs in the run up to the election (Priddy, 2020, p. 1), with 44 relating directly to Brexit.[1] The UQ tabled by Labour's Yvette Cooper, granted after the meaningful vote delay, committed the government to put the vote before the House of Commons before 21 January. In his answer to Cooper's question, the Department of Exiting the EU minister, Robin Walker, further committed the government:

> if Parliament were to reject the deal, the Government would be required to make a statement on our proposed next steps and table a motion in neutral terms on that statement (HC Debates, 11 December 2018, c.151).

This was a difficult period for executive–legislative relations, but the New Year brought even greater tension and a resurgent House of Commons. This was signalled most forcefully on 9 January when the government tabled its business motion for five further days of debate on the Prime Minister's Brexit deal, to be followed by the long-awaited meaningful vote. The Speaker allowed an amendment by Conservative backbencher Dominic Grieve, requiring the government to table a new motion within three sitting days, setting out the way forward, should they lose the vote. When Conservative loyalists challenged the decision, Bercow maintained that it was standard practice and that the Speaker's judgements should 'not [be] questioned by Members of the House' (HC Debates, 9 January 2019, c.366). He would later admit, however, that parliamentary officials had advised him not to allow a vote on Grieve's amendment, justifying his decision as a means of ensuring the government did not 'exert unfettered control' over parliament (Bercow, 2020, p. 373).

When the amendment passed by a narrow margin of just 11 votes (308 votes to 297), it marked the second time in just a few weeks that Grieve had upset the government's planned parliamentary timetable. *The Guardian's* description of Theresa May as an 'increasingly boxed-in Prime Minister' (Stewart and Walker, 2019) was very apt.

When the vote was finally held, the government suffered a massive defeat (202 votes to 432), the heaviest defeat in 'the parliamentary era' (Stewart, 2019). It was indeed the biggest loss since official parliamentary records began. If the

---

[1] Figures from parliamentary search tool using the terms 'Urgent questions' AND brexit session : 17/19

government were not humiliated enough by the size of the defeat, Jeremy Corbyn's decision to table a motion of no-confidence in the Prime Minister intensified the hostile atmosphere on the green benches. During the debate, Conservative backbenchers did not defend so much on May's leadership as a question whether a general election was the correct solution. The motion was defeated by 19 votes and May reiterated her desire to have individual meetings with the opposition party leaders and with 'groups of MPs who represent the widest possible range of views' (May, 2019a), in the hope of finding a way forward for her withdrawal deal. Jeremy Corbyn would later refuse to take part. Promising the House that she would approach discussions constructively, May warned that 'we must focus on ideas that are genuinely negotiable and have sufficient support' (HC Debates, 16 January 2019, c.1126). She also stuck to what would become an increasingly common line, that the only way to prevent a no-deal Brexit was for MPs to vote *for* the government's deal.

What was unusual about this tumultuous parliamentary period though was that, although it was clear that the position of the government was much weaker than normal, the House of Commons was equally weak. Although it was proving itself capable of frustrating the government and thwarting its attempts to forge ahead with May's negotiated Brexit deal, it too found itself thwarted by an overwhelming lack of consensus on an appropriate road to Brexit. Corbyn appealed to the House after the first meaningful vote defeat, saying that 'it is not enough for the House to vote against the deal before us, and against no deal; we also have to be *for* something' (HC Debates, 15 January 2019, c1109, emphasis added). Such was the deadlock that Ken Clarke told MPs that they were facing a 'constitutional crisis' (HC Debates, 29 January 2019, c.693).

At the end of January 2019, MPs debated the Brexit deal for a second time. Among the seven amendments selected by the Speaker for discussion were those tabled by Dominic Grieve and Yvette Cooper. Both amendments were designed to give the Commons the opportunity to avoid a no deal Brexit, by providing MPs with space in the parliamentary timetable the following week to debate and vote on a set of alternatives to May's deal (Grieve's amendment) and to let MPs decide whether to extend Article 50 in a binding vote (Cooper). For Grieve, it would provide 'the House the space in which to find where the majority lies' (HC Debates, 29 January 2019, c.674), but for the Prime Minister, it was an attempt to 'usurp the proper role of the Executive' (HC Debates, 29 January 2019, c.673). When MPs voted that evening, they demonstrated that a majority were against a no-deal Brexit (Conservative backbencher Caroline Spelman's amendment) and also against the current iteration of the Northern Ireland backstop (Graham Brady's amendment) but the other amendments failed. During a further general debate on Brexit on 14 February, MPs gain tried again to amend a government motion on Brexit. Although unsuccessful, Jeremy Corbyn warned the Prime Minister to stop 'ignoring Parliament' (HC Debates, 14 February 2019, c.1159).

2. Backbench MPs continue to push back against the government

In a change of strategy to try to prevent a no-deal Brexit, Yvette Cooper presented a Private Member's Bill in the Commons—the European Union (Withdrawal) (No. 4) Bill. This was a presentation bill and as such was the type of legislation which would normally be used by MPs simply to draw attention to an issue. The bill had cross-party support and was drafted with Conservative MP Oliver Letwin. It outlined a mechanism through which the Commons could instruct the Prime Minister to ask for an extension to the Article 50 period if the government lost the meaningful vote on the deal for a second time. It was a continuation of MPs' parliamentary action to try to prevent a no-deal Brexit. As the end of February approached, it looked as though the government might be starting to heed some of the Commons' concerns. Conservative MP Alberto Costa resigned from his position as Parliamentary Private Secretary to the Secretary of State for Scotland, David Mundell, in order to table an amendment to guarantee the implementation of citizens' rights and the government agreed to support it. The Prime Minister also committed to some of the provisions set out in the Cooper-Letwin bill, which would not progress beyond its first reading stage.

After negotiating further assurances in relation to the Northern Ireland backstop, May gave MPs the opportunity to vote on her Brexit deal for a second time on 12 March—just 17 days before the UK was expected to leave the EU. In what was becoming a remarkably familiar line, she told MPs that they faced 'a very clear choice: vote for and support this deal . . . or risk no deal' (HC Debates, 12 March 2019, c.209). After five hours of debate, they overwhelmingly rejected the deal once again, by 391 votes to 242. Although this was a smaller defeat for the government compared to the first attempt, it was still a reverse of a scale not typically seen in British parliamentary politics. A total of 75 Conservative MPs, plus the DUP, had walked through the no lobby, alongside the other opposition parties. Labour's Emma Reynolds summed up the general feeling on the backbenches:

> This last-minute deal, which really has not changed much, is just the latest chapter in the Tory party's Brexit divisions and melodrama. When the Prime Minister says that she is listening to Parliament, she is actually listening to hard-line Tory Brexiteers and her confidence and supply partners, the DUP. When she says that she is acting in the national interest, she is actually putting her party's interests above the prosperity of our constituents. She encourages us to come together, but she has done

little to reach out across the House to appeal to Labour Members and other Opposition MPs (HC Debates, 12 March 2019, c.277).

May told MPs that she 'profoundly regret[ted] the decision' (HC Debates, 12 March 2019, c.295), but that she would stand by the concessions she had made about the next appropriate parliamentary steps. Fearing that the government would simply put the same deal before the House for the third time and worried that parliament was being 'shabbily treated' by the government (Bercow, 2020, p. 382), the Speaker once again intervened, citing the convention that the same question cannot be put before MPs twice in any session.

3. A state of gridlock

By the end of March, MPs had formally voted against leaving the EU on the Prime Minister's terms on two occasions by staggering majorities. They had also voted firmly against leaving the EU without any deal at all. As the clock ticked down to the supposed exit day of 29 March, the government talked of a short extension to the Article 50 period. It was clear what MPs did not want, but it remained unclear what path out of the EU could be acceptable to parliamentarians and uncertain if a short extension would suffice to attain sufficiency of consensus. It quickly became apparent that the government would not seek a compromise, tabling a motion making an extension of the Article 50 period conditional on MPs voting for the government's deal. Labour MP Mary Creagh told the House that the government was holding them 'prisoner' (HC Debates, 13 March 2019, c.468). The following day MPs again tabled amendments pressing for alternatives including a second referendum, but all were defeated. They did, however, agree to the government's motion to ask the EU for a delay to the Brexit period beyond 29 March.

By this point not only the scale of the intra-party divisions, but also the scale of inter-party cooperation, was far higher than is the norm for British parliamentary politics. Whereas MPs usually work on a cross-party basis on shared policy demands, the poor handling of the withdrawal process by the government united MPs on all sides of the debate against the Prime Minister's deal. Damien Green admitted candidly that most of the MPs involved in cross-party efforts to make progress had 'not found [themselves] signing amendments together much in the past' (HC Debates, 13 March 2019, c.422). The Conservative MP, Oliver Letwin, for example, supported the government's deal in every meaningful vote, yet still worked with Yvette Cooper to give the Commons a voice in finding a better, more workable alternative to that same deal and ensuring that a no-deal Brexit was taken off the table. For some, this was an indication that the party system was no longer fit for purpose. Labour's Jess Phillips told MPs that it had been 'blown to pieces' by the Brexit debate (HC Debates, 13 March 2019, c.435).

4. Finding a way through the impasse

Since the beginning of the year, there had been a continual tension between the wishes of many MPs to explore alternative options for a way forward and the government's continued insistence that the only way forward was to vote for the deal. The Chair of the Brexit select committee, Hilary Benn, had found his committee's requests for a series of indicative votes on alternatives firmly declined by the Prime Minister. On 14 March, Benn tried once again to push for indicative votes, tabling an amendment to allow MPs to take control of the parliamentary timetable in order to do so. Although his amendment was selected by the Speaker, MPs narrowly rejected the move.

It would take two more weeks before Benn would get his wish. In a debate on 25 March, Oliver Letwin moved an amendment calling for business on 27 March to be set aside for MPs to hold a series of indicative votes. Government Minister David Lidington told the House that it would 'upset the balance between legislature and executive in a way that would set an unwelcome precedent' (HC Debates, 25 March 2019, c.68) but backbenchers queried the claim that the government had a longstanding constitutional right to determine Commons business (see HC Debates, 25 March 2019, cc.80, 81). Letwin's amendment passed comfortably (329 votes to 302) in what Vince Cable described as a 'major constitutional innovation' (HC Debates, 25 March 2019, c.144).

5. The Commons takes control

The indicative votes were just that: indicative rather than definitive. A vote in favour would not bind the government to any course of action but would show where the majority Brexit view lay. It was left to the Speaker to decide which motions to select; eight were chosen and announced to the House on the afternoon of 27 March. A business motion moved by Oliver Letwin set aside not just that day but also the following Monday if no majority view was found. For MPs like Letwin, it was the culmination of an attempt to prove that sovereignty lay with parliament, rather than with the government (see HC Debates, 27 March 2019, c.343, 344). When the results of the votes were announced later that evening, not a single alternative had been able to secure a majority. The narrowest result, Ken Clarke's customs union proposal, was defeated by eight votes. Several proposals had received more support from MPs than May's deal had just a few weeks before, but they had not been able to achieve the necessary majority.

Later that week the Prime Minister tried and failed for a third time to gain Commons approval for her Brexit deal. To get around the Speaker's restrictions on putting the same question twice, the government asked MPs to vote only on the withdrawal agreement and not on the political declaration. Despite asking MPs to 'look into [their] hearts and decide what is best for our constituents and our country' (HC Debates, 29 March 2019, c.769), the third meaningful vote was defeated by 286 votes to 344. May summarised the extreme parliamentary stale-mate in her address to the House immediately afterwards:

> I fear that we are reaching the limits of this process in this House. This House has rejected no deal; it has rejected no Brexit; on Wednesday it rejected all the variations of the deal on the table; and today it has rejected approving the withdrawal agreement alone and continuing a process on the future (HC Debates, 29 March 2019, c.775).

Her words would be mirrored by activity in the Commons the following week when Oliver Letwin put a motion before the House to pursue a second round of indicative votes. This time the Speaker selected only four motions for MPs to consider: a customs union, a Common Market 2.0 motion (proposing member-ship of the European Free Trade Association and the European Economic Area plus a comprehensive customs arrangement with the EU), a confirmatory public vote and an SNP motion asking for an extension to the Brexit process or a clear vote between no-deal and a revocation of Article 50. All four were defeated, but Ken Clarke's customs union motion lost out by a very narrow margin of just three votes. Also significant was the motion for a confirmatory public vote, defeated by just 12 votes (292 votes to 280). A sizeable number of MPs now clearly favoured giving the British public a further say. At this point, though, the UK was set to leave the EU in 11 days, yet MPs had rejected May's Brexit deal and every alternative proposal put before them. MPs said it would be an 'outrage' if the government tried to hold a fourth vote (HC Debates, 1 April 2019, c.880). Exasperated by the failure of his own motion in the evening's votes, Conservative Nick Boles announced his resignation from the Conservative Party, crossing the floor of the Commons to a round of applause from opposition MPs.

The following day Yvette Cooper introduced another Private Member's Bill, the European Union (Withdrawal) (No. 5) Bill, backed by MPs from all parties including Letwin, Grieve and Benn, requesting another Article 50 extension. The bill aimed to give clarity to the process of asking for an extension to exit day and to ensure that the Commons would continue to have a role to play in the process. Cooper's bill completed its Commons stages in a single day, passing its third reading by just a single vote. Moving on to the House of Lords, it received Royal Assent just five days later. This forced the government to bring forward a motion extending the Article 50 deadline to 30 June, which was passed with a hefty majority. A new date of 31 October would later be agreed with the EU.

6. An increasingly fractured government and an isolated Prime Minister

As the stalemate extended into May 2019, the government hoped to hold a fourth meaningful vote and to introduce the necessary Brexit legislation (the Withdrawal Agreement Bill). The already difficult parliamentary context was exacerbated though by the momentum forming for the Prime Minister's departure. Already a group of 14 Conservative MPs had written to May to warn against including a customs union in any compromise deal with the opposition parties. It was no surprise, then, that at a meeting with the 1922 Committee of Conservative MPs, the Prime Minister agreed to formalise a timetable for her departure.

Despite the overt lack of support now for May's leadership from both the Conservative Party and from the Commons, the Prime Minister still outlined her plans for a 'new deal' to MPs (HC Debates, 22 May 2019, c.731). She outlined a ten-point plan to 'end the political impasse' which would be enshrined in the forthcoming Withdrawal Agreement legislation including a commitment to replace the Northern Ireland backstop by December 2020, a workers' rights bill and a guarantee that MPs would be able to vote on any treaties governing the UK's future relationship with the EU. Jeremy Corbyn told her that she had lost the 'authority to deliver' (HC Debates, 22 May 2019, c.734) and that, with no guarantee that her replacement would stand by any of these guarantees, it was a case of too little, too late. Just two days later, May formally announced her departure saying that she had done everything she could to convince MPs to back her deal (May, 2019*b*). The Conservative Party's disastrous performance at the European Parliament elections just a few days later was a sign that the public had lost any faith they had in the government delivering the Brexit they had promised. Following a ballot of MPs and party members, Boris Johnson was elected as the next leader of the Conservative Party, taking over from Theresa May as Prime Minister at the end of July.

7. A new Prime Minister facing the same parliamentary problems

Boris Johnson's first speech from Downing Street saw him on a mission to prove 'the doubters, the doomsters [and] the gloomsters' that they were wrong about the government's chances of honouring the 2016 referendum (Johnson, 2019*a*). Promising to leave by 31 October with 'no ifs or buts' (Johnson, 2019*a*) he had just 99 days to succeed in what his predecessor had failed to do over the last three years. In his first appearance before MPs in the Commons, Johnson promised to 'turbo charge' the Brexit process after the summer recess (HC Debates, 25 July 2019, c.1458). At the end of August, however, he announced that the Queen had approved a prorogation of parliament for most of September and early October. MPs were understandably concerned about such a move, which would inhibit parliamentary scrutiny at a critical time. As well as the lack of progress on parliament's approval of the Brexit deal, other legislation was also building up, including the Trade Bill and the Agriculture Bill. The Commons Speaker told the press that it was 'blindingly obvious' that the aim of prorogation was to prevent scrutiny of Brexit (BBC, 2019).

The Prime Minister's determination to prorogue parliament was matched by a similarly determined Commons which did not want the government to go unscrutinised. When the House returned in early September, Hilary Benn introduced another piece of private member's legislation—the European Union (Withdrawal) (No. 6) Bill—giving the Prime Minister until 19 October to pass his Brexit deal, to pass a no-deal motion, or to seek a further extension to Article 50. The bill, which even went so far as to set out word-for-word the text of the letter which the Prime Minister would be required to send to the European Council President, demonstrated that the Commons would not be relinquishing its new found power over the government any time soon. It set 31 January 2020 as the new deadline to leave the EU.

Passing Benn's bill required Oliver Letwin to secure an emergency debate in the Commons, in which MPs passed a motion to take control of parliamentary business once more. When the tellers announced the result (328 votes to 301), it was clear that the responsibility fell on the shoulders of 21 Conservative MPs who had joined their opposition colleagues in the 'aye' lobby. They included a now familiar set of faces (Grieve, Letwin and Clarke) but also a broader contingent of former cabinet ministers and previously loyal MPs (Anne Milton, Philip Hammond and Ed Vaizey). All would lose the party whip that night and sit as independent Conservative MPs.[2] Their expulsion only served to exacerbate the government's minority position in the Commons. When two ministers, Jo Johnson and Amber Rudd, resigned from the Cabinet Johnson's position in the Commons fell even further. The previous parliamentary session seemed to be repeating itself.

8. The bumpy road to a general election

In his formal response to the vote on Letwin's motion, the Prime Minister told MPs they had left him with no choice but to push for a general election. Putting

---

[2]Sam Gyimah joined the Liberal Democrats and he was joined by former colleague Antoinette Sandbach a few weeks later.

the blame squarely in parliament's hands, he accused MPs of 'wrecking' the Brexit deal and bringing 'more dither, more delay and more confusion' (HC Debates, 3 September 2019, c.140). A government motion was subsequently tabled in line with the provisions of the FTPA. As Benn's bill passed its second reading and committee stage the next day, Johnson moved the motion for an early election. When the result was announced, the Prime Minister found himself in the strange position of having won the vote (298 votes to 56) but losing the prize of a general election as he had not met the threshold of 434 votes specified in the legislation.

The bill received Royal Assent on 9 September, the day on which parliament was due to be prorogued. Dominic Grieve successfully lobbied the Speaker for an emergency debate on the prorogation, forcing the government to come to the House and explain themselves. Raising his concerns with Bercow about the unprecedented parliamentary manoeuvre, he questioned the Prime Minister's motives, citing the difference between his public statements and 'what the evidence suggests is the reality' (HC Debates, 9 September 2019, c.519). He was duly granted an emergency debate on the matter in which he requested copies of all formal and informal communication from government be presented to parliament through a humble address. The motion was agreed to by 311 votes to 302. Johnson then tried once again to get the House to agree to an early general election. Referring to Benn's legislation as the 'surrender bill', he told MPs that an election was 'the only way to break the deadlock in the House' (HC Debates, 9 September 2019, c.616). For a second time, the government won the vote, largely thanks to Labour's abstention (293 votes to 46) but failed to achieve the majority required under the FTPA. The SNP leader in the Commons congratulated Johnson for managing to lose 'every vote he has brought to the House since he became Prime Minister' (HC Debates, 9 September 2019, c.640). Bercow would later describe Johnson's treatment of parliament as a 'constitutional outrage' (Proctor, 2019).

When the Supreme Court unanimously ruled that the prorogation had prevented parliament from exercising 'its constitutional functions' and was thus unlawful, MPs returned to the Commons for what the Speaker said was the 'most peculiar atmosphere' he had ever known (Bercow, 2020, p. 1). The Prime Minister was met with cries of 'resign!' from the opposition benches (see HC Debates, 25 September 2019, c.774) and challenged them to table a no-confidence motion. The resulting hostile atmosphere in the House meant that, when the government tried to adjourn the Commons for Conservative party conference, MPs refused, defeating the motion by 289 votes to 306.

9. A new parliamentary session

As a new parliamentary session began in mid-October 2019, following a lawful prorogation, MPs agreed to sit on a Saturday for the first time in 37 years to debate the government's new Brexit deal and have a further attempt at a meaningful vote. The Speaker selected another cross-party amendment, moved by Oliver Letwin, to give the House the chance to scrutinise the text of the necessary withdrawal legislation before having any meaningful vote. As was now becoming a regular occurrence for Letwin's amendments, the House gave its seal of approval (322 votes to 306) and, as such, the meaningful vote could not be put to the House. The government announced its intention to proceed with the vote the following week but the Speaker disallowed it on the grounds that it 'would be repetitive and disorderly to do so' (HC Debates, 21 October 2019, c.696). By then, the Prime Minister had anyway been obliged to follow the measures set out in the Benn legislation, sending a letter to the European Council requesting an extension to Article 50, which the Council later agreed to, giving a new Brexit date of 31 January 2020.

A few days later, the EU (Withdrawal Agreement) Bill came before MPs. The government had allocated just three days for the bill to complete its scrutiny, something all parties warned was 'simply not good enough' for such important legislation which had only been printed the evening before (HC Debates, 21 October 2019, c.735; c.884). Although the bill passed its second reading with some ease, the programme motion for its committee stage was defeated (308 votes to 322). After the vote, Jeremy Corbyn described the Prime Minister as the 'author of his own misfortune' (HC Debates, 21 October 2019, c.926) and the government decided to pause the further progress of the bill.

Frustrated once more by the Commons, the government put forward a third general election motion on the grounds that parliament had 'run its course' and was not 'capable of delivering on the priorities of the people' (HC Debates, 29 October 2019, c.54). Jeremy Corbyn pledged that Labour would not support an election motion until no-deal had been taken off the table and it was clear that people (particularly students) would not be disenfranchised by an election date right before Christmas, while the SNP wanted to force the Prime Minister to stop Brexit rather than risk giving him a mandate or majority to finish it. Only the Liberal Democrats expressed their support for an election. It was no surprise, then, that once again the required majority was not reached. Most Labour MPs abstained, along with several of the former Conservative MPs who had had the whip withdrawn. Johnson told MPs the result was 'utterly bewildering' and that the government would introduce a general election bill instead, to finally end the 'dysfunctional parliament' (HC Debates, 29 October 2019 c.79). As a standard piece of legislation, the Early Parliamentary General Election Bill required only a simple majority of MPs to vote in favour. Specifying 12 December 2019 as polling day under the FTPA, the two-clause bill passed its Commons stages in a single day, its third reading supported by 438 votes to 20. Johnson had finally managed to circumvent the Act which the party's manifesto would later commit to removing altogether.

10. The 2019 general election and parliament

As MPs returned to their constituencies to campaign in the 2019 general election, the Conservative government had set a series of political and parliamentary records. Over the preceding two years, over a quarter of the Cabinet had resigned, over 100 backbench MPs had voted to remove a Prime Minister from her position, the government had been defeated by the largest margin in parliamentary history and it had been censured by the Supreme Court for an unlawful prorogation. MPs were not relishing the thought of another general election so soon but it was the inevitable consequence of the state of gridlock and inertia which had brought the government's legislative programme to a standstill.

The campaign itself was mired in a sense of distrust or disbelief from the public at the behaviour of their elected representatives. For some, there was an irony in the perpetual voting on Brexit, given that the public had only had the chance to vote once in the referendum (e.g. HC Debates, 14 March 2019, c.609). MPs had become ever more conscious of the public's view of the Commons as the 2017 parliament had progressed. They voiced their constituents' concerns about the 'childish antics' of MPs (HC Debates, 29 January 2019, c.686) and the general sense of exasperation with parliament. Some felt that it was now their duty to let the public decide what the composition of the new parliament, and thus their preferred path out of the European Union, should be. Johnson's campaign slogan of 'Get Brexit Done' tied neatly with this sense of frustration that constituents had been relaying to their MPs.

As the results came in during the early hours of 13 December, it was clear that the 2019 parliament would be a very different beast to its predecessor. The large majority for the Conservatives put Prime Minister Boris Johnson in a much stronger parliamentary position, providing the parliamentary buffer needed to progress smoothly with the EU withdrawal process. Many of the Conservative rebels, such as Ken Clarke and Oliver Letwin, who had been such persistent thorns in the government's side, had already announced their intention to stand down at the election. Others stood as independent or Liberal Democrat candidates. All of them failed to win their seats. They included Dominic Grieve, the architect of so many government defeats, who lost his Beaconsfield seat to Conservative candidate Joy Morrissey. Ten of the suspended Conservative MPs had the party whip restored in October 2019 but just four of these (Steve Brine, Greg Clark, Stephen Hammond and Caroline Nokes) contested the election. John Bercow, the Commons Speaker who had granted so many backbench amendments, also stood down from parliament. The Prime Minister therefore found himself relieved of the three major bugbears of his premiership so far; the lack of a parliamentary majority, the activist Speaker and most of the rebellious backbenchers, had now gone.

11. Conclusion

The 2019 general election marked the end of an extremely volatile period of parliamentary politics. Pete Wishart's description of the events of the 2017 parliament as a very 'British parliamentary coup', one 'conducted with points of order and copies of Erskine May rather than through military means', was very apt (HC Debates, 1 April 2019, c.804). Armed with the support of the Commons Speaker, MPs had provided a visible demonstration to the government that it did not have unfettered power. Although they were unable to put forward an alternative to the government's Brexit deal that an absolute majority of MPs could get behind, they had shown the government that if it treated the parliament with contempt it would be quickly reined in. The power of the Commons was wholly unusual, but the resurgence was to be short-lived. With an 'overwhelming mandate' from the people at the general election, the Prime Minister's promise of a 'parliament that works for you' (Johnson, 2019*b*) was confirmed by the passage of the troublesome Withdrawal Agreement Bill in January 2020 with a majority of 99. It seems unlikely that the relationship between parliament and government will be as fraught for the foreseeable future, but the memories of what the Commons can do to a struggling government will no doubt linger on.

References

BBC (2017, 13 December) 'Brexit Bill: Government Loses Key Vote after Tory Rebellion', accessed at https://www.bbc.co.uk/news/uk-politics-42346192 on 3 April 2020.

BBC (2018, 5 December) 'Theresa May Suffers Three Brexit Defeats in the Commons', accessed at https://www.bbc.co.uk/news/uk-politics-46446694 on 3 April 2020.

BBC (2019, 28 August) 'Parliament Suspension: Queen Approves PM's Plan', accessed at https://www.bbc.co.uk/news/uk-politics-49493632 on 10 May 2020.

Bercow, J. (2020) *Unspeakable: The Autobiography*, London, Weidenfeld and Nicolson.

Cabinet Office (2017, 26 June) 'Confidence and Supply Agreement between the Conservative and Unionist Party and the Democratic Unionist Party', accessed at https://www.gov.uk/government/publications/conservative-and-dup-agreement-and-uk-. accessed at government-financial-support-for-northern-ireland/agreement-between-the-conservative-and-unionist-party-and-the-democratic-unionist-party-on-support-for-the-government-in-parliament#confidence-and-supply-agreement-in-the-uk-parliament on 24 April 2020.

HC Debates (13 November 2017) c.37.

HC Debates (10 December 2018) c.23.

HC Debates (10 December 2018) c.28.

HC Debates (10 December 2018) c.31.

HC Debates (10 December 2018) c40.

HC Debates (11 December 2018) c.151.

HC Debates (9 January 2019) c.366.

HC Debates (15 January 2019) c.1109.

HC Debates (16 January 2019) c.1126.

HC Debates (29 January 2019) c.674.

HC Debates (29 January 2019) c.686.

HC Debates (29 January 2019) c.693.

HC Debates (14 February 2019) c.1159.

HC Debates (12 March 2019) c.209.

HC Debates (12 March 2019) c.277.

HC Debates (12 March 2019) c.295.

HC Debates (13 March 2019) c.468.

HC Debates (14 March 2019) c.609.

HC Debates (25 March 2019) c.68.

HC Debates (25 March 2019) cc.80–81.

HC Debates (25 March 2019) c.144.

HC Debates (27 March 2019) cc.343–344.

HC Debates (29 March 2019) c.769.

HC Debates (29 March 2019) c.775.

HC Debates (1 April 2019) c.804.

HC Debates (1 April 2019) c.880.

HC Debates (22 May 2019) c.731.

HC Debates (22 May 2019) c.734.

HC Debates (25 July 2019) c.1458.

HC Debates (3 September 2019) c.140.

HC Debates (9 September 2019) c.519.

HC Debates (9 September 2019) c.616.

HC Debates (9 September 2019) c.640.

HC Debates (25 September 2019) c.774.

HC Debates (21 October 2019) c.696.

HC Debates (21 October 2019) c.735; c.884.

HC Debates (21 October 2019) c.926.

HC Debates (29 October 2019) c.54.

HC Debates (29 October 2019) c.79.

Johnson, B. (2019a, 24 July) 'Boris Johnson's First Speech as Prime Minister', accessed at https://www.gov.uk/government/speeches/boris-johnsons-first-speech-as-prime-minister-24-july-2019 on 20 April 2020.

Johnson, B. (2019b, 13 December) 'PM Statement in Downing Street', accessed at https://www.gov.uk/government/speeches/pm-statement-in-downing-street-13-december-2019 on 20 April 2020.

May, T. (2017, 12 September) 'PM Statement on EU Withdrawal Bill', accessed at https://www.gov.uk/government/news/pm-statement-on-eu-withdrawal-bill-12-sept-2017 on 20 April 2020.

May, T. (2019a, 16 January) 'PM's Statement at Downing Street', accessed at https://www.gov.uk/government/speeches/pms-statement-at-downing-street-16-january-2019 on 14 April 2020.

May, T. (2019b, 24 May) 'PM's Statement in Downing Street', accessed at https://www.gov.uk/government/speeches/prime-ministers-statement-in-downing-street-24-may-2019 on 20 April 2020.

Priddy, S. (2020, 7 April) *Number of Urgent Questions in the Commons since 1997*, London, House of Commons Library, CBP 08344, accessed at: file:///C:/Users/Team%20Knowhow/Downloads/CBP-8344.pdf on 11 April 2020.

Proctor, K. (2019, 28 August) 'Boris Johnson's Move to Prorogue Parliament a 'Constitutional Outrage' Says Speaker', *The Guardian*, accessed at https://www.theguardian.com/politics/2019/aug/28/boris-johnsons-move-to-prorogue-parliament-a-constitutional-outrage-says-speaker on 22 April 2020.

Sharman, J. (2017, 13 December) 'Stephen Hammond: Tory MP Sacked as Conservative vice-chairman after Brexit Rebellion', *The Independent*, accessed at https://www.independent.co.uk/news/uk/politics/stephen-hammond-fired-sacked-brexit-rebellion-tory-mp-theresa-may-latest-a8108691.html on 26 April 2020.

Stewart, H. and Walker, P. (2019, 10 January) 'Brexit: May Loses Grip on Deal after Fresh Commons Humiliation', *The Guardian*, accessed at https://www.theguardian.com/politics/2019/jan/09/may-loses-grip-on-brexit-deal-after-fresh-commons-humiliation on 24 April 2020.

Stewart, H. (2019, 16 January) 'May Suffers Heaviest Parliamentary Defeat of a British PM in the Democratic Era', *The Guardian*, accessed at https://www.theguardian.com/politics/2019/jan/15/theresa-may-loses-brexit-deal-vote-by-majority-of-230 on 13 April 2020.

SAM POWER, TIM BALE AND PAUL WEBB*

'Mistake overturned, so I call it a lesson learned':[1] The Conservatives

When all is said and done, what might be the most surprising thing about the Conservative Party's victory in 2019 was how unsurprising it was. As the UK voted on 12 December, almost every poll had the Tories ahead by at least six percentage points (BBC, 2019). And yet much was made during the campaign itself of the result being supposedly hard to call (Pienaar, 2019). This was partly perhaps because commentators were chastened by unexpected results in 2015 and 2017. But it was also because, in early October, the British Election Study (BES) had shown that the electorate was the 'most volatile in modern times' (British Election Study, 2019), with even the godfather of psephology (indeed, the inventor of the term) Sir David Butler stating that he had 'never felt more confused and uncertain' about an electoral outcome (Payne, 2019).

Yet the dawn which broke on 13 December brought Conservatives what for some of them must have been delayed gratification: this was the victory that 2017 was supposed to have been. The difference, as Johnson's former colleague from City Hall Guto Harri argued, was in the execution: 'he's got the same deck of cards as Theresa May, but he's played them differently' (McTague, 2019).

1. 'I'm not the artist; I'm merely the subject—it is for you to apply the rich *chiaroscuro* to your canvas'[2]

One of the more interesting analogies made during the general election came from an unusual source. Matthew McGregor—a veteran digital political strategist

---

*Sam Power, Department of Politics, University of Sussex, s.d.power@sussex.ac.uk; Tim Bale, School of Politics and International Relations, Queen Mary University of London, t.bale@qmul.ac.uk; Paul Webb, Department of Politics, University of Sussex, p.webb@sussex.ac.uk

[1]Lyrics by Alicia Keys (2007).

[2]Remarks made to a journalist by Boris Johnson when asked why it had been such a dull campaign (reported by McTague, 2019).

© *The Author(s) 2020. Published by Oxford University Press on behalf of the Hansard Society; all rights reserved.*
For permissions, please e-mail: journals.permissions@oup.com
doi:10.1093/pa/gsaa022

who had worked on Obama's re-election campaign in 2012, but also extensively for the Labour Party and Blue State Digital—argued that to understand everything you needed to know about the Conservative Party strategy in 2019, you should go back not to 2017 but rather to 2008:

> I worked for the Labour Party in 2008, for Boris Johnson's first mayoral run . . . and they had very little to say. I mean the entire campaign was, 'I'm going to get rid of bendy buses' . . . he makes himself a very, very big character outside of election time and then in election campaigns he makes himself as small a target as he possibly can and just tries to dance his way through without taking too many hits. So, they've built up all the momentum before the election campaign and now they're trying to coast through quietly. (Commons People, 2019)

It might well be the case, nonetheless, that Conservative Campaign Headquarters (CCHQ) had also learned the hard lessons from a 2017 campaign that put Theresa May front and centre—in terms of direct mail and leaflets, if not during TV debates. Part of this approach was down to Isaac Levido, the election strategist who had worked on the 2015 Cameron campaign and Scott Morrison's surprise re-election in Australia earlier in 2019. Levido was said to favour a 'safety-first' approach and 'insisted on strict message discipline . . . rarely veering from [Johnson's] slogan to "Get Brexit Done", and dodging the most difficult television interviews that risked tripping him up' (Donaldson and Ross, 2019). The campaign, full of 'clunking metaphors' (Johnson, 2019) such as driving a JCB through a wall to symbolise breaking the parliamentary deadlock was, in fact, 'classic Johnson, giving the appearance of chaotic joviality' whilst in reality 'saying nothing to distract from the campaign script' (McTague, 2019).

The Conservative Party manifesto itself is a neat encapsulation of this approach. It came in at just over 60 pages, nearly half that of Labour's, and was so bereft of detail that PoliticsHome dubbed it the 'meh-nifesto' (Langford, 2019). It contained relatively modest spending proposals of £2.9 billion, especially when compared with the Liberal Democrats' £63 billion and Labour's £83 billion. This made some in CCHQ anxious, with Labour being perceived as the party of change and the Tories as the party of more of the same (BBC, 2020). But it reflected a calculated gamble. Whilst the Tories might well have been seen as failing to properly address nearly ten years of austerity, they hoped that Labour's more full-hearted approach to public spending would simply be seen as unrealistic (Partington, 2019).

Ultimately, that gamble paid off. Moments like Culture Secretary Nicky Morgan coming unstuck on *Good Morning Britain* with regards to how many of the promised 50,000 new nurses were in actuality 'new', represented little more than one of a few fleeting 'gotcha' moments of the campaign, rather than more fundamental dissections of a manifesto which was otherwise seen as a more viable offer than Labour's. Michael Gove, whilst disagreeing that the manifesto was 'light', admitted as much when suggesting that it was 'written in such a way as to make sure that people had a clear sense of the direction we wanted to take the country and also to avoid some of the rows and distractions that had derailed Theresa's campaign in 2017' (BBC, 2020). It was, indeed, left to the public to apply the rich chiaroscuro to the (relatively) blank canvas.

Whilst surely a hangover from the failures of 2017, this strategy might also have reflected an acceptance amongst party higher-ups, including Johnson himself, that he could be a rather 'marmite' figure. We know from work conducted by the campaign organisation Who Targets Me that all parties were relentlessly A/B testing all kinds of messaging during the early stages of the campaign on Facebook (Doward, 2019). This led to the Conservatives adopting varied marketing strategies, depending on the constituencies they were targeting. In Leave-voting constituencies, adverts solely featuring Johnson were favoured, whereas in Remain-voting constituencies, (negative) adverts solely featuring the opposition were favoured (Who Targets Me, 2019).

In terms of campaign management, then, there was a pretty basic cost–benefit analysis at play. There was simply more to be lost than gained from Johnson being overly visible on the election trail. If that meant taking short-term reputational damage from, say, appearing only as an ice sculpture at a Channel 4 debate on climate change, or refusing a sit-down interview with BBC Rottweiler Andrew Neil, then so be it. As Michael Gove put it, when asked whether it was a mistake for Johnson not to be questioned by Neil (BBC, 2020):

> No. We won ... with the best will in the world ... the purpose of running an election campaign is to win so that you can govern the country well, not to agree to every broadcast bit.

Indeed, those rare occasions when Johnson did encounter significant scrutiny suggested the Tories' less-is-more strategy was a sensible one. The final days of the campaign witnessed farcical scenes featuring Johnson seeking refuge in a large fridge to hide from a particularly enthusiastic *Good Morning Britain* reporter, as well as a slightly more sinister pocketing of a reporter's phone when he confronted the PM with a picture of a child forced to sleep on a hospital floor.

Despite all this, when Johnson did put himself forward for scrutiny in head-to-head leaders' debates he performed as well, if not marginally better than Jeremy Corbyn, at least in as much as these things can be measured. Both the BBC and ITV debates were effectively fought to a 'score draw'. YouGov found 51% of voters backing Johnson as the winner in the ITV debates (Ibbetson, 2020) whereas the BBC debates (Smith, 2019)—held a full three weeks later—had Johnson on 52% to Corbyn's 48%. If, on the issues there was little between the two, when the public were asked who would make the best prime minister, there was considerably more daylight. According to a post-election poll conducted by Lord Ashcroft, 49% of voters said that Johnson would make the best prime minister, with just 31% saying the same of Corbyn (Ashcroft, 2019a). Finally, a more light-hearted poll, released just days before the election might have been the clearest indication of the public's true feelings, suggesting Johnson was simply seen as the best of a not particularly desirable bunch. YouGov (2019a) asked 'If you had to, which of the main party leaders would you most like to spend Christmas Day with?'; here, excluding 'don't knows', Johnson was the clear winner. He stood alone at 22%, with Corbyn on just 14%, Farage on 10% and Swinson and Sturgeon on 8%.

With any election, you do need a little bit of luck, and many problems that the Conservatives faced—or might have faced—were quickly nullified by weaknesses in their opposition. For example, the first week of the campaign got off to a rocky start when Welsh Secretary Alun Cairns resigned over claims that he was aware of a former aide's hand in 'sabotaging' a rape trial and Jacob Rees-Mogg apologised when appearing to imply that Grenfell Tower victims lacked common sense (O'Donoghue, 2019). However, at the same time, Corbyn had to contend with two (former) MPs doing the rounds of the weekend politics shows urging voters not to plump for the Labour Party. Similarly, the London Bridge terror attack might well have been a moment in which cuts to defencing and policing were brought front and centre, but in the eyes of many, Corbyn now lacked the moral authority to make that argument. The Conservatives might also have been tripped up by a rather unhelpfully timed visit from Donald Trump but he—aside from suggesting that the US would not 'take' the NHS 'if you handed it to us on a silver platter' and describing Johnson as 'very capable'—largely stood aside from the fray (Langford, 2019).

2.   The organisational strengths

From Johnson's victory in the leadership contest, we know, and have always known, that one thing Johnson can do is excite the Conservative base—and the organisational shortcomings that plagued the Conservative campaign in 2017 were lessened here. Whilst membership was still well below that of Labour (as of July 2019 the Conservatives had around 180,000), it still represented a modest increase on the 2017 number which stood at circa 150,000. Moreover, Labour membership, whilst still impressive, had reportedly fallen off considerably since 'peak Jeremy'. PoliticsHome, in July 2019, had the 'bleakest' report that Labour membership had dropped to 485,000, from the 518,659 reported in the 2018 accounting returns to the Electoral Commission (Schofield, 2019), and nearly a full 80,000 down from the high of 564,443 reported in December 2017 (Audickas *et al.*, 2019). The revival of Tory membership numbers did not, however, mean that the party's grassroots activity during the election campaign matched, let alone surpassed, that of the Labour Party—nor, in proportionate terms, were its members generally as active as any other party's bar the UK Independence Party's (UKIP) or the Brexit Party's, as Table 4.1 shows. Tory members reported having done an average of 1.4 campaign activities in 2019, which is significantly below Labour's score of 2.4 activities. And there is little comfort to be gained from the fact that UKIP and the Brexit Party fared even worse in these terms, given that many of their members or supporters will have lived in seats where there was no candidate from their parties. Moreover, Conservative footsoldiers were generally less inclined to involve themselves in campaign activity than they were in 2017 or 2015 (Bale *et al.*, 2019, p. 100). Party Members Project data reveal that some 57% of an enlarged Conservative membership admitted to having devoted no time at all to campaigning in 2019, compared to 44% in 2017 and just 29% in Cameron's victorious campaign of 2015. Although the trend has been similarly negative across most of the parties, it has been more pronounced for the Tories. For instance, the respective figures for non-campaigners among Labour's members are 27% in 2015, 33% in 2017 and 40% in 2019.

On the other hand, there was one vitally important aspect of the campaign in which the Tories were able to completely dominate their opponents: money. The Conservative Party managed to raise far more in large donations than Labour, or indeed, anyone else. If we look at the final six weeks of the campaign, we can see from figures reported to the Electoral Commission as pre-poll donations that the Conservatives raised considerably more than their nearest rivals (Figure 4.1). Indeed, the Conservative Party's near £19.5 million dwarfed the amount raised by Labour (£5.1 million), the Brexit Party (£4 million) and Liberal Democrats (£1.2 million) combined. In fact, the sum raised by the Conservatives is actually greater than the sum total of donations to all parties (including the Tories) during the pre-poll period in 2017 (£18.7 million).

On top of this, when the accounts for the Q4 accounting period (2019) were released by the Electoral Commission, the enthusiasm that (large) donors had for the Conservative Party at this election was clear to see. The near £37.7 million (excluding public funds) that they managed to raise was, again, far higher than all other parties put together, which stood at just under £31.1 million (Electoral Commission, 2020).

While it should come as no surprise that the Conservative Party is better at raising money through large donations than other political parties, the scale of money raised shows a level of support that had been lacking in 2017. The £37.7 million raised in the final quarter of 2019 also represents an increase in the total amount raised by the Conservative Party in 2017 *as a whole* through donations and fundraising (£34.9 million). The party, as an organisational force, was simply much more capable of exciting its donor base than last time around.

Table 4.1 Which of the following things did party members do for their parties during the 2019 General Election campaign?

Activity	Conservative	Labour	Liberal Democrat	UKIP/ Brexit	Green	SNP	Total
'Liked' something by party/candidate on FB	39.4 (+0.02)	56.4 (−7.5)	45.5 (−17.7)	35.0 (+0.2)	48.0 (−15.6)	65.7 (−5.0)	48.4 (−9.0)
Tweeted/retweeted party messages	22.8 (−1.5)	39.4 (+0.5)	32.1 (−8.0)	18.2 (−0.6)	33.8 (−6.0)	37.1 (−6.6)	30.7 (−5.0)
Displayed election poster in window	13.6 (−8.0)	40.2 (−16.0)	31.0 (−17.2)	11.6 (−22.0)	22.4 (−17.3)	46.1 (−12.9)	27.7 (−16.7)
Delivered leaflets	20.8 (−9.7)	27.7 (−3.9)	32.9 (−11.1)	8.5 (−19.2)	17.6 (−5.3)	27.6 (−2.8)	22.6 (−9.7)
Attended public meeting or hustings	19.4 (−0.4)	24.3 (−0.8)	21.6 (−1.5)	16.2 (−13.8)	18.5 (−1.0)	27.5 (−7.2)	21.3 (−3.9)
Drove voters to polling stations	3.3 (+1.0)	4.1 (−0.5)	2.1 (−0.6)	1.0 (−3.8)	0.8 (−1.2)	5.6 (+0.1)	2.9 (−0.7)
Canvassed face to face or by phone	15.3 (−8.0)	23.8 (−3.0)	17.1 (−5.5)	6.9 (−9.3)	9.9 (−4.1)	20.9 (+0.9)	16.0 (−5.0)
Helped run party committee room	3.8 (−3.2)	5.2 (+1.2)	6.4 (+0.9)	1.4 (−3.4)	2.8 (+0.4)	5.7 (+1.3)	4.2 (−0.6)
Stood as candidate (councillor or MP)	0.9 (−1.3)	2.2 (+1.4)	2.7 (−0.9)	1.3 (−3.5)	2.3 (−1.0)	0.3 (−0.7)	1.6 (−0.7)
Other	5.0 (−5.2)	4.0 (−9.8)	7.3 (−8.9)	4.0 (−2.2)	5.5 (−5.2)	5.6 (−4.1)	5.1 (−6.7)
None	20.4 (−4.3)	13.1 (+4.2)	14.8 (+4.0)	31.1 (+5.5)	20.5 (+3.5)	9.0 (+0.7)	18.1 (+3.5)
Campaign Activism Index—Mean	1.39 (−0.29)	2.23 (−0.29)	1.91 (−0.62)	1.00 (−0.76)	1.56 (−0.51)	2.37 (−0.32)	1.75 (−0.52)
Number	1191	1377	1044	1112	1023	1038	6785

Notes: All activities figures are percentages. Figures in brackets are changes since 2017. Campaign activism index is based on an additive scale that runs from 0 (no activity during the election campaign) to 9 (maximal activity during the campaign, excluding 'other'). All relationships between party and type of campaign activity reported in this table are significant at $p < 0.001$.
Source: Party Members Project Survey (2019).

3.   Was it 'Brexit Wot Won It'? Winning the four-party politics of England and Wales

Organisation aside, it was the Conservatives' superior reading of the electoral landscape that represented their biggest strength in this election. As Curtice (2019) pointed out, Brexit reshaped 'the basis of party support – again'.

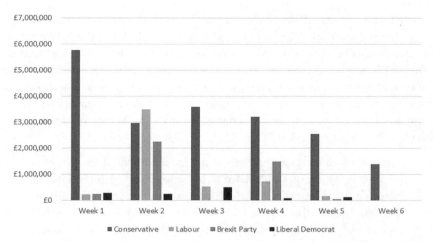

Figure 4.1 Weekly donations at the 2019 general election reported to the Electoral Commission as pre-poll donations
Source: Electoral Commission (2019).

The election began with a gamble, initially on the part of the Liberal Democrats and then, when the writing was on the wall, Labour, that Remain and Leave affiliations would wreak havoc on traditional party loyalties. The problem was that the 'havoc' proved somewhat unidirectional.

Labour banked on the fact that when push came to shove, voters were far more Remain than they were Conservative and far more Labour than they were Leave. On both counts, they were only half right. A snap post-election poll conducted by YouGov (Chorley, 2019), found that just 65% of Remainers who had backed the Conservative Party in 2017 backed them again. On the Remain side for Labour, 79% stuck with the party. However, if we look at the Leave numbers, we see that 92% of Leavers stuck with the Conservatives, while just 52% stuck with Labour, with 33% moving directly to a prime minister promising to 'Get Brexit Done'. Moreover, the Remain vote was quite inefficiently split among Liberal Democrats, the Greens, the nationalist parties and the Labour Party. Of the aforementioned 2017 Conservative Remainers, 22% went to the Liberal Democrats, with the number that moved to Labour in single figures; a similar post-election poll conducted by Lord Ashcroft also showed 21% of Tory Remainers moving to the Liberal Democrats, with 8% moving to Labour (Ashcroft, 2019a). Ultimately, the Conservatives retained the support of enough Tory Remainers who simply could not countenance voting for a Corbyn-led Labour Party, whereas Labour lost a larger number of Leavers, whilst failing to compensate for those losses from defecting Remainers.

The Conservatives' ability to chart a path between these distinct, but overlapping, electoral coalitions suggests that the true turning point of the 2019 election occurred weeks before campaigning began when Boris Johnson managed to conclude a Withdrawal Agreement with the European Union that would win the backing of his parliamentary party, minus those he was prepared to expel. As such, voters could be sure that the election of a Conservative majority government would mean, at last, the UK's departure from the European Union. Isaac Levido certainly argues as much:

> That deal was a real game-changer; it unified a number of the fringes of our voter coalition that we needed to bring together - namely, some of those that voted for us in 2017, but that were considering voting for the Lib Dems because they were concerned about no deal. Similarly, we had a lot of our 2017 voters, who were considering voting for the Brexit Party (BBC, 2020).

Johnson's deal was not all that new or different to a range of deals negotiated, and was rejected by Theresa May and her team prior to her downfall (Boffey *et al.*, 2019). Indeed, the most significant change from that negotiated by May was that, despite Johnson's protestations to the contrary, it effectively agreed to locate a customs border between Britain and Northern Ireland. But, notwithstanding the furious chagrin of the DUP, politics is as much about elite cues and perceptions of success, as about the substance of policy detail. And with the European Research Group (ERG) and the right-wing press (broadly) on board, Johnson could both trumpet his deal and turn it into a snappy slogan during the campaign itself.

4.   A Brexit (Party) pact?

The Conservatives also benefited from the announcement during the second week of the campaign that the Brexit Party would not contest those seats that May had managed to win or hold onto in 2017. The decision itself caused much hullaballoo about the extent to which a backroom deal had been made between the Tories (who categorically denied it) and the Brexit Party, with Nigel Farage even suggesting that allies of Johnson had offered the party eight peerages in return for standing down Brexit Party candidates (Hughes and Parker, 2019). Richard Tice, Brexit Party Chairman and widely seen as Farage's deputy, suggested that back channels were indeed open prior to their decision (BBC, 2020):

> I wasn't offered a peerage, but it did start with me because they started a sort of decapitation strategy with me at the top as chairman by suggesting that I take a safe seat ... and indeed the seat of Rutland was mentioned ... that was part of their ruthless behaviour. Deep down, there are levels of – bordering on corruption with a very small 'c' [*sic*].

However, analysing the exact effects of the Brexit Party's self-denying ordinance is tricky. Though it certainly meant that the Leave vote did not split as much as the Remain vote, the precise electoral consequences are less clear. Although some are left in little doubt that the Brexit Party decision represents the single most important moment of the campaign—that 'Farage won it for Johnson' (Loucaides, 2019)—the numbers tell a slightly different story. YouGov's Curtis (2019), for example, pointed to the fact that the Brexit Party was only standing down in Tory-held seats. The state of the polls prior to the announcement, it was argued, implied a 4% swing from the Labour Party to the Tories, which meant that in seats the Conservatives hoped to gain—and many of which they ended up winning—the Brexit Party would still be standing. In fact, of the 212 seats that the Conservative Party held from 2017 with Labour in second place, 86 had a Leave vote above 60% and in only five of those seats was the Conservative majority less than 10,000 (Connolly, 2019).

It might well have been the case, then, that the Brexit Party announcement did very little to affect the overall outcome, short of a few seats here or there. Indeed, the effect the Brexit Party had in 2019 may well have been to prevent an even larger Tory majority. Of the 189 seats that the Labour Party managed to retain, there were 38 seats in which the combined total of the Brexit Party and the Conservatives was higher than Labour's (Connolly, 2019). Of course, not every Brexit Party voter was a Conservative in disguise—as Ford and Goodwin (2014) were quick to point out when it came to UKIP support—but there were many Labour seats such as those of Ian Lavery, Yvette Cooper and former leader Ed Miliband that were won on vastly diminished majorities and were likely saved by the Brexit Party splitting the Leave vote.

5. Taking the 'red wall'

Many of the abovementioned seats made up the so-called 'red wall' (Onward, 2019), the crumbling of which on 12 December made for the main drama of the broadcasters' election night coverage. This was arguably an earthquake waiting to happen as culture and national identity cut new—and for the Conservatives profitable—paths in politics. That the election was about Brexit, there can be little doubt; but the underlying issues and trends for which Brexit acted as a filter had been bubbling under for some time. The Conservatives, in successfully pitching 2019 as a Brexit election (in a way that they failed to do in 2017) and then subsequently nullifying the Brexit Party challenge, managed to traverse this new landscape, although how long that landscape will remain as it stands now is an open question.

It may well do. Beyond the traditional left–right divide that underlies party competition and voting behaviour in Britain, it has long since become common-place to recognise the impact of a second line of conflict between 'materialists' and 'postmaterialists' (Inglehart, 1997), or between 'Green-Alternative-Liberal' and 'Traditional-Authoritarian-Nationalist' (GALTAN) voters (Hooghe *et al.*, 2002). Ford and Jennings (2020) have suggested that these new faultlines have evolved due to four key sociodemographic developments: first, an educational ex-pansion which has (1) driven the widening of a graduate class and (2) led to the decline of school leavers often employed in manual labour; second, an increase in mass migration which has led to an enlargement of ethnic diversity amongst elec-torates; third, the ageing of society, which has contributed to deepening genera-tional divides in terms of both education and political values; and finally, a growing divide between prospering cities and declining towns and rural areas. These socio-demographic changes have helped boost the rise of the populist radi-cal right—represented in the UK by the UKIP and then the Brexit Party. That radical right was able to pull together a coalition of voters from the left and (to a greater extent) the right disillusioned with 'progressive' politics (broadly de-fined), thereby exploiting the divide 'between nationalists and cosmopolitans, lib-erals and conservatives, and cultural traditionalists and multiculturalists' (Ford and Goodwin, 2017, p. 28; see also Norris and Inglehart, 2019). However, the Conservative Party moved quickly under Boris Johnson (and even to some extent under Theresa May) to steal their thunder—a move made easier, some argue, by Labour: according to one of its defeated MPs (Engel, 2019):

> Left behind? They just wanted to be left alone! They looked at their own values, their own sense of right and wrong, and they preferred it to the confusion and chaos of what the political elites in London seemed to be obsessed with: antisemitism, transgenderism and net-zero carbon admissions. It's not that they disagreed with the parties' positions on them, it's that they have absolutely no bearing on their daily lives.

The Conservative appeal amongst these voters is born out in polling. Over the past few elections, the Conservatives had been closing the gap on Labour amongst DE voters (essentially, lower working class and those not in work); in 2015, the Conservatives only won 29% of these voters to Labour's 37%, whilst in 2017 the figures stood at 41% and 44%, respectively. By 2019, the Conservative vote amongst DE electors had risen to 47% with Labour's falling to 34% (Chorley, 2019). Seats that the Conservatives gained from Labour in ei-ther 2017 or 2019 (Table 4.2) also had higher than average levels of depriva-tion, while house prices and wages were substantially below the national average and the seats contained very low numbers of graduates. Constituencies

Table 4.2 Safe seats and seats that switched hands between the Conservatives and Labour at the 2017 and 2019 general elections

	Seats consistently held by Labour	Labour gained from Con in GE2017 or GE2019	Con gained from Labour in GE2017 or GE2019	Seats consistently held by Conservatives
Deprivation	Much higher than average levels of deprivation	Slightly lower than average levels of deprivation	Higher than average levels of deprivation	Much lower than average levels of deprivation
Housing	Low numbers own outright or own with a mortgage. High numbers of private renters. High levels of social housing.	Average numbers own outright or own with mortgage. High numbers of private renters. Low levels of social housing.	Average numbers own outright or own with mortgage. Low numbers of private renters. High levels of social housing.	High numbers own outright or own with a mortgage. Low numbers of private renters. Very low levels of social housing.
House prices	Below average	Average (though wide variation)	Substantially below average	Above average
Wages	Slightly below average	Average	Substantially below average	Above average
Age	High working-age population. Low numbers of pensioners	High working-age population. Quite low numbers of pensioners	Quite low working-age population. Quite high numbers of pensioners	Low working-age population. High numbers of pensioners
Ethnicity	Substantially above-average BAME population	Above-average BAME population	Below average BAME population	Below average BAME population
Education	Average number of graduates	Very high numbers of graduates	Very low numbers of graduates	Quite high numbers of graduates

Source: Cooper and Cooper (2020).

with these kinds of demographics 25 years ago, would have reasonably been described as the Labour 'heartlands'.[3]

This is also representative of a shift in electoral geography (Ford and Jennings, 2020, p. 1713). Here we see young, ethnically diverse, graduate populations with socially liberal views agglomerating around cities and voting for leftist and/or socially liberal parties like Labour, the Greens and the Liberal Democrats, whereas the older, more ethnically homogeneous, non-graduate voters holding populist and socially conservative values opting for the Brexit Party and UKIP but, crucially, in 2019 the Conservatives (Ford and Jennings, 2020; see also Jennings and Stoker, 2016, 2019). This benefited the Conservatives both sociologically and institutionally. Whilst in the early 2000s, New Labour benefited from a First Past the Post electoral system that worked very well for them in terms of vote distribution, the boot is now firmly on the other foot. Conservative voters are now far more efficiently distributed across the UK, which minimises wasted 'surplus' votes in safe seats and 'redundant votes' in seats the Tories lose (Smith, 2020; see also Electoral Reform Society, 2020). The 'bias' in the electoral geography that favoured Labour in the Blair–Brown years had swung decisively towards the Tories.

The Conservatives managed to claim large numbers of seats across the 'red wall', largely in the North and Midlands, due in large part to having a Brexit pitch that appealed—and a leader that seemed far less unappealing than Labour's; of the 54 seats the Tories took from Labour in 2019, 50 of them had voted Leave in 2016 (Goodwin, 2019). After his brief moment of catch-up in the leader popularity stakes during the 2017 general election campaign, Corbyn had regularly ranked lower than his Conservative counterpart thereafter (YouGov, 2019b). British Election Study data gathered during the 2019 campaign showed that he was less well-liked than Boris Johnson in almost all demographic groups, excepting under 25-year-olds, Londoners and Scots. This means, among other things, that Corbyn was less well-regarded than his direct rival for the premiership among working-class voters and those northern and midland regions across which the 'red wall' stretched (Table 4.3). Given the growing body of evidence that confirms the significance of leader effects on voting behaviour, this was highly significant (Garcia, 2012; Curtice and Lisi, 2015).

However, Tory success also owed much to longer-term institutional and sociological trends. These trends underpinned the Brexit vote, and may even point the way towards a future realignment in British politics. In Table 4.4, we bring together several of the various attitudinal and demographic factors reckoned to

---

[3]We also see that those seats Labour gained from the Conservatives in either 2017 or 2019 are also indicative of this shifting electoral landscape in that they contain a high number of graduates, lower levels of deprivation and a high working-age population.

Table 4.3 Who was the best-liked major party leader, 2019?

	Johnson	Corbyn	Swinson
Men	4.33	2.55	2.86
Women	4.01	2.79	2.91
ABC1	3.94	2.79	3.06
C2DE	4.44	2.55	2.58
Graduate	3.40	3.11	3.35
Non-graduates	4.78	2.34	2.53
18–25	*2.51*	*4.24*	*3.43*
26–35	3.39	3.14	3.37
36–45	3.88	2.57	3.09
46–55	4.42	2.24	2.58
56–65	5.00	1.77	2.29
Over 65	5.94	1.29	2.26
North East	4.21	2.83	2.75
North West	3.97	3.11	2.64
Yorks & Humber	4.09	2.81	2.73
East Midlands	4.71	2.37	2.80
West Midlands	4.75	2.45	2.75
East of England	4.83	2.22	2.83
London	*3.34*	*3.52*	*3.35*
South East	4.65	2.08	2.96
South West	4.68	2.34	2.92
Wales	4.08	2.88	2.66
Scotland	*2.63*	*2.86*	*2.94*
Total	4.17 (*n* = 30,227)	2.67 (*n* = 29,947)	2.88 (*n* = 26,818)

Notes: All figures are mean scores for a scale on which respondents were asked to rate leaders from 0 (strongly dislike) to 10 (strongly like). The italicized rows are the only categories in which Corbyn has a higher mean score than Johnson.
Source: BES Internet panel, Wave 19 (December 2019).

influence voting behaviour in a logistic regression model of voting for the Conservative Party in 2019.

It confirms much of what we would expect. Using measures of perceived competence of the two direct rivals for the keys of Number 10 as indicators of leadership evaluations, we see that the higher that respondents rated Johnson, the greater the probability of them having voted for the Conservatives, whereas the opposite is true for Corbyn. We also see that more right-wing and socially authoritarian respondents were more likely to have voted Conservative. Compared to those who voted Leave in the 2016 EU referendum, those who voted Remain were significantly less likely to have voted Conservative in 2019.

We can also take into account people's evaluations of the country's economic performance, given the widespread evidence that, however much 'values voting' has grown in importance recently, these kinds of 'valence effects' continue to

Table 4.4 Logistic regression model of the Conservative Party vote, December 2019

Predictor	Logistic regression coefficient	Standard Error	Significance	Odds ratio
Competence: Johnson (0=incompetent, 10=competent)	0.159	0.021	0.000	1.172
Competence: Corbyn (0=incompetent, 10=competent)	−0.304	0.019	0.000	0.738
Left-right scale (0=left, 10=right)	0.215	0.032	0.000	1.240
Libertarianism-authoritarianism scale (0=liberal, 10=authoritarian)	0.118	0.027	0.000	1.125
EU referendum vote (Ref: = Leave)	−0.487	0.130	0.000	0.615
Expected general economic situation in country in next 12 months (ref: will get a lot better)				
Will get a lot worse	−1.379	0.466	0.003	0.252
Will get a little worse	−1.190	0.457	0.009	0.304
Will stay the same	−0.519	0.462	0.262	0.595
Will get a little better	0.265	0.493	0.592	1.303
Age (years)	0.008	0.003	0.016	1.008
Graduate (Ref: = non-graduate)	0.021	0.117	0.858	1.021
Gender (Ref: = female)	0.223	0.106	0.036	1.250
Social Grade ABC1 (Ref: = C2DE)	0.113	0.115	0.327	1.119
Constant	0.562	0.547	0.304	1.754

Dependent variable: 1 = Voted Conservative, 0 = Voted for other party.
 Nagelkerke R^2 = 0.535, Cox-Snell R^2 = 0.369, n = 3719

Notes: The Left-Right and Libertarian-Authoritarian variables are simple additive scales constructed from well-known batteries of survey questions first devised in the 1990s by Heath *et al*. (1994).
Source: BES Internet panel, Waves 17 and 19 (November and December 2019).

impact voting behaviour in contemporary Britain (Clarke *et al.*, 2004, 2009; Whiteley *et al.*, 2013; Green and Jennings, 2017). Here, we find that, compared to those who expected the economy to get a lot better over the next year, those who expected it to get either a lot or a little worse were significantly less likely to have voted Tory in 2019.

Finally, of the four major demographic controls entered into the model, only one of them had a statistically significant effect on voting for Conservative candidates. Whether people were male or female, graduate or non-graduate or manual or non-manual employees made no difference. What mattered was age: the older a voter was, the more likely they were to have opted for the Tories.

6. Must the Conservatives win?

This is an election result that some see as tantamount to Labour's last rites. But it is worth remembering that politics can change very quickly. In the wake of a crushing defeat in the 1959 general election, political scientists Mark Abrams and Richard Rose (1960) published their now classic reading of the runes *Must Labour Lose?*—only for Wilson to sweep to victory in 1964. In 1994, Anthony Heath and colleagues wondered if the 1992 election constituted *Labour's Last Chance?* Thirteen years of New Labour dominance followed not long thereafter. And in 2005 Geoffrey Wheatcroft published *The Strange Death of Tory England*; a few months later, David Cameron became leader of the Conservatives and the rest, as they say, is history.

Just as 2017 was the election in which everything went wrong for the Tories and 2019 was the election where everything went right, it might not do so next time around. They have a potentially fragile and fissiparous coalition of support, from traditional Tory shires to the previously solidly Labour North East, and of Leavers and Remainers. Table 4.2 shows the stark challenge that keeping these voters together will present: the column representing seats gained from Labour in 2017 and 2019 and the one showing consistently held Conservative seats present very real contrasts in terms of policy and demographics.

In short, the Conservatives have a lot of plates to spin—and, likely, five years to keep them spinning. Boris Johnson acknowledged these challenges on the steps of Downing Street as dawn broke on 13 December when he observed that many of the votes that re-elected him had been loaned to his party and, as such, should not be taken for granted (Johnson, 2019). Although it might be easier for those who have at last broken their habit of voting Labour to vote Conservative next time too, it might just as well prove to be the case that, for these voters at least, the Tories end up being a one-time fling—'a temporary and transactional swing to the Conserva*tives*, rather than a conversion to conserva*tism*' (Ashcroft, 2019b). Moreover, many of these people voted for the Conservatives on the promise that they would 'Get Brexit Done' and for an 'oven ready' Brexit deal, which is actually, at best, parboiled. Moreover, the government, we should not forget, were facing a divided Labour opposition, with an unprecedently unpopular leader and a confusing pitch on the major issue of the day. Come the next election, the Tories might not be so lucky.

That said, the Conservative Party still has more reasons to be cheerful than the Labour Party. The election showed that it had grasped many of the more fundamental challenges that the UK's changing electoral landscape presents. Whether it can cope with the challenges presented by the government remains, however, to be seen.

Acknowledgement

This work was supported by the Economic and Social Research Council (grant number ES/M007537/1). Tim and Paul would also like to thank their colleague on the Project, Dr Monica Poletti.

References

Abrams, M. and Rose, R. (1960) *Must Labour Lose?* Harmondsworth, Penguin.

Ashcroft, L. (2019a) 'Lord Ashcroft: How Britain Voted and Why. My 2019 Post-vote Poll', accessed at https://www.conservativehome.com/platform/2019/12/lord-ashcroft-how-britain-voted-and-why-my-2019-post-vote-poll.html on 28 February 2020.

Ashcroft, L. (2019b) 'Lord Ashcroft: Would Victories for Johnson and Trump Herald the Triumph of Conservatism', accessed at https://www.conservativehome.com/platform/2019/12/lord-ashcroft-will-victories-for-johnson-and-trump-herald-the-triumph-of-conservatism.html on 28 February 2020.

Audickas, L., Dempsey, N. and Loft, P. (2019) 'Membership of UK Political Parties', accessed at https://researchbriefings.parliament.uk/ResearchBriefing/Summary/SN05125 on 28 February 2020.

Bale, T., Webb, P. and Poletti, M. (2019) *Footsoldiers: Political Party Membership in the 21st Century*, London, Routledge.

BBC (2020, February 9) 'The Inside Story of Election 19' accessed at https://www.bbc.co.uk/sounds/play/m000f5rr on 28 February 2020.

BBC (2019, December 11) 'General Election Poll Tracker: How Do the Parties Compare?' accessed at https://www.bbc.co.uk/news/uk-politics-49798197 on 28 February 2020.

Boffey, D., Henley, J., O'Carroll, L. and Mason, R. (2019) 'Boris Johnson 'on brink of Brexit deal' after Border Concessions', accessed at https://www.theguardian.com/politics/2019/oct/15/boris-johnson-close-to-brexit-deal-after-border-concessions on 6 March 2020.

British Election Study (2019) 'Press Release: Most Volatile British Electorate in Modern Times', accessed at https://www.britishelectionstudy.com/bes-resources/press-release-most-volatile-british-electorate-in-modern-times/#.XlzzQRP7Rp8 on 28 February 2020.

Chorley, M. (2019, December 17) 'General Election Results: Working Class Switched to Tories', accessed at https://www.thetimes.co.uk/edition/news/general-election-results-working-class-switched-to-tories-kfwptc6cr on 28 February 2020.

Clarke, H., Sanders, D., Stewart, M. and Whiteley, P. (2004) *Political Choice in Britain*, Oxford, Oxford University Press.

Clarke, H., Sanders, D., Stewart, M. and Whiteley, P. (2009) *Performance Politics and the British Voter*, Cambridge, Cambridge University Press.

Commons People (2019) 'Weak Leadership. Inexperienced Strategists. Poor Policy – A Chastening Week For The Election Campaigns', accessed at https://audioboom.com/

posts/7435766-weak-leadership-inexperienced-strategists-poor-policy-a-chastening-we ek-for-the-election-camp on 28 February 2020.

Connolly, J. (2019, December 19) 'What Impact Did the Brexit Party Have on the General Election Result?', accessed at https://blogs.spectator.co.uk/article/what-impact-did-the-brexit-party-have-on-the-general-election-result- on 28 February 2020.

Cooper, C. and Cooper, L. (2020) 'The Devastating Defeat: Why Labour Lost and How It Can Win Again', accessed at https://www.europeforthemany.com/tdd-web.pdf on 28 February 2020.

Curtice, J. (2019) 'Brexit Reshapes The Basis of Party Support – Again', accessed at https://whatukthinks.org/eu/brexit-reshapes-the-basis-of-party-support-again/ on 28 February 2020.

Curtice, J. and Lisi, M. (2015) 'The Impact of Leaders in Parliamentary and Presidential Regimes'. In Costa Lobo, M. and Curtice, J. (eds.) *Personality Politics: The Role of Leader Evaluations in Democratic Elections*, Oxford, Oxford University Press, pp. 63–86.

Curtis, C. (2019) 'Farage's Election Stand-down Will Make Little Difference', accessed at https://yougov.co.uk/topics/politics/articles-reports/2019/11/11/unless-polls-move-todays-announcement-farage-will- on 28 February 2020.

Donaldson, K. and Ross, T. (2019, December 13) 'The Ruthless Vote Machine Behind Boris Johnson's Big Win', accessed at https://www.bloomberg.com/news/articles/2019-12-13/rampant-johnson-gets-roars-and-hugs-while-opponent-faces-despair on 28 February 2020.

Doward, J. (2019) 'Voters 'used as lab rats' in political Facebook adverts, warn analysts', accessed at https://www.britishelectionstudy.com/bes-resources/press-release-most-vo latile-british-electorate-in-modern-times/#.XlzzQRP7Rp8 on 28 February 2020.

Electoral Commission (2019) 'Donations and Loans Received by Political Parties and Non-party Campaigners in the UK', accessed at https://www.electoralcommission.org. uk/media-centre/donations-and-loans-received-political-parties-and-non-party-cam paigners-uk-fourth-weekly-pre-poll on 13 May 2020.

Electoral Commission (2020) 'Record year and quarter for political party donations and loans in Great Britain', accessed at https://www.electoralcommission.org.uk/media-cen tre/record-year-and-quarter-political-party-donations-and-loans-great-britain on 28 February 2020.

Electoral Reform Society (2020) *Voters Left Voiceless: The 2019 General Election*, London, Electoral Reform Society.

Engel, N. (2019, December 16) 'The Working Classes are Sick of Being Told What to Think', accessed at https://www.thetimes.co.uk/edition/comment/the-working-classes-are-sick-of-being-told-what-to-think-9cz8l95xt on 28 February 2020.

Ford, R. and Goodwin, M. (2014) *Revolt on the Right: Understanding Support for the Radical Right in Britain*, Abingdon, Routledge.

Ford, R. and Goodwin, M. (2017) 'Britain after Brexit', *Journal of Democracy*, **28**, 17–30.

Ford, R. and Jennings, W. (2020) 'The Changing Cleavage Politics of Western Europe', *Annual Review of Political Science*, **23**, 295–1720.

Garcia, D. (2012) 'Party and Leader Effects in Parliamentary Elections: Towards a Reassessment', *Politics*, **32**, 175–185.

Goodwin, M. (2019, December 24), 'Nine Lessons from the Election: Boris was Lucky – but He Also Played His Hand Right', accessed at https://blogs.spectator.co.uk/article/nine-lessons-from-the-election-boris-was-lucky—but-he-also-played-his-hand-right on 28 February 2020.

Green, J. and Jennings, W. (2017) *The Politics of Competence: Parties, Public Opinion and Voters*, Cambridge, Cambridge University Press.

Hooghe, L., Marks, G. and Wilson, C. J. (2002) 'Does Left/Right Structure Party Positions on European Integration?', *Comparative Political Studies*, **35**, 965–989.

Heath, A., Evans, G. and Martin, J. (1994) 'The Measurement of Core Beliefs and Values: The Development of Balances Socialist/Laissez Faire and Libertarian/Authoritarian Scales', *British Journal of Political Science*, **24**, 115–132.

Hughes, L. and Parker, G. (2019) 'Farage Claims Tories Dangled Titles for Brexit Party Support' accessed at https://www.ft.com/content/2c8bb0a8-06fc-11ea-a984-fbbacad9e7dd on 28 February 2020.

Ibbetson, C. (2020) 'It's a Draw, But Our Poll Shows Corbyn Came Across As More in Touch' accessed at https://yougov.co.uk/topics/politics/articles-reports/2019/11/21/corbyn-draws-boris on 28 February 2020.

Inglehart, R. (1997) *Modernization and Postmodernization: Cultural, Economic, and Political Change in 43 Societies*, Princeton, Princeton University Press.

Jennings, W. and Stoker, G. (2016) 'The Bifurcation of Politics: Two Englands', *The Political Quarterly*, **87**, 372–382.

Jennings, W. and Stoker, G. (2019) 'The Divergent Dynamics of Cities and Towns: Geographic Polarisation and Brexit', *The Political Quarterly*, **90**, 155–166.

Johnson, B. (2019) 'Boris Johnson: Perhaps My Campaign Was 'Clunking'. But Sometimes, Clunking Is What You Need', accessed at https://www.spectator.co.uk/article/boris-johnson-perhaps-my-campaign-was-clunking-but-sometimes-clunking-is-what-you-need on 28 February 2020.

Keys, A. (2007) *Lesson Learned*, New York, Universal Publishing Group.

Langford, E. (2019) 'AT-A-GLANCE: The Key Moments of the 2019 Election Campaign', accessed at https://www.politicshome.com/news/uk/politics/news/108505/glance-key-moments-2019-election-campaign on 6 March 2020.

Loucaides, D. (2019) 'The Brexit Party Folded, But Make No Mistake: Farage Won It for Johnson', accessed at https://www.theguardian.com/commentisfree/2019/dec/13/brexit-party-nigel-farage-boris-johnson-labour-leavers on 28 February 2020.

McTague, T. (2019) 'It's Boris Johnson's Britain Now', accessed at https://www.theatlantic.com/international/archive/2019/12/boris-johnson-britain-uk-election/603466/ on 28 February 2020.

Norris, P. and Inglehart, R. (2019) *Cultural Backlash: Trump, Brexit and Authoritarian Populism*, Cambridge, Cambridge University Press.

O'Donoghue, D. (2019) 'Nine key moments from the 2019 general election campaign', accessed at https://www.pressandjournal.co.uk/fp/news/politics/uk-politics/1908847/nine-key-moments-from-the-2019-general-election-campaign/ on 6 March 2020.

Onward (2019) 'Realignment: How Did the Tories, Win, How Did the Red Wall Fall, and What Does It Mean for the Future?' accessed at https://www.ukonward.com/wp-content/uploads/2019/12/Realignment-Onward-deck-1.pdf on 14 March 2020.

Partington, R. (2019) 'Conservative Party Manifesto: What It Says and What It Means', accessed at https://www.theguardian.com/politics/2019/nov/24/conservative-manifesto-the-key-points-policies-boris-johnson on 6 March 2020.

Payne, S. (2019) 'UK Set for 'Most Unpredictable Election' in Decades, Study Finds', accessed at https://www.ft.com/content/3c889084-e9bf-11e9-85f4-d00e5018f061 on 28 February 2020.

Pienaar, J. (2019) 'General Election 2019: A Campaign Unlike Any Other?', accessed at https://www.bbc.co.uk/news/election-2019-50432050 on 6 March 2020.

Schofield, K. (2019) 'EXCL Labour Membership Dips Below Half a Million as Tens of Thousands Leave Party', accessed at https://www.politicshome.com/news/uk/political-parties/labour-party/news/105507/excl-labour-membership-dips-below-half-million on 28 February 2020.

Smith, M. (2019) 'YouGov Snap Poll Finds Another Close Result as Viewers Split on Who Won BBC Leaders Debate', accessed at https://yougov.co.uk/topics/politics/articles-reports/2019/12/06/yougov-due-release-bbc-debate-snap-poll-930pm, on 28 February 2020.

Smith, T. (2020) 'Why Did the Conservatives' Large Lead in Vote Shares Produce Only an 80-Seat Majority?', accessed at https://www.democraticaudit.com/2020/01/22/why-did-the-conservatives-large-lead-in-vote-shares-produce-only-an-80-seat-majority/ on 16 March 2020.

Who Targets Me (2019) 'Boris Johnson is Marmite (and the Tory Facebook ads know it)', accessed at https://medium.com/@WhoTargetsMe/boris-johnson-is-marmite-and-the-tory-facebook-ads-know-it-b15de3d1f174 on 28 February 2020.

YouGov (2019a) 'If You Had To, Which of the Main Party Leaders Would You Spend Christmas Day With?', accessed at https://yougov.co.uk/topics/politics/survey-results/daily/2019/12/09/aa68a/1 on 28 February 2020.

YouGov (2019b) 'Political Tracker Polls, Best Prime Minister', accessed at https://d25d2506sfb94s.cloudfront.net/cumulus_uploads/document/xqkhf8r3eb/YG%20Trackers%20-%20Best%20Prime%20Minister.pdf on 14 March 2020.

Wheatcroft, G. (2005) *The Strange Death of Tory England*, London, Allen Lane.

Whiteley, P., Clarke, H., Sanders, D. and Stewart, M. (2013) *Affluence, Austerity and Electoral Change in Britain*, Cambridge, Cambridge University Press.

Britain Votes (2019) 84–102

EUNICE GOES*

Labour's 2019 Campaign: A Defeat of Epic Proportions

When the Prime Minister Boris Johnson called an early election, few Labour candidates were expecting a victory or even a repeat of the better than expected results obtained in the 2017 general election. Equally few, however, were prepared for the party to suffer such a comprehensively devastating defeat. Yet Labour obtained its worst election result since 1935, attracting less than one-third of the votes cast and electing only 202 MPs. Crucially, Labour lost 61 seats (and won one), many in traditional heartlands in northern England and in the Midlands, but the party also lost a sizeable number of seats in Scotland and Wales.

Unsurprisingly, as soon as the electoral results arrived, the blame game began. For many observers and Labour candidates, the leader of the party, Jeremy Corbyn, was the main cause of Labour's defeat. After all, he agreed to hold an election at the worst possible time, led a disorganised campaign and was extremely unpopular with voters. 'Corbynistas', on the other hand, blamed Labour's pro-European faction, which forced the party to adopt a new policy on Brexit which, in their view explains the loss of dozens of seats in the North of England and Midlands.

Doubtless, these factors contributed to Labour's devastating defeat; however, other long-term factors, such as a decade of turbulent politics, structural changes to politics and the emergence of new cleavages contributed to Labour's fourth consecutive defeat since 2010. This chapter will explain the short-term and long-term factors that led to Labour's defeat but it will start by contextualising Labour's state of readiness for the election and analysing Labour's 2019 electoral campaign.

1. From hubris to chaos

Labour's better-than-expected results at the 2017 general election offered some breathing space to its leader. The planned plots to oust Corbyn were put on hold and so were the 'Save Jeremy' campaign devised by his team (Shipman, 2018,

*Eunice Goes, School of Communications, Arts and Social Sciences, Richmond University, Eunice.goes@richmond.ac.uk

doi:10.1093/pa/gsaa023

p. 448). Moreover, as the new intake of MPs was supportive of his agenda, Corbyn was able to tighten his control over the party. Over time, the Left became the dominant voice of the party's National Executive Committee and main decision-making structures of the party.

When the party met in Brighton for its annual conference in September 2017 the mood was, to use the words of Corbyn's former adviser Andrew Fisher, 'hubristic' (Evening Standard, 2020). Reflecting that mood, Corbyn told delegates that Labour had become 'a government-in-waiting' that was 'setting the agenda and winning the arguments for a new common sense about the direction our country should take' (Corbyn, 2019c).

The Shadow Chancellor, John McDonnell, responded to Corbyn's call by turbo-charging the party's policy-making engine and by focussing on improving the party's economic credibility. He led workshops on alternative forms of ownerships, listened to economists on productivity and launched several 'tea-charm offensives' to the City of London and to Britain's boardrooms in the hope of reassuring them that business was 'better off with Labour'.

But McDonnell's efforts to turn Labour into a credible government in waiting were undermined by two major crises which paralysed the party for the best part of the two years that preceded the 2019 election. The first one was Corbyn's failure to tackle decisively anti-semitic behaviour within the party; the second was his inability to develop a coherent approach to Brexit, the most important question facing the country at the time.

The crisis of anti-Semitism emerged soon after Corbyn's election as Labour leader in 2015 but it had acquired dramatic proportions by the summer of 2018. The party tried slowly, albeit with little resolve, to address the issue by adopting new internal rules to discipline members found guilty of anti-semitic behaviour. But those efforts backfired when, in March 2018, Jeremy Corbyn expressed his opposition to the defacing of an anti-semitic mural. The backbencher Luciana Berger questioned the leader's office about Corbyn's apparent endorsement of the mural. Corbyn's office backtracked immediately and apologised but this reaction was deemed inadequate by Berger and other MPs. Even McDonnell and Momentum condemned Corbyn's office for Labour's failure to deal with anti-semitic behaviour in a decisive manner (Kogan, 2019, pp. 349–351).

The mural incident was not the final one in the party's anti-Semitism crisis. In the summer of 2018, Labour's internal debate about the adoption of the International Holocaust Remembrance Alliance's (IHRA) definition of anti-semitism into the party's code showed that Corbyn had not yet tackled the problem. The NEC's proposed amendments to the definition were challenged by several frontbenchers who wanted Labour to adopt the full IHRA definition and by 68 British Rabbis, who published a letter in the *Guardian* (2018) condemning the party's new code. Needless to say, the media coverage of the controversy did Labour no favours.

This was a wound that continued to bleed. Another key moment in Labour's anti-Semitism crisis emerged in February 2019, when Luciana Berger, together with seven other Labour backbenchers, defected from the party claiming institutional anti-Semitism. Labour's anti-Semitism crisis escalated further when three months later, the Equality and Human Rights Commission launched an investigation into Labour's anti-semitic behaviour. The extent of the party's anti-semitic crisis was highlighted by the decision of the Jewish Labour Movement to refuse to campaign for the party at the 2019 election, quickly followed by the recommendation by the Chief Rabbi Ephraim Mirvis to his congregants to vote for whichever party that is more likely to defeat Labour. Following this, Labour's reputation as an anti-racist party was in tatters.

The second problem that undermined Labour's popularity was Brexit. The party's 2017 manifesto accepted the results of the referendum on membership of the European Union (EU) as well as the end of free movement, while making some positive noises about a softer Brexit and the benefits of immigration (Labour Party, 2017). This ambivalent position was electorally astute (Mellon *et al.*, 2018, p. 735), but following the general election, Corbyn was under pressure to adopt a more pro-European stance. Confronted with a divided parliamentary party on the most important issue of the day, Corbyn's approach to Brexit was marked by obfuscation in the period between the two general elections. The party's Shadow Brexit Secretary, Keir Starmer, told Labour's 2018 conference in Liverpool that 'nobody is ruling out Remain as an option' in a second referendum. Corbyn appeared less enthused by such a move.

It took months of campaigning by pro-European groups and trade unions, and the disastrous results of the European Parliament elections in June 2019, for Labour to adopt a clearer policy on Brexit. Finally, at the party's 2019 annual conference, Corbyn announced that a Labour government would first negotiate a new withdrawal agreement with Brussels and then it would subject that deal to a new referendum where voters would also be given the option to vote to remain in the EU. But to the surprise of many, the Labour leader announced that he would remain neutral on the question and would implement the will of the people.

Labour's new Brexit policy, which reflected the views of the majority of Labour members (Bale *et al.*, 2020, p. 70; Fieldhouse, 2019), was greeted with relief by activists who had been campaigning for the last two years for a new referendum on EU membership. However, Labour's new position was announced just a few weeks before the general election and meant that the party had little time to explain it to voters. As a result, many candidates feared the worst. For candidates who represented Leave seats, it was clear that their voters would react angrily at the party's blatant disrespect for the results of the 2016 referendum on EU membership (Cruddas, 2019). Others feared that Corbyn's neutrality on the issue made him look indecisive and opportunistic.

The party's handling of these crises undermined Labour's popularity, even among 'Corbynistas'. The infectious enthusiasm of the youngsters who chanted 'Oh, Jeremy Corbyn!' at music festivals in 2017 waned as a result of the party's inability to discipline anti-semitic behaviour, ambivalence over Brexit and resistance to democratising its policy-making structures. Indeed, as the Leader of the Opposition's Office tightened its grip over the party's policy-making machine, disillusion grew amongst activists.

That disillusion was well captured by the convener of the left-wing grassroot movement Compass, Neal Lawson, who remarked that the 'Labour leader's office today is at least as powerful, and unaccountable, as it was under Blair and Brown. Whatever else it is, this is not bottom-up democracy' (2019, p. 180). In a similar vein, Jeremy Gilbert, an academic who supported Corbyn, admitted that the leader's office was 'acquiring a reputation for secrecy, authoritarianism and narrow-mindedness that may have well been an inevitable product of seeking success within the Westminster system, but which threatens to demoralise the membership base' (2019, p. 87). This account was confirmed by Andrew Fisher's letter of resignation from the party, in which he accused the leader's office of a 'lack of professionalism, competence and human decency' (quoted by Line and Bloom, 2019).

The scale of Labour's unpopularity was extraordinary given the inability of the then Prime Minister Theresa May to get her withdrawal agreement supported by her party and approved in parliament. But instead of capitalising on May's failings and unpopularity, Labour was consumed by its own internal crisis and was therefore unable to mount any effective opposition to the government.

2. Falling into the fox's trap

In the meantime, the Conservatives got their act together following Theresa May's resignation and Boris Johnson's election as leader of the party in the summer of 2019. Johnson faced the same institutional and political limitations (i.e. he did not control a parliamentary majority) as of May, but his style of governing was radically different. Instead of dithering and last-minute charm offensives to parliamentarians, Johnson relished the confrontation with the House of Commons and the Supreme Court over his decision to prorogue parliament in the hope of getting his EU withdrawal agreement approved with as little scrutiny as possible.

Johnson's use of prerogative power to prorogue parliament for five weeks was adjudged to have been exercised unlawfully by the Supreme Court on 24 September. Forced to retreat, the Prime Minister, in October, reluctantly asked the EU for another extension for article 50, delaying Britain's departure, but his strategy of forcing an early election eventually paid-off. Labour, together with the other opposition parties was totally unprepared for this turn of events. In reality, they fell into Johnson's wily fox trap by reluctantly agreeing to an early election to be held in early December.

But the timing of the election could not have been worse for Labour. The party was trailing behind the Conservatives by 15 percentage points (YouGov, 2019*a*). Corbyn's personal ratings were even more problematic. In one survey, he ranked as the most unpopular leader of the opposition since 1977 (Skinner *et al.*, 2019). The same survey showed that 76% of public opinion was 'dissatisfied' with Corbyn as opposition leader and 77% believed he was doing a bad job at handling's Britain's withdrawal from the EU. At the start of the electoral campaign, only 21% of voters thought that Corbyn would be the best Prime Minister (YouGov, 2019*a*).

3. The advent calendar campaign

With these polling figures, it is not surprising that Labour launched its electoral campaign almost a week before the Conservative Party. Party strategists hoped to reverse the trend in the opinion polls with an offensive campaign strategy and by diverting voters' attention from Brexit with a populist-themed campaign adapted to the festive season. To use the words of one of the party's strategists, the aim of the campaign was to channel the 'Christmas cheer and spirit' into the election, with 'Vote Labour' bobble hats, mulled wine in flasks on the doorstep, Christmas jumpers and all manner of creative ideas' (Ryle, 2019).

Labour's electoral promises would be presented as if displayed in an Advent Calendar: each day the party would announce a brand-new policy idea which would target a different segment of the electorate. In this spirit, Corbyn launched the party's Christmas-themed campaign, sprinkled with small doses of populist anger against the ruling elites. In the speech that launched the party's campaign at Battersea's Arts Centre, he announced a 'once-in-a-generation chance to transform our country' and promised to go after 'the tax-dodgers, the landlords, the bad bosses, big polluters' (Corbyn, 2019*b*).

Labour's strategy involved avoiding Brexit as a campaigning theme. Aware that the party's new stance on Brexit was not easy to explain to voters, Corbyn used his second speech of the campaign to promise that a Labour government would get 'Brexit sorted within six months' (2019*a*). In a parallel move, Momentum launched a video where an enthusiastic young man explained Labour's 'simple' approach to Brexit in 30 seconds but for the rest of the campaign, the party tried to avoid the subject. It turns out that these efforts were insufficient as most voters thought that Labour's Brexit policy was unclear (Abraham, 2019).

Having decided to treat Brexit as an aside, Labour's offensive campaign strategy had four main components: Corbyn's visits; the daily announcements from the party's headquarters; the ground campaign and the digital campaign. To some extent, the tactics deployed at the 2017 election were fine-tuned; however, there was an important difference. Instead of adopting the defensive strategy used in 2017 (Middleton, 2019, p. 508), this time Labour conducted an offensive campaign. Labour strategists believed that Labour could have won more seats in 2017 if the party had adopted a more offensive strategy.

This reasoning explains the decision to conduct most of Corbyn's visits in marginal or Conservative-held seats. Over the six-week campaign (from 31 October to 11 December), he only visited 29 Labour-held seats, out of his visits to 80 seats.[1] Corbyn spent most of the campaign visiting marginal seats and Conservative seats like Harlow, Ashfield, Telford, Milton Keynes, Loughborough or seats held by the Scottish National Party (SNP) in Scotland (which he visited twice), but his visits to Labour-held seats in the North East of England and the Midlands were rarer. But Corbyn's offensive visits strategy was also the result of the unwillingness of Labour candidates to be seen side-by-side with Corbyn (Labour MP, 2020).

Corbyn enjoyed a few good moments on the campaign trail. For example, when Yorkshire and the Midlands were hit by flooding, Corbyn was able to present himself as an empathetic leader who visited the affected areas. This image contrasted to that of the Prime Minister, who stayed away from the media glare. But these positive moments were rare. In truth, the crowds at Corbyn events were smaller and less enthusiastic than in 2017, and his media performances were lacklustre and in some of them (e.g. his BBC interview with Andrew Neil), he came across as impatient and angry.

In terms of digital campaign, Labour relied on the grassroot movement Momentum's infrastructure which had been upgraded since the 2017 campaign. Momentum launched the new website MyCampaignMap.com which directed activists to their nearest marginal seats and was used to set up more than 21,000 canvassing events. Momentum also launched the 'Labour Legends' campaign, which recruited 1,400 individuals who volunteered a week of their time to campaign for the party (Clarke, 2019), and trained thousands of activists on how to have persuasive conversations with voters, using techniques borrowed from the campaign team of the American presidential candidate Bernie Sanders.

---

[1] The number of visits was calculated by looking at Labour's press releases, Corbyn's Instagram, Facebook and Twitter feeds, as well as the national and local media coverage.

However, Momentum's contribution to the campaign was not the asset it had been in the previous election. Halfway through the electoral campaign, the site MyCampaignMap.com adopted Labour's offensive strategy and started to divert activists from defensive seats to participate in 'Unseat Campaigns' in places like Wimbledon, Hendon, Uxbridge and Chingford and Woodford Green, which Labour had few chances of winning. In addition, the Bernie Sanders' inspired training sessions turned out to be less effective. Many activists were turning up to campaign events not knowing how to handle hostile voters, and some did not know the name of the candidate they were campaigning for.

There was also significant variation in the number of footsoldiers on the ground. In London and in the South East of England, Labour candidates could rely on the support of hundreds of Labour and Momentum activists, but it was far more difficult and expensive to send footsoldiers to campaign in seats in the North East and the Midlands. Indeed, in seats which had not been targeted by the party's headquarters (Proctor, 2020), Labour candidates could rely only on a relatively small pool of party members to conduct the campaign.

But Labour's main campaign problems were not created by Momentum. The party's campaign was also in the words of one observer 'shambolically organised' (Rodgers, 2020). Information was concentrated in Corbyn's office, and consequently there was, according to a post-mortem, a 'lack of communication and preparation over key policy lines, lack of clarity of how campaigns could secure the data of newly registered voters, the unreliability of digital tools' and inadequate training of activists' (Somerville, 2020).

The daily policy announcements did not help as it contributed to a campaign without a coherent and focussed narrative (Rodgers, 2019). Apart from Fisher and McDonnell few people knew which flagship policies would be announced on a daily basis (Stewart, 2020). Without guidance from the party, candidates around the country were forced to improvise. As Chris Bryant put it, 'you never knew if you were getting a ring or a satsuma' out of the Advent Calendar (2020).

Labour thought that these shortcomings could be overcome by the launch of the party manifesto. To that end, the party organised a big manifesto launch event in Birmingham on 21 November which involved the entire shadow cabinet. The manifesto, entitled *It's Time For Real Change*, was more radical than Labour's 2017 manifesto and it promised free broadband to all, a Green Industrial Revolution, the nationalisation of the railways, water and electricity, a four-day week, the scrapping of university tuition fees, the rise of the minimum wage, a windfall tax on oil companies, the promise of building 100,000 new council houses every year until 2024, higher investment in the NHS and other public services, pay rises for nurses, teachers and police officers, pension justice for women and crucially a second referendum on Brexit (Labour Party, 2019).

The media reaction to this Christmas themed manifesto was either negative or tepid. Most newspapers perceived it to be too radical and too costly. For example, the *Daily Mail* called it the 'Marxist Manifesto' and 'Corbyn's 83% Tax Robbery'; the *Daily Express* called it 'The £80 BN Raid on Your Wallets', the *Financial Times* claimed that Labour's manifesto stirred the 'spectre of the 1970s for business', while *The Guardian* neutrally claimed that Corbyn had unveiled 'Labour's most radical manifesto for decades'. The only supporting newspaper was the *Daily Mirror* whose front page claimed that Labour was 'On Your Side'.

4. Alarm bells start ringing

By the end of November, alarm bells started to ring at Labour headquarters. The ground and digital campaigns, together with the manifesto launch had a very modest effect upon the party's lack of popularity. If Labour's approval ratings were slowly rising in the polls, so were the Conservatives'. But the real bombshell of the campaign was YouGov's multilevel with poststratification poll (see the Introduction to this volume) released in late November. The model, which confirmed Labour's internal polling and the success of the Conservatives' strategy of targeting seats in Labour's 'red wall', projected a comfortable Conservative majority of 359 whilst Labour was expected to win only 211 seats (Wells, 2019).

This devastating projection led to a change in the party's strategy in the last two weeks of the campaign. The party shifted campaigning resources to defend constituencies which thus far had been deemed safe and started to focus on 'bread and butter issues' like council housing, more local buses and free prescriptions that were more likely to attract traditional working-class voters in the 'red wall'. Because many of the seats under threat were strong Leave constituencies the party also started to place more pro-Leave voices at the centre of the campaign. For instance, Ian Lavery led a tour of Leave areas, whereas figures like Richard Burgon, Laura Pidcock, Angela Rayner, Jon Trickett were given more prominent roles in Labour's media strategy. In contrast, figures associated with the Remain campaign, like Keir Starmer, Emily Thornberry, Diane Abbott, were told to keep off the airwaves.

By the last week of the campaign, morale was extremely low among Labour activists and campaigners. Opinion polls suggested that the Conservatives retained a solid lead over Labour and the feedback from the candidates and canvassers confirmed that trend. Nonetheless, Corbyn pursued with his gruelling schedule of visits, having spent the last day of campaign visiting Scotland and Middlesbrough for the second time (Stewart, 2019).

On election day, Labour was preparing for bad news, but the electoral results went beyond the party's worst fears. Labour attracted only a 32.9% share of the vote across Great Britain (32.1% of the UK vote), with only 202 MPs elected, the lowest number of seats won since 1935. Labour retained only 72% of its 2017 voters. The loss of ultra-safe and traditional Labour seats like Bolsover, Sedgefield, Blyth Valley, Don Valley, Leigh, Workington and Bishop Auckland came to symbolise Labour's existential crisis. However, the results showed that Labour's crisis extended well beyond the famous 'red wall'. The party lost seats everywhere and to every party and lost votes across all demographic groups (Cooper and Cooper, 2020, p. 12).

Faced with such devastating results, Corbyn announced his resignation from the leadership of the party but failed to take responsibility for Labour's defeat. In reality, his office blamed Keir Starmer for forcing the party to adopt a new Brexit stance which seemed to disrespect the result of the 2016 referendum. This interpretation of Labour's crushing defeat was rejected by many. Indeed, three-quarters of Labour councillors said that Labour's national leadership was the main reason for voters leaving the party (Butler, 2020). And for those candidates who lost their seats or who were re-elected on small majorities, the blame lay mostly with Corbyn, who was not only unpopular but seen as an ineffective leader (Merrick, 2020). This view was encapsulated by Alan Johnson's outburst against Corbyn whom, he said, 'couldn't lead the working class out of a paper bag' (ITV News, 2019) let alone to electoral victory.

But the scale of Labour's defeat cannot be attributed to a single factor or simply to contextual factors like Brexit or a poorly run electoral campaign, especially because this was the party's fourth consecutive defeat since 2010. The following section will analyse the short-term and contextual factors as well as the long-term trends that explain Labour's results.

5. Explaining the results

The electoral results and survey and polling data show that there was an amalgam of reasons, both contextual and structural, which led so many voters to abandon Labour. Among the different factors that can explain the party's defeat, Corbyn's reputation, the party's Brexit policy, a transactional manifesto which overpromised, a poorly run campaign together with long-term factors like structural political changes and new trends in voting behaviour, standout. These different factors did not work in isolation. In some instances—for instance, the Brexit and Corbyn factors—they reinforced each other.

Doubtless, Brexit influenced voting behaviour. This was after all the issue that had dominated British politics since 2016 and the reason why an early election was called. Thus, it is not surprising that of the 60 seats that Labour lost, 52 represented Leave areas, though the party also lost Remain voters (Cooper and Cooper, 2020, p. 16). One analysis of the electoral results showed that only 14% of Leave voters voted for Labour in 2019 (down from 24% in 2017) and only 49% of Remain voters voted for the party (House of Commons, 2020). Lord Ashcroft's polls, outlined in the opening results chapter, indicate a higher vote share for Labour among Leave voters, of 26%, compared with 47% of Remain voters. What is clear from both sets of figures is that Labour's support among Leave voters was woefully low. Leavers did not see Brexit as 'getting done' by Labour.

Analysis by the Resolution Foundation shows that 'changes in Labour's vote shares were more shaped by their Brexit vote' than in the 2017 general election, but other factors, like voters' perception of the competence of party leaders, were also contributing factors (Bell, 2019; see also Curtis 2019). Lord Ashcroft's (2020) analysis of Labour's defeat also claimed that two-thirds of Labour Party members, including three-quarters of those who voted for Corbyn as leader, said that Brexit dominated the election and had a bigger effect on the result than on how people felt about the parties, leaders and other policies (Ashcroft, 2020).

However, it is not clear whether a pro-Leave position would have resulted in retaining seats in Leave areas. Lord Ashcroft's survey indicated that 85% of Labour voters said they would have probably voted the same way had Brexit not been an issue (Ashcroft, 2020). In truth, candidates and activists who campaigned claimed that the Brexit factor could not be disentangled from voters' attitudes towards the leader of the opposition. As Curtice explained, the 'lack of leadership' was a very big problem for Labour because, among other reasons, it led to indecision on Brexit and perceptions of competence and electability (2020).

Perceptions of competence influence voting behaviour (Stewart and Clarke, 1992, p. 467), especially 'when major events heighten the relevance of competence' (Green and Jennings, 2018, p. 11), when parties prime questions of competence and performance and when high salience events 'politicise the handling of an issue and make managerial competence' more important (Green and Jennings, 2018, p. 221). After three years of parliamentary deadlock around Brexit, it can be argued that perceptions of competence seemed to be particularly relevant to voters in 2019. In truth, the Conservative Party primed competence as an important benchmark to evaluate party electability and centred its campaign on the promise of 'getting Brexit done'.

It is then not surprising that most analyses of Labour's defeat identified Corbyn's reputation as a leader as the main reason why so many voters abandoned the party. YouGov's (2019*a*) report showed that Corbyn's leadership was the main reason why Labour voters defected (Curtis, 2019). Lord Ashcroft's (2020) report also showed that 53% of Labour defectors did not want Jeremy

Corbyn to be Prime Minister. The same survey suggested that voters found Corbyn unpatriotic and lacking in leadership qualities.

Corbyn's unpopularity had many facets. As George Eaton (2019) explained, he was not trusted on national security; he was perceived as an unpatriotic, weak leader unable to manage a divided party and who did not look prime-ministerial. An illustration of the multi-faceted nature of popular hostility to Corbyn was offered by the former Labour whip, Graham Jones' canvassing experiences: 'door one wouldn't vote for him because he was scruffy; the next person wouldn't vote for him because of antisemitism in the party; the next because of connections to Hamas; and the next because he seemed unable to lead' (Jones quoted Syal *et al.*, 2019).

Labour's ambitious manifesto was also invoked as one the causes of its defeat, the party's manifesto promises viewed as undeliverable, unrealistic and too expensive by many (Curtis, 2019). Similarly, Lord Ashcroft's (2020) study identified Labour's manifesto as a cause of Labour's unpopularity. Labour's badly organised campaign also played a role, especially because it contrasted with the Conservatives' laser-focussed 'Get Brexit Done' campaign, though it must be said that electoral campaigns are rarely game changers. At best, campaigns have a mobilising effect which is reflected in the media coverage (Banducci and Karp, 2003, p. 463).

But Labour's 2019 results cannot be fully understood by considering only the short-term factors that influenced voting behaviour, especially because this was the party's fourth consecutive electoral defeat. Indeed, it is important to consider that the election took place following ten years of high political turbulence. As the four general elections (two of which delivered hung parliaments), a referendum on Scottish independence and a national referendum on Britain's relationship with the EU vividly illustrate, the British party system has suffered in the last decade several 'electoral shocks' which rendered voting behaviour more fluid, volatile and unpredictable (Fieldhouse *et al.*, 2020, p. 30).

In truth, the instability of the party system predates this decade of political turbulence (Goes, 2019, pp. 295–297). Hyper-globalisation, the rise in immigration flows and the adaptation by political parties to these changes led to class and partisan dealignments which in turn altered voting behaviour. In particular, the emergence in the last two decades of a globalisation cleavage led to significant changes in voter behaviour not only in Britain but also in most European party systems (Jennings and Stoker, 2016; Kriesi *et al.*, 2006; Hobolt, 2016, p. 1260; Cutts *et al.*, 2020, p. 17).

As globalisation created 'winners' and 'losers' in society their antagonism manifested itself at economic, cultural and political levels. Thus, as shown by Kriesi *et al.*, the 'losers of globalisation', who tend to be older, with fewer qualifications and live in rural, suburban or post-industrial areas, are more likely to vote for parties that defend tighter immigration controls, economic protection-ism and authoritarian values, whereas the 'winners', who tend to be younger, with university qualifications and live in ethnically diverse urban areas, are more inclined to vote for parties that favour European integration, support immigra-tion and cosmopolitan and libertarian values (2006, p. 924).

It was precisely this globalisation cleavage which transformed the demographic and geographic profile of Labour support in the last two decades. Indeed, as Evans and Tilley show, the working classes started to desert the Labour Party after 2001 (2017, p. 153), but the 2015 general election was the first election since the war when the 'working class voted for Labour at a lower rate than some middle-class groups' (2017, p. 152). This new pattern of class voting was again in evi-dence at the 2019 general election. In terms of social class, Labour attracted only 33% of the vote of those categorised as C2DE, while the Conservatives attracted 48% of that social class. The old electoral laws of social class had been reversed. The Conservatives enjoyed significantly more support among the working class than did Labour. Meanwhile, Labour attracted 33% of the ABC1 social class, compared with 43% support for the Conservatives in that middle-class category (YouGov, 2019b). Labour's support was evenly spread across the social classes, too thinly in both cases.

New social class voting patterns are accompanied by age, educational and geo-graphical dimensions, confirming Kriesi *et al.*'s globalisation cleavages. Age was the key indicator of voting behaviour at the 2019 election: 56% of 18- to 24-year-old voted Labour, while only 22% of the over-60s did likewise. Only 25% of vot-ers without educational qualifications voted for Labour, while 43% of Labour voters had university degrees (McDonnell and Curtis, 2019). Age is correlated with education, as younger people tend to have higher educational qualifications. In terms of the geographical dimension, Jennings and Stoker showed that, at the previous two elections, support for Labour had tended to be concentrated partic-ularly in urban areas connected to global growth, but declined in a cluster of coastal, post-industrial, suburban and rural areas (2017, p. 361; see also Jennings and Stoker, 2019 , p. 156). This trend was confirmed and consolidated in 2019.

To understand how the globalisation cleavage played out at the 2019 election, we need to consider that the new pattern of class voting reflects economic and so-cial values and also cultural identities normally expressed in public attitudes to immigration (Evans and Tilley, 2017, p. 186). Analysis by Evans and Chzhen con-firmed the expression of this new class voting, by correlating the decline in Labour's support in the 2005 and 2010 elections to popular disquiet with levels of immigration (2013, p.19). In 2019, that globalisation cleavage is associated with the Brexit factor.

A closer look at Labour's share of the vote in some of the 'red wall' seats over the last two decades shows us again the impact of globalisation in voting

Table 5.1 Labour share of the vote in English 'red wall' seats, 2001–2019 (%)

Constituency	2001	2005	2010	2015	2017	2019
Ashfield	58.1	48.6	33.7	41.0	42.6	24.4
Barrow Furness	55.7	47.6	48.1	42.3	47.5	39.3
Bassetlaw	55.3	56.6	50.5	48.6	52.6	27.5
Bishop Auckland	58.8	50.0	39.0	41.4	48.1	35.9
Blyth Valley	59.7	55.0	44.5	46.3	55.9	40.9
Bolsover	68.6	65.2	50.0	51.2	51.9	35.9
Burnley	49.3	38.6	31.3	37.6	46.7	36.9
Darlington	56.3	52.4	39.4	42.9	50.6	40.5
Don Valley	54.6	52.7	37.9	46.2	53.0	35.2
Leigh	64.5	63.3	48.0	53.9	56.2	41.1
NW Durham	62.5	53.9	42.3	46.9	52.8	41.9
Redcar	60.3	51.4	42.3	43.9	55.5	37.4
Sedgefield	64.9	58.9	45.1	47.2	53.4	36.3
Stockton South	53.0	47.8	38.3	37.0	48.5	41.1
Workington	55.5	50.5	45.0	42.3	51.1	39.2

Source: House of Commons (2001, 2005, 2011, 2015, 2019, 2020).

behaviour. As Table 5.1 shows Labour's decline in support started in 2005, but became spectacularly visible following the 2008 global financial crisis and the 2016 referendum on EU membership and was confirmed at the 2017 and 2019 general elections.

In the 15 seats displayed in Table 5.1, a pattern of electoral decline in Labour's working-class heartlands can be identified between 2001 and 2019. In 2001, Labour won its comfortable electoral victory but by 2005, the large influx of immigrants from the new EU accession countries started to erode support for Labour in some of these seats. By 2010, two years after the global financial crisis, Labour suffered a devastating defeat which continued in 2015 but two years later there was surprising surge in support for Labour. In 2019, the decline in Labour support resumed, expressed in dramatic fashion.

In seats like Ashfield, Redcar, Leigh, North West Durham and Stockton South, Labour registered notable vote share gains in 2017, but two years later Labour lost those seats to the Conservatives for the first time, in some cases in spectacular fashion. Labour's woeful results in Leave-voting former heartlands indicate Brexit salience (see Curtice in this volume). In 2017, Labour promised to respect the results of the EU referendum and to reverse austerity measures and was rewarded with very big majorities in those seats, but in 2019, the promise of a second referendum on EU membership and lack of clarity over Labour's position on Brexit proved unappealing, restoring the pattern of decline in the Labour vote in these areas. Thus, to a certain extent what was expressed in the last two general elections was not simply a Brexit effect but the long-term impact of the globalisation cleavage in the voting behaviour of traditional Labour voters (see also Flinders in this volume).

6. Conclusion: Labour on life support

Labour's decline in its traditional heartlands and concomitant transformation into a party of the 'winners of globalisation' led the backbencher Jon Cruddas to conclude that 'paradoxically Corbyn completed Tony Blair's project' of transforming Labour into a party of the urban middle classes (2019). This is an interesting conclusion but there is no denying that these new trends in class, age and geographical vote pose an almost existential challenge to the Labour Party. As Lord Liddle argued, 'Labour is still a viable party, but it might never again be a party of government' (2020). Simply put, Labour cannot be a party of government by relying solely on the support of middle-class voters in English cities.

Corbyn's successor as Labour leader, Keir Starmer, elected in April 2020, was elevated to restore the party's much battered credibility. As the candidate who attracted support from all Labour wings and won the leadership election with a resounding victory, the immediate expectations of Starmer were the unification of a bitterly divided party and the capacity to offer a more professional and forensic opposition to the Conservative government. Nonetheless, as the new Labour leader admitted in his acceptance speech, he faces a proverbial mountain to climb.

To turn Labour into a party of government again, Starmer has to craft a political programme which keeps the urban, educated middle classes on board while bringing back into Labour's fold the suburban, post-industrial communitarian working-class voters of the North of England, Midlands, Wales and also Scotland who have abandoned the party since 2005. This is a tall order. After all, these two sets of very different voters will struggle to find common ground on issues of law and order, immigration and national security but may agree on a social, democratic, economic approach that addresses the devastating socio-economic impact of a pandemic-led recession and of Britain's withdrawal from the EU, the effects of which will be acute at the time of the next election. If that is the case, Starmer, may, but only just, find the solution to the electoral puzzle that has kept Labour out of power since 2010.

Acknowledgements

I would like to thank Lord Liddle, Lord Giddens, Jon Cruddas, Bridget Phillipson, Chris Bryant, Sienna Rodgers, Michael Chessum, Luke Cooper,

Natalie Sedacca and other Labour MPs, councillors and party members who asked to remain anonymous, for sharing their time and insights. All mistakes in analysis are, of course, my own.

References

Abraham, T. (2019) 'Most Brits Uncertain on Labour', *YouGov*, 5 November, accessed at https://yougov.co.uk/topics/politics/articles-reports/2019/11/05/most-brits-uncertain-labours-brexit-policy on 10 January 2020.

Ashcroft, L. (2020) 'Diagnosis of Defeat: Labour's Turn to the Smell the Coffee', *Lord Ashcroft Polls*, 12 February 2020, accessed at https://lordashcroftpolls.com/wp-content/uploads/2020/02/DIAGNOSIS-OF-DEFEAT-LORD-ASHCROFT-POLLS-1.pdf on 17 February 2020.

Bale, T., Webb, P. and Poletti, M. (2020) *Footsoldiers: Political Party Membership in the 21st Century*, London, Routledge.

Banducci, S. A. and Karp, J. A. (2003) 'How Elections Change the Way Citizens View the Political System: Campaigns, Media Effects and Electoral Outcomes in Comparative Perspective', *British Journal of Political Science*, 33, 443–467.

Bell, T. (2019, December 13) 'Election Dissection: Top of the Charts', *Resolution Foundation*, accessed at https://www.resolutionfoundation.org/comment/election-dis section/ on 17 March 2020.

Bryant, C. (2020) 'Corbyn's Legacy', Mile End Institute Event, 'What Next for Labour', 20 January 2020. London.

Butler, P. (2020, February 6) 'Labour and Jeremy Corbyn under Fire from Councillors' Leader', *The Guardian*, accessed at https://www.theguardian.com/politics/2020/feb/06/labour-and-jeremy-corbyn-under-fire-from-councillors-leader on 20 February 2020.

Clarke, L. (2019, November 30) 'Inside Momentum's Data-Driven March to Put Corbyn in Number 10', *Wired*, accessed at https://www.wired.co.uk/article/momentum-labour-party-my-campaign-map on 10 February 2020.

Cooper, L. and Cooper, C. (2020) 'The Devastating Defeat: Why Labour Lost and How It Can Win Again: Part 1, Europe for the Many', 12, accessed at https://www.europeforthe many.com/the-devastating-defeat/ on 1 February 2020.

Corbyn, J. (2019a, November 5) 'Brexit Speech', *Harlow*, accessed at https://labour.org.uk/press/jeremy-corbyns-brexit-speech-in-harlow/ on 31 March 2020.

Corbyn, J. (2019b, October 31) 'First Major Speech of the General Election Campaign', *Battersea Arts Centre*, 31 October, accessed at https://labour.org.uk/press/jeremy-corbyns-first-major-speech-of-the-general-election-campaign/ on 1 February 2020.

Corbyn, J. (2019c) 'Speech to the 2017 Labour Party Annual Conference', 27 September 2019, accessed at https://labour.org.uk/press/jeremy-corbyn-speech-to-labour-party-conference/ on 30 November 2019.

Cruddas, J. (2019) Private Interview, 8 October 2019. House of Commons, London.

Curtice, J. (2020) 'Why Labour Lost', *Coffee House, The Spectator* Blog, accessed at https://blogs.spectator.co.uk/2020/01/why-labour-lost/ on 18 January 2020.

Curtis, C. (2019) 'In Their Own Words: Why Voters Abandoned Labour', *YouGov*, 23 December, accessed at https://yougov.co.uk/topics/politics/articles-reports/2019/12/23/their-own-words-why-voters-abandoned-labour on 10 January 2020.

Cutts, D., Goodwin, M., Heath, O. and Surridge, P. (2020) 'Brexit, the 2019 General Election and the Realignment of British Politics', *The Political Quarterly*, **91**, 7–23.

Eaton, G. (2019, December 15) 'How Labour Lost – And How It Can Recover from an Epic Defeat', *New Statesman,* accessed at https://www.newstatesman.com/politics/uk/2019/12/why-labour-lost-and-how-it-can-recover-epic-defeat on 10 January 2020.

Evans, G. and Tilley, J. (2017) *The New Politics of Class: The Political Exclusion of the British Working Class*, Oxford, Oxford University Press.

Evans, G. and Chzhen, K. (2013) 'Explaining Voters' Defection from Labour over the 2005-2010 Electoral Cycle: Leadership, Economics and the Rising Importance of Immigration', *Political Studies*, **61**, 138–122.

Evening Standard (2020) 'Corbyn Adviser Says 'Hubris Cost Us'', 22 January 2020, accessed at https://www.standard.co.uk/news/londoners-diary/the-londoner-corbyn-adviser-says-hubris-cost-us-a4341276.html on 10 April 2020.

Fieldhouse, E., Green, J., Evans, G., Mellon, J., Prosser, C., Schmitt, H. and Van Der Eijk, C. (2020) *Electoral Shocks: The Volatile Voter in a Turbulent World*, Oxford, Oxford University Press.

Fieldhouse, E. (2019) 'Labour's Electoral Dilemma', *British Election Study*, 19 October, accessed at https://www.britishelectionstudy.com/bes-findings/labours-electoral-dilemma/#.XlVexpP7Ts0 on 31 March 2020.

Gilbert, J. (2019) 'Acid Corbynism for Beginners'. In Perryman, M. (ed), *Corbynism from Below*, London, Lawrence and Wishart, pp. 80–103.

Goes, E. (2019) 'The British Party System(s): Fragmented, Unstable and Very Capricious'. In Lisi, M. (ed), *Party System Change, the European Crisis and the State of Democracy*, Abingdon, Routledge, pp. 289–309.

Green, J. and Jennings, W. (2018) *The Politics of Competence: Parties: Public Opinion and Voters*, Cambridge, Cambridge University Press.

Guardian (2018, July 18) 'Letter to the Editor: Labour Party Must Listen to the Jewish Community on Defining Antisemitism', accessed at https://www.theguardian.com/politics/2018/jul/16/labour-party-must-listen-to-the-jewish-community-on-defining-antisemitism on 10 April 2020.

House of Commons (2020) *General Elections 2019: Results and Analysis*, London, House of Commons Library.

House of Commons (2019) *General Elections 2017: Results and Analysis*, Briefing Paper CBP 7979, London, House of Commons Library.

House of Commons (2015) *General Election 2015*, Briefing Paper, Number CBP7186, London, House of Commons Library.

House of Commons (2011) *General Election 2010*, Final Edition, Research Paper 10/36, London, House of Commons Library.

House of Commons (2005) *General Election 2005*, Final Edition, Research Paper 05/33, London, House of Commons Library.

House of Commons (2001) *General Election Results, 7 June 2001*, Research Paper 01/54, London, House of Commons Library.

Hobolt, S. B. (2016) 'The Brexit Vote: A Divided Nation, a Divided Continent', *Journal of European Public Policy*, **23**, 1259–1277.

ITV News (2019, December 13) 'He Couldn't Lead the Working Class Out of a Paper Bag': Alan Johnson Launches Fierce Attack On Corbyn and Momentum', accessed at https://www.itv.com/news/2019-12-13/alan-johnson-momentum-jeremy-corbyn-itv-news/ on 10 April 2020.

Jennings, W. and Stoker, G. (2019) 'The Divergent Dynamics of Cities and Towns: Geographical Polarisation and Brexit', *The Political Quarterly*, **90**, 155–166.

Jennings, W. and Stoker, G. (2017) 'Tilting towards the Cosmopolitan Axis? Political Change in England and the 2017 General Election', *The Political Quarterly*, **88**, 359–339.

Kogan, D. (2019) *Power and Protest: The Battle for the Labour Party*, London, Bloomsbury.

Kriesi, H., Grande, E., Lachat, R., Dolezal, M., Bornschier, S. and Frey, T. (2006) 'Globalisation and the Transformation of the National Political Space: Six European Countries Compared', *European Journal of Political Research*, **45**, 921–956.

Labour, MP. Private Interview, 10 March 2020. House of Commons, London.

Labour Party (2019) *It's Time for Real Chance: The Labour Party Manifesto 2019*, London, Labour Party, accessed at https://labour.org.uk/wp-content/uploads/2019/11/Real-Change-Labour-Manifesto-2019.pdf on 28 February 2020.

Labour Party (2017) *For the Many Not the Few: The Labour Party Manifesto 2017*, London, Labour Party.

Lawson, N. (2019) 'Labouring under Illusions'. In Perryman, M. (ed) *Corbynism from Below*, London, Lawrence and Wishart.

Liddle, L. (2020) Private Interview, 8 January 2020.

Line, H. and Bloom, D. (2019) 'Top Jeremy Corbyn Aid Resigns Attacking 'Blizzard of Lies' in the Party', Mirror, 22 September 2019, accessed at https://www.mirror.co.uk/news/politics/top-jeremy-corbyn-aide-resigns-20141185, on 6 January 2020.

Mellon, J., Evans, G., Fieldhouse, E., Green, J. and Prosser, C. (2018) 'Brexit or Corbyn? Campaign and Inter-Election Vote Switching in the 2017 UK General Election', *Parliamentary Affairs*, **71**, 719–737.

McDonnell, A. and Curtis, C. (2019) 'How Britain Voted in the 2019 General Election', *YouGov*, 17 December, accessed at https://yougov.co.uk/topics/politics/articles-reports/2019/12/17/how-britain-voted-2019-general-election on 10 January 2020.

Merrick, R. (2020) Corbyn's 'Cabal' of Top Aides Sabotaged Election Campaign, Says Labour Leader's Close Friend', *The Independent*, 8 February, accessed at https://www.independent.co.uk/news/uk/politics/corbyn-general-election-labour-alan-simpson-seamus-milne-karie-murphy-a9324066.html on 12 March 2020.

Middleton, A. (2019) 'For the Many Not the Few: Strategising the Campaign Trail at the 2017 General Election', *Parliamentary Affairs*, **72**, 501–521.

Proctor, K. (2020) 'Labour's Canvassing Strategy Had 'Major Deficiencies': Leaked Report Says', *The Guardian*, 7 February, accessed at https://www.theguardian.com/politics/2020/feb/07/labours-canvassing-strategy-had-major-deficiencies-leaked-report-says on 12 March 2020.

Rodgers, S. (2020) 'Corbyn's Legacy', Mile End Institute event, 'What Next for Labour?' 20 January 2020.

Rodgers, S. (2019) 'How Labour Lost the Red Wall', *The House Magazine*, 16 December, accessed at https://www.politicshome.com/news/uk/political-parties/labour-party/house/house-magazine/108584/sienna-rodgers-how-labour-lost on 10 January 2020.

Ryle, J. (2019) 'Labour Must Make This a Christmas Election, Not a Brexit Election', *LabourList*, 29 October, accessed at https://labourlist.org/2019/10/labour-must-make-this-a-christmas-election-not-a-brexit-election/ on 11 January 2020.

Shipman, T. (2018) Fallout: A Year of *Political Mayhem*, London: William Collins.

Skinner, G., Pedley, K., Gottfried, G. and Garrett, C. (2019, September 20) 'Jeremy Corbyn Has Lowest Leadership Satisfaction Rating For Any Opposition Leader Since 1977', *Ipsos MORI*, accessed at https://www.ipsos.com/ipsos-mori/en-uk/jeremy-corbyn-has-lowest-leadership-satisfaction-rating-any-opposition-leader-1977 on 10 March 2020.

Somerville, E. (2020, February 8) 'Labour Campaign Weaknesses Exposed as 'Major Deficiencies In Election', *I Newspaper*, accessed at https://inews.co.uk/news/labour-election-defeat-jeremy-corbyn-canvassers-1393517 on 27 February 2020.

Stewart, H. (2020, February 21) 'Crushed By Brexit: How Labour Lost the Election', *The Guardian*, accessed at https://www.theguardian.com/politics/2020/jan/21/crushed-by-brexit-how-labour-lost-the-election on 27 February 2020.

Stewart, H. (2019, December 13) 'Clashing Egos and policy incontinence': Inside Labour's Campaign', *The Guardian*, accessed at https://www.theguardian.com/politics/2019/dec/13/inside-labours-campaign-behind on 6 January 2020.

Stewart, M. C. and Clarke, H. D. (1992) 'The (Un) Importance of Party Leaders: Leader Images and Party Choice in the 1987 British Election', *Journal of Politics*, **54**, 447–470.

Syal, R., Mason, R., Stewart, H. and Perraudin, F. (2019, December 17) 'Corbyn, Antisemitism and Brexit: Labour MPs on Why They Lost', *The Guardian*, accessed at https://www.theguardian.com/politics/2019/dec/17/corbyn-antisemitism-and-brexit-labour-mps-on-why-they-lost on 10 January 2020.

YouGov (2019a) 'Westminster Voting Intention Tracker 2017–2019', accessed at https://yougov.co.uk/topics/politics/articles-reports/2020/02/05/political-trackers-31-jan-2-feb-2020-update on 21 February 2020.

YouGov (2019b, December 17) 'How Britain voted in the 2019 General Election', accessed at https://yougov.co.uk/topics/politics/articles-reports/2019/12/17/how-britain-voted-2019-general-election on 31 March 2020.

Wells, A. (2019, November 27) 'YouGov MRP: Conservatives 359, Labour 211, SNP 43, LD 13, Plaid 4, Green 1', accessed athttps://yougov.co.uk/topics/politics/articles-reports/2019/11/27/yougov-mrp-conservatives-359-labour-211-snp-43-ld-   on   27 January 2020.

DAVID CUTTS AND ANDREW RUSSELL*

Relevant Again but Still Unpopular? The Liberal Democrats' 2019 Election Campaign

The year 2019 was supposed to be the year of the Liberal Democrats' rehabilitation. They had apparently emerged from the long, dark shadows cast by their coalition with the Conservatives, and their electoral trouncing in 2015 and poor showing in 2017. They had enjoyed a period of stability, and remarkable progress, under the leadership of Vince Cable who inherited a party that had been worn down to a husk. As Labour shifted to the left and the Conservatives chose full-on Euroscepticism and inner turmoil, the Liberal Democrats started to grow. A rearguard action in local government, European Election success and victory in a Westminster by-election saw off a centre party threat seeking to claim their territory. Brexit—and the need to stop it—was the party's passport back to the top table of British politics. When Cable stood down as leader, he was succeeded by a candidate who seemed to fit the bill for what the party most desired. Jo Swinson was young, female and had a reputation in the Westminster circle for competence and empathy. Under Swinson, the Liberal Democrats grasped the opportunity with both hands to reinvent themselves as the only GB wide, unambiguously anti-Brexit party. With pre-election polls placing them on the coattails of Labour, the Liberal Democrats then went for the jugular. Swinson began the campaign in spectacularly upbeat fashion, reasserting that a majority Liberal Democrat government would revoke Article 50 and announcing that she was running to be the new Prime Minister. A few weeks later, the party's campaign had turned to ashes, the number of Westminster Liberal Democrats actually fell and Swinson herself, for the second time in four years, lost her own seat to the Scottish National Party (SNP). Everything that might have gone wrong went spectacularly awry. So what was to blame for the Liberal Democrats' failure to sustain pre-election expectations? Why in the so-called 'Brexit election' did the party whose raison d'être was

*David Cutts, Department of Political Science, University of Birmingham, d.cutts@bham.ac.uk; Andrew Russell, Department of Politics, University of Liverpool, Andrew.Russell@liverpool.ac.uk

doi:10.1093/pa/gsaa024

to stop Britain leaving the European Union (EU) fail to make significant electoral headway? Why did the Liberal Democrats get their political and electoral strategy so badly wrong? We examine what happened and why and assess whether this represented another missed opportunity, or whether the failings of the campaign mask the underlying story of slow, relative and partial, recovery in Liberal Democrat fortunes.

1. Building momentum

After Tim Farron's resignation, Sir Vince Cable was elected unopposed as leader, with the unenviable task of reconnecting with an increasingly polarised and divided electorate. The Cable era can be divided into two parts. Initially, Cable was keen to play the 'statesmanlike' card by making a virtue out of his longevity in public life. On Brexit, for instance, he immediately painted himself as the 'political adult' in the room and while ruling out formal pacts with the others sought to call out 'sensible grown-ups' from both parties who shared his and the party's position to keep Britain in the single market and customs union. He recognised that the party needed more media exposure to rally the troops and sought to provide clearer political messaging and policy positions in order to keep the Liberal Democrat badge in the forefront of public debate and people's minds. Yet, despite all the positive rhetoric, optimism and denial that he was merely a short-term caretaker, the reality was something different. The first 18 months of Cable's leadership was pedestrian, lacklustre and did little to raise the party's profile. The Liberal Democrats poll rating barely moved much above 8% while the 2018 local election results were, in terms of its nationwide share of the vote, one of the worst local election performances by the Liberal Democrats since their formation. Unsurprisingly, a year on from becoming leader, Cable confirmed that he would stand down after Brexit was resolved or stopped and after he had transformed the inner workings of the party. Yet, writing off Cable proved to be premature.

During the first half of 2019, both the Conservatives and Labour hit internal strife and showed signs of fracturing as they faced increasing public derision over Brexit. When the inevitable happened, the new Independent Group of 11 MPs was vocal in expressing their desire not to join the Liberal Democrats, claiming the party brand had been damaged by coalition with the Conservatives. Cable responded in a measured manner, calling for electoral alliances around shared interests such as a second Brexit referendum but noted the structural electoral hurdles for two centrist parties competing for the same voters. His decision in mid-March to step down after the local elections, to make way for a new generation, simultaneously enabled the party to talk about renewal and a fresh start but strategically was designed to offset the novelty of its new centrist opponent. And with Change UK not standing in the local elections and Brexit dominating political discourse, the door seemed ajar for the Liberal Democrats to make a political statement.

Over the next month, the Liberal Democrats not only gained significant electoral impetus but also they mortally damaged their Centrist adversaries. First, through local election success—704 net gains and 12 councils—the party won 16% of seats up for election, with 1,351 councillors returned and now controlled 23 councils, its highest number since 2010. With visibility increasing, a seemingly decisive shift in the national polls occurred. The Liberal Democrats immediately sought to build on this through the launch of their European election manifesto and campaign slogan, 'Bollocks to Brexit', which generated even more media exposure. Like the local elections, it was the Liberal Democrats that cannibalised the pro-Remain vote in the European elections, winning 16 seats, its largest number since 1979. With 3.4 million votes and 20% of the national vote, the party topped the poll in London and was the largest party in 44 local areas, 29 of which were in the capital and the South East. Cable passed the baton onto Swinson with the Liberal Democrats seemingly back in the electoral fight.

2.   Swinson: shifting position

Emboldened by the legitimacy given to it from pro-Remain supporters in local and European elections, a record membership of 120,000 and the subsequent considerable uptick in national polls, the Liberal Democrats became increasingly visible and garnered far more national media attention. Swinson hit the ground running with success in the Brecon and Radnorshire by-election while defections from Change UK and, in time, from three Conservative MPs who crossed the floor of the House also provided publicity and a legitimacy boost.

From the early days of Swinson's leadership, there were two distinct shifts from the Cable regime. On becoming leader, Swinson unequivocally set out her stall to 'Stop Brexit' and remove any ambiguity about the Liberal Democrats' pro-Remain credentials. Part of the reasoning was to exploit the uncertainty around Labour's 'renegotiation strategy' position and their shift towards a 'second referendum' position with strings attached. As a consequence, the Liberal Democrats signalled to Remain voters that they would revoke Article 50 if they won outright power and would revert to supporting a second referendum with a Remain option if they fell short.

The Liberal Democrats also adopted an unambiguous equidistance stance to lure recruits from both Labour and the Conservatives by ruling out supporting a Johnson- or Corbyn-led administration. Compared to Cable, Swinson also 'ratcheted up' the anti-Corbyn tone and rhetoric. She consistently dismissed a Corbyn-led caretaker government to avoid a no-deal Brexit and instead put forward other alternative caretaker PMs. Eyeing disenchanted Labour voters,

Swinson went beyond Corbyn's reluctance to back a second referendum. She also signposted the Labour leadership's handling of anti-Semitism and its damaging economic policies, while portraying Corbyn as a threat to national security, using examples of his response to the Salisbury poisoning incident and support for authoritarian regimes.

Both the Revoke policy and the rigid equidistance stance represented political gambles. Each risked alienating potential Conservative and Labour tactical switchers. They also jeopardised message clarity and handed their rivals potential attack lines warning that supporting the Liberal Democrats could let in their opponent by mistake. With both leaders and parties not overwhelmingly popular in their own right, the Liberal Democrats began to project Swinson as a competent, decisive leader who owned policy positions like Revoke and was not afraid to make tough choices. When the Labour leadership bowed to pressure from Swinson and the SNP for an early general election, it was clear that the party would go 'all in' on this one-club electoral strategy.

3.   The political and electoral strategy

After their 2017 general election performance, the Liberal Democrats still needed to climb an electoral mountain even to get back to the point prior to entering coalition with the Conservatives. There were 17 seats where the party needed a swing of 10% or less, 12 of which were won by the Conservatives in 2017. On a swing of 20% or less, this figure increased to 52 seats with 40 held by the Conservatives, 7 by Labour and 5 by nationalist parties in Scotland and Wales. Of these 35 most marginal, only Dorset West and St Albans had not been held by the Liberal Democrats between 2001 and 2010. Despite evidence of growing individual switching, for any Liberal Democrat revival to occur, it was highly likely it would be in the places where local credibility remained a factor. But there were other problems to overcome. As Figure 6.1 shows, only 16 of the 52 seats where the Liberal Democrats required a swing of 20% or less had a Remain vote above 55%. Nine of these 16 seats were held by Labour or the SNP. Yet, 22 of these seats had a majority for Leave, with 12 recording a Leave vote of 55% or more. Ten of these 12 were held by the Conservatives. If the Liberal Democrats were to make an electoral breakthrough, they needed the support of both a highly efficient tactical 'Remain Alliance' and disgruntled moderate Leave voters. This was a monumental challenge.

To overcome the millstone of credibility, part of the electoral strategy involved trying to persuade switching MPs to remain in their incumbent seats and fight on the Liberal Democrat badge. Two of its new MPs (Sandbach and Wollaston) fought where they were originally elected. Other high-profile defectors were parachuted into Remain seats where party polling suggested they had a viable

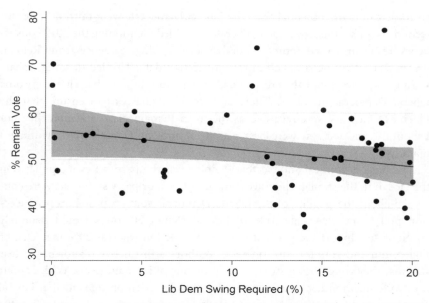

Figure 6.1 Liberal Democrat 2019 possible constituency targets (swing 20% or less) by 2016 % Remain vote

chance of winning or causing an upset. Three of these MPs (Berger, Gyimah and Ummuna) were strategically placed into strong London Remain seats, while Smith and Lee moved to Remain Altrincham and Sale West and Wokingham, respectively.

The party sought to offset credibility concerns by re-selecting either former MPs or those who stood in key target seats last time out. It hoped that the personal votes of former MPs would simultaneously nullify any incumbent advantage and act as a focal point for tactical pro-Remain switching in these seats. The Liberal Democrats also relied on their trusted local base to help spring a surprise. Recent local gains against the Conservatives in North Devon and Winchester provided some hope that this would translate to the parliamentary level. And the party agreed a Unite to Remain electoral pact with the Greens and Plaid Cymru in 60 seats where only one of these party's candidates would stand to maximize the chances of getting MPs who opposed Brexit elected. With a free-run in 43 of these seats, the party hoped it would boost its electoral chances in key targets.

A key plank of the party's electoral strategy was to minimize the potential squeezing from its rivals. Evidence from the British Election Study (Fieldhouse *et al.*, 2019) suggested that the Liberal Democrats drew 49% of its vote from Labour and 20% from Conservative 2017 voters in the European elections. Holding onto these voters who switched was vital. Again, credibility was critical, given that in many potential seats the Liberal Democrats were third or a distant second. To offset this, the party deliberately avoided mentioning the 2017 constituency result and used more favourable local polling, evidence from Remain driven tactical voting sites and European election data. This led to some embarrassing enquiries about the creative use of data and dubious bar charts in some Liberal Democrat literature. The dual credibility goal was to ensure that the Liberal Democrats were regarded as the main Remain party and that they not Labour (in most cases) were best placed to stop the Conservatives winning a majority.

The biggest political and electoral gamble was the party's Revoke policy. On the face of it, the strategy did have some merit. Senior party strategists were concerned about the fragility of the Liberal Democrat vote—a post-European election poll found that only 31% of Liberal Democrat voters would definitely continue to support the party at the general election whereas 29% may change their mind and vote for someone else. Without a distinctive platform, the fear was that they risked being swallowed up by one of its main rivals. With Labour now offering another referendum, the Revoke position meant the Liberal Democrats could continue to present itself as the true party of Remain. Given its weak partisan base and desire to build support in Labour seats, shoring up its vote through this Remain narrative seemed a credible option. Leaving aside the judgment on whether the party's new policy was sufficiently liberal or democratic, it was a clear risk nevertheless. Only 54% of those who voted Liberal Democrat in June 2019 either approved or strongly approved of cancelling Brexit.[1] While the policy appealed to voters in much of London and its wealthy suburban belt, outside of four or five London seats, it still needed to convert Labour and Green voters en masse to translate votes into seats. There was also a worry that a policy of revoking Article 50 could seriously backfire in Conservative battlegrounds. At the individual level, it was inconceivable that such a policy would appeal to Leavers while the Conservative Remain vote could also be turned off by such as hard-line policy. At the aggregate level, many of its previous strongholds in the South West of England were strong Leave areas. To win back these seats and others elsewhere, the Liberal Democrats were now reliant on the Remain vote mobilizing behind them and the Brexit party splitting the Leave vote. In Scotland, the Liberal Democrats had to 'out-Remain' the Remain SNP in a country where growing support for the SNP's IndyRef2 platform was likely to split the Remain vote and lead to the party battling other parties for the Remain plus Union voter (see the Mitchell and Henderson contribution to this volume).

---

[1]To the BES question of whether parliament should cancel Brexit, 54% of Liberal Democrat voters in June 2019 either approved or strongly approved. For Labour switchers, it was 57% but far less for Conservative switchers (46%).

Away from Brexit, it would still need to appease core Labour voters in any tactical coalition, given the Liberal Democrats austerity record. For all the talk of individual volatility, it still looked electorally complicated for the Liberal Democrats when the anchor of credibility was not present (Cutts and Russell, 2018).

4. The electoral outcome

The 2019 general election saw the Conservatives gain 43.6% of the UK vote and win an 80-seat majority with 48 net gains. Labour saw their vote plummet by almost 8 percentage points to 32.1% and 60 seat losses. While the combined Conservative and Labour vote share did not reach the heights of 2017, more than 75% of voters still supported the two main parties. With the SNP also gaining ground in Scotland, internal party fears that the Liberal Democrat vote could be squeezed during the election campaign became reality. Nonetheless, the party did poll nearly 3.7 million votes, 1.31 million more than in 2017 despite the 2-point decline in turnout and increased its vote share by 4.2 percentage points to 11.5% (Table 6.1). The improvement was steady but not the spectacular increase hoped for prior to the campaign. To put this into perspective, the Liberal Democrat vote was higher than in 2015 and 2017 but half of what it achieved nine years ago pre-coalition and lower than at any election between 1974 and 2010. Two years previously, the party lost support but achieved a net gain of four seats due to effective targeting. In 2019, support increased in 574 of the 611 constituencies where the Liberal Democrats stood candidates. Yet the party suffered a net loss of one seat, gaining three seats and losing four, and the number of Liberal Democrat MPs in Westminster fell to 11.

For the second time in four years, Swinson experienced defeat in her East Dunbartonshire seat. In 2015, her vote held up relatively well when other Liberal Democrat incumbents suffered dramatic drops in support. This time, with her as party leader, the effect was hugely symbolic and catastrophic. The SNP was extremely effective at squeezing the Labour vote and building an anti-Swinson alliance to secure victory. The loss of Stephen Lloyd in Eastbourne was less surprising and less high profile, while defeat for Tom Brake in Carshalton and Wallington appeared to be a tactical blunder. Internal Liberal Democrat analysis suggested that Brake would hold the seat and central office then deployed valuable resources to nearby Wimbledon where the party was challenging the Conservatives. Warning signs emerged on polling day as efforts were made to save Brake but to no avail. Elsewhere, with Norman Lamb not standing in Norfolk North, the Liberal Democrat vote plunged by more than 18 percentage points as the Conservatives regained the seat.

The Liberal Democrats did gain North East Fife from the SNP helped by pro-Union Conservative tactical switching and narrowly held onto Caithness,

Table 6.1 Summary of Liberal Democrat general election performance, 1992–2019

LD	1992	1997	2001	2005	2010	2015	2017	2019
Votes (000)	5999	5243	4814	5985	6836	2416	2372	3696
UK vote (%)	17.8	16.8	18.3	22.0	23.0	7.9	7.4	11.5
Seats won	20	46	52	62	57	8	12	11
Seats won (%)	3.2	7.0	7.9	9.6	8.8	1.2	1.8	1.7
Votes: seats[a]	1.12	2.74	2.84	2.82	2.48	1.01	1.62	0.96
Lost deposits	11/632	13/639	1/639	1/626	0/631	341/631	375/629	136/611

Note: These are UK-wide vote share percentages so differ slightly from the GB-only figures reported by David Denver in 'Results'.
[a]Votes: Seats ratio derived from dividing LD seats won by LD share of the vote. In 1992, the Liberal Democrats stood in 632 constituencies; and in 2017, they stood in 629. In 2019, the party only stood in 611 seats following their pact with Plaid Cymru and the Greens.

Sutherland and Easter Ross and Edinburgh West. Across England, the two gains in ultra-Remain Richmond Park and St Albans were secured with comfortable majorities with both Liberal Democrat candidates polling more than 50% of the vote. In 6 of the 11 seats won, the party gained more than half of the votes cast. Elsewhere the party fell agonisingly short in four seats: Cheltenham, Sheffield Hallam, Wimbledon and Winchester. Wimbledon was one of seven seats (excluding Buckingham) where the party increased their vote by more than 20 percentage points but failed to win the seat. Despite some strong performances, all the Labour and Conservatives defectors who stood as Liberal Democrats in 2019 fell short. Perhaps the worst kept secret of the Liberal Democrat campaign was the big effort in Esher and Walton to unseat the incumbent, prominent Conservative Brexiteer Dominic Raab but despite increasing their vote by almost 28 points the party narrowly failed.

Two years ago, the Liberal Democrats polled more than 30% of the vote in 28 constituencies, lost 375 deposits and only came second in 38 seats. In 2019, the party did advance, winning more than 30% of the vote in 51 seats and losing deposits in only 138 constituencies. They are now second in 91 seats, 80 of which where the Conservatives are the incumbent. Of those second places, the Liberal Democrats are now 10% behind the winning party in 15 seats compared to 9 two years ago. Ten seats are ultra-marginal (5% or less behind the incumbent) with eight of these held by the Conservatives. Optimists might claim the Liberal Democrats have the platform to make serious electoral inroads into the Conservatives next time.

At the national and regional levels, the Liberal Democrat vote remains uneven and the post 2010 north-south divide in party support is widening (Table 6.2). Despite holding four seats in Scotland, its vote continued to be squeezed in the

Table 6.2 Liberal Democrat performance, 2019 general election: national and regional breakdown

National and Regional	2019 % LD Vote	2017 % LD Vote	Change 2017–19	Seats 2019	Seats 2017	Change 2017–19
Country						
UK	11.5	7.4	+4.2	11/632	12/632	−1
England	12.4	7.8	+4.6	7/533	8/533	−1
Scotland	9.5	6.8	+2.8	4/59	4/59	0
Wales	6.0	4.5	+1.5	0/40	0/40	0
Region						
East Midlands	7.8	4.3	+3.5	0/46	0/46	0
Eastern	13.4	7.9	+5.5	1/58	1/58	0
London	14.9	8.8	+6.1	3/73	3/73	0
North East	6.8	4.6	+2.3	0/29	0/29	0
North West	7.9	5.4	+2.5	1/75	1/75	0
South East	18.2	10.5	+7.7	1/84	2/84	−1
South West	18.2	14.9	+3.2	1/55	1/55	0
West Midlands	7.9	4.4	+3.5	0/59	0/59	0
Yorkshire and the Humber	8.1	5.0	+3.1	0/54	0/54	0

face of SNP resurgence and pro-Union supporters opting for the Conservatives unless the Liberal Democrats were better placed. Liberal Democrat support rose by less than 3 points in Scotland but it fared far worse in Wales. Even accounting for the Unite to Remain pact, the party lost Brecon and Radnorshire, 16 deposits in the 32 seats they stood and only managed to increase their vote by 1.5 percentage points across the country.

The Liberal Democrats gained support across all regions in England, with the largest growth in London and the South East. Of the 29 seats where the party is now fewer than 10 percentage points behind the incumbent, 14 are in London and the South East (and only eight of the party's 138 lost deposits nationally were suffered in these areas). The Liberal Democrats continue to poll relatively strongly in its area of traditional strength, notably the South West with 11 of the 55 seats in the region recording Liberal Democrat vote shares of 30% or more. However, as in 2017, party support continues to bottom-out with increases below the national average. Aside from regaining Bath in 2017, they failed to recover lost ground elsewhere and the task seems to be getting more difficult. Only 5 of the 29 seats where the Liberal Democrats are 10% behind the incumbent now are in the South West with the Conservatives retaining huge majorities in previous Liberal Democrat strongholds.

Liberal Democrat support continues to hold up in eastern England and remains above the national average but elsewhere the picture looks bleak. Across the North of England and the Midlands, party support is anything from 3.4% to as much as 4.7% below the national vote share. In 2017, the difference between the five northern and midland regions and the four southern regions of England was roughly 6.5 points. By 2019, this gap had grown to 9 percentage points. To re-iterate the growing divide, around 87% of lost party deposits in England were in the North and Midlands. Forty per cent of all UK wide lost party deposits were in the North West and Yorkshire and the Humber. The Liberal Democrats failed to record any constituency vote shares above 30% across the whole of the Midlands. Only 4 of the 29 seats where the party was second and less than 10% behind the winner in 2019 are in the North of England. There remains a clear geographic divide in Liberal Democrat representation. For the second successive election, Westmoreland and Lonsdale is the only northern English Liberal Democrat seat.

5.   The constituency battleground

Table 6.3 examines the Liberal Democrats' 2019 performance by seat type. In 2015 and 2017, while incumbency mattered, those seeking re-election were not guaranteed immunity from any national surge because of their personal standing in the seat (Cutts and Russell, 2017). The loss of Swinson and Brake reinforces this. Nonetheless, where a Liberal Democrat incumbent stood again, support rose by a modest 2 percentage points, lower than the national increase in party support and roughly half that achieved by incumbent candidates in 2017. For Liberal Democrat candidates in a number of incumbent seats, support had begun to reach its ceiling. Moreover, the party was far less defensive than two years ago targeting many more seats including some where the Liberal Democrats were languishing in third place. In non-held seats, support increased by more than 4 points. Evidence suggests that the floor of the Liberal Democrat vote (the 375 seats where the party lost its deposit in 2017) rose by 3.1 percentage points. Yet closer inspection suggests that, while being in second place mattered, the role of political agency continues to be more important.

Heading into the 2019 general election, the Liberal Democrats were second in 38 seats, 29 of which were Conservative–Liberal Democrat battlegrounds. Previously, the tactical unwind of the centre-left vote in these battleground seats was a major factor in the party's collapse. Likewise in 2017, while success against the Conservatives transpired where the Liberal Democrats were able to curb the Labour vote, some tactical unwind occurred, with Labour even relegating the Liberal Democrats to third place in five seats (Cutts and Russell, 2017). In 2019, tactical unwind not only stopped but had reversed, although in modest and uneven fashion. In the 29 Conservative–Liberal Democrat battlegrounds, the party made above-average headway, increasing support by 5.7 points. There is, however, a lot of unevenness, with the party losing ground in five seats and

Table 6.3 Liberal Democrat performance by incumbency and seat type, 2019 general election

Seats	2019 % LD Vote	2017 % LD Vote	Change ±17–19
Incumbency			
LD 2017 incumbent seats (12)	44.6	44.2	+0.4
LD incumbent candidates (10)	44.9	42.9	+2.0
LD non-held seats (599)	10.9	6.6	+4.3
Seat type (LDs second place)			
LD all second place (38)	33.1	29.1	+4.0
Con-LD seats (29)	35.4	29.7	+5.7
Lab-LD seats (7)	24.5	26.1	−1.6
SNP/PC-LD seats (2)	30.2	30.9	−0.7
Historical Legacy			
LD legacy February 1974 seats (13)[a]	19.9	21.9	−2.0
LD heartland 1992 seats (18)	26.2	27.0	−0.8
LD breakthrough 1997 seats (28)[a]	31.8	28.5	+3.3
LD pre-coalition 2010 (56)[a]	27.6	27.6	0.0

Notes: Percentages derived from summing LD votes cast/Total Valid Votes Cast × 100. The 2017 constituencies exclude Buckingham and Brighton Pavilion as the LDs did not stand a candidate in either constituency. In 2019, the Liberal Democrats stood in 611 seats.
[a]Legacy seats are one less because the party did not stand in Isle of Wight; in 2010 they are one less because the party did not stand in Bristol West.

simultaneously recording double-digit increases in another six. In the two seats, the Liberal Democrats won, both the Conservatives and Labour lost support. Across the 29 seats, the Conservatives marginally increased their support but Labour saw their vote drop by 6.6 points, with their vote declining in all but one of these constituencies. The Liberal Democrats clearly began to regain some of the centre-left tactical switchers that had left it after 2010 but its failure to make any deep inroads into the Conservative vote placed a ceiling on its ability to win seats.

In the seven seats, they were directly challenging Labour the party simply failed to breakthrough and lost 1.7 percentage points of their vote. Again, Liberal Democrat vote change was uneven with four of the seven seats recording a decline in support. Two recorded little change while the party's vote rose by nearly 10 points in Hornsey and Wood Green. Labour also experienced a decline in support but only by 2.2 percentage points. Clearly, the failure to secure the marginal seats of Cambridge and Sheffield Hallam and to make further inroads against Labour generally was a considerable setback.

The tactic of re-selecting a previous Liberal Democrat MP to stand in the seat they once represented had limited success. Of those, only Sarah Olney in Richmond Park saw a substantial increase in support and actually won back the seat. In two potentially winnable seats—Ceredigion and St Ives—previous MPs lost ground. The Liberal Democrat retreat in their traditional heartlands continued although there are signs that the rate of decline is beginning to slow as support reaches its floor. Of the 14 Liberal constituencies held in February 1974, Orkney and Shetland remained the only seat held. The Liberal Democrats largely stood still in all 1,992 seats despite regaining North East Fife. Many of these seats were the foundation for party growth during 1990s and 2000s but were wiped out during the coalition years. In 2019, the drop in Liberal Democrat voting looks to have bottomed-out but there are few signs of any long-term recovery. On the contrary, for the second successive election, the Liberal Democrats improved their performance in the 'breakthrough' seats which the party won in 1997 at the peak of the anti-Conservative tactical alliance. They recorded on average more than 30% of the vote in these predominantly Conservative-leaning constituencies and increased their support overall by more than 3 points. Across the 56 seats that the party won in 2010 and stood a candidate in 2019, there was little evidence of any resurgence. This is mainly because any growth where the party was fighting the Conservatives was largely offset by more challenging conditions in seats where Labour and the SNP were the primary competitors. Despite the churn, 8 of the 11 seats won in 2019 were held by the party in 2010; 5 were first gained in 1997; 4 of the 11 seats also elected Liberal Democrat representatives 27 years ago. The story, therefore, remains similar to two years ago: while the party has failed to recover in its traditional heartland areas, the Liberal Democrats historical legacy still remains vital to both its support and Westminster representation.

6.   Brexit and the Liberal Democrat vote

After the 2019 election, only 1 of the 11 seats represented by Liberal Democrat MPs voted Leave in the 2016 EU Referendum. In 6 of the other 10 seats it now holds, support for Remain in the referendum exceeded 60%. Three of the four losses were Leave seats. In 2017, there was a positive relationship (correlation of 0.15* significant at 99% level) between Liberal Democrat constituency vote change and Remain vote, albeit the line was relatively flat. Two years later, the relationship is slightly stronger (0.24* significant at 99% level) although there is some indication that the Liberal Democrat vote increased more in softer Remain seats as well as in those places that strongly voted Remain (see Figure 6.2).

Overall, party support was on average more than 6 percentage points higher in Remain areas than in Leave seats and around 4 percentage points higher than the party's national vote share. When broken down into 'soft' (50–59.9%) and 'hard' (with a 60%+ vote) categorisations, it is evident that the party's vote was 5.5 points lower in 'hard Brexit' than 'soft Brexit' areas but both saw increases in Liberal Democrat support (see Table 6.4). Many of these included seats where Labour was fighting off a Conservative surge. Even on this limited evidence (and

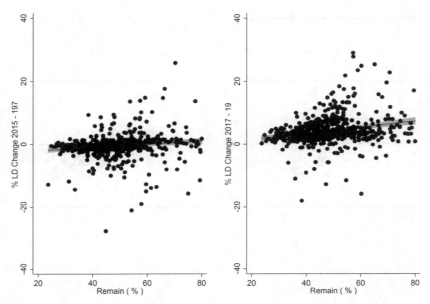

Figure 6.2 Liberal Democrat vote change 2015–2017 and 2017–2019, by % Remain vote

acknowledging ecological fallacy issues), it is probable that while Remain voters did not abandon Labour for the Liberal Democrats in droves, the party's ability to lift the floor of its vote harmed Labour. The party increased their vote share, on average, by 5.6% across Remain constituencies but the growth was nearly 1 percentage point stronger in 'soft' than 'hard Remain' seats. In a sizeable minority of these 'hard Brexit' seats, the SNP was rampant which restricted growth. Many others were safe Labour seats of which more than 30 were in London. The party simply lacked the longstanding credibility in these seats as a viable voting option so any possible surge in support was always going to have a ceiling.

Figure 6.3 provides further insight into how Brexit shaped Liberal Democrat support in the 2019 election against their main rivals. Here, we mark England and Wales constituencies as to whether they backed Remain (hollow triangle, where support for Leave <45%); were comparatively evenly balanced (hollow square, where support for Leave ≥45% and ≤55%) or whether they backed Leave (black circle, where support for Leave >55%). For the Liberal Democrats, there is a significant negative effect for Conservative and Labour vote change on Liberal Democrat vote change, suggesting that Liberal Democrat support held up better in seats where their rivals did not make as much ground. In 2019, we can see how the Liberal Democrats made modest gains in Leave and largely working-class seats from an extremely low base predominantly where the Conservatives gained moderate support and Labour collapsed. In Remain and

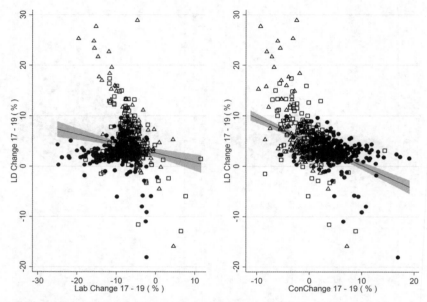

Figure 6.3 How Brexit shaped Liberal Democrat gains and losses, 2019 general election

largely middle-class seats, there are places where the Liberal Democrats saw their vote surge while Labour fell away but there are also a number of strong Remain areas where the Labour vote held up. Liberal Democrat gains and Conservative losses are predominantly in the evenly balanced Brexit areas and Remain seats notwithstanding a small cluster of the latter where the party made little progress. While this did not translate into Liberal Democrat seats in 2019, it does illustrate Britain's changing electoral map where previous Conservative middle class, largely Remain areas might be potentially vulnerable to the Liberal Democrats in future elections.

7. Why did it go wrong for the Liberal Democrats?

7.1 Jo Swinson's disastrous campaign

Leaders are critical nowadays in British elections but they are especially vital for third parties. Not only do they enable them to reach out to the electorate but they provide a vehicle to enhance electoral credibility and create goodwill towards the party brand. Traditionally, the Liberal Democrats always did better when they were given more exposure with the popularity of the leader a key determinant in the party's success. With Johnson marmite for many and Corbyn unpalatable for more, the Liberal Democrats sensed an opportunity. Notwithstanding internal

Table 6.4 Liberal Democrat performance in Remain and Leave seats, 2019 general election

Seats	2019 % LD Vote	Change ±17–19
Remain/Leave		
All Leave seats (381)	9.2	+3.3
All Remain seats (230)	15.4	+5.6
Leave		
'Soft Brexit' seats 50.1–59.9% (231)	11.0	+3.8
'Hard Brexit' seats 60%+ (150)	6.5	+2.6
Remain		
'Soft Remain' seats 50.1–59.9% (145)	15.6	+5.9
'Hard Remain' seats 60%+ (85)	15.0	+5.0

Note: 611 seats where the Liberal Democrats stood candidates.

party enthusiasm for Swinson, many saw her relative obscurity both an advantage and a vehicle through which the Liberal Democrats could capture votes from disenchanted voters. As a consequence, the party's campaign, branding and literature were built around her. From the orange battlebus emblazoned with her photo and the phrase 'Jo Swinson's Liberal Democrats' to personalising high-profile policy announcements on free childcare for those aged two to four, the 'presidential style' campaign was all about selling Swinson the person to the public at large.

Far from being an electoral asset, Swinson quickly became a liability. At the party's formal election campaign launch, Swinson insisted she was running to become Prime Minister. The comment haunted her throughout the campaign with many considering it arrogant and unrealistic. As the party's polling began to slide, Swinson resolutely kept talking up her Prime Ministerial chances, which served to make her sound fanciful and out of touch. This was largely of the party's own making but there was also a bind the Liberal Democrats now consistently find themselves in, since their time in coalition. The party ruled out working with a Johnson-led Conservative administration and a Labour one led by Corbyn but did not explicitly dismiss other alternatives. While this permitted some deflection on questions of potential coalition building, it meant that the party needed to persuade voters to support it in their own right and selling Swinson as a potential, credible Prime Minister was an important plank in this strategy. Crucially, Swinson's approval ratings barely got above 25% throughout her period as leader. In the early days, many polled could not make a judgement but as the public got to know and see Swinson more, the more unimpressed they became. Whereas Swinson's net approval rating was below Corbyn, ultimately, only 19% of the public approved of Swinson, a figure below even 21% for the Labour leader. Swinson simply failed to cut through.

Swinson's inability to free herself from the shackles of the Conservative–Liberal Democrat 2010–2015 coalition also damaged the party's appeal. Swinson's own track record in the austerity government dogged her throughout the campaign. Not only she was the subject of a concerted online campaign from Labour supporters and activists, she faced anger from voters in person. During her BBC Question Time appearance, Swinson came under repeated attack from younger audience members for supporting austerity and was forced to say 'sorry that we did not win more of those fights in coalition' (Independent, 2019*a*). Swinson was also confronted by a student in Glasgow who blamed her and the Liberal Democrats for enabling austerity cuts and then later in the campaign by a protestor in Streatham over the effect of the coalition government's policies on young people. There was also a sense that the apology for austerity cuts became more sincere as the campaign progressed. Early on, Swinson not only spoke about being upfront about the Liberal Democrats failings in coalition but also defended their role in government pointing to policy successes such as same-sex marriage and taking lower incomes out of paying tax. A few weeks later the tone changed. The week before polling day, Swinson apologised for voting for austerity cuts, supporting policies such as the 'bedroom tax' and admitted that austerity went too far (Independent, 2019*b*). Austerity remained a millstone around the party's neck. Among key voters that the party needed onside, austerity still mattered and Swinson represented the era when the Liberal Democrats were the poster boys of economic cuts. If the Liberal Democrats wanted to draw a line under this period, Swinson was emblematic of why this could not happen.

Swinson's exclusion from the first televised head-to-head election debate was a damaging blow. It might have provided a critical space for the Liberal Democrat leader's credibility, just as it did for Nick Clegg in 2010. A three-way leaders' debate could have given the party and Swinson equal footing with her main rivals on a national stage. The vigour with which the party attacked and contested the decision suggested that they thought it might be a pivotal moment. Given the 'presidential nature' of the Liberal Democrat campaign, it represented a prize opportunity for Swinson to present herself as the moderate, progressive leader reaching out to discontented voters. Nevertheless, in different TV debate formats, it was not as if Swinson 'stole the show', so it is not guaranteed that Swinson and the Liberal Democrats would have gained a huge advantage from taking part.

7.2 Party strategy

Aside from adopting a backfiring 'Presidential style' campaign, the biggest strategic error was the policy to revoke Article 50. Throughout the campaign, it came under sustained attack from both the main parties. On the one hand, it was counterproductive because it could only be implemented if the party won a majority which was highly unlikely. It also muddied the Liberal Democrats' Brexit message which was previously simple and clear. It both hurt and contradicted the moderate, pragmatic appeal of the party's image to voters. Opponents questioned whether winning a majority at Westminster under first-past-the-post constituted an unequivocal mandate. For the Liberal Democrats, a party that had long supported proportional representation recognizing such a mandate seemed inconsistent and in the long run an act of self-harm. Polling two weeks before election day suggested that 28% of the public supported the Liberal Democrats' position of revoking Article 50 and stopping Brexit completely (YouGov, 2019). Yet, only 50% of Remain voters backed it while 35% opposed. More than four-fifths of Leave voters unsurprisingly did not support the policy. The policy was clearly polarising and caused a great deal of public resentment. Moreover, there was barely any support among Conservative voters, with only 3% in agreement and 90% opposed. The policy of revoking Article 50 arguably placed a ceiling on party support and hampered efforts to persuade large numbers of Conservative moderates to lend them their vote. To make matters worse, in the final weeks of the campaign, the Liberal Democrats began to row back and returned to what Layla Moran called 'Plan A' of a second referendum. This shifted position reaffirmed that it 'bombed' with those voters the party wanted to win over.

Like previous efforts to be equidistant, such a stance simply failed to reap electoral rewards. While criticisms of Boris Johnson and his Brexit policy was wholly unsurprising, the acerbic tone levelled at Corbyn and Labour was strategically a little more difficult to fathom. Early on it appeared that the party saw an electoral opening. By winning over Labour Remain voters and moderates from other parties, the Liberal Democrats could do irreparable damage to Labour. Yet while Corbyn was clearly unpopular, it became abundantly evident as the campaign progressed that he was the only leading politician—and Labour the only party—that could achieve what the Liberal Democrats wanted—to stop Brexit. Despite this, the attacks continued diluting the party's supposedly unequivocal anti-Brexit stance. This had two damaging knock-on effects. Firstly, many Labour Remainers simply saw through Liberal Democrat attempts to position themselves in key seats as the only viable Remain option. As Lord Ashcroft's (2019) post-election polling shows, 84% of 2017 Labour Remainers stayed with Labour. Secondly, for Remain Conservatives, already nervous about a Corbyn-led Labour government, constant confirmation from the Liberal Democrats about how bad it would be scared them off from switching. When the opposition is unpopular, it makes it difficult for a third party to win seats from the incumbent. Further fuelling that unpopularity and supporting an extreme policy which could lead to resentment from voters in those key seats it is trying to attract, made little strategic sense and unsurprisingly failed. On the face of it, cooperation with Labour together with a carefully thought out political strategy to get a 'people's vote' with Remain on the ballot through a Labour-led administration might have changed electoral dynamics. Simply put, equidistance gave the party a high-risk shot at a 'home run' return to the Kennedy days of Westminster representation, but ultimately it was somewhat easily and predictably 'struck out' by far cannier rivals.

7.3 The campaign

The party went into the election with a highly ambitious 80-seat target strategy as internal strategists believed that the electoral momentum was with them. It staked that volatility would triumph over local credibility with scores of voters abandoning place-based political loyalties as they switched to them. Yet, despite the odd surge and the leapfrogging of Labour in some seats, longstanding credibility once again proved far more vital. As the campaign went on, the target list was amended week by week based on internal polling and local canvass returns with layers of key seats withdrawn central support. Come polling day, only a select few target seats remained, illustrating how hopelessly optimistic the original strategy was. Some of the damage was done early on. Nigel Farage's decision to remove the Brexit party from standing in Conservative-held seats was out of Liberal Democrat control but might have been anticipated as Farage had come under severe pressure from donors, high-profile supporters and the Brexit-leaning media in advance of the campaign. For the Liberal Democrats, already struggling to unify the Remain vote in marginal battlegrounds, a united Leave vote was far too powerful to overcome.

Other problems were of the Liberal Democrats' own making. In an attempt to offset an absence of local credibility, the Liberal Democrats used European election constituency results, internal polling and external multilevel regression with post-stratification (MRP) polling from tactical voting websites and local constituency polls to tell voters it was them, not Labour, most likely to oust Conservative incumbents. The party's use of data and badly drawn bar charts angered opposition activists and voters alike and quickly attracted media attention with Swinson having to face down accusations of misleading voters. It became an unwelcome distraction. And if Labour suspicions about the Liberal Democrats pro-Remain credentials at all costs were already somewhat waning, candidate disputes in Canterbury and High Peak added fuel to the anti-Labour conspiracy. While the decision to stand a candidate against pro-Remain Labour MP Rosie Duffield in marginal Canterbury did not stop her winning, her compatriot in High Peak was not so lucky, losing by 600 votes with the new Liberal Democrat candidate decisively winning more than 5% of the vote. Even though there was no formal Remain pact with Labour, it seemed to contradict the Liberal Democrats' widely

Table 6.5 Best party on issues: YouGov tracking poll, 25–26 November 2019 (%)

Issue	Conservatives	Labour	Lib Dems	Others	None	DK
Health	26	35	6	3	8	21
Immigration	30	18	8	14	7	24
Law and order	36	19	6	5	8	26
Education	26	30	9	3	8	24
Taxation	34	24	7	3	8	24
Unemployment	28	27	5	4	9	27
Economy	37	19	7	4	8	26
Housing	22	32	6	3	9	28
Britain's EU exit	31	13	11	13	11	20
Defence and security	39	15	5	5	7	30

aired stated ambition of stopping Brexit and opened it up to accusations that its real goal was to damage Labour.

Beyond revoking Article 50, the Liberal Democrats' manifesto remixed and extended some 2017 policies such as 1p in the pound on income tax to raise £7 billion for NHS and free childcare for two to four year olds. Like 2017, there was a renewed attempt to win back centre-left voters who had deserted the party since 2010, with proposals to generate 80% of electricity from renewables, freeze train fares, recruit 20,000 new teachers, lift the minimum wage for those on zero-hour contracts and build 300,000 new homes a year. On the economy though, the Liberal Democrats were more fiscally conservative than their rivals, with stringent borrowing limits. Any additional revenue was due to come from the 'Brexit bonus' from remaining in the EU. Although the Liberal Democrats' efforts to showcase their broader policy portfolio were somewhat overshadowed by 'Brexit', longstanding problems on political identity and policy appeal remained. Like 2017, aside from Europe where 11% of respondents named the Liberal Democrats as the best party, the Liberal Democrats were unable to make much headway in challenging their rivals' ownership of salient issues (see Table 6.5). There were some improvements on Education but apart from Europe all other issues remained in single digits. Simply put, there were few signs that the policies presented in the manifesto translated to the public and little evidence that the party had managed to address longstanding concerns by showcasing a distinctive identity.

8. Conclusion

After being routed in 2015, the Liberal Democrats were on life support, battling for electoral survival. Two years ago, the party had stabilised but was still in a critical condition. In 2019, the Liberal Democrats seemed to be on the precipice of a full recovery but remain in intensive care. Most of the damage was self-inflicted. The campaign proved to be a disaster and much of the political strategy was ill-thought out. Embarking on a 'Presidential style' campaign with a leader whose popularity plummeted on close public inspection damaged the party's ability to reach out to disenchanted voters (and suggests no-one in Liberal Democrat HQ had paid any attention to Theresa May's disastrous campaign of 2017). Its seemingly kamikaze Revoke policy muddied the Liberal Democrat Brexit message, polarised the public and undermined the party's moderate-pragmatic brand. The unrelenting personal attacks on Corbyn backfired, as Conservative and Labour voters hardened their positions for different reasons. Tactical mistakes, targeting blunders and data misrepresentation combined to make this a campaign to forget. Swinson's own defeat in a seat the party was adamant throughout they would defend exemplified the campaign's shortcomings. However, these failings actually mask some small but important advances. Leaving aside the drop in representation, the party saw an upsurge in support and is in a far healthier position than two years ago. Amidst Britain's changing electoral geography, it is now in prime position against the Conservatives in a cluster of seats and has an opportunity to develop its local brand in many others. There are also strong signs of growth among longstanding demographics, particularly graduates living in suburban, cosmopolitan areas who in recent elections looked elsewhere. Despite the disappointment, there are reasons to be optimistic.

Yet longstanding issues persist. The party's social and partisan base remains relatively weak and it is still largely reliant on votes that are lent rather than owned. Aside from Europe, the party continues to lack a political identity, focussing instead on quick fix, eye-catching proposals rather than building a long-term policy platform that appeals to those who share wider liberal values. Excluding its high-profile Remain credentials, it remains the case that, outside the most avid of political observers, most voters would be unable to say what the Liberal Democrats stand for, or recollect any of their policies. The association with the Coalition and its austerity policies also continues to damage the party's brand with key sections of the electorate.

After three consecutive election setbacks, now ought to be the time to change direction and adopt a different approach. The Liberal Democrats need to rethink their political identity, probably embrace a more centre-left agenda and possibly abandon equidistance. Given the changing electoral map, it makes political sense to take a more strident anti-Conservative line and forge new alliances with those on centre left of British politics. With Corbyn gone and a new leader with reputational competence and 'soft Left' credentials at the helm, the task of persuading moderates in Conservative facing seats to switch should now be easier. But the party needs to be careful as they too could lose ground to Labour in the places where they have made progress if credibility is weak.

And if Labour surges, winning back Labour-held seats may prove impossible. This will be doubly difficult if the party does not choose to break with the past. The logic here suggests the next Liberal Democrat leader ought to have been elected since the Coalition years so that they and the party can move forward without the baggage of austerity. While the Liberal Democrats are not awash with potential candidates, recent electoral churn means that there are a number of credible options. Rebuilding the connection with Labour and Green supporters could be the difference between making significant electoral gains or remaining a spectator on the sidelines.

The Liberal Democrats still face a monumental task. With Brexit seemingly done and dusted, political and economic fallout from the COVID-19 pandemic is likely to dominate the political discourse. With traditional left-right debates about the role, size and funding of the state likely to usurp recent cultural drivers of voting, the Liberal Democrats will face a renewed challenge of connecting with the public, providing policy distinctiveness and retaining political relevance. The 2019 election demonstrated that even when the Liberal Democrats recovered their relevance they still found it difficult to be popular. How the party defines and positions itself in the next few years could dictate its viability and long-term future. The Liberal Democrats might be on the road to recovery but the path ahead remains hazardous.

References

Ashcroft, L. (2019, December 13) 'How Britain Voted and Why', accessed at https://lordashcroftpolls.com/2019/12/how-britain-voted-and-why-my-2019-general-election-post-vote-poll/ on 20 April 2020.

Cutts, D. and Russell, A. (2017) 'The Liberal Democrats: Green Shoots of Recovery or Still on Life Support?', In Tonge, J., Bandeira, C. and Wilks-Heeg, S. (eds.) *Britain Votes 2017*, Oxford, Oxford University Press, pp. 72–90.

Cutts, D. and Russell, A. (2018) 'The 'Exit from Brexit' illusion: why the Liberal Democrats cannot capture the 48%, LSE Blog (British Politics and Policy)', accessed at https://blogs.lse.ac.uk/brexit/2018/11/09/the-exit-from-brexit-illusion-why-the-liberal-democrats-cannot-capture-the-48/ on 19 April 2020.

Fieldhouse, E., Green, J., Evans, G., Mellon, J. and Prosser, C. (2019) 'British Election Study Internet Panel Wave 16', accessed at https://www.britishelectionstudy.com/data-object/wave-16-of-the-2014-2019-british-election-study-internet-panel/ on 2 April 2020.

Independent (2019a, November 22) 'Question Time Debate: Jo Swinson admits "getting it wrong on austerity"', accessed at https://www.independent.co.uk/news/uk/politics/election-debate-jo-swinson-become-prime-minister-regret-austerity-a9214526.html on 20 April 2020.

Independent (2019b, December 4) 'Jo Swinson knows she will lose', accessed at https://www.independent.co.uk/news/uk/politics/election-jo-swinson-interview-andrew-neil-liberal-democrats-coalition-welfare-cuts-a9233351.html on 19 April 2020.

YouGov (2019) 'Sunday Times Survey Results', accessed at https://3859gp38qzh51h504x6gvv0o-wpengine.netdna-ssl.com/files/2019/12/YouGov-Sunday-Time-opinion-poll-late-November-2019.pdf on 20 April 2020.

Britain Votes (2019) 125–141

JAMES DENNISON*

How Niche Parties React to Losing Their Niche: The Cases of the Brexit Party, the Green Party and Change UK

This contribution considers how niche parties react when they lose their niche, using the cases of three parties in the turbulent period prior to the 2019 UK general election: the Brexit Party, the Green Party and Change UK. I overview the background of these parties before showing that each lost its respective policy niches to larger, more established parties. I show that each responded with some combination of directly *competing* with the mainstream party; electorally *cooperating* with them or other parties; or *diversifying* into something distinct from their mainstream analogue. I explain how each party's approach partially explains their 2019 general election result, as well as European Parliament elections result, using British Election Study data. I suggest that this 'compete, cooperate or diversify' approach provides a theoretical framework for understanding how niche parties are likely to react to losing their niche elsewhere.

1. Niche parties in the UK prior to the 2019 UK general election

Even though they ultimately received relatively few votes, the pivotal role played by 'niche parties' during the 2017–2019 parliament does much to explain the outcome of the election and the subsequent direction of British politics. Such parties have received various academic definitions, with perhaps the most succinct being that they are 'parties that compete primarily on a small number of non-economic issues' (Wagner, 2012, p. 845). There have been a number of attempts in the academic literature to make sense of niche parties. Adams *et al.* (2006) show that niche parties, first, do not respond to shifts in public opinion by changing their policy positions, whereas mainstream parties do, and, secondly, are electorally punished when moderating their positions, unlike mainstream parties (see also,

*James Dennison, Department of Sociology, University of Stockholm; Migration Policy Centre, European University Institute; Center for European Studies, Harvard University, James.dennison@eui.eu

doi:10.1093/pa/gsaa026

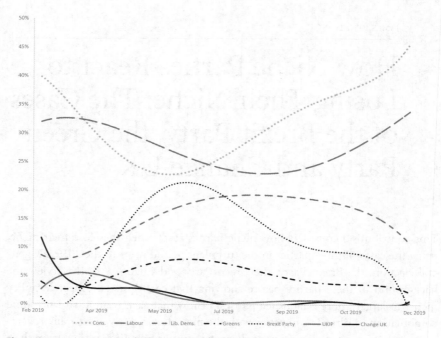

Figure 7.1 General election polling, February 2019–December 2019
Source: Wikipedia aggregation of polls.

Ezrow, 2008). Meguid (2005) argued that the electoral fortunes of niche parties are subject to strategic manipulation of the salience of issues by mainstream parties, which may adopt 'accommodative' or 'adversarial' strategies in response (see also, Abou-Chadi, 2016). However, to date, there have been no analyses of how niche parties react to the actions of mainstream parties. Although in the notably specific context of a first-past-the-post electoral system, the tumultuous period in British politics prior to the 2019 elections in which a number of 'niche parties' rose and fell in prominence (see Figure 7.1) provides three cases to investigate their reactions.

2.   How the Brexit Party won Britain's most valuable niche

On 15 January 2019, Theresa May's Conservative government lost the first 'meaningful vote' on its Withdrawal Agreement with the European Union (EU) by a margin of 230 MPs, the largest defeat of a government in modern parliamentary history. The crushing defeat, the first of three on the UK–EU deal, came 14 months after the High Court of Justice ruled that the government would have to put any withdrawal agreement to a vote in parliament, upending the government's Brexit strategy, casting the referendum result into doubt and leading to painful parliamentary wrangling between and within the mainstream parties.

Five days later, Nigel Farage, the former leader of the UK Independence Party (UKIP) warned of attempts by Conservative and Labour MPs to rule out no deal, form a committee to take over the Brexit process entirely, or even end it altogether (Farage, 2019). He went on to state:

> A lot of new parties have been formed in the course of the last year or two. A registration has been put into the Electoral Commission for 'The Brexit Party' [...] it's got my full support in every way [...] I want to make it really clear to all those people in Westminster on both parties that if they think they can betray Brexit and get away with it scot-free, they can't.

Elsewhere, Farage argued that there was widespread electoral demand for a party with a clear position on Brexit, compared to the 'political elite [that] want to stop Brexit in its tracks [while] the Prime Minister doesn't have the strength or inclination to see this through' (Wooding, 2019). Survey data largely supported his claim; in early 2019, nearly half of the UK electorate believed that 'no party was best able to handle' the issue that they considered most important—usually Brexit—up from 20% two years earlier (see Figure 7.2). Meanwhile, the percentage listing the Conservatives had fallen from around a third to 13% and the figure for UKIP had slowly risen to 8%.

Farage by this point had entirely separated himself from UKIP. In the aftermath of the 2016 referendum, he had given the Conservatives his tacit support to pursue Brexit unencumbered by electoral competition to its right. Eventually, in 2018, he left UKIP as it unsuccessfully attempted to both compete directly on Brexit with the Conservatives, who were still fairly trusted on the issue, and diversify into a more explicitly Islamophobic populist radical right party that publicly courted controversial far-right figures (Dennison, 2018).

On 5 February 2019, the Brexit Party was officially registered with the Electoral Commission. Farage, appearing on various news outlets, stated that he would stand as a candidate for the European Parliament in May should Brexit be delayed. As the government failed to pass its second and third 'meaningful votes', some Conservative MPs openly suggested they might vote for the Brexit Party in the now inevitable European elections amid chaos inside the Conservative party. Farage, by then officially party leader after Islamophobic social media activity by the founder had been uncovered, held the official party launch two days after a six-month extension was agreed between the EU and UK. Referring to his former party, Farage concluded that 'middle England, decent people' would not vote for a party 'completely obsessed' by Islam with a 'fairly loutish fringe' and associated

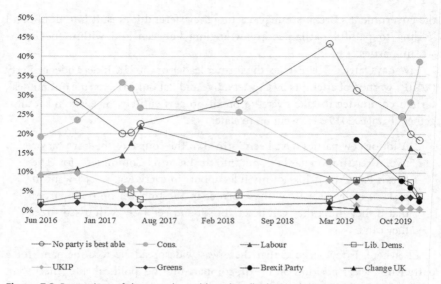

Figure 7.2 Perceptions of the party best able to handle the single most important issue facing the country, June 2016–December 2019
Q: 'Which party is best able to handle the issue that you think is the single most important one affecting the country at the present time?'
Source: Fieldhouse *et al.* (2020).

'with violence, criminal records and thuggery' (Halliday and Walker, 2019). He stated, 'In terms of policy, there's no difference [from UKIP], but in terms of personnel there is a vast difference'.

These personnel, introduced as candidates for the upcoming elections, represented a broad range of professions, while others with political backgrounds included the sister of high-profile Tory Brexiteer Jacob Rees-Mogg and 'radical libertarian' campaigner Claire Fox, underscoring the party's single-issue credentials. Seven Members of the European Parliament (MEPs) defecting from UKIP followed. The party took steps to keep the focus purely on Brexit, including, aside from its easily interpretable name, withholding any manifesto until after the European Parliament elections and, even more unusually, having only three members so as to avoid the division that defined the internal politics of UKIP. Farage himself maintained control over the selection of the executive committee and candidates. The party itself was controlled by a parent company, The Brexit Party Limited, which had just two directors, Farage and the party's chairman Richard Tice (an election candidate), along with five undisclosed shareholders. Crucially, as it would later turn out, the company's memorandum of association gave the leader freedom to work with other democratic parties 'for particular purposes consistent with its aims', presumably working with a future 'hard-Brexit' Conservative Party (McTague, 2019). Published following a freedom of information request, the party's constitution described its broader policy objectives in vaguely Thatcherite terms.

Over the following weeks, other high-profile candidates were gradually announced, maintaining media coverage of the new party. The party was soon able to claim over 100,000 'registered supporters' and topped every opinion poll for the European elections from late April onward. Estimates for the Conservatives declined from nearly 30% at the end of February to just over 10% by the election, while those for UKIP declined from 17% to around 3%. Meanwhile, Farage toured Leave voting areas, holding rallies focussed squarely on the undemocratic 'betrayal' of the Leave vote by a Remain parliament and no longer bothering with criticism of the EU itself. Promising that a vote for the Brexit Party was the best way to express desire for a 'proper', 'clean' or 'World Trade Organisation (WTO) terms' Brexit, Farage was met with crowds chanting his name.

At the 2019 European Parliament elections, the Brexit Party won 30.5% of votes, 10.9 percentage points more than the second-placed Liberal Democrats. This share netted 29 seats, four in 10 of the total British delegation. The party's predecessors, UKIP, managed 3.2% of the vote. The Brexit Party won the most seats in every constituency in England and Wales, except London and picked up an additional seat in Remain-leaning Scotland. Post-election surveys made clear that the Brexit Party had unequivocally won the most prized niche in British politics in the space of just two months. The Brexit Party won 70.3% of Leave voters and 82% of those who *both* voted Leave in 2016 *and* saw 'Europe' as the most important issue affecting Britain. In terms of so-called EU referendum identities, now more common than party identities, the Brexit Party won 75% of Leave identifiers. The Conservatives won <9% of each of these groups (Fieldhouse et al., 2020).

The socio-demographic and attitudinal leanings of Brexit Party voters were reasonably consistent with those of UKIP voters in previous European elections. The average age, 59, was six years older than that of the average voter, 56% of the party's voters were male, the party's votes disproportionally came from the south, their income was only slightly lower than that of the average voter and the mean self-placement on a 0–10 left–right spectrum was 6.33 (Fieldhouse *et al.*, 2020). The Brexit Party's voters placed Theresa May at 4.1 and the Conservatives at 4.7 on a 0–10 scale of likeability, while 70% stated that the government was handling the Brexit process badly. More measured, however, were attitudes to the deal itself. Less than half believed that the government's deal with the EU did 'not at all' honour the result of the EU referendum, suggesting ire was directed more at the inability to 'leave' rather than the nature of the deal itself. Perhaps most significantly of all, 64% of Brexit Party voters stated in June that they planned to vote for the party again at the next general election.

3. From losing Britain's biggest niche to unilateral electoral cooperation

In the month following the European Parliament election, the Brexit Party regularly topped polling for the next general election, with one poll estimating that the party would win 306 MPs, 20 short of an outright majority while the party came within just 683 votes of upsetting Labour in a by-election on 7 June, with 29% of the vote. Owing to the Brexit Party's drubbing of the Conservatives, who received just 8% of the vote, at the European Parliament elections, Theresa May announced that she would resign as Prime Minister (see Denver, this volume). Attention thereafter turned to the Conservative leadership election, with commentators speculating about which candidate might be best able to win votes back from Farage's party. Polling showed that at least a third of Conservative Party members would vote for the Brexit Party if there were a general election before the UK had left the EU.

By aping many of the noises being made by the Brexit Party, Boris Johnson, promising a 'do-or-die' Brexit, even if proroguing parliament were required, quickly became the choice of hard-line Brexiteers within the Conservative Party and, thus, the favourite to win the contest. Farage's initial strategic reaction to events was competitive. The Brexit Party leader rubbished the Brexit credentials of the Tories and the idea of an electoral pact with them, asking 'Just to keep the Tories inside No 10 and us in the EU? . . . I don't trust any of them to deliver a genuine Brexit and unless that situation changes, we are gearing up as an organisation to fight every seat in the country' (Adu, 2019). Having praised the campaign of Rory Stewart, the main candidate supporting May's deal, he reserved his 'strongest criticism' for Boris Johnson, labelling him 'untrustworthy' after voting 'aye' at the third meaningful vote and being 'very confused' about the EU's single market during the 2016 referendum campaign.

Installed as Prime Minister in late July, Boris Johnson took a hard-line stance by proroguing parliament and removing the whip from 21 Conservative MPs who had voted in favour of the Benn Bill, which legislated against a no-deal Brexit. One former Conservative cabinet minister announced her intention to resign as an MP, stating: 'My concerns about the Conservative Party becoming the Brexit Party have come to pass'. Johnson announced his intention to seek an early election, something that MPs then rejected thrice before forcing the government to request an extension until 31 January 2020. Johnson did so, while washing his hands of responsibility for 'parliament's letter, not my letter'. During this period, the intensity and complexity of parliamentary wrangling and the novelty of Johnson's premiership overshadowed the Brexit Party. One of the main exceptions came as Johnson's government put a minimally revised deal—lambasted by Farage as 'appalling'—to parliamentary vote, passing second reading on 22

October. Though the Brexit Party at this stage maintained a highly competitive stance towards the Conservatives, Johnson had done what May had been unable to do, in receiving the support of a majority of MPs for a deal, leaving it 'frozen' at second reading, just seven days before the House of Commons finally agreed to a general election and with the Conservatives again seen as the best party to deal with Brexit (see Figure 7.2).

Cowed by the possible loss of their niche, the Brexit party turned from electoral competition to cooperation as the best way to maintain relevance. The calls for cooperation were initially aggressive and maintained attempts to undermine their rival's credibility on the issue. On 2 November, Farage issued an 'ultimatum' to the Prime Minister that the Brexit Party would stand candidates across the country unless he scrapped the deal with the EU. Johnson flatly rejected electoral cooperation and underlined his sole ability in parliament to 'Get Brexit Done'. The next day Farage stated that he personally would not run in the election, allowing him to campaign across the country, while attacking Johnson's deal as 'not Brexit', otherwise 'we wouldn't need to fight against him in this election' (Sandle, 2019). Simultaneously, he contradicted this dogmatism by suggesting that his own offer of a 'Leave alliance', reportedly made as early as September, had been rejected. Meanwhile, the Conservatives polling lead steadily increased as pro-Brexit voters again faced the inescapable logic of first-past-the-post.

On 11 November, the last day for candidates to register, Farage declared that his party would not field candidates in the 317 seats in which there was an incumbent Conservative MP. He justified the decision by citing recent promises by Johnson that the one-year post-Brexit transition period would not be extended and that there would be greater regulatory divergence with the EU. Even most Brexit Party candidates, whose campaigns were abruptly ended, expressed support for the decision, given the obvious electoral arithmetic; indeed, much of the pressure to not field a full slate of candidates came from within the Brexit Party. However, with a one-sided 'Leave alliance' of sorts in place, Farage refocussed on attacking Labour for 'betraying' its Leave-supporting voters. Underscoring the party's decline into second-tier players that fulfilled a niche-within-a-niche, Farage initially responded ambiguously when asked if he would vote for the Conservatives.

At the general election, the party contested 275 seats, winning 644,257 votes and 2% of the national vote share (5.1% in seats in which it stood candidates). The party gained around 30% in two Barnsley seats, though Labour maintained healthy majorities in each case. In terms of socio-demographic and attitudinal profile, Brexit Party voters were similar to their European Parliament voters. Indeed 83% of Brexit Party voters at the general election had voted for them seven months earlier at the European Parliament election, with another 10% opting for UKIP.

In the aftermath of the election, there was considerable speculation about whether Farage's decision had cost Labour or the Conservatives more seats. Proponents of the former theory, in some cases seemingly keen to explain the Labour Party's loss as a Brexit one-off rather than a rejection of the direction of the party itself, claimed that 'Farage won it for Johnson', arguing that the Brexit Party won the votes of 'Labour leavers' who would never vote Conservative. One aggregate-level analysis estimated that Farage's decision to stand down ultimately doubled Johnson's majority (Norris, 2019). However, later-released individual-level data puts into doubt these arguments (Fieldhouse *et al.*, 2020). Whereas 'only' 45% of all voters placed Corbyn at nought on a zero to ten scale of likeability, 73% of Brexit Party voters did so and only 4% reported liking him (giving him six or higher). In contrast, 69% of Brexit Party voters reported liking Boris Johnson and only 6% placed him at zero. That said, 29% had voted for Labour in 2017, <37% who had voted Conservative but more than the 22% who had voted for UKIP, at that point struggling. Overall, the Brexit Party's voters typically had little history of voting Labour and, even if they did, would have been unlikely to do so again with Jeremy Corbyn as Labour leader, instead of feeling considerable sympathy with Boris Johnson.

Finally, with Brexit complete and electoral competition and cooperation now moot, Farage spent the aftermath of the election pointing to his plans for the ultimate diversification of the Brexit Party, renaming it the 'Reform Party', a name already registered prior to the election, with the first priority of reform to be the House of Lords. Whether constitutional reform has the niche-issue vote potential as Brexit had very much remains to be seen.

4.   The Greens: balancing competition, cooperation and diversification

Unlike the other niche parties at the 2019 general election, the Green Party of England and Wales (GPEW) had already lost their most significant niche of anti-austerity politics in the previous parliament following the election of Jeremy Corbyn as leader of the Labour Party (Dennison, 2015, 2016, 2018). As a result, the party had experienced balancing competition, cooperation and diversification. At the party's 2017 autumn conference, the GPEW explicitly debated how best to perform this balance going forward. Caroline Lucas, the party's co-leader, defended the strategy of cooperation that had seen the party stand aside in 22 marginal seats in which the Labour or Liberal Democrat candidate supported electoral reform, arguing that the decision had avoided a Conservative majority. Delegates argued it had caused a negative impact on the overall vote share, which indeed had more than halved, with a subsequent loss in funding. In reality, these losses were more to do with the loss of their niche and, partially as a result, greater tactical voting in 2017. Some went so far to describe the fangled 'progressive alliance' as 'treachery' or 'surrender', particularly as the other parties failed to return the favour. Delegates passed a motion calling for 'new tests' on future pacts and for the party leadership to stop referring to Green participation in any 'progressive alliance'. Continuing the strategic balancing act of the last parliament, Lucas refocussed on diversification, stating that by 'focusing on the environment and Brexit' the Greens would win voters back and arguing that 'Corbyn's position on Brexit betrays young people'. Outside of the party, in early 2018, pro-Corbyn *Guardian* columnist, Owen Jones, called for the collapse of the Green Party into the Labour Party stating 'In the political era before 2015 the Greens functioned as a left-wing alternative to Labour; but the ascent of Corbynism has rather dented that purpose. Truthfully, the Green party's prospects are poor' (Jones, 2018).

In May, despite Jones' predictions, the GPEW saw their councillors increased by 8 to 39 on a vote share of 6.5% at the 2018 local elections. Caroline Lucas, in her second leadership stint, announced that she would not be standing at the party's upcoming biennial leadership contest, after two years dedicated in large part to internal restructuring and performing a three-way strategic balancing act of 'competition, cooperation and diversification'. She stated 'We have not been eclipsed by the rise of Jeremy Corbyn, but instead have used these unique circumstances to push for even more radical change' before highlighting the Greens' positions on post-material issues like shorter working weeks, ending 'pointless jobs', environmentalism, peace and drug legalisation, as well as electoral reform. Incumbent co-leader Jonathan Bartley and two-time London mayoral candidate and London Assembly member, Siân Berry, by this point both also councillors, were declared new co-leaders that September, with over three-quarters of the party vote. Bartley used his victory speech to criticise 'treacherous' Corbyn who had 'fudged' the issues of Brexit, airport expansion, nuclear power and electoral reform, as well as overlooking wealth redistribution. Finally, Bartley criticised Labour's commitment to credit-fuelled growth and subsidies for both fossil fuels' and the arms trade—perhaps attempts by the former advisor to John Major to pique the interest of more fiscally conservative voters, in the vein of the German Greens.

As the unforeseen 2019 European Parliament election approached, the Greens again began to find their relevance increase. The party gained a 'sensational' 184 seats at the English local elections, the biggest percentage gain of any party and leading to membership surge of over 10,000 members. The party's European campaign completely diversified from the socio-economic focus of the preceding decade, now put simply as 'Yes to Europe, No to Climate Chaos'. Party co-leader, Berry, stated 'The Greens are the most united, strongest pro-EU party on the ballot'. Survey evidence suggested that the British public, or at least the portion that felt able to express a view on the subject, agreed, consistently placing the party as

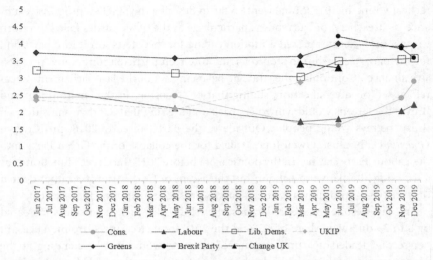

Figure 7.3 Perceptions of the extent of unity and division in political parties, June 2017–December 2019
Q: 'How united or divided are each of these parties?' (i) very divided; (ii) fairly divided; (iii) neither divided nor united; (iv) fairly united; (v) very united.
Source: Fieldhouse *et al.* (2020).

the most united in British politics (see Figure 7.3). Vince Cable, leader of the Liberal Democrats, proposed running joint tickets with the Greens and Change UK on the issue of a second referendum; however, the party turned down the offer, citing ideological differences and the Greens' focus on climate change. Behind the scenes, the Greens did not want to risk wasting the more proportional nature of the electoral system and had the wind in their sails following an uptick in the salience of their original environmental niche, amid widespread flooding and increasing global awareness of climate issues (see Figure 7.4).

At the 2019 European Parliament elections, the GPEW won an impressive 12% of the vote (an increase of five points) and seven seats (up from three), with over 1.8 million voters choosing them. Compared to the mean voter at the election, the average Green party voter was five years younger and five percentage points more likely to be female, while on average placing themselves at 3.5 on a 0–10 left–right spectrum. Lucas explained the result with the party's twin campaign on the climate and the EU, though Green parties across the EU had performed well. The party's general election polling was by now regularly into double figures for the first time since early 2015.

The party's post-Corbyn diversification had until then been primarily in terms of salience, with more attention being given to Europe, the environment and post-material policies, rather than positioning. Most of these policies were

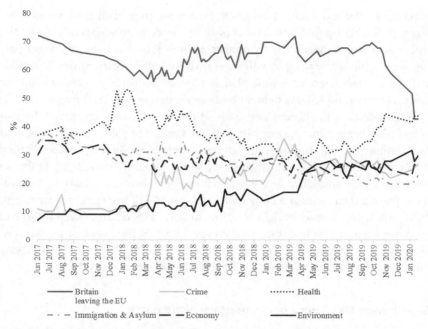

Figure 7.4 Most important issues facing the country, June 2017–January 2020
Q. 'Which of the following do you think are the most important issues facing the country at this time? Please tick up to three' Source: YouGov Top Issue Tracker.

already in place while the party was still operating as an anti-austerity niche party. However, by late September, the Greens also held a unique position in Europe after the Liberal Democrats changed their policy from favouring a second referendum to immediate revocation of Article 50 to remain in the EU. Lucas (2019), wasted no time in labelling the move as 'arrogant, self-indulgent, cynical and very dangerous'.

By mid-November, however, the Greens had managed to build a 'Remain alliance' with the Liberal Democrats and Plaid Cymru across 60 seats, which would see the Greens given a free run in eight seats and stand aside in 43. The alliance, called 'United to Remain' and led by now-Liberal Democrat Heidi Allen, was criticised by Labour shadow chancellor John McDonnell who stated 'To those Greens and others who are getting into bed with the Lib Dems: I remember what the Lib Dems did when they were in government. I say, go and ask any disabled person in this country' (Proctor, 2019).

During the election campaign, and with the environment now considered the third most important issue affecting Britain by the public, the Greens focussed a full 45.9% of its social media activity on environmental issues (Deacon *et al.*, 2019). Berry encapsulated the party's strategic refocus by telling activists that making the election about climate was even more important than Brexit. This was only further buoyed by their inclusion in a leaders' debate specifically on the issue of climate change in late November. However, by this point, the other parties were again attempting to win over environmental voters, with Labour describing its centrepiece economic plan as a 'green industrial revolution' and the Liberal Democrats pledging tighter deadlines for net-zero carbon emissions.

At the election, the Greens won 2.7% of the national vote, up from 1.9% two years earlier, again returning one MP, Caroline Lucas. The party saved its deposit in 31 constituencies, up from five, though was unable to produce a genuine electoral threat for a second seat. Green voters held a similar profile to those at the European Parliament elections, albeit less skewed either socio-demographically or attitudinally, placing themselves at a fairly centrist 4.0 on a 0–10 left–right spectrum, with 15% considering themselves right of centre. In 2017, 39% of 2019 Green voters had voted for Labour, 17% had voted Conservative and 25% had voted Green. Notably, Green Party voters expressed strong dislike for Jeremy Corbyn, with 82% placing him at less than five on a 0–10 likeability scale (Fieldhouse *et al.*, 2020).

5. Change UK: a very parliamentary niche party

For a group receiving 18% in a nationwide poll five days after being formed, it seems fair to say that the 2019 general election, nine months later, did not turn out as planned for The Independent Group (TIG; later known as Change UK—TIG and, finally, TIG for Change). Initially, a coalition of seven MPs simultaneously resigning from a Labour Party they described as 'hijacked by the machine politics of the hard left', 'institutionally antisemitic' with a culture of 'bullying and bigotry' and 'facilitating Brexit', the group was immediately compared to the Social Democratic Party of the 1980s. Although the launch was overshadowed by one MP making a racial *faux-pas*, over the next two days another Labour MP and three Tory MPs, whose party was at that point still considering a no-deal Brexit, joined TIG. In total, four of the party's MPs had recently been deselected by their constituency Labour Party. In the following weeks, the group remained squarely in the media limelight and attracted large donations and revolting councillors, as pro-EU forces sensed that they may now somehow be able to overcome parliamentary Brexit gridlock in their favour and anti-Corbyn Labour supporters hoped the group might offer the centre-left a fresh start.

Immediately, commentators speculated over how TIG and the Liberal Democrats would interact with each other, given their ideological similarity, the precedent of the Social Democratic Party (SDP)-Liberal alliance and merger and that both had equal parliamentary representation. Three of the group's most high-profile parliamentarians, Chuka Umunna, Chris Leslie and Anna Soubry, adopted a competitive stance. Umunna and Leslie immediately ruled out a merger and highlighted their group's ambition to 'build a new alternative', while

Soubry urged Liberal Democrats to join their group. Meanwhile, the Labour Party quickly attempted to stymie further defections by announcing that it would back moves for a second referendum.

The group officially registered as a party in March. This was again overshadowed by its proposed 'Change UK – The Independent Group' name being challenged by petition website change.org. The new party, with ex-Conservative Heidi Allen chosen as its interim leader, declared it would put forward a large number of candidates if there were forthcoming European elections. Liberal Democrat Jo Swinson called for the two parties to find ways of 'working together', a proposal rejected by TIG on the grounds that the party's brand was still damaged by its participation in the 2010–2015 coalition. A reportedly leaked internal party strategy document explicitly outlined how they planned to win over Liberal Democrat activists, members and resources.

With the European Parliament elections now seemingly inevitable, TIG again rejected offers of electoral cooperation from the Liberal Democrats, this time to stand joint pro-Remain candidates. Instead, on 23 April, TIG announced a full list of 73 candidates, including former Labour, Conservative and Liberal Democrat MPs, and a broad range of professional backgrounds, including Boris Johnson's sister and a former BBC correspondent, to some extent echoing the Brexit Party's earlier launch. Two of the candidates were quickly forced to step down after 'inappropriate' past tweets were discovered. At a question-and-answer session, the party claimed that, for now, only a party commitment to a second referendum mattered and the new policies would be announced soon.

Soon after, the party's 'TIG' logo and its use of a hashtag were both rejected by the Electoral Commission, meaning that its candidates would have to run with blank spaces next to their names in the upcoming elections. More broadly, the party's unclear branding and name were negatively compared to those of the immediately understandable Brexit Party. Even Rachel Johnson, the party's lead candidate for the South West, publicly criticised the name and party leadership, likening the outfit to a sinking ship. Meanwhile, the lead candidate for Scotland defected to the Liberal Democrats and encouraged others to do the same after homophobic remarks by another candidate, the former Deputy Prime Minister of Poland, were uncovered. More problematically, as shown in Figure 7.5, less than half of voters were able to correctly name the party's official Brexit position, the lowest of any party.

6. Losing their niche and splintering into cooperation, competition and diversification

At the European Parliament elections, Change UK achieved a disappointing 3.3% of the vote, seventh place and no seats. In contrast, the Liberal Democrats comfortably came in second place with 19.6% of the vote in an election obviously

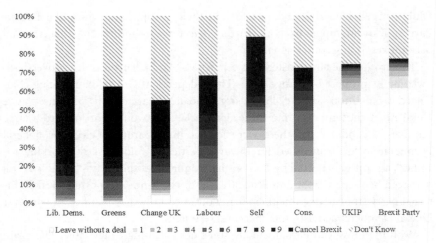

Figure 7.5 Attitudes to Brexit by party supported, June 2019
Q: 'Some people want to leave the European Union immediately without a deal. Other people would like to cancel Brexit and remain in the EU. Where would you place yourself and the political parties on this scale?'
Source: Fieldhouse *et al.* (2020).

characterised by the painful consequences of the 2016 referendum. The party's voters were slightly younger than average, gender-balanced, with above-average incomes and disproportionately likely to hail from London or the South East of England, while placing themselves at a very centrist 4.8 on at 0–10 left–right spectrum on average (Fieldhouse *et al.*, 2020). At the 2017 general election, half of 2019 Change UK voters had chosen Labour, 36% the Conservatives and 10% the Liberal Democrats. At the December 2019 general election, 40% would go on to vote for Labour, 18% for the Conservatives and 33% for the Liberal Democrats.

With the battle to win the pro-Remain niche over, Change UK's MPs split into three ways over the correct course of action for the party. Before the result, Allen and Umunna were already openly hinting at electoral cooperation with the Liberal Democrats at the next general election and stating their remorse over the lack of a pact. Another group preferring to maintain competition with the Liberal Democrats was led by Anna Soubry who soon became party leader, attacking Allen's remarks as 'bizarre'. Meanwhile, a third preferred to diversify by returning to its initial parliamentary niche of being a loose independent group. One commentator wryly pointed out that 'bluntly, the decision is likely to be made for' all three splinters (Bush, 2019). Eventually, five TIG MPs joined the Liberal Democrats, including Umunna and Allen. Three of these had initially joined a non-party parliamentary group called 'The Independents', set up by a handful of former TIG MPs and operating for the rest of the Parliament as a 'cooperative of independents'. At the 2019 general election, the remaining three MPs of Change UK, now known as

TIG for Change, failed to retain any of their seats, with their best result being Anna Soubry's 8.5%. Soon after, Soubry announced the party's deregistration.

7. Conclusion

The three niche parties in the UK prior to the 2019 general election reacted to losing their niche with some combination of 'compete, cooperate or diversify'. The rapid success of the Brexit Party directly led to Boris Johnson's election as leader of the Conservatives, robbing them of their Brexiteer niche. This led them to first attempt to undermine Johnson's Brexiteer credentials, with little success, before demanding cooperation on their own terms and then resigning themselves to unilateral electoral cooperation. After the election, party leader Farage hinted at diversification into the 'Reform Party'. The GPEW, which had lost its anti-austerity, far left niche to Labour in 2016, spent 2017–2019 continuing the strategic balancing act that had maintained place in second tier of the party system. Diversification to focussing on issues like Europe and (back to) the environment proved successful as the salience of both issues rose, while they formed a more favourable 'remain alliance' than the 'progressive alliance' of two years earlier. Finally, Change UK (under various other names) took a highly competitive stance towards its obvious rivals, the Liberal Democrats, before its pro-Remain niche had been properly secured. With the obvious loss of this niche in the aftermath of the European Parliament elections, its 11 MPs divided into those cooperating via joining their erstwhile rivals, continuing to compete as a party or diversifying into a 'non-party' called 'The Independents'.

The three different approaches partially resulted from the different leadership structures of the parties, with Farage able to dictate transition from one strategy to another, the pluralist Greens forced to balance various forces and the 'very parliamentary' niche party of TIG having more leaders than members, each clustering around one strategy after the party lost its niche. The 'compete, cooperate or diversify' theoretical framework seems to also work well for the fates of recent British niche parties, such as UKIP in its heyday, or the Greens in the early 1990s, although it may not work so well in more proportional electoral systems in which niche parties do not risk 'dividing the vote', making cooperation less imperative. The model also highlights the difficulties faced by niche parties when they lose their niche, with only the Greens, after three years of a difficult balancing act, able to claim some level of success at the 2019 general election.

Acknowledgment

I would like to acknowledge the generous support of the Swedish Research Council (Vetenskapsrídet; grant no. 2019/00504).

References

Abou-Chadi, T. (2016) 'Niche Party Success and Mainstream Party Policy Shifts – How Green and Radical Right Parties Differ in Their Impact', *British Journal of Political Science*, **46**, 417–436.

Adams, J., Clark, M., Ezrow, L. and Glasgow, G. (2006) 'Are Niche Parties Fundamentally Different from Mainstream Parties? the Causes and the Electoral Consequences of Western European Parties' Policy Shifts, 1976', *American Journal of Political Science*, **50**, 513–529.

Adu, A. (2019) 'Brexit Pact', *The Sun*, accessed at https://www.thesun.co.uk/news/9309594/tories-pact-nigel-farage-general-election-johnson/ on 27 April 2020.

Bush, S. (2019) 'Terrible Election Results and Nearing Zero in the Polls: What is the Future of Change UK?' *New Statesman*, accessed at https://www.newstatesman.com/politics/uk/2019/06/terrible-election-results-and-nearing-zero-polls-what-future-change-uk on 27 April 2020.

Deacon, D. J., Goode, D., Smith, D., Wring, D., Downey, J. and Vaccari, C. (2019) 'General Election 2019: Report 5: 7 November–11 December', *Centre for Research in Communication and Culture*, Loughborough, Loughborough University.

Dennison, J. (2015) 'The Other Insurgency? The Greens and the Election', *Parliamentary Affairs*, **68**, 188–205.

Dennison, J. (2016) *The Greens in British Politics: Protest, anti-Austerity and the Divided Left*. Basingstoke, Palgrave Macmillan.

Dennison, J. (2018) 'The Rug Pulled from under Them. UKIP and the Greens', *Parliamentary Affairs*, **71**, 91–108.

Ezrow, L. (2008) 'Research Note: On the Inverse Relationship between Votes and Proximity for Niche Parties', *European Journal of Political Research*, **47**, 206–220.

Farage, N. (2019, 20 January) The Nigel Farage Show, LBC. Accessed at https://www.youtube.com/watch?v=HZxJ5J9Jt1Q on 4 June 2020.

Fieldhouse, E., Green, J., Evans, G., Mellon, J. and Prosser, C. (2020) 'British Election Study Internet Panel Waves 1–19', accessed at https://www.britishelectionstudy.com/data-objects/panel-study-data/ on 25 April 2020.

Halliday, J. and Walker, P. (2019) 'Annunziata Rees-Mogg to Stand as MEP for Farage's Brexit Party'. *The Guardian*, accessed at https://www.theguardian.com/politics/2019/apr/12/annunziata-rees-mogg-to-stand-as-mep-for-farages-brexit-party on 27 April 2020.

Jones, O. (2018, 22 February) 'The Greens' Best Hope is to Sign Up with Labour', *The Guardian*, accessed at https://www.theguardian.com/commentisfree/2018/feb/22/greens-labour-jeremy-corbyn on 27 April 2020.

Lucas, C. (2019, 18 September) 'Lib Dem 'Revoke and Remain' Stance is Arrogant', *The Guardian*, accessed at https://www.theguardian.com/politics/2019/sep/18/caroline-lucas-lib-dems-revoke-and-remain-stance-brexit-is-arrogant on 27 April 2020.

McTague, T. (2019) 'Nigel Farage's Startup Politics', *Politico,* accessed at https://www.politico.eu/article/nigel-farage-brexit-party-start-up-politics-eu-election/ on 27 April 2020.

Meguid, B. (2005) 'Competition between Unequals: The Role of Mainstream Party Strategy in Niche Party Success', *American Political Science Review,* **99,** 347–359.

Norris, P. (2019) 'Was Farage the Midwife Delivering Johnson's Victory? The Brexit Party and the Size of the Conservative Majority', *LSE British Political and Policy,* accessed at https://blogs.lse.ac.uk/politicsandpolicy/ge2019-brexit-party-impact/ on 27 April 2020.

Proctor, K. (2019, 7 November) 'Lib Dems, Greens and Plaid Cymru reveal Remain Election Pact'. *The Guardian,* accessed at https://www.theguardian.com/politics/2019/nov/07/lib-dems-greens-and-plaid-cymru-reveal-remain-election-pact on 27 April 2020.

Sandle, P. (2019) 'Brexit Party Leader Nigel Farage Will Not Run in UK Election', *Reuters,* accessed at https://www.reuters.com/article/uk-britain-election-farage/brexit-party-leader-nigel-farage-will-not-run-in-uk-election-idUSKBN1XD05Y on 27 April 2020.

Wagner, M. (2012) 'Defining and Measuring Niche Parties', *Party Politics,* **18,** 845–864.

Wooding, D. (2019) 'Newkip'. *The Sun,* accessed at https://www.thesun.co.uk/news/brexit/8236819/nigel-farage-new-brexit-party/ on 27 April 2020.

Britain Votes (2019) 142–156

JAMES MITCHELL AND AILSA HENDERSON[*]

Tribes and Turbulence: The 2019 UK General Election in Scotland

Recent trips to the polls in Scotland seem to evoke a series of binaries: Yes versus No, Remain versus Leave, Indyref versus Brexit, surges and losses. The 2019 UK election is no exception for it allows us to look at simple themes, such as whether the Scottish National Party (SNP) would regain those seats it lost in 2017 and offer more nuanced analysis about the relative importance of different constitutional issues on voter choice. In what follows, we outline the wider political context of the 2019 election, the relevant themes within the campaign and then explore the results, at each point identifying the various challenges facing parties and how they navigated an electorate that now finds itself divided into four tribes: Yes/Remain, Yes/Leave, No/Remain and No/Leave.

1. Background and summary results

In the early years of devolution, it was assumed that elections to the Commons would be first order and elections to the Scottish Parliament would be second order.[1] Allied with a more proportional electoral system, the SNP was expected to perform better in elections to Holyrood but struggle to challenge Labour's dominance representing Scotland in the Commons. Holyrood elections created opportunities for the SNP unavailable in elections to the Commons. The 'blackmail' potential would be augmented by a 'governing potential', the possibility of becoming the governing party in Edinburgh (Mitchell *et al.*, 2011, pp. 10–33). The SNP averaged under 20% of the vote in the first three Commons elections after devolution but its constituency vote in Holyrood averaged close to 30%, seemingly confirming the second-order thesis.

[*]James Mitchell, Politics and International Relations, University of Edinburgh, james.mitchell@ed.ac.uk; Ailsa Henderson, Politics and International Relations, University of Edinburgh, ailsa.henderson@ed.ac.uk

[1]The extent to which Holyrood elections are second order was challenged from the first elections to the Scottish Parliament. Paterson *et al.* (2001, p. 44) concluded that the 'first Scottish election was neither clearly first order nor was it undoubtedly second order'.

doi:10.1093/pa/gsaa027

These expectations have been challenged and patterns disrupted in recent elections. The SNP landslide in 2015 reduced its Labour, Conservative and Liberal Democrat opponents to one seat each. The independence referendum that took place eight months before had caused this dramatic change. But this was only the first shock to the Scottish party system. The Brexit referendum in 2016 had a similar, though less significant, impact. The 2017 general election witnessed the SNP lose a quarter of its vote from two years before, falling from 50% to 36.9% and losing 21 seats. The Conservatives pushed Labour into third place in Scotland for the first time since 1935.[2] The 2019 European elections offered continued pain for Labour. Their least-worst swing was −6 in Orkney and worst was −24 in North Lanarkshire. They were in fourth place in two-thirds of councils and sixth in a further 12. At the time, this was attributed to ambiguous or inconsistent policies on both Brexit and independence.

These two issues—Brexit and Scottish independence—have recently dominated Scottish politics, creating remarkable turbulence in electoral behaviour over the last five years. However, there has been little shift in public opinion on independence or Brexit. Indeed, there is evidence that opinion on independence has become more entrenched. But while these issues continue to be the major drivers of Scottish electoral behaviour, the importance of each has varied in impact over the last three general elections.

The turbulent nature of Scottish electoral behaviour is evident in the last three UK general elections (Table 8.1). We have to go back to Labour's 1997 landslide to see significant shifts in share of the vote when Labour increased its Scottish share of the vote by 6.6 points from 1992 and the Conservatives' share tumbled by 8.2 points. The succession of dramatic changes over three elections suggests an unsettled electorate. The days when becoming a Scottish MP was an assured job for life for some have gone at least for the moment.

There has been only one election to the Scottish Parliament over the same period. In May 2016, the SNP retained its position as Scotland's largest party but lost the overall majority of seats it had won five years before. The SNP formed a minority government with 63 seats in the 129 seat Parliament. The Conservative Party gained most, winning 31 seats (up 16 from 2011) and seven ahead of Labour (down 13). With six seats, the Scottish Greens, beneficiaries of the more proportional electoral system, pushed the Liberal Democrats with five seats into the fifth position. It is far from clear that Holyrood elections are second-order contests though turnout remains lower and smaller parties perform better in Holyrood elections, but the latter could be explained by the electoral system. It

---

[2]It is sometimes mistakenly assumed that the Conservatives were the largest party in 1955 but this is an ahistorical reading of results that lumps together support for the Scottish Unionist Party (forerunner of today's Scottish Conservative and Unionist Party) and other Unionists/Liberal Unionists. Labour was Scotland's largest party since 1935 until 2015.

Table 8.1 Vote shares and seats in Scotland, 2015, 2017 and 2019 UK general elections

	2015		2017		2019	
	% vote (change)	Seats (change)	% vote (change)	Seats (change)	% vote (change)	Seats (change)
Conservative	14.9 (−1.8)	1 (−)	28.6 (+13.7)	13 (+12)	25.1 (−3.5)	6 (−7)
Labour	24.3 (−17.7)	1 (−40)	27.1 (+2.8)	7 (+6)	18.6 (−8.5)	1 (−6)
Liberal Democrats	7.5 (−11.3)	1 (−10)	6.8 (−0.7)	4 (+3)	9.5 (+2.8)	4 (−)
SNP	50.0 (+30.1)	56 (+50)	36.9 (−13.1)	35 (−21)	45.0 (+8.1)	48 (+13)

Note: Figures in brackets refer to (change from previous election).

appears that Scottish concerns are driving Scottish elections at Holyrood and at Westminster as never before. The disadvantages faced by the SNP in elections to the Commons have declined significantly.

The Scottish and European questions have each become simple binary choices: for or against independence and for or against European Union (EU) membership. This polarisation has worked to the advantage of the SNP and Conservatives as each has a clearly defined position on these questions. Ironically, the main thrust of Conservative campaigning in Scotland has been to keep the Scottish question alive, presenting the party as the most effective opposition to the SNP and seeking to marginalise Labour and the Liberal Democrats in the process. In early August 2019, for example, the outgoing Scottish Conservative leader, Ruth Davidson, accused Labour of 'rank betrayal' by opening the door to a second independence referendum, after Shadow Chancellor John McDonnell said Labour would not block a referendum if the Scottish Parliament and Scottish people decide that (*The Herald*, 2019). In the past, the Conservatives had been damaged electorally as the Unionist Party *par excellence* in Scotland (Mitchell, 1990) but its hardline position on the union was now working to its advantage. If anything, the Liberal Democrats have also hardened their opposition to independence in recent years. The party continued to pay lip service to federalism but made no effort to develop or prioritise the policy and its rhetoric has become vehemently anti-SNP and anti-independence. The old Liberal insistence that it was neither unionist nor nationalist but federalist has all but disappeared.

Brexit presented major challenges for the Scottish Tories. While the Scottish Tory leadership had opposed Brexit during the 2016 referendum, it fell into line after the referendum result but got caught up in the internal party battles over the nature of the Brexit deal. Ruth Davidson insisted that any deal must be the same throughout the UK and argued against any special provisions for Northern Ireland, fearing this would set a precedent for a different arrangement for Scotland that the Scottish government proposed (*Express*, 2017). Davidson undermined Theresa May's tactic of threatening to withdraw from negotiations with the EU by saying it was 'certainly possible' that the Scottish Tories might oppose policy decided by the UK Cabinet. The key issue that arose was whether the group of Scottish Tory MPs elected in 2017 would back May or Davidson in such a scenario. Newspaper reports suggested that the Scottish Tories might break away from the party south of the border, a platform on which her main opponent had stood in the Scottish Tory leadership contest in 2011 and which Davidson had then strongly opposed (*The Telegraph*, 2017; Convery 2014). In the aftermath of the 2017 election, it had been widely reported that the new group of Scottish Tory MPs would act as a bloc and be accountable to Davidson (*The Guardian*, 2017; *The Courier*, 2017). This view was encouraged by the Scottish leader's claim that the group of Scottish Tory MPs would argue Scotland's case 'forcefully' with the Prime Minister and the assertion that the Scottish party had 'complete autonomy over policy, candidates, campaigning, finance', while the party's MPs would take the Tory whip in the Commons (BBC News, 2017). But it soon became clear that the MPs saw themselves primarily as accountable to the leadership in London rather than Edinburgh. This became even more obvious after Boris Johnson became the leader and effectively took back control of the party in Scotland. Most Scottish Tory MPs subsequently adopted a hardline position on Brexit.

The SNP also had challenges. It had all but swept the board when independence had cast its shadow over the 2015 election by attracting a high turnout amongst the 45% who had voted 'Yes' in the 2014 referendum. Its three main opponents fought amongst themselves (and against lower turnout) for the 55% who had voted 'No'. But the Brexit referendum in 2016 pushed that issue up the agenda, adding an unhelpful dimension for the SNP. In 2017, this meant that supporters of independence who also supported Brexit would be cross-pressured. There was less incentive to vote amongst supporters of independence, while politics operated in the shadow of the Brexit referendum. The SNP had misread the public mood and came out of the 2017 election bruised, losing 21 seats. As the results in Table 8.2 show, over 40% of those who had voted Yes in 2014 and Leave in 2016, voted for a party other than the SNP, with more than half turning to Labour, although SNP won almost 80% of those who had voted SNP in 2015 and Remain in 2016 (Henderson and Mitchell, 2018) and a similar proportion of Yes/Remain voters. As the political agenda shifted to Brexit, the SNP was in danger of arguing for independence when many of its erstwhile voters opposed the SNP policy on EU membership or thought independence was not the key issue in 2017.

Labour has suffered the classic third-party squeeze on both independence and Brexit, not helped by a perceived lack of clarity on its Brexit position. While Labour's policy remains steadfastly opposed to Scottish independence, many of its former voters supported the idea. Labour's best prospects lay in changing the focus of attention away from these issues, framing the election on other matters.

Table 8.2 Voting in the 2017 UK general election in Scotland, by constitutional preferences (%)

	Yes Remain	Yes Leave	No Remain	No Leave
Conservative	3	15	32	69
Labour	17	24	42	19
Liberal Democrats	2	3	13	5
SNP	77	58	13	5
Other	1	0	0	2
N	439	286	571	354

Notes: The 2019 Scottish Election Survey asked respondents in wave 1 to recall how they voted in the previous UK general election (2017), in the 2014 independence referendum and the 2016 Brexit referendum. Respondents who did not vote in all three contests are therefore excluded from this table.
Source: Scottish Election Study 2019.

In 2019, the NHS was mentioned as a very important issue for 67% of its voters, with independence only in fifth place as a matter of importance. The problem for Labour was that its own voters were atypical of the electorate as a whole in listing matters of importance in the election (Ipsos MORI, 2019). Half of Labour's lost deposits across Britain were in Scotland and the Liberal Democrats lost 13 deposits in Scotland.

While the Liberal Democrats strived to present themselves as *the* European party *par excellence* by promising to reverse the Brexit process without a referendum, they struggled to convince voters that they were credible as the main pro-Remain party in Scotland compared with the SNP. The Scottish Greens are now the fourth party in Holyrood but continue to struggle to break through at Westminster. The party contested 22 candidates across Scotland in 2019, up from only three contested two years before but lost all deposits (the Scottish Greens' best result was in Edinburgh East where they won 4.3%). The Brexit Party won a seat at the European Parliament elections in May 2019 with 14.8% of the vote, coming second behind the SNP (37.8%). In the general election, the Brexit Party contested 15 seats and UKIP only seven. Louis Stedman-Bryce, Brexit Party MEP for Scotland, resigned from the party just before the UK election because he felt that the party had failed to represent Leave voters by standing down in Tory-held seats and because the party's candidate in Glenrothes was homophobic. The Brexit Party and UKIP lost all deposits and the best result for a Brexit Party candidate was for the Glenrothes candidate who had been dropped during the campaign by the party.

2. Results on the ground

As ever, the aggregate results hid many variations across constituencies in Scotland. The SNP gained 14 seats but also lost a seat. The SNP had come from fourth to take North East Fife in 2015. Stephen Gethins, the SNP's high-profile Westminster spokesperson on Brexit, held the seat two years later by two votes to make it the most marginal constituency in the UK. The seat had previously been held by Menzies Campbell, former Liberal Democrat leader, from 1987 until his retirement in 2015 and had long been a battleground between Liberal Democrats and Tories. The equivalent seat in Holyrood is held by Willie Rennie, Scottish Liberal Democrat leader. The Liberal Democrat strategy had been to appeal to the sizeable Conservative support in the constituency to vote tactically. This resulted in the Conservatives suffering their largest decrease in Tory support in the UK at the election. The Scottish Greens changed their minds and decided not to contest the seat in favour of the SNP though it was far from clear that Green-inclined voters in places like St Andrews would necessarily follow Green Party activists in supporting the SNP.

In nearby Kirkcaldy and Cowdenbeath, held by Gordon Brown until he retired, Neale Hanvey was suspended from the SNP after social media posts were discovered in which he compared Israeli treatment of the Palestinian people to the holocaust and included an image of George Soros as a puppet master (BBC News, 2019). The SNP had taken the seat in 2015 but Labour had regained it in 2017 with a tiny majority of 259 over the SNP. The SNP leadership instructed local activists to campaign instead in North East Fife for Stephen Gethins. Hanvey and local activists ignored the SNP leadership and he fought the seat as an independent, although his name appeared on the ballot paper as SNP candidate as his suspension came after the close of nominations. He won the seat, defeating Labour's Shadow Scottish Secretary with a 1243 majority.

While the SNP lost a seat in the east of Scotland to the Liberal Democrats, it gained Jo Swinson's East Dunbartonshire seat in the west. Swinson, UK Liberal Democrat leader, had lost the seat in 2015 to John Nicolson of the SNP but regained it in 2017. Nicolson chose not to stand in East Dunbartonshire but instead became SNP candidate in Ochil and South Perthshire (though he confused the two seats speaking at hustings in Ochil a fortnight before polling). He nonetheless won the seat from the Conservatives, while Amy Callaghan won his old seat for the SNP in a tight contest with the Liberal Democrat leader.

Ian Murray managed to hold onto Edinburgh South for Labour with a significantly reduced but still substantial majority over the SNP and returned to being Labour's only Scottish MP, a position he held after 2015. The constituency includes predominantly middle-class areas of Edinburgh such as Morningside and Colinton (its median income is 14% higher than the Scottish average) leading to exaggerated comments that Murray had the largest Tory majority in Scotland with reference to tactical voting to keep the SNP from taking the seat. Murray had a high profile as a critic of Jeremy Corbyn and strongly anti-Brexit (which is helpful in a constituency that voted 78% Remain). He is also avowedly anti-independence, but the constituency is less hostile to independence than it is to Brexit, and the way in which these two issues are navigated will likely determine his future success in the constituency.

3. Polls and expectations

Polls consistently placed the SNP ahead of the other parties throughout the short parliament elected in 2017 (Figure 8.1). The SNP lead over its main challenger was under 10 points in only six polls early in the period between the 2017 and 2019 elections and was 20 points or more on five occasions. SNP support dipped in late 2017 and through the following year, with odd exceptions, it appeared to have passed its peak. But from early in 2019, its support increased and rarely fell much below 40%. Its 45% share of the vote in the election was higher than any poll had shown it throughout the short parliament.

Labour and Conservatives competed to be the main challengers to the SNP in share of the vote, though the electoral system, which historically had worked to Labour's great advantage, has been seriously undermining the party since 2015. Scottish Conservative support dipped over the winter of 2017–2018 and there was no evidence that the party was able to build on its 2017 election performance. The Tories appeared to have peaked in 2017. Even before Ruth Davidson's resignation as leader in August 2019, the Scottish Tories looked likely to struggle to hold onto the seats they had

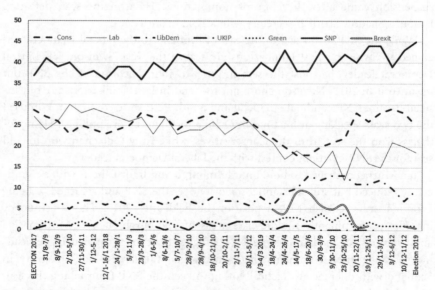

Figure 8.1 Opinion polls in Scotland, June 2017–December 2019
Source: Electoral Calculus.

gained, although they picked up some support in the polls towards the end of 2019 under the new Acting Leader, Jackson Carlaw. The party went into the election looking likely to lose seats but as the campaign progressed, the Conservatives became increasingly confident that they would hold and indeed gain seats, including Lanark and Hamilton East where the Tory candidate dispensed with a dog whistle and trumpeted her belief that the area was a 'solid unionist royalist Rangers supporting heartland' (*The Times*, 2019). But the constituency result, a 5,187 SNP majority, suggested that this old-style Protestant unionist vote was not so easily mobilised.

On winning the Edinburgh Central Scottish parliamentary constituency in 2016, Ruth Davidson had acknowledged that she was 'under no illusion that everybody who voted for me in that seat is a true-blue, dyed-in-the-wool Tory, and neither are they in places up and down Scotland' but had voted for her and her party 'to do a very specific job, and that is to hold the SNP to account' (BBC News, 2016). The Tories had essentially rebalanced, if not quite renounced, their message as the Scottish Conservative and Unionist Party in favour of its unionist message. The independence referendum and continued importance of the issue provided the Tories with a fillip after decades of decline and an opportunity to build support for the party's wider agenda. But the party played it safely under Davidson's leadership, emphasising its unionism rather than seek to convert unionists who had voted for the party into Conservatives.

Labour too had its challenges. The party made a recovery in 2017 winning six additional seats at the expense of the SNP. Labour came within 1.5 points of the Conservatives in 2017 but the party's six-seat gains amounted to half of the number of extra seats captured by the Tories. Labour's best showing in the polls, in the 18 months between the 2017 and 2019 elections, had come early in the parliament when it led the Tories for second place from the autumn of 2017 until spring 2018. But Labour failed to maintain that lead and slipped back into third place. The result of the European elections in May 2019 saw Labour support collapse in Scotland. The party came in fifth with 9.3%, behind the SNP (37.8%); Brexit Party (14.8%); Liberal Democrats (13.9%); and the Conservatives (11.6%).

4.   Campaign foci

Polls showed that Brexit was the dominant issue in the election in Scotland, as across the UK. Two weeks before polling day, 56% of Scottish respondents cited Brexit as the issue which would be 'very important' in helping decide how to vote. This was followed by health on 44% and independence/devolution coming in third on 34%. Brexit was the dominant issue even amongst those intending to vote SNP with 55% citing the issue and with independence and health on 46%

and 45%, respectively. Brexit was even more emphatically the number one issue for Conservative-inclined voters, despite the Scottish Tories making opposition to independence/an independence referendum central to their campaign (Ipsos MORI, 2019).

The SNP manifesto maintained that 'An SNP election victory will be a clear instruction by the people of Scotland that a new referendum on independence should be held next year, on a precise date to be determined by the Scottish Parliament' (Scottish National Party, 2019, p. 10) and insisted that the SNP already had a mandate for a second independence referendum given the material change in conditions brought about by Brexit. In the fortnight before the official launch of the campaign, SNP leader Nicola Sturgeon repeatedly used the #indyref2020 hashtag and on 27 October tweeted that '#indyref2020' would be at the 'heart of the @SNP campaign'. But the SNP messages were quite different during the campaign. Brexit dominated news releases issued by SNP headquarters and tweets from the SNP leader during the election and #indyref2020 was dropped. There was only one further explicit tweet from Sturgeon referring to #indyref after the official start of the campaign and that was in response to Labour's changing position on an independence referendum. Labour had initially said it would oppose another independence referendum in its first term in office, then shifted to opposing one in its first two years in office, provoking the SNP leader to tweet that, 'By the end of the week, at this rate, Corbyn will be demanding #indyref2020.'

Sturgeon's references to a second independence referendum were at best ambiguous during the campaign. This typically involved urging voters to support the SNP 'to put Scotland's future in Scotland's hands' rather than arguing explicitly for a referendum and avoided suggesting that a referendum would be held in 2020. Even references to 'independence' were rare.[3] There was little surprise in this shift in focus, given polling evidence that most voters, including many potential SNP voters, were not keen on a referendum in the immediate future. Scottish voters tended to divide evenly on whether there should be a further referendum in the next five years in Panelbase polls towards the end of 2019 (What Scotland Thinks, 2019). In an Ipsos MORI poll taken two weeks before the 2019 election, 43% strongly opposed and 7% opposed an independence referendum in the next five year and only 33% strongly supported and 9% supported one, while Scotland split 50:50 on independence. Sturgeon had failed to convince enough of her own supporters, far less anyone else, of the case for another referendum (Ipsos MORI,

---

[3]When independence appeared, it was in retweets from Sturgeon. At the start of the campaign, Sturgeon responded to a tweet by a party colleague who had paid tribute to a party activist who had died who had 'worked incredibly hard for @theSNP and the independence cause'.

2019). It was not surprising that the SNP quietly dropped direct references to a referendum during the election.

A range of other matters was mentioned much more often in Sturgeon's tweets but Brexit was the dominant issue and was linked to a range of policy matters. Escaping Brexit, escaping Boris Johnson and escaping the Tories featured heavily in a campaign that reversed past SNP campaign emphasis on positive campaigning (Pattie *et al.*, 2011). But while the SNP might struggle to claim it had a mandate for an independence referendum in 2020 based on its campaign, it could at least take solace in the outcome of the Conservative campaign. The Tories emphasised opposition to an independence referendum, arguing persistently and unambiguously that if people voted SNP, they would be giving the SNP a mandate for a second referendum. The Conservative campaign was largely a rerun of recent Tory campaigns in Scotland. Campaign literature throughout Scotland was consistent to the point of uniformity leaving very limited space for other issues. The message was conveyed with military discipline and repetitively. Uniform campaign literature was delivered across Scotland with little scope for individual candidates to offer an alternative from the dominant message of opposition to an independence referendum. This included a facsimile of a handwritten letter to all voters from Ruth Davidson, even though she had already announced her resignation as leader.

While the Scottish Tories could not avoid Brexit, given it was the dominant theme of the party across Britain, it posed challenges for them given that the leadership of the Scottish Tories and most of their Members of the Scottish Parliament (MSPs) had opposed Brexit in the 2016 referendum. During that referendum, Ruth Davidson, credited with having revived the fortunes of the party north of the border, had been a leading figure in the Remain campaign during the 2016 referendum and had not hidden her opposition to and indeed contempt for Boris Johnson. During the UK Tory leadership contest after Theresa May stood down, Davidson initially backed Sajid Javid, then Michael Gove after Javid was knocked out of the contest before supporting Jeremy Hunt, along with 18 of the 31 Scottish Tory MSPs, in a vain bid to block Boris Johnson. Davidson resigned as a leader at the end of August but her successor was not in post at the time of the election, leaving Jackson Carlaw, her deputy, as Acting Leader.[4]

Carlaw faced the election in 2019 not confirmed as party leader and with a low profile, in part due to the massive effort that the Scottish Conservatives and media had put into building the party around Ruth Davidson. Richard Leonard suffered similarly from a low profile. He became Scottish Labour leader in November 2017, in a contest in which he was portrayed as Corbyn's candidate against Anas Sarwar, the 'New Labour' candidate. This contest had followed the

---

[4]Carlaw would go on to win the election as Scottish Tory leader in February 2020.

Table 8.3 Satisfaction with the Prime Minister/First Minister/party leaders (%)

	Satisfied	Do not know	Dissatisfied
Boris Johnson	22	4	74
Jeremy Corbyn	22	9	69
Jo Swinson	27	25	48
Nicola Sturgeon	48	4	48
Jackson Carlaw	18	39	43
Richard Leonard	17	33	50
Willie Rennie	31	31	38

Source: Ipsos MORI for STV, 27 November 2019.

Table 8.4 Voting in the 2019 UK general election in Scotland by preferences on Scottish and European questions (%)

	Yes Remain	Yes Leave	No Remain	No Leave
Conservative	1	27	23	67
Labour	9	16	29	14
Liberal Democrats	2	3	20	7
SNP	88	50	25	9
Other	1	3	1	3
N	550	250	636	362

Source: Scottish Election Study 2019.

sudden and unexpected resignation of Kezia Dugdale, who had been elected Scottish Labour leader in August 2015. Leonard had only been elected to Holyrood in 2016 as a List member for Central Scotland. He had little support amongst Labour MSPs and struggled to gain traction amongst the electorate. Willie Rennie, Scottish Liberal Democrat leader, had an advantage over other opposition leaders in Scotland and his own UK party leader in having been a leader since 2011. Surveys showed that Sturgeon had by far the most positive satisfaction ratings in Scotland, as Table 8.3 indicates.

5.   The impact of the Scottish and Brexit referendums

As noted above, the Scottish and Brexit questions overshadowed the election. How this played out for each party depended on the relative importance of each issue combined with the party's position on these and how they each dealt with the challenges they faced. Taking the four main parties and two key issues, we can see how each party performed across the two questions (Table 8.4).

The SNP won 88% support (up from 77% in 2017) amongst those who supported its policies of independence and remaining in the EU but won only half the vote of those who supported independence but supported leaving the EU, down from 58% in 2017 (see Tables 8.2 and 8.4 for 2017 and 2019 figures). Over a quarter of voters who wanted independence and Brexit voted for the Conservative Party, up from 15% in 2017, suggesting that such voters saw Brexit as more important than independence. The Conservatives won 67% amongst those who accepted its position of opposing independence and EU membership, only slightly down in 2017. It is no surprise to find that the Conservatives again hardly polled at all amongst supporters of independence and the EU though the SNP managed to win almost 1 in 10 of those who opposed both independence and EU membership, slightly up in 2017.

The Liberal Democrats might have expected to do well amongst opponents of independence who supported remaining in the EU given the clear position that party had adopted on these issues. In fact, the Liberal Democrats won only one in five such voters, fewer than any of the other three main parties amongst this group, though an improvement on 2017 when they won 13%. Labour's best result was amongst those who opposed independence and supported membership of the EU, but the party only won 29% of this group, the largest collection of voters, significantly down from the 42% in this group won in 2017.

The SNP shift in focus onto Brexit during the campaign played down its support for a second independence referendum. This appealed to the majority on the issue that had the highest salience for the public. Once the election was over, however, the SNP returned to its demand for a referendum. In a speech delivered the day after the election, Nicola Sturgeon claimed that the SNP victory 'renews, reinforces and strengthens the mandate we have from previous elections to offer the people of Scotland a choice over their future'. Given the lack of priority during the campaign attached to a second independence referendum, the SNP proposed a novel form of mandate theory to claim there should be a second referendum, by noting that the Conservatives had 'said that a vote for them was to deny people in Scotland the right to decide our own future' (SNP News release, 13 December 2019). As the election receded into the past, the SNP increasingly claimed a mandate for a referendum in 2020 on the basis of the election result.

What Table 8.4 does not capture, however, is the differing ways that the two constitutional issues affected political parties. This is more obvious when we look at three parties in particular: the SNP, Conservatives and Labour. In their early analysis of 2019 Scottish Election Study results, Johns *et al.* (2020) noted that Conservative voters were far more likely to say that Brexit was the most important issue when determining how they would vote, indeed they were six times more likely to mention Brexit rather than independence. For the SNP, however, independence was seen as most important by over one-third but Brexit was cited by just over a quarter. This suggests that the SNP were taking a significant body of independence supporters for granted and focussing during the campaign on reaching out to others on Brexit. The two constitutional issues together helped to earn support for the SNP. These are, it should be noted, self-reported assessments, separate from models of voting behaviour as such.

Labour, however, is in a slightly different position. Labour voters were more likely to say that Brexit rather than independence determined their view (over 40% versus over 15%). When the Scottish Election Study team modelled support for Labour defectors, however (Henderson *et al.*, 2020), it is clear that Labour's failure to capture the shift in support for independence—within the electorate as a whole but also amongst its previous voters—was, all things being equal, an important source of declining support. Critically, it was not how individuals had voted in 2014 but how they felt about independence in 2019 that cost Labour. Those who were least Left-wing and those who disliked Corbyn were also more likely to defect to other parties. This makes clear that it was not Labour's ambivalence on Brexit but its hostility to independence, that cost it most votes in 2019 which, coming on top of losses incurred since 2015, has left the party in a parlous position.

6. Conclusion

As Scotland moved on to the Holyrood election in 2021, the same issues that dominated the political agenda in December 2019 looked likely to determine the outcome of the election. Arguments over another independence referendum and about Brexit and its form looked set to continue to polarise opinion. Other matters seemed likely to be crowded out or subsumed within these constitutional questions. The SNP and Conservatives share an interest in keeping the Scottish and European questions uppermost in the electorate's mind but this could also present dangers for each party. The SNP leadership could face pressure from within the party and wider movement if polls continue to show that support for independence remains static or if it is unable to deliver a second referendum. The Conservatives face dangers if Brexit turns out, or more accurately is perceived to be damaging, especially in those parts of Scotland in which it has made gains in recent years or if its emphasis on independence contributes to the SNP's claim that it has a mandate for a second referendum.

Labour has changed its leader in London but with a Corbyn-supporting Scottish leader and a new Deputy Scottish leader on the Blairite wing of the party, it may continue to expend energy on internal battles. As with the Liberal Democrats, Labour has yet to articulate a position on the Scottish and European questions that might allow it to cut out a distinct and convincing alternative to the positions of the SNP and Conservatives. The impact of the COVID-19 crisis is difficult to assess at the time of writing but the recent past suggests that this global pandemic will be presented to the electorate through these constitutional prisms. While this much seems likely, recent history suggests that the turbulent nature of Scottish politics makes prediction hazardous. Tribes and turbulence can have unpredictable dynamics.

Funding

Scottish Election Study (ESRC award ES/N018060/1).

References

BBC News (2016, 6 May) 'Holyrood 2016: Scottish Tory Leader Ruth Davidson Wins Edinburgh Central', accessed at https://www.bbc.co.uk/news/election-2016-scotland-36219380 on 19 April 2020.

BBC News (2017, 10 June) 'Davidson Says Scots Tory MPs Will Argue Scotland's Case "forcefully"', accessed at https://www.bbc.co.uk/news/uk-scotland-scotland-politics-40232374 on 19 April 2020.

BBC News (2019, 29 November) 'SNP Members Urged Not to Campaign for Axed Candidate', accessed at https://www.bbc.co.uk/news/election-2019-50711777 on 19 April 2020.

Convery, A. (2014) 'The 2011 Scottish Conservative Party Leadership Election: Dilemmas for Statewide Parties in Regional Contexts', *Parliamentary Affairs*, **67**, 306–327.

The Courier (2017, 12 June) 'Exclusive: Scottish Conservative MPs to Be Led by David Mundell and Report to Ruth Davidson', accessed at https://www.thecourier.co.uk/fp/news/politics/scottish-politics/446686/exclusive-scottish-conservative-mps-led-david-mundell-report-ruth-davidson/ on 19 April 2020.

Express (2017, 5 December) 'Davidson Wades into Brexit Row as May Battles Cabinet', accessed at https://www.express.co.uk/news/uk/888226/brexit-deal-northern-ireland-scotland-single-market-ruth-davidson-theresa-may on 19 April 2020.

The Guardian (2017, 11 June) 'Scottish Tories expected to act as a bloc to protect Scotland's interests', accessed at https://www.theguardian.com/politics/2017/jun/11/scottish-tories-expected-vote-bloc-protect-scotlands-interests on 19 April 2020.

Henderson, A. and Mitchell, J. (2018) 'Referendums as Critical Junctures? Scottish Voting in British Elections'. In Tonge, J., Leston-Bandeira, C. and Wilks-Heeg, S. (eds.) *Britain Votes 2017*, Oxford, Oxford University Press, pp.109–24.

Henderson, A., Johns, R., Larner, J. and Carman, C. (2020) 'Scottish Labour as a Case Study in Party Failure: Evidence from the 2019 UK General Election in Scotland', *Scottish Affairs*, **29**, 127–140.

The Herald (2019, 6 August) 'Labour Would Not Block a Second Scottish Independence Referendum', accessed at https://www.heraldscotland.com/news/17819772.john-mcdonnell-labour-not-block-independence-referendum/ on 19 April 2020.

Ipsos MORI (2019, 27 November) 'Scottish Political Monitor for Scottish Television', accessed at https://www.ipsos.com/ipsos-mori/en-uk/scotland-voting-intention-snp-pole-position-run-election on 20 April 2020.

Johns, R., Henderson, A., Larner, J. and Carman, C. (2020) 'Brexit or Independence: Scotland's General Election', *Political Insight*, **11**, 28–31.

Mitchell, J. (1990) *Conservatives and the Union*, Edinburgh, Edinburgh University Press.

Mitchell, J., Bennie, L. and Johns, R. (2011) *The Scottish National Party: Transition to Power*, Oxford, Oxford University Press.

Paterson, L., Brown, A., Curtice, J., Hinds, K., McCrone, D., Park, A., Sprogston, K. and Surridge, P. (2001) *New Scotland, New Politics?*, Edinburgh, Polygon.

Pattie, C., Denver, D., Johns, R. and Mitchell, J. (2011) 'Raising the Tone? The Impact of "Positive" and "Negative" Campaigning on Voting in the 2007 Scottish Parliament Election', *Electoral Studies*, **30**, 333–343.

Scottish National Party (2019) *Stronger for Scotland*. SNP manifesto for the 2019 election, Edinburgh, SNP.

The Telegraph (2017, 10 June) 'Ruth Davidson Planning Scottish Tory Breakaway as She Challenges Theresa May's Brexit Plan', accessed at https://www.telegraph.co.uk/news/2017/06/09/ruth-davidson-planning-scottish-tory-breakaway-challenges-theresa/ on 19 April 2020.

The Times (2020, 9 December) 'Brexit and Scottish Independence Have the Marginal Seat of Lanark & Hamilton East Feeling Blue', accessed at https://www.thetimes.co.uk/article/brexit-and-scottish-independence-have-the-marginal-seat-of-lanark-amp-hamilton-east-feeling-blue-09k8qjnpx on 19 April 2020.

What Scotland Thinks (2019) accessed at https://whatscotlandthinks.org/questions/when-do-you-think-anotherscottish-independencereferendum-should-be-held-asked-a/ on 20 April 2020.

Britain Votes (2019) 157–171

JONATHAN BRADBURY*

The Election in Wales: Campaign and Party Performance

It is often forgotten that Boris Johnson cut his general election teeth, aged 32, standing as the Conservative candidate for Clwyd South in north Wales in the 1997 general election. He managed a respectable second place in losing to Labour amidst the New Labour landslide and it was to be another four years before he finally entered parliament. But as Johnson hit the campaign trail yet again in November 2019 it was as an incumbent Prime Minister seeking the parliamentary majority that had eluded his predecessor, Theresa May, in 2017. Just as May had noted, Johnson was aware that Wales offered a possible source of the gains that were needed, with several Labour marginal seats across both north and south Wales. While Labour still held 28 of the 40 seats in Wales and the Conservatives just eight, the Conservative vote share had steadily risen with each general election since 1997, to reach just over a third in 2017. Labour had proven themselves time and again a resilient force in Wales but 2019 looked as if it could be the time the dam broke.

When the results appeared on the morning of 13 December, Labour was still the largest party in Wales, but in the election as a whole Johnson emerged with an 80-seat majority and part of the story of that success could be found in Wales. The dam had not fully broken but the Conservatives had achieved their highest vote share in Wales since 1900 and their highest number of MPs in Wales since 1983. Simon Baynes, the Conservative candidate in Clwyd South, had finally succeeded where his boss had failed 22 years before and Conservative victories across north Wales contributed to the knocking down of key parts of Labour's 'red wall' that helped to achieve the Conservative majority. How did the Conservative erosion of Labour's fortress happen, and how did political actors view its likely causes and consequences? In answering these questions, we must address the ways in which the UK election campaign played out in Wales. To do this, the chapter will first review the election campaign and party strategies in Wales and

*Jonathan Bradbury, Department of Political and Cultural Studies, Swansea University, j.p.bradbury@ swansea.ac.uk

doi:10.1093/pa/gsaa025

then examine party performance, before turning to the post-election debate. The focus here is on revealing what the parties in Wales did, analysing perceptions of the causes of the result and its implications.

1. The campaign

It is important to note of course that Boris Johnson was fighting the long election campaign from the moment he became Prime Minister in July 2019, heading a minority Conservative government. His first target had been the Brexit Party, which in Wales, as in England, had emerged victorious in the European elections in May. Johnson set about establishing that the Brexit Party was no longer needed and that the Conservatives under him would deliver on the defining issue of the day: negotiation of withdrawal from the EU and then the UK's departure from it. Following this, he set about winning the battle in the polls against Labour by first, promising to deliver Brexit, and secondly, offering a targeted set of spending priorities on the NHS, police and education. In contrast, Jeremy Corbyn as Labour leader fashioned a complex position over Brexit to try and address the conundrum that most Labour MPs wanted to remain in the EU while most Labour seats had voted to leave in the 2016 referendum. The policy involved renegotiation, followed by a second referendum,

Johnson's hopes in Wales were bolstered by the fact that, to the horror of the Labour establishment, there had been a 52.5% Leave vote in Wales in the 2016 referendum, just as there had been in the UK as a whole. The Labour Party, successful in holding back Theresa May's efforts in 2017 in Wales under Welsh First Minister, Carwyn Jones, was now under the leadership of Mark Drakeford. Plaid Cymru offered a potential heightened threat, having come second in the European elections in Wales, ahead of Labour, on a Remain platform and were now under a charismatic new leader, Adam Price. But the polls had been steadily encouraging and the expectation was that Brexit would be the key issue, a matter on which the Conservatives hoped to capture all the Leave support against a set of parties either not offering clarity or still supporting Remain.

When the election campaign began the hopes of the Conservatives appeared to be borne out. The first Welsh opinion poll in early November indicated a Labour lead over the Conservatives of just 1% (Table 9.1). There was still a reasonably strong showing for the Brexit Party, third in the poll on 15%. The projection from the poll, on the basis of a uniform swing since the 2017 election, was that the Conservatives would gain nine seats from Labour, including five seats in the north (Alyn and Deeside, Clwyd South, Delyn, Vale of Clwyd and Wrexham) and four in the south (Newport West, Cardiff North, Bridgend and Gower) (Scully, 2019). This would have taken the Conservatives to 17 out of Wales' 40 seats. It was also predicted that Labour would lose Ynys Mon to Plaid Cymru, meaning that they would lose ten seats overall, and be reduced to a total of 18

Table 9.1 Welsh Political Barometer opinion polls: shares of the vote during the election campaign (%)

	Cons	Lab	Lib Dem	Plaid Cymru	Brexit	Others
31 Oct–4 Nov. (N=1,136)	28	29	12	12	15	4
22–25 Nov. (N=1,116)	32	38	9	11	8	2
6–9 Dec. (N=1,020)	37	40	6	10	5	2

Source: ITV Cymru Wales and Cardiff University, carried out by YouGov.

seats. Plaid Cymru were predicted to stay on four seats as the poll also predicted that the Liberal Democrats would take Ceredigion from them. As revealing were Welsh views on who would make the best Prime Minister, with 41% choosing Boris Johnson and just 26% Jeremy Corbyn. Voters' feelings about who they blamed for Brexit having not yet happened did not point to any particular electoral implications, as 46% blamed MPs on all sides, 20% Boris Johnson and the Conservative government and 14% Jeremy Corbyn and the Labour party.

The Welsh Conservative campaign had early problems. Alun Cairns resigned as Secretary of State on 6 November, following accusations that he had supported the nomination of a party staff member, Ross England, as a Conservative candidate for the National Assembly despite knowing about his role in the collapse of a rape court case. Cairns was not replaced and as a result there was no Welsh figurehead to the campaign. At the same time, they had a string of candidacy difficulties. Cairns continued to stand as a candidate in the Vale of Glamorgan and attracted considerable media attention. Francesca O'Brien, the candidate in Gower, received calls to stand down over reports that in 2014 she had written on her Facebook page, after watching the TV programme Benefits Street: 'my blood is boiling, these people need putting down' (*Western Mail*, 5 November 2019: 8). The party in Wales stood by her nonetheless.

The Conservatives were also seeking to get two seats back that they had won in 2017 but subsequently lost. In Aberconwy, Guto Bebb gave up the party whip over Brexit but was standing down at the election. The Conservatives had also lost Brecon and Radnorshire as recently as August 2019 to the Liberal Democrats, after the 2017 Conservative victor, Chris Davies, was convicted in April 2019 of submitting false expense claims. Davies re-emerged as the party's candidate in Ynys Mon, only to pull out just prior to the election, leaving the party to scramble around for a new candidate.

The Welsh Conservative Party's manifesto, 'Get Brexit Done, Unleash Wales' Potential', was launched in the target seat of Wrexham on 24 November (Welsh Conservative Party 2019) and the two themes, of getting Brexit done and unleashing a tide of investment in Wales in the aftermath, were repeated throughout the campaign. This was backed up by a strong focus on developing the Welsh economy and passing on the targeted funding increases on the police, health and education to the Welsh budget to improve public services. In so doing they also promoted some specific policies that suggested the direct interest of a UK Conservative government in improving Wales' fortunes over the heads of the Labour-led government in the National Assembly for Wales. This drew on the already agreed UK government-backed city or growth deals for Cardiff, Swansea, mid Wales and north Wales. The election saw the promotion specifically of the Marches Growth deal to improve cross-border road infrastructure.

Closely related to this, Johnson, along with other key party visitors to Wales, including the then chancellor Sajid Javid, repeatedly focused on the transport needs of south and north Wales. In the south they stressed that even though the Welsh government had abandoned the M4 relief road plan to explore alternatives, the UK government had allocated the funding necessary from the UK level and wanted to make it happen. Speaking on a campaign trip to Caerphilly, Johnson told journalists that 'we're going to rely on our superior powers of persuasion. I think people looking at the congestion now...the Brynglas tunnels, it's been famously said, are the nostrils of the Welsh dragon which are currently stuffed-up. We intend to apply the Vicks inhaler. I think the overwhelming case is to get it done' (*Western Mail*, 12 December 2019). The Conservatives also promised to fund a West Wales Parkway railway station outside Swansea and along the north Wales coast they pledged to upgrade the A55 through the National Road Fund. The final component of the narrative was damning criticism of Labour's left ideology in Wales and their record both on the economy and in public service performance, as revealed, as one example, in relatively poor education results. In contrast, as Johnson said in his Wrexham address, 'We will put Wales first, we will put you first... the Welsh dragon will roar louder than ever before' (*Western Mail*, 25 November 2019).

On the face of it, Labour's Welsh campaign was a fairly coherent alternative. It was led by Mark Drakeford and provided a close fit with policies being championed by the British leadership. The manifesto, *Standing up for Wales*, also launched in Wrexham, committed Labour to a green industrial revolution with investment in renewable energy, promised a boost to small and medium enterprises through the Development Bank Wales, and publicly owned railways (Labour Party 2019). Corbyn's spending promises offered an extra £3.4 billion for the Welsh government budget, to be spent on health, education and other public services, allowing the provision of free social care and the scrapping of tuition fees. There were commitments to end the pay cap for the public sector, get rid of universal credit, introduce free broadband for every home and business and legislate for a real living wage of at least £10 an hour. Drakeford was proud that the Welsh government had been the first in the UK to declare a climate emergency and this priority ran through everything the party would do in government in Wales.

In choosing the manifesto title, 'Standing up for Wales', Drakeford consciously repeated the slogan used by his predecessor, Carwyn Jones, at the 2017 election. Jones had used this to suggest that in voting for Labour candidates, voters should see their vote as primarily for MPs who would represent Wales at Westminster and less as MPs who would support Jeremy Corbyn as Prime Minister. On this occasion, Drakeford did in part stand out from the Corbyn leadership by identifying a specifically Welsh position over Brexit. Drakeford had originally supported Corbyn's Brexit stance but he was alone in his cabinet in doing so and changed his mind. In contrast to Corbyn's neutrality, if and when a second referendum was held by a Labour government, Drakeford (2019, p. 21) committed the Welsh party to clearly campaigning for Remain, insisting 'Welsh Labour will campaign wholeheartedly and unapologetically to Remain, because we believe Wales is better off as part of Europe'. As Shipton (2019a) observed, this was significant because 'belated as this was, it enabled strongly Remain Welsh Labour candidates to appear credible when they said they had the backing of their party in a way the European Parliament candidates hadn't. . .Welsh Labour simply declared itself a Remain party'. Other than over Brexit though, Drakeford did not depart from the British party line. He had been the first Welsh Labour cabinet member to support Corbyn's candidacy in 2015 and strongly supported Corbyn now. He declined to redevelop Carwyn Jones' 2017 rhetorical narrative of appealing to voters to support Wales in voting for Labour rather than Jeremy Corbyn for prime minister. The Corbyn agenda largely stood to succeed or fail on its own merits in Wales, just as it did anywhere else.

Both the Conservatives and Labour were parties standing for office that had to incorporate their positions on Brexit within broader programmes for government. In contrast, the other parties defined themselves more explicitly in relation to how they would influence the handling of Brexit by whichever government took office. On the one hand, the Brexit Party provided the option to vote for keeping the political class to their promise on leaving the EU. As the election proceeded, the party leader, Nigel Farage, stood candidates down in many seats where the Conservatives were expected to win, to leave a focus on Labour held Leave seats. Their argument was that the Brexit Party was in the best position to challenge Labour in such seats. This had big implications for Wales as 21 of the 29 seats that voted Leave in 2016 had a sitting Labour MP. Welsh Labour's hardening of their pro-Remain position in a second referendum underlined the Brexit Party's resolve to campaign in these seats, threatening both Labour's position, as well as, potentially at least, Conservative prospects for taking any of these where they were target seats. Throughout the campaign the Conservatives attacked the

Brexit Party for threatening to split the Leave vote and allow Labour MPs to sneak back in.

On the other side, on 7 November it was announced that the pro-EU electoral pact between the Liberal Democrats and Greens, seen in England across 49 seats, was being extended to Wales to include Plaid Cymru. The pact covered 11 seats in all, meaning that in each case two of the parties would stand aside for the other to stand as the clear pro-Remain candidate for a second referendum. Plaid Cymru were the biggest winners from this, gaining a free run in seven seats, the Liberal Democrats in three and the Greens one. This replicated the electoral pact between the three parties in the Brecon and Radnorshire by-election held earlier in 2019, in which the Liberal Democrat candidate, Welsh party leader Jane Dodds, had been given a free run and won. The declared intention was to give a Remain voting candidate the biggest chance of victory in each case; but the anti-Brexit coalition was always incomplete without Labour joining. This was never a realistic option given Labour's history in Wales and Labour actively sought to blunt its appeal. A Welsh Labour spokesperson suggested that at its core the 'pact appears to be nothing more than Plaid and the Lib Dems propping each other up in seats they're worried about losing. Plaid are worried about Arfon. The Lib Dems don't think they'll hold Brecon and Radnorshire' (BBC, 2019). The pact did not cover Ceredigion, where Plaid Cymru held the seat and the Liberal Democrats were the main competitors. The pact was not supported by everyone, with the Liberal Democrat candidate in Pontypridd resigning and running as an independent.

Among the electoral pact partners, Plaid Cymru achieved the most visibility during the campaign, led ably by both the Assembly party leader, Adam Price, and the UK parliamentary leader, Liz Saville Roberts. As well as seeking to defend their four seats, two of which were very marginal, they had the modest target of trying to win one more, Ynys Mon, where they launched their campaign on 4 November. As well as campaigning against Brexit, they consistently highlighted the Corbyn leadership's greater interest in higher spending in Scotland than in Wales, as well as the deficiencies in Labour's Welsh government record. Their manifesto, *Wales, It's Us* (Plaid Cymru, 2019) promoted policies focused on an economic strategy based on investing in renewable energy, infrastructure and digital technology; a free national social care service; universal free child care and a new £35 a week payment for every child in low-income families; a programme of affordable homes investment and rent relief for people who pay more than 30% of their income on rent; devolution of the police and welsh justice system; and the creation of a new £50 million crime prevention fund to recruit 1,600 new police officers. As usual, Plaid were competing on the same left of centre class and nation ground as Labour but they were realistic that there were still very few constituencies where they had an established platform on which to compete. Adam

Price's eye was on preparing the ground for a bigger shot at the 2021 Assembly elections.

The campaign overall lacked drama and colour. Perhaps this was a function of it being a winter election and politicians being tired at the end of a long year. Leaders' debates also failed to take off. These were curious affairs, as the Conservatives called on David Davies, Conservative chair of the Welsh Affairs select committee, to represent them in lieu of the departed Cairns. Labour, by custom put up their shadow secretary of state, as opposed to the Labour First Minister. But on this occasion the shadow secretary of state, Christina Rees, was not deployed, nor was the possible alternative of Mark Drakeford. Instead, the party preferred to use Nick Thomas Symonds, MP for Torfaen. Pitched against Adam Price and Jane Dodds, the still very unknown leader of the Liberal Democrats, it all looked a bit random; more like occasional editions of the BBC's Question Time than the major set piece election events such debates originally were intended to be.

As the campaign went on Labour under Corbyn was at least rallying on the campaign trail and in Wales, as usual, the party was putting in a large organisational effort. A second opinion poll, released on 25 November, showed Labour up nine points from the first poll and the Conservatives up four points (see Table 9.1). Labour's relative improvement appeared to be limiting the likely damage as at this point just four seats were predicted to change hands, two in north Wales (Vale of Clwyd and Wrexham) and two in south Wales (Cardiff North and Gower). Corbyn was clearly more popular than at the start of the campaign. The poll indicated that 38% of Welsh electors saw Johnson as the best Prime Minister and 35% Corbyn. By now, it was apparent that there was a similar trend happening in Wales as in England in that the two main parties were squeezing the smaller ones, notably the Brexit Party.

However, the third and final opinion poll, released in early December, suggested that in comparison with the 2017 election there had been no Corbyn surge, and there was no particular mitigating Welsh Labour appeal. The third poll predicted a further two point rise for Labour to 40% but a five point rise for the Conservatives to further squeeze the other parties. Labour was again predicted heavy losses, this time eight seats: five in north Wales (Wrexham, Vale of Clwyd, Delyn, Clwyd South and Alyn and Deeside) and three in south Wales (Bridgend, Gower and Cardiff North).

By this point, open criticism of the Labour campaign specifically in Wales was beginning to break out into the press. Welsh Labour made a strong case for how hard they had fought the election, in that they had targeted resources on defensive Labour/Tory marginal and target seats, with a focus generally on both north Wales and south Wales seats. They claimed that there had been over 2,000 campaign events, over 150 key campaign visits and strenuous efforts at doorstep and telephone canvassing. Amidst criticism of Drakeford personally, it was claimed that he had visited 30 constituencies. But critics pointed out how little Corbyn had visited Wales during the campaign; that Drakeford had been pretty invisible; and that the 'Standing up for Wales' campaign had lacked substance and had not been well communicated. Organisational problems were raised: that the campaign launch had been in Cardiff South and Penarth, convenient to the Assembly, but a safe seat and with very few people present; leaflets had not been printed in time to deliver before postal votes were sent out; there had been a shortage of leaflets in key seats; and the example was raised of busing campaigners into campaign in Arfon, which was not a key seat. On the eve of the poll a senior Welsh Labour politician claimed: 'Lessons have to be learnt. Members and staff have worked really hard but there is a lack of strategic leadership within Transport House'. Communications staff in Transport House, Welsh Labour's headquarters in Cardiff, also briefed the media that Corbyn had made it harder for them in Wales. (*Western Mail,* 11 December 2019). The omens on election eve were that Brexit, a campaign that did not take off and organisational problems might well make the difference this time.

2. Party performance

Labour were the largest party in Wales but they did indeed lose six seats (see Table 9.2). In the south they limited the damage to Bridgend but in the north they lost a clutch of seats: Ynys Mon, Vale of Clwyd, Clwyd South, Delyn and Wrexham. The northern seats were seen as part of the hitherto apparently unbreachable Labour 'red wall' and the loss of Wrexham was particularly totemic, having been held by the party since the 1930s. Apart from Alyn and Deeside, in north east Wales, held with a majority of just 213 votes, all of Labour's seats were now across south Wales. In the seats held, Labour's strongest performances came in the four Cardiff seats, with Cardiff Central the safest Labour seat in Wales, with a majority of 17,179. However, even in all the seats Labour retained, there was a swing to the Conservatives. In the south east this included large swings in Torfaen (8.3%), Newport East (8.1%) and Islwyn (7.9%); in the valleys there was a 7.7% swing in the Rhondda, 7.9% in Merthyr Tydfil and Rhymney, and 7.6% in Ogmore; and in the industrial south west swings in Aberavon of 8.6%, Llanelli 8.8% and Neath 8.8%. Overall, Labour's share of the vote in Wales of 40.9% was eight points down on 2017. This was still better than their results in Wales in 2010 and 2015 and they were still the largest party in Wales. Nevertheless, their seat tally of 22 of the 40 seats was the party's worst since 1983. It was a grim night for the party.

Meanwhile, Boris Johnson could rightly see the election in Wales as a cause for celebration. The party regained the two seats that they had lost between the 2017

Table 9.2 UK General Election Result in Wales, 2019

	Seats	Change from 2017	Vote share (%)	Change in % vote share since 2017
Conservative	14	+6	36.1	+2.5
Labour	22	−6	40.9	−8.0
Lib Democrat	0	−	6.0	+1.5
Plaid Cymru	4	−	9.9	−0.5
Brexit	0	−	5.4	+5.4
Others	0	−	1.7	−0.8

and 2019 elections, Aberconwy and Brecon and Radnorshire. Beyond that they won the six seats from Labour to take 14 in all; Bridgend in the south and the five north Wales seats, including Ynys Mon which had been a Plaid Cymru target. Local constituency difficulties largely melted away as Alun Cairns won the Vale of Glamorgan with an increased majority, though the problems in Gower were a factor in them not winning the seat back. This meant that the Conservatives held all but two of the seats across north Wales, and down the eastern half of Wales you could walk continuously from Wrexham in the north to Monmouth in the south and never leave Conservative held seats. In addition, they held two of the Pembrokeshire and Carmarthen seats in the far south west. The Conservatives lay in second place in 21 of Labour's 22 seats, having reduced Labour's majorities in all. They also cut Plaid Cymru's majority in Carmarthen East to less than 2,000 votes. The Conservatives came out of the election looking genuinely like a competitive party nationwide. Overall, the Conservative vote share of 36.1% represented a further 2.5 percentage point increase from 2017 and their best share of the vote since 1979. Labour may have still been the largest party in Wales but the Conservative performance impressed.

The results reflected a squeeze of support for other parties. This left Plaid Cymru deeply disappointed at once again not making a breakthrough. They took comfort from increasing their majorities in Arfon at the expense of Labour and Ceredigion at the expense of the Liberal Democrats, as well as holding on to their two other seats. But beyond winning their four seats they came second nowhere and third in 15 seats spread across north and south Wales. Plaid came third even in their top target seat of Ynys Mon. The Liberal Democrats virtually disappeared as a serious party, coming second only in two seats, competitive only in Brecon and Radnor and third in only nine seats (including Ceredigion, where they were passed by the Conservatives). Perhaps the most significant of the results for the smaller parties was that for the Brexit Party. Their vote was squeezed down to 5.4% by election day, with some votes going to the Conservatives and some to

Labour as the campaign wore on. Even so their performance was 3.4 percentage points higher than UKIP in 2017 and included a second place in Blaenau Gwent and nine third place finishes, all in Labour held seats in south Wales.

It is hard to say conclusively, but the Brexit Party's performance may have made the difference in four seats where Labour held on from the Conservative challenger by fewer votes than were won by the Brexit party candidate coming in third place. These were one in the north (Alyn and Deeside) and three in south Wales (Newport East, Newport West and Torfaen). But for Nigel Farage's insistence that the Brexit Party had a role to play in the election, the Labour and Conservative parties may have ended up even on 18 seats each. This reflects more broadly that the election was a night of fine margins. These four Labour holds were all with majorities of less than 2,000 votes but the six Conservative gains from Labour were also all with majorities of 2,131 votes or fewer. So often in tight elections the small margins had broken Labour's way. The Brexit Party may have saved Labour even more blushes, but overall the fine margins for once favoured the Conservatives.

In the first election poll, 60% of voters had said that Brexit was the most important issue to them and consistently during the campaign it remained the top issue, followed by health. In reflecting on the results further it would appear that they seem to suggest that the party's positions on the issue of Brexit helped the Conservatives the most (see Table 9.3). In the 2016 European Union referendum, 29 of Wales' constituencies had voted Leave. Seven of the eight seats that the Conservatives retained were Leave voting seats (the exception was Monmouth) and all six of the seats that the Conservatives won from Labour were Leave voting seats. Labour retained 15 Leave seats and Plaid Cymru one, though in all cases with substantially reduced majorities. Eleven constituencies had voted Remain in 2016. None of these changed hands in the 2019 election. It is likely that in these cases Labour candidates were helped by Welsh Labour's unequivocal pro-Remain position as it allowed candidates to reflect this. Two marginal seats that stayed Labour were Gower and Cardiff North. Anna McMorrin in Cardiff North campaigned explicitly as the pro-Remain candidate and it was reported that 'the Liberal Democrat candidate has nobly suggested to his supporters that they might consider voting for Ms McMorrin in the spirt of opposing Brexit' (Shipton, 2019b). Generally, however, the numbers suggested that Labour probably lost more than it gained in Wales from not clearly supporting the completion of Brexit. Voters in all parts of Wales moved from Labour to the Conservatives and party positions on Brexit appear to have played a big part.

The election post-mortem started almost immediately in the Labour Party, reflecting much pent-up frustration at Corbyn's leadership and the reception candidates had found in canvassing for their leader. Several Welsh Labour MPs publicly criticised him. Chris Bryant, MP for the Rhondda, said 'During the last

Table 9.3 Party performances in Wales, according to Leave or Remain constituency voting in the 2016 EU Referendum

	Leave voting constituencies	Remain voting constituencies
Labour Hold	15	7
Cons Hold	5	1
Cons Hold (lost between 2017 and 2019)	2	0
Cons Gain from Labour	6	0
PC Hold	1	3
Total	29	11

Source: Adapted from House of Commons Library: *Brexit: Estimates of Votes by Constituency*.

general election in 2017, people on the doorstep would call him a terrorist sympathiser. This time round it was "He is a terrorist". A lot of that may be unfair, but the Labour Party has a lot of soul searching to do, and so does Jeremy Corbyn. For a lot of Labour voters, the Labour Party has swayed a long way from the party they have known and loved. Whether that is over Brexit or our defence policy or our patriotism' (*Western Mail*, 14 December 2019, pp. 4–5). Anna McMorrin asserted: 'It's on the watch of this leadership of our party that we have lost decent hardworking MPs who fought every day for their constituents and the millions of people who need a Labour government and I hope that he will take responsibility so we can move on and rebuild the party' (*Western Mail*, 14 December 2019, p. 4).

The most entertaining attack came from former Labour MP for Pontypridd, Kim Howells, who was deeply critical of Corbyn's post-election decision that he would stay on until a new leader had been elected: 'It is just insane, but it is an indication of that smug, sanctimonious, deluded, middle class, London group of MPs who run the Labour party and have ruined it' (*Western Mail*, 17 December 2019). He attacked Corbyn for his lack of patriotism, always finding fault in Britain and siding with Britain's enemies. Alun Davies, AM for Blaenau Gwent, wrote in his blog: 'We need to recognise that this defeat was not only a defeat for the man, but a defeat for what he stood for as well. His failure was personal, political, policy and principle. Corbyn must go but for Labour to recover Corbynism must go as well' (*Western Mail*, 17 December 2019).

In response, the left of the party sought to defend the election policy agenda generally and blame the specific issue of Brexit that made the election very hard for Labour. Mark Drakeford described the results as 'deeply disappointing' but argued that the losses in Wales were by relatively small margins of 2,000 or less, with Labour still the largest party. The seats that the Conservatives had won he considered to be ones that had only been lent to the Conservatives and they wanted them back. He acknowledged 'we have a particular issue in the north of Wales as well, we know we have to address, and we'll be thinking hard and we've been thinking that already' (*Western Mail*, 20 December 2019).

The Conservatives celebrated while the other parties felt utterly marginalised by the two-party battle. Only Plaid Cymru still had a foothold in the party system and looked forward immediately to the 2021 Assembly elections. Observers of

Table 9.4 UK General Election results in Wales, 1979–2019

	Con	Lab	Lib Dem (formerly Lib and Lib-SDP)	Plaid Cymru	Others (incl. UKIP and Green)
1979					
Vote share (%)	32.2	47.0	10.6	8.1	2.2
Seats	11	21	1	2	1
1983					
Vote share (%)	31.0	37.5	23.2	7.8	0.4
Seats	14	20	2	2	0
1987					
Vote share (%)	29.5	45.1	17.9	7.3	0.2
Seats	8	24	3	3	0
1992					
Vote share (%)	28.6	49.5	12.4	8.8	0.7
Seats	6	27	1	4	0
1997					
Vote share (%)	19.6	54.7	12.4	9.9	3.4
Seats	0	34	2	4	0
2001					
Vote Share	21.0	48.6	13.8	14.3	2.3
Seats	0	34	2	4	0
2005					
Vote share (%)	21.4	42.7	18.4	12.6	4.9
Seats	3	29	4	3	1
2010					
Vote share (%)	26.1	36.2	20.1	11.3	6.2
Seats	8	26	3	3	0
2015					
Vote share (%)	27.2	36.9	6.5	12.1	17.3
Seats	11	25	1	3	0
2017					
Vote share (%)	33.6	48.9	4.5	10.4	2.5
Seats	8	28	0	4	0
2019					
Vote share (%)	36.1	40.9	6.0	9.9	7.1
Seats	14	22	0	4	0

Turnout: 1979: 79.4%; 1983:76.1%; 1987: 78.9%; 1992:79.7%; 1997: 73.6%; 2001: 60.6%; 2005: 62.4%; 2010: 64.9%; 2015: 65.6%; 2017: 68.6%; 2019: 66.6%.

representative democracy in Wales could take some generally positive conclusions from the election. The turnout was a bit lower than in 2017 but it was a winter election. The number of women MPs increased by three to 14 (35%) overall, just slightly above the proportion for the House of Commons as a whole. Sarah Atherton (Wrexham), Virginia Crosbie (Ynys Mon) and Fay Jones (Brecon and Radnorshire) were the Conservatives' first female MPs ever elected in Wales. There were still no BME MPs though. The seats to vote shares were more proportional than in previous elections, with Labour winning 55% of the seats on 40.9% of the vote, the Conservatives 35% of the seats on 36.1% of the vote, and Plaid Cymru 10% of seats on 9.9% of the vote. Labour clearly still received a bonus in how the simple plurality system worked.

The election indicated overall that Labour resilience generally was still there but, as Table 9.4 shows, the historic trend suggests that Labour has now had a relatively bad result in Wales in three of the last four elections. Its decline from total dominance was emphasised in 2019 by its lowest seat haul since 1983, because for once Labour relatively speaking lost out more at the margins. Overall, the trend appears to be towards a more competitive two-party system between Labour and the Conservatives with Plaid Cymru as the third party, strong in its core areas but otherwise still struggling to break a duopoly.

3. Conclusion

The fulfilment of Boris Johnson's desire for a decisive majority in order to 'Get Brexit Done' was aided by the results in Wales. Whether this outcome included specifically Welsh factors is a matter for debate. There was a Welsh campaign, characterised by party strategies, manifestos and leaders' debates, conducted amid an awareness that the electorate invariably returned Labour as the largest party. It would be hard to say that the distinct Welsh Conservative campaign offered a great deal to the Conservatives' UK-wide cause; but it is likely that the reach of Johnson's British-wide message and campaign, tailored to Wales, was important in positively making a difference to Conservative fortunes in Wales. This was the factor that made the difference from 2017. At the same time, the Welsh Labour campaign had its problems. It was not as effective as the Labour campaign in 2017 and it is likely that this in fact was the most significant specifically Welsh dimension to the election that made a difference. Having said that clearly Corbyn was not as effective as in 2017 as well.

The implications of the result fed into British-wide analyses of political change. The trend towards support for the (small 'u' unionist) centre-ground of Welsh politics seen in 2017 was confirmed; it is simply that the Conservatives won more of it than in the previous contest. The implications of this were hard to predict. Labour was still the largest party with a proven record of resilience. They could improve their performance after a slightly under-par election organisation-ally, and with a different British leader and Brexit behind them the party could yet increase their vote share again. Nevertheless, the Conservatives clearly had a more solid platform for the future. This certainly had implications for future UK elections, and possibly also for Conservative fortunes in the National Assembly elections in 2021.

In this context, it is perhaps worth reflecting on the 2019 election in Wales specifically as a success for Johnson. In launching the party's manifesto on Bangor-on-Dee's racecourse in late November, he had commented that 'I started this project 22 years ago'. In a way that Theresa May had signally failed to under-stand from walking holiday visits, Johnson had got both what the Welsh elector-ate disliked about the Conservative Party and what it might support ingrained in his DNA from the oldest form of political training; the party apprenticeship of taking a good political beating in an unwinnable seat. As a result, when it mat-tered, he had a brand of populist Toryism that cut through to appeal to both con-ventional Conservative voters and tap into anti-Welsh establishment feeling. This was done concisely and cleverly, in a language which was engaging and insistent without forcing people to feel like they were being disloyal to their country. This more than anything else may be the defining legacy of the 2019 election in Wales.

References

BBC. (2019) 'General election: Plaid, Lib Dems and Greens in pro-EU pact in 11 Welsh seats', 7 November 2019, accessed at https://www.bbc.co.uk/news/uk-wales-50325815 on 7 January 2020.

Drakeford, M. (2019) 'Richer Lives, Greener Future for all and a Chance to Stay in the EU', *Western Mail*, 11 December, p. 21.

Cymru Plaid., (2019) *Wales, It's Us*, Cardiff, Plaid Cymru.

Scully, R. (2019, 4 November) 'The First Welsh Poll of the General Election', accessed at https://blogs.cardiff.ac.uk/electionsinwales/2019/11/04/the-first-welsh-poll-of-the-gen eral-election-2/ on 2 April 2020.

Shipton, M. (2019a), 'Don't Assume the Odds-on Favourite will Cruise to Victory', *Western Mail*, 30 October, pp. 22–23.

Shipton, M. (2019b) 'Brexit will be Determining Factor in this Historic Election', *Western Mail*, 12 December, p. 9.

Welsh Conservative Party (2019) *Get Brexit Done, Unleash Wales' Potential*, Cardiff, Welsh Conservatives.

Welsh Labour. (2019) *Standing up for Wales*. 2019 Election Manifesto, Cardiff, Welsh Labour.

Western Mail (2019, 5 November) 'Top Tories Standing by Election Hopeful in Facebook "put them Down" Row', p. 8.

Western Mail (2019, 26 November) 'Johnson Pledges Key Roads Boost as he Launches Welsh Manifesto', pp. 6–7.

Western Mail (2019, 11 December) 'Labour Activists Accuse Party of Poor Campaign', p. 8.

Western Mail (2019, 12 December) 'Boris Johnson Visits Caerphilly in Last Push for Election Votes' pp. 6–7.

Western Mail (2019, 14 December) 'Corbyn to Resign as Leader in Early 2020 after Polls Nightmare', pp. 4–5.

Western Mail (2019, 14 December) 'Leader under Fire as Labour Endures a Battering in Wales Despite Keeping Control of Cardiff', p. 4.

Western Mail (2019, 17 December) 'Former Labour Minister's Scathing Attack on Corbyn', p. 6.

Western Mail (2019, 20 December) 'Interview with Mark Drakeford', pp. 8–9.

Britain Votes (2019) 172–188

JONATHAN TONGE AND JOCELYN EVANS*

Northern Ireland: From the Centre to the Margins?

Northern Ireland's election had dramatic outcomes and important consequences for the restoration of devolved power-sharing. For the first time, Unionist MPs elected to Westminster were in the minority. Nine nationalists won seats, seven taken by Sinn Féin (SF) who refused to take up their positions in the House of Commons, with the Social Democratic and Labour Party (SDLP) recording two constituency triumphs. Eight unionists, all from the Democratic Unionist Party (DUP) were returned, along with one member of the Alliance Party, not part of either the unionist or nationalist bloc. The once dominant Ulster Unionist Party (UUP) failed to win a seat for the third time in the last four elections.

The previous general election result in Northern Ireland impacted across the UK, with the DUP holding the balance of power at Westminster and entering a confidence-and-supply arrangement with the Conservative government (HM Government, 2017). The story of 2019 was of a reversion to type, with all of Northern Ireland's MPs marginalised. The question begged was how they could articulate Northern Ireland's interests when their contingent was miniscule compared with the size of the Conservatives' majority. As those MPs headed to Westminster (or not, in SF's case), the focus switched to the legislature in Belfast. With the DUP's glory days in London over and the Northern Irish electorate impatient with the absence of devolved government (and blaming either of the main two parties), the need for the revival of a local power base was apparent. One month after the election, the Northern Ireland Assembly, absent since January 2017, was duly restored.

This analysis of the general election examines how the contest developed in Northern Ireland, discusses why four seats changed hands and assesses the implications of the outcome. It examines how arguments over Brexit, unionist, nationalist and pro-Remain pacts, election tactics, a blame game over Stormont's absence and traditional sectarian politics dominated the campaign. In assessing the results, the chapter draws extensively upon data from the 2019 Economic and Social Research Council's Northern Ireland general election study, based upon

*Jonathan Tonge, Department of Politics, University of Liverpool, J.Tonge@liverpool.ac.uk; Jocelyn Evans, School of Politics and International Studies, University of Leeds, j.a.j.evans@leeds.ac.uk

doi:10.1093/pa/gsaa036

2,003 post-election interviews with a representative sample of the electorate.[1] All data, other than the overall and constituency results, are taken from the study unless indicated otherwise.

1. The results

Table 10.1 shows the overall results, in terms of votes, percentage shares and seats. The DUP had a tough defence to mount, having won a record ten seats in 2017. The party lost two of its three Belfast seats, including the North Belfast constituency of Westminster leader Nigel Dodds. SF's return of seven seats matched its 2017 haul and included the notable Dodds scalp but the party's vote share fell everywhere beyond North Belfast. The SDLP regained the Westminster representation it had lost for the first time in 2017. Party leader Colum Eastwood thrashed SF to retake Foyle and Claire Hanna triumphed easily in South Belfast, so two nationalist voices are now heard in the Commons. Table 10.2 shows party fortunes in each constituency.

Table 10.1 The 2019 general election result in Northern Ireland

Party	Votes	Percentage of vote	Percentage change from 2017	Seats	Seat change from 2017
DUP	244,127	30.6	−5.4	8	−2
SF	181,853	22.8	−6.7	7	—
Alliance	134,115	16.8	+8.8	1	+1
SDLP	118,737	14.9	+3.1	2	+2
UUP	93,123	11.7	+1.4	0	0
Others	31,412	3.2	−1.5	0	−1

[1]The Northern Ireland general election survey was conducted between 28 December 2019 and 11 February 2020. The Principal Investigator was Professor Jonathan Tonge (University of Liverpool) with co-investigators Professor Peter Shirlow (Liverpool) Professor Bernadette Hayes (Aberdeen) Professor Jocelyn Evans (Leeds) and Dr Paul Mitchell (LSE). It involved interviews with a representative sample of 2,003 respondents, in 90 electoral wards across Northern Ireland's 18 constituencies. The study covers voters and non-voters at the election. It was funded mainly by the Economic and Social Research Council, award ES/T015527/1, with further support from the Heseltine Institute at the University of Liverpool. Data available at https://beta.ukdataservice.ac.uk/datacatalogue/studies/study?id=8619

Table 10.2 Northern Ireland constituency results, 2019 general election (percentage vote shares)

Constituency		DUP	UUP	Alliance	SF	SDLP	OTH	Change in winning party's vote share	Turnout (%)	Turnout change from 2017
Belfast East	DUP HOLD	49.2	5.9	44.9	—	—	—	−6.6	64.3	−3.2
Belfast North	SF GAIN FROM DUP	43.1		9.8	47.1	—	—	+5.4	68.4	−0.8
Belfast South	SDLP GAIN FROM DUP	24.7	2.7	14.3	—	57.2	—	+31.3	67.9	−1.8
Belfast West	SF HOLD	13.5	—	4.9	53.8	7.7	20.1	−12.9	59.4	−6.0
East Antrim	DUP HOLD	45.3	14.7	27.3	5.7	2.4	3.6	−12.0	57.7	−2.9
East Londonderry	DUP HOLD	40.1	9.2	15.1	15.6	15.7	4.4	−8.0	57.0	−4.2
Fermanagh and S Tyrone	SF HOLD	—	43.2	5.2	43.3	6.8	1.5	−3.9	70.1	−5.7
Foyle	SDLP GAIN FROM SF	10.1	2.3	2.7	20.7	57.0	7.1	+17.7	63.7	−1.7
Lagan Valley	DUP HOLD	43.1	19.0	28.8	2.4	3.9	2.8	−16.5	60.2	−2.0
Mid Ulster	SF HOLD	24.5	5.9	7.9	45.9	14.3	1.5	−8.6	63.8	−4.4
Newry and Armagh	SF HOLD	21.7	8.2	8.3	40.0	18.6	3.2	−8.0	62.9	−5.6
North Antrim	DUP HOLD	47.4	18.5	14.1	12.8	6.7	0.5	−11.5	57.5	−6.6
North Down	ALLIANCE GAIN FROM IND. UNIONIST	37.9	12.1	45.2	—	—	4.8	+35.9	60.9	−0.1
South Antrim	DUP HOLD	35.3	29.0	19.1	11.4	5.3	—	−3.0	60.2	−3.1
South Down	SF HOLD	15.3	6.6	13.9	32.4	29.2	2.5	−7.5	63.1	−4.1
Strangford	DUP HOLD	47.2	10.7	28.4	1.5	5.3	6.9	−14.8	56.3	−4.1
Upper Bann	DUP HOLD	41.0	12.4	12.9	24.6	9.2	—	−2.5	60.7	−3.2
West Tyrone	SF HOLD	40.2	6.7	9.7	40.2	17.8	3.7	−10.6	62.4	−5.8

Table 10.3 Party gains and losses in constituency vote share, 2019 general election in Northern Ireland

Party	Seats contested	Vote share up	Vote share down
DUP	17	1	16
SF	15	1	14
Alliance	18	17	1
SDLP	15	10	5
UUP	16	10*	6

*UUP 'increases' include two seats uncontested in 2017.

1.1   The rise of Alliance

Perhaps the most striking feature of the results was the rise from fifth to third place, in vote share, of the Alliance Party, rejecting unionism and nationalism. Naomi Long's party gained North Down with 45% of the vote. In 2017, the party's share in the constituency was in single percentage figures. Alliance's overall 9-point general election increase in vote share added to the party's 11-point European and 5-point council election increases in 2019. Alliance improved its vote share in 17 of the 18 constituencies. With those rejecting unionist or nationalist labels outnumbering those who do identify as either, by 40% to 28% and 25%, respectively, Alliance has a large and growing electoral reservoir in which to fish. Half of those declining to identify as unionist or nationalist did not vote in 2019. Of the half that did, Alliance outscored its closest challenger by two-to-one. As Table 10.3 shows, as Alliance improved its position, the DUP and SF fell back.

Alliance has, belatedly, come a long way. After 45 years marooned on an average 7% vote share, the three elections in 2019 saw the party average 16%, attracting more than 300,000 votes across the trio of contests and gaining 62,000 votes between the 2017 and 2019 general elections. While the UUP's relatively liberal pro-Union political territory might appear to be most at risk from the Alliance surge, UUP defectors from the 2017 election provided only 3% of the supporters of Naomi Long's party at the general election. This was a much smaller rate of desertion than the 18% shifting from the DUP (which obviously had the most votes to lose) at the previous contest and 12% from SF. Former SDLP voters provided another 5%, while 8% of Alliance's new voters had not voted in the 2017 election. Alliance garnered the support of a quarter of all non-voters from two years earlier. The party has the youngest voter base, with half aged 45 years and under. Alliance's supporters are slightly more likely to be Protestant than Catholic, with percentage support among those of no religion twice that of any other main party. The proportion of Alliance Party voters who are graduates (31%) is double than that among DUP and SF supporters. Only the SDLP's support comes close.

Alliance's vision is one in which constitutional questions are displaced by local issues. It stresses a desire for a united community and integration, emphasising it is 'not an orange or green party' (Alliance Party, 2019, p. 3). Alliance's appeal is as a big tent for liberal unionists, moderate nationalists and those neither unionist nor nationalist, although it is not always clear whether the party is attempting to *accommodate* existing affiliations or promote Northern Irishness to *overcome* British unionist and Irish nationalist identities. The party's voters embrace each identity: 32% British; 34% Irish and 28% Northern Irish. While 'neither unionist nor nationalist' ideological identification is the main choice of Alliance voters, 44% do adopt traditional unionist or nationalist identifications.

2.   Continuing polarisation

Does the strong Alliance performance indicate that Northern Ireland's electorate is thawing in terms of sectarian division? Table 10.4 shows the unionist, nationalist and non-aligned shares of the vote, in relation to Protestant, Catholic and no-religion proportions of each constituency, while Table 10.5 indicates the correlations between Protestant religious community background and the unionist bloc vote and Catholic religious community background and nationalist bloc vote.

As Table 10.5 shows, heralding a thaw and hailing the arrival of electoral spring would be premature. Despite a modest weakening, the association between religious community background and unionist and nationalist bloc votes remains very strong. Support for the DUP or UUP remains very extensive among those identified as holding a Protestant community background at the last census (admittedly dated now, having been conducted in 2011) and the same applies to backing for SF and the SDLP among those from a Catholic background. In the 2019 Northern Ireland election survey, no Catholics 'admitted' voting for either the DUP or UUP, an absence of selection reciprocated by Protestants in terms of SF, with only 1% backing the SDLP. Table 10.6 provides party support by religion.

More than two decades after the Good Friday Agreement, progress towards electoral rapprochement, in terms of voting for a party on the other side of the sectarian divide, appears virtually non-existent. Any thawing is likely to be via the diminution of religious communal identification and the willingness to vote for a non-bloc party, not the propensity to vote for the 'other' side's bloc parties.

Nonetheless, the 2019 election did produce more constituency outliers in terms of the religion–vote relationship, plotted in Figures 10.1 (Protestant–unionist vote) and 10.2 (Catholic–nationalist vote). A weakening of the relationship would see much greater scattering but most constituencies remain close to the line. The labelled constituencies are ones where the distance from the trend

Table 10.4 Unionist, nationalist and non-unionist/non-nationalist constituency percentage vote shares, 2019 general election in Northern Ireland

Constituency	Protestant, percentage of constituency	Unionist vote (%)	Roman Catholic, percentage of constituency	Nationalist vote (%)	No religion	Non-Unionist or Non-Nationalist vote (%)
Belfast East	75.4	55.1	12.7	N/A	10.5	44.9
Belfast North	45.7	43.1	46.9	47.1	6.4	9.8
Belfast South	43.7	27.4	44.0	58.4	9.5	14.2
Belfast West	16.7	13.5	80.1	65.7	2.7	20.8
East Antrim	70.1	62.8	20.4	8.1	8.5	29.1
East Londonderry	53.3	49.3	41.7	35.7	4.4	9.0
Fermanagh and S Tyrone	39.1	43.2	57.7	50.1	2.6	6.7
Foyle	22.0	12.5	75.1	82.0	2.1	5.5
Lagan Valley	71.9	64.9	19.0	6.3	8.1	28.8
Mid Ulster	30.8	30.4	66.7	60.2	2.1	9.4
Newry and Armagh	30.6	30.0	66.4	61.7	2.5	8.3
North Antrim	66.0	65.9	28.4	19.4	4.8	14.7
North Down	74.4	54.8	12.6	N/A	11.8	45.2
South Antrim	59.8	64.3	31.9	16.7	7.6	19.0
South Down	26.9	21.9	69.3	64.2	3.4	13.9
Strangford	73.1	62.7	17.3	6.8	8.7	30.5
Upper Bann	50.0	53.3	44.0	33.8	5.1	12.9
West Tyrone	30.2	28.6	68.0	60.4	1.5	11.0

Note: The Conservative Party and UKIP are classed as unionist. Aontu, as an anti-abortion Irish republican party, is classed as nationalist. People Before Profit, the Greens and an Independent are classed as non-unionist and non-nationalist.
Source: For religious composition of constituencies: Russell (2013).

Table 10.5 Correlations between religious community background and unionist or nationalist bloc vote, 2005–2019 general elections in Northern Ireland

	2005	2010	2015	2017	2019
Catholic-nationalist	0.98	0.99	0.99	0.99	0.95
Protestant-unionist	0.97	0.94	0.92	0.96	0.93

*All significant at P < 0.001.

lines is ±10% or more. Belfast South is an outlier for both communities. With a pro-Remain pact between the SDLP and SF, the latter standing aside, nationalists voted wholesale for the SDLP. The below–par unionist vote may have reflected

Table 10.6 Voting by religion, 2019 general election in Northern Ireland (%)

	Catholics	Protestants
DUP	0	54
UUP	0	24
SF	51	0
SDLP	28	1
Alliance	13	17
Other	8	4

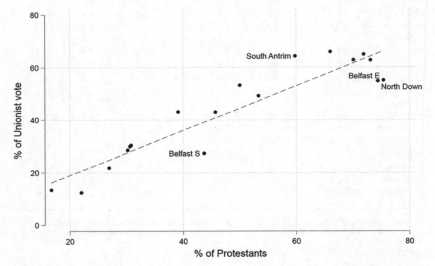

Figure 10.1 The unionist vote and percentage of Protestants in each constituency, 2019 general election in Northern Ireland

some acceptance of the situation by liberal Protestants in a middle-class constituency. This was the only seat where Alliance's vote share dropped. In North Down, the liberal Protestant vote went to the Alliance candidate, Stephen Farry, with all other pro-Remain parties standing aside, explaining why the unionist vote was below what might have been expected given the constituency's religious background profile. In East Belfast, the high-profile Alliance Party leader, Naomi Long, polled very strongly as she had at the previous three contests. South Antrim was the site of the only DUP versus UUP close contest, a scenario which mobilised unionists, reflected in a total unionist vote beyond what might have been expected. Regarding the other nationalist outliers beyond Belfast South, Foyle reflects how nationalists came out in large numbers, in what appeared a

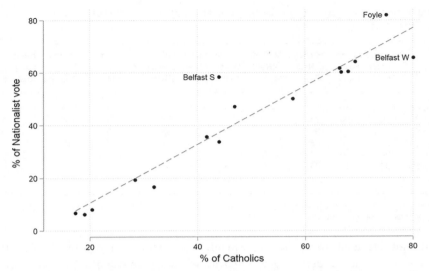

Figure 10.2 The nationalist vote and percentage of Catholics in each constituency, 2019 general election in Northern Ireland

marginal seat, to ensure a huge victory for the SDLP at the expense of SF, who had captured the seat for the first time in 2017 by a mere 169 votes. The nationalist vote in West Belfast is lower than that might be expected because of the sizeable (16%) vote share for the left-wing People Before Profit.

Although it has been suggested that British or Irish political parties might usefully stand in Northern Ireland to break the 'place apart' sectarian logjam, the idea does not really fly and divides voters on sectarian lines. Voters for SF are five times more likely to be against British parties standing than support the idea, but, by two-to-one, they back Irish parties, such as Fianna Fáil and Fine Gael, contesting elections in Northern Ireland. Two-thirds of DUP voters oppose Irish political parties contesting elections in Northern Ireland with only 9% in favour. They back other British parties standing by 44–26%.

Young people are the least enamoured with the current political dispensation. Among 18– to 24-year olds, two-thirds did not vote at the 2019 general election, a proportion identical to that at the 2017 contest and a majority decline to identify as unionist or nationalist. While neither had a particularly successful election, the DUP and SF continue to be perceived as the stouter representatives of their ethno-national bloc, explaining their continued dominance in a system favouring ethnic tribune parties (Mitchell *et al.*, 2009).

Considerable polarisation is evident in the perceptions of performances of party leaders, which appear highly conditioned by communal background. Almost one-third of DUP voters rated Arlene Foster at ten out of ten, on a zero

Table 10.7 Views of party leaders by party voted for, 2019 general election in Northern Ireland (0-10 scale) (%)

	Arlene Foster DUP	Arlene Foster DUP	Michelle O'Neill SF	Michelle O'Neill SF	Steve Aiken UUP	Steve Aiken UUP	Colum Eastwood SDLP	Colum Eastwood SDLP	Naomi Long Alliance	Naomi Long Alliance
Score	0–5	6–10	0–5	6–10	0–5	6–10	0–5	6–10	0–5	6–10
DUP	10	90	98	2	55	45	93	7	71	29
UUP	30	70	99	1	7	93	85	15	68	32
SF	98	2	13	87	95	5	57	43	55	45
SDLP	94	6	54	46	88	12	5	95	31	69
Alliance	83	17	75	25	75	25	64	36	12	88

'On a scale of 0–10 where 0 means you don't rate that leader at all and 10 where you rate that very highly indeed, please give your views on these political leaders'

(do not rate at all) to ten (rate very highly) scale. More than two-thirds of DUP voters rated their leader at eight or above and more than half of UUP voters also rated Foster at seven or higher. In contrast, a clear majority (56%) of SF voters gave the DUP leader the minimum rating of zero and 44% of SDLP voters did likewise. Only 2% of SF voters rated Foster at six or above. Forty per cent of those same voters gave UUP leader Steve Aiken zero, even though he had only been in the job for 33 days when the election took place.

The antipathy was reciprocated. Some 43% of DUP voters ranked SF's northern leader, Michelle O'Neill at zero and 75% rated her no higher than two out of ten. Meanwhile, the majority (55%) of SF voters ranked their leader at eight or above. Only 1% of unionist voters gave O'Neill a positive rating (i.e. six or above). SDLP leader Colum Eastwood must have felt positively loved in comparison, with 9% of unionist voters rating him at six out of ten or higher.

Alliance's Naomi Long escaped the worst of the opprobrium, making her overall the most popular—or least unpopular—party leader. Even here, 12% of DUP and 15% of SF curmudgeons gave her a zero. UUP voters are the most negative (68% rate Long only between zero and five). SDLP voters are much warmer, two-thirds offering a positive ranking for Long of six or above. Table 10.7 provides the scoring for the main party leaders.

3.   Brexit pacts, an 'economic united Ireland' and constitutional futures

The election campaign featured rows over Brexit-related pacts, tinged with an older Orange versus Green sectarian flavour. The DUP defended its confidence-and-supply deal with the Conservative government as attracting a large amount of extra funding, highlighting the substantial extra cash for health, schools and employment (Democratic Unionist Party, 2019). Towards its end, however, the DUP had been dismissively cast aside by Prime Minister Johnson, who reached a Brexit deal which aligned Northern Ireland much more closely to the EU than the rest of the UK. Johnson had promised the DUP the opposite at their party conference one year earlier.

Amid much derision aimed towards the DUP for its pro-Brexit strategy having resulted in a Brexit now disowned, the election was marked by 'Remain pacts'. Despite having criticised SF for decades for abstaining from Westminster, the SDLP standing aside for SF in North Belfast was justified by Colum Eastwood's party on the grounds it was better no-one attend parliament than a Brexiteer. Abstention remains totemic for SF and there are no moves to change policy and allow their MPs to swear an oath of allegiance to a British monarch. Even though the election survey data suggest a slight overall majority of SF voters support their party taking seats (it was unionist voters who were opposed), the issue is not being debated within SF ranks. Those who think SF should take their seats still voted SF regardless. Moreover, the large Conservative majority would offer no traction at Westminster. No Northern Ireland representatives were invited onto the Commons Brexit committee following the election.

SF's returning of the SDLP's favour in South Belfast led to unionist complaints that Remain pacts were 'pan-nationalist' fronts, thinly veiled anti-DUP decapitation tactics. However, the DUP was content to see pan-unionist fronts. The UUP stood aside to try and aid the DUP in North Belfast and the DUP reciprocated for the UUP in a similarly unsuccessful pact in Fermanagh and South Tyrone. Unionism versus nationalism was thus mapped onto the Remain versus Leave battles. For all the noise, most unionist and nationalist voters are not opposed to pacts. While there are many undecideds, only 22% of DUP voters dislike them and just 12% of UUP voters are similarly hostile. On the other side of the divide, 29% of SF and 21% of SDLP voters reject pan-nationalist pacts.

Brexit was indeed the issue identified as most important at the election by the electorate, followed, amid an acute local health crisis, by the National Health Service (NHS) and then the older constitutional question of Northern Ireland's place in the UK versus Irish unity. However, DUP voters placed the NHS above Brexit in the order of importance. The latter was listed in the top two concerns of only 35% of DUP supporters, reflecting the belief of some that predicted negative consequences of EU would not ensue. The DUP opposed Boris Johnson's form of Brexit more than parties which supported Remain. A sense of betrayal was apparent. Only 4% of DUP voters (and unionist voters more broadly) rejected the confidence-and-supply deal at its outset. DUP members favour the Conservatives to Labour by seven-to-one (Tonge *et al.*, 2014). Yet the Conservative–DUP deal had seemingly ended in tears with Northern Ireland still closely and uniquely aligned to the EU, creating possible trade barriers within the UK internal market.

The Prime Minister's deal with the Taoiseach and the EU accepted the semi-detachment of Northern Ireland via, effectively, a border in the Irish Sea, terms that Johnson (2018) had told the DUP conference one year earlier 'no British Conservative government could or should sign up to'. The nationalist perspective was that the DUP had acted as midwife to a Brexit rejected by a majority in Northern Ireland and so deserved electoral sanction.

Recognising the new realities after the election, however, the DUP appeared more sanguine over what the Prime Minister had agreed. The party's new Westminster leader, Jeffrey Donaldson (2020) commented that 'customs checks doesn't mean that you change the constitutional status of a part of the United Kingdom' and spoke about 'exploiting the opportunities' of bespoke EU and UK market access. It appeared that most DUP voters still backed Brexit, but with some slippage in support for Leave and with backers of Arlene Foster's party eschewing possible consequences. Support for Brexit fell from 67% reported at the 2016 referendum (Garry, 2017) to 56% of the 2019 DUP general election supporters saying they still favoured EU departure. Among all DUP voters, only 31% said checks on goods travelling between Northern Ireland and Ireland would be acceptable, eschewing a hard border and only 22% accepted the 'East-West border' of Johnson's EU deal, checks on goods transported between Great Britain and Northern Ireland. Even a majority (53%) of SF's voters rejected East-West checks, despite the argument that treating trade between Great Britain and Northern Ireland as 'exports' suited the party's ultimate constitutional agenda in representing a shift towards an economic united Ireland. Naturally, SF voters overwhelmingly opposed greater friction in trade across the border in Ireland.

4.   The restoration of the devolved power-sharing Assembly

The election result and context made the rapid restoration of the devolved Northern Ireland Assembly and Executive inevitable. The DUP's Westminster influence was removed. Its vote share had dropped, as had SF's, as electors appeared unimpressed at their absence from the region's political institutions. The Secretary of State threatened new Assembly elections if the parties did not return to government in Northern Ireland which, given the desertions of the DUP and SF by some voters, did not augur well for the big two. Some contentious issues had been dealt with at Westminster, which had legalised same-sex marriage and abortion in Northern Ireland. Amid an unaddressed local health crisis, there was overwhelming support for the return of the devolved institutions among electors, only 2% not wanting them back. SF's return as a party of government in the North preceded a strong showing at the election in the South, as the party topped the poll in the election there in February 2020.

The consequence of the pressure from the voters and the British and Irish governments was a restoration of devolved government one month after the election, under the 'New Decade, New Approach' deal (HM Government, 2020). The extent of change from previous Assembly arrangements appeared modest. Irish language and Ulster-Scots provisions were introduced, with a commissioner for each. An Office of Identity and Cultural Expression was established. These arrangements looked akin to a draft plan rejected internally by the DUP in 2018, indicating how it was the political and electoral context that had changed far more than legislative proposals. There were slight alterations to veto rights over legislation. Provision for an official opposition was bolstered, but all the main parties chose to enter the ruling Executive anyway. That Executive would be given more time to recover in the event of future collapse before fresh elections were required. New Assembly sub-committees were created on Brexit and a Bill of Rights. However, the Secretary of State presiding over Stormont's restoration, Julian Smith, was sacked two months after the election. Smith had agreed to implement the 2014 Stormont House Agreement to address conflict legacy issues. Its provisions included continuing investigations into the past actions in the Troubles, regardless of perpetrator. Potential further prosecutions of British soldiers did not find favour among sections of the Conservative Party.

The 'New Decade New Approach' accord nonetheless promised a sustained devolved government. Beyond how to deal with the past, its major controversy concerned the level of new funding. Northern Ireland's extra one billion pounds of funding extracted by the DUP as between 2017 and 2019 had bypassed the Barnett Formula (Birrell and Heenan, 2019) and added to a level of subsidy per head which already exceeded that found elsewhere in the UK (Keep, 2016). The parties re-entering devolved government received a similar windfall.

One of the divisions that had beset the Assembly previously was in the rearview mirror at least. The blocking of same-sex marriage by unionist members of the Northern Ireland Assembly, using a Petition of Concern which requires cross-community support for a measure, had been overcome by Westminster passing legislation, introduced by the Labour MP, Conor McGinn, permitting such unions. February 2020 saw Northern Ireland's first same-sex marriage. More voters from each of the main five parties supported the change than were opposed. Overall, one-quarter of electors still disagreed with legalisation, but even among those aged 65 years and over, only 43% thought it the wrong decision, with a mere 8% of 18- to 24-year olds opposed to the change. Abortion, however, remained a potentially awkward issue for the Assembly. It was also legalised in Northern Ireland via direct Westminster legislation towards the end of the Assembly hiatus. Ironically, the legislation introduced by Labour MP, Stella Creasy, converted Northern Ireland's abortion legislation from the most restrictive in Western Europe to the most permissive in terms of time limits. None of the main parties' bases support this extension of time limits for abortion to 28 weeks but only one-third of electors wish to return to the previous position of abortion being permitted only when the mother's life was in danger.

Meanwhile, divisions over an Irish Language Act remained acute. Only 8% of DUP and UUP voters believed there should be one. A mere 3% of SF and SDLP voters believed there should not. 'New Decade New Approach' fudged the issue by introducing Irish language and Ulster-Scots provisions and dedicated language commissioners akin to what a separate bill might provide, but via amendments to existing legislation rather than the standalone act demanded by SF and Irish language activists.

However, inter-communal relations beyond elections, parties and language issues appeared healthier. Almost 70% of respondents said they 'would not mind' if a close relative married outside their religion and an unconcerned majority was present among supporters of all parties. Only 7% stated they would 'mind a lot'. One-third of respondents said they would prefer to send their children to a single-religion school but almost half preferred a mixed-religion establishment.

5. A border poll?

The election took place amid speculation that Brexit would advance the cause of a united Ireland. The 1998 Good Friday Agreement permits the Secretary of State for Northern Ireland to call a border poll if it appears that public opinion on a united Ireland may be in favour. Supporters of Irish unity can play a long game. If a border poll is lost, another can—but does not automatically have to be—called seven years later. SF called for a referendum within five years. Yet the prospect of Irish unity still appeared distant. Table 10.8 shows the level of support for Irish unification by ideological association and Table 10.9 by party voted for.

The seemingly low support for a united Ireland appeared to offer unionists hope of a celebrating a bicentenary for Northern Ireland, let alone the 2021 centenary. That only 29% of electors say they would vote for a united Ireland in a border poll tomorrow, against 52% saying they would vote for Northern Ireland to remain part of the UK, might provide reassurance. When 'don't knows' are removed, the figures break down at 65 to 35% in favour of the status quo. If the results include only those who voted in the 2019 election, people we might reasonably assume would also show up on referendum day, 61% back Northern Ireland staying in the UK, against 39% wanting Irish unity. The findings offer an antidote to post-Brexit speculation concerning the imminence of Irish unity. From a very different perspective, hardline republicans might also claim vindication in dissenting from SF's strategy of accepting the northern consent principle.

The SF leadership has not claimed a united Ireland is inevitable but rather that unity is to be striven and prepared for. The party's approach is that a prospectus

Table 10.8 How would you vote in a border poll tomorrow, by self-identification as unionist, nationalist, or neither? (%)

	All	Unionist	Nationalist	Neither unionist nor nationalist
NI stay in UK	65	99	8	73
United Ireland	35	1	92	27

* This and subsequent tables exclude replies saying 'don't know'.

Table 10.9 How would you vote in a border poll tomorrow, by party voted for in the 2019 general election in Northern Ireland? (%)

	NI in UK	United Ireland
DUP	99	1
UUP	99	1
SF	8	92
SDLP	19	81
Alliance	70	30

for a united Ireland needs to be constructed in advance of a referendum on the constitutional question. Ideally, this would involve unionists but whether many would participate in discussions over the dissolution of 'their' country is debatable. Detailed consideration of the data perhaps offers more hope to republicans. First, although supporters of the constitutional status quo enjoy a big lead over backers of Irish unity, the indication that only a bare overall majority of Northern Ireland's citizens say they would vote for the maintenance of the union is hardly a resounding endorsement of a political entity. Secondly, there has been a 2% rise in support for Irish unification since the 2017 election. That appears modest but if such a rate of increase is maintained every two-and-a-half years, it would produce a majority for a united Ireland within a quarter-of-a-century. Thirdly, nearly 17% of respondents said they did not know how they would vote, giving a big number of electors to work upon.

The pro-unity election study figure of 29% is the highest so far from an interview-based survey. Online surveys have produced much higher levels of support for unification (e.g. Ashcroft, 2019). Given that a border poll in the gift of the British Secretary of State, who is required to call one when he or she believes that there may be a majority for a united Ireland, agreed criteria on how judgements of public opinion are formulated would be useful. At the general election, the combined support for nationalist and republican parties—those that favour a united Ireland—totalled 39%, 10% above support reported for a united Ireland

Table 10.10 Ideology, by party voted for, 2019 general election in Northern Ireland (%)

	Unionist	Nationalist	Neither
DUP	77	0	23
UUP	74	1	25
SF	0	80	20
SDLP	2	58	40
Alliance	25	19	56
All electors	31	26	43

in the 2019 general election study, but below online polling, while the combined unionist vote amounted to 42%, again 10% below the percentage saying they would vote for the union in a border poll. There are plenty who are constitutionally ambiguous or undecided, not reflected in the voting figures. While 81% of voters opted for unionist or nationalist parties at the general election, the largest section of the electorate—as distinct from voters—claims to be 'neither unionist nor nationalist' (Table 10.10) and breaks almost three-to-one in favour of the constitutional status quo. Among actual voters in 2019, SF needs to convert 12 in every 100 voters to back unity to bridge the 24-point gap between those who are pro-Union and pro-United Ireland. The most obvious group to target is those who say they are neither unionist nor nationalist but who do vote.

Nationalist parties combined were outpolled by unionist ones in first preference votes in both the 2019 council and European elections, by 44% to 36% each time. While plausible in the long-term, Irish unity still looks somewhat distant, even though unionists have lost their overall seat majorities at both Westminster and Stormont. The most obvious recent shifts have been, first, towards ideological dealignment and secondly, in movement to the constitutionally neutral Alliance Party whose support base resides principally among the 'neither' category and whose backers favour Northern Ireland's current status by more than two-to-one.The election study nonetheless indicates the considerable extent to which Irish identity is now held within a polity once seen as an acutely British part of the UK, as Table 10.11 indicates. There is little difference in size between the sections of the population holding British or Irish identities.Table 10.11 also indicates the continuing polarisation of identities. The eschewal of Britishness by nationalist party voters and the similar refusal of unionists to adopt an Irish identity are unsurprising. Perhaps, starker though is that while the hybrid Northern Irish identity has grown marginally since the 2017 general election, it is a minority taste even among those voting for a multi-ethnic party in Alliance. That said, Northern Irish identity is held by at least some of the supporters of each of the main parties.

Table 10.11 Primary national identity in Northern Ireland, by party voted for, 2019 general election in Northern Ireland (%)

	British	Irish	Northern Irish	Ulster	European	Other
DUP	79	0	19	2	0	0
UUP	74	1	20	3	2	0
SF	0	88	10	0	2	0
SDLP	2	73	20	1	4	0
Alliance	32	34	28	2	4	0
All electors	35	36	24	2	2	1

6. Conclusion

There were several election consequences for Northern Ireland. The first was the marginalisation of its elected representatives at Westminster, with the DUP removed from its pivotal Westminster role, SF absent as always and the three other MPs up against a large Conservative majority. Secondly, and interlinked, was that isolation at Westminster renewed the focus upon restoration of devolved power sharing, quickly restored as all parties recognised the need for a local power base. Thirdly, all three elections, council, European and Westminster, in Northern Ireland in 2019 confirmed the growth of the political centre, in the form of Alliance, steadfastly eschewing unionist and nationalist ideologies and in so doing refusing electoral pacts with parties on either side of the divide. Alliance finally appeared capable of tapping into some of the ever-growing number of those declining traditional ideological affiliations. The party was helped by frustration over the absence of devolution, with the DUP and SF seemingly blamed. Despite the rise of an 'other' party, the revived Assembly is still based upon the Good Friday Agreement framework of management of the unionist versus nationalist fracture. Finally, the shift towards Irish economic unity under a bespoke Brexit for Northern Ireland ensures that a constitutional United Ireland remains a salient issue. The Secretary of State can call a border poll under the terms of the Good Friday Agreement if it appears likely there is a majority favouring a United Ireland. That still seems unlikely anytime soon but, with SF a significant political force on either side of the border, the constitutional referendums in both jurisdictions required prior to reunification remain a live long-term prospect.

References

Alliance Party (2019) *Demand Better*. Westminster Election Manifesto, Belfast, Northern Ireland, Alliance Party.

Ashcroft, L. (2019) 'My Northern Ireland Survey Finds the Union on a Knife-edge', accessed at www.lordashcroftpolls.com on 1 April 2020.

Birrell, D. and Heenan, D. (2019) 'The Confidence and Supply Agreement between the Conservative Party and the Democratic Unionist Party: Implications for the Barnett Formula and Intergovernmental Relations in the UK', *Parliamentary Affairs*. 10.1093/pa/gsz012.

Democratic Unionist Party (2019) *Let's Get the UK Moving Again*, Westminster Election Manifesto, Belfast, Northern Ireland, Democratic Unionist Party.

Donaldson, J. (2020) 'Spotlight' , BBC1 Northern Ireland, Belfast, 3 March.

Garry, J. (2017) 'The EU Referendum Vote in Northern Ireland: Implications for Our Understanding of Citizens' Views and Behaviour', *Northern Ireland Assembly Knowledge Exchange Seminar Series*, accessed at http://www.niassembly.gov.uk/globalas sets/documents/raise/knowledge_exchange/briefing_papers/series6/garry121016.pdf on 24 April 2020.

HM Government (2017) 'Confidence and Supply Agreement between the Conservative and Unionist Party and the Democratic Unionist Party', accessed at https://www.gov. uk/government/publications/conservative-and-dup-agreement-and-uk-government-fi nancial-support-for-northern-ireland on 26 April 2020.

HM Government (2020) *New Decade New Approach*, London, HMSO, accessed athttps:// assets.publishing.service.gov.uk/government/uploads/system/uploads/attachment_data /file/856998/2020-01-08_a_new_decade__a_new_approach.pdf on 20 April 2020.

Johnson, B. (2018) Speech to the Democratic Unionist Party Annual Conference, Belfast, accessed at https://www.youtube.com/watch? v=FRGBU2TNc_k on 31 March 2020.

Keep, M. (2016) 'Public Expenditure by Country and Region', House of Commons Library Briefing Paper, London, House of Common, 04033, November.

Mitchell, P., Evans, G. and O'Leary, B. (2009) 'Extremist Outbidding in Ethnic Party Systems is Not Inevitable: Tribune Parties in Northern Ireland', *Political Studies*, **57**, 397–421.

Russell, R. (2013) 'Census 2011: Key Statistics at Assembly Area Level', *Northern Ireland Research and Information Service Information Paper NIAR 161-13*, accessed at http:// www.niassembly.gov.uk/globalassets/documents/raise/publications/2012/general/7013. pdf on 27 January 2020.

Tonge, J., Braniff, M., Hennessey, T., McAuley, J. and Whiting, S. (2014) *The Democratic Unionist Party: From Protest to Power*, Oxford, Oxford University Press.

Britain Votes (2019) 189–207

JUSTIN FISHER*

Party Finance in 2019: Advantage Conservative Party

With only two and half years since the previous election, there might have been a temptation to think little would change in terms of party finance. Certainly, there were no major reviews or legislative change. But, the fallout from the 2015 election continued and was finally resolved in court, with the ruling affecting party behaviour in terms of allocating campaign expenditure. And, just as in 2017, the snap election established Conservative financial dominance. But 2019 did more than that. The Conservatives' financial advantage became even more marked, buoyed by further growth in corporate donations. For Labour, the legacy of the Corbyn leadership was a very positive increase in income from party members but equally a heavy reliance on one union for campaign donations.

1. Developments in party finance

Unlike the previous three parliaments, there was no major review of party finance (Fisher, 2010, 2015) nor a substantive change in the law (Fisher, 2018a). This is not surprising, given the brevity of the 2017 parliament and the other demands on parliamentary time. However, there was—nevertheless—an important development, which had implications for how some parties interpreted existing legislation. The development related to the appropriate allocation of campaign expenditure to candidates or parties. As Fisher (2018a, pp. 173–176) outlined, this had been a growing issue in British politics. Ostensibly, the distinction is clear—that which promotes a party is counted as national (party) expenditure, while that which promotes the candidate is counted as constituency-level. In reality, the distinction is not so neat. Nor indeed is it a new concern, with the issue first being tested in court in 1952 (Fisher, 2018a, pp. 173, 174). And, as Fisher (2018a, pp. 174–176) explains, over the last 30 years, developments in technology and campaign techniques have become such that the boundaries between national and constituency-level spending have become less distinct. This is a consequence of newer technologically driven practices such as telephone voter identification, nationally sent direct mail and targeted advertisements in social

*Justin Fisher, Department of Social and Political Sciences, Brunel University, Justin.fisher@brunel.ac.uk

doi:10.1093/pa/gsaa028

media (Fisher *et al.*, 2007, 2011; Fisher, 2018*a*) as well as longer-standing practices including national party figures—especially party leaders—focussing their election tours on marginal seats (Butler and Kavanagh, 1974, p. 224; Fisher and Denver, 2008, p. 816) and party volunteers descending on target seats to assist with campaigns. In the last example, parties would often assist with travel for these volunteers. In all five aspects of campaigning, expenditure was ascribed principally to the national party, rather than the candidate; the view being that they promoted the party rather than the candidate explicitly.

As Fisher (2018*a*) argues, these developments have been important for three reasons. First, the national campaign has been effectively subsumed into supporting constituency-level activities (Fisher, 2010, 2015). Secondly, and as a consequence, the distinctions between expenditure on national and constituency-level campaigns have become increasingly blurred and the ability to ascribe expenditure meaningfully as being national or constituency-level has become increasingly challenging. Thirdly, the increasing blurring has led some to claim that the candidate spending limits in constituencies are now effectively meaningless, since so much national spending is devoted to supporting campaigns in individual constituencies.

Such circumstances have led to calls for reform such that national-level activity which is focussed on constituencies should count as candidate expenditure. On the face of it, it is a potentially appealing idea. The reality, however, is more complex (Fisher, 2018*b*, pp. 61–64). If implemented, then national parties would need to apportion all their direct mail, telephone calls, billboard placement, newspaper advertisements and social media activity to various constituencies. This is not straightforward. Regional or local newspapers frequently cut across constituency boundaries so can be argued to not be constituency-level expenditure. Equally, billboards whether fixed or mobile, can be seen by anyone walking or driving past. Direct mail, telephone calls and social media advertisements may be easier to ascribe but there are potentially high administrative costs in so doing and, of course, such apportionment would need to be available for auditing. There are also other consequences: such a move would effectively centralise all constituency-level spending, since in order to comply, the central party would need to control both national and constituency-level spending. It would also almost certainly lead to election spending being even more concentrated in parties' target seats than is already the case. Since this accounts for only a minority of seats, the vast bulk of voters would enjoy very little of the beneficial effects of campaigning, which would be likely to have an impact on turnout. As things stand, the distinction between national- and constituency-level spending means that sufficient money is spent in non-targeted seats not to depress turnout overall (Fisher *et al.*, 2016; Trumm and Sudulich, 2018). So, the current system is imperfect and open to manipulation by national parties. However, it is not at all clear that removing the distinction between national- and constituency-level expenditure would deliver preferable alternatives, especially if it resulted in campaigns being subject to repeated legal challenge.

For all these more abstract discussions, however, new developments following the 2015 election became a matter for the courts and a judgement in 2019 had potentially significant ramifications. It related to the case of the Thanet South constituency and the 2015 election (Fisher, 2018a, p. 176). Specifically, it related to the reporting of the candidate's election expenses during the short campaign (post-dissolution). The Crown Prosecution Service concluded that there was sufficient evidence to authorise charges against three people—the candidate, his election agent and a Conservative Party official. In the end, the candidate and agent were found not guilty of making a false election expenses declaration. However, the Conservative Party official, Marion Little, was found guilty of encouraging or assisting an election offence. The judge noted that the overspending of the candidate's permitted election expenses was substantial, and that the official had created dishonest documents and presented them to the candidate and his agent for signing. By so doing, she had 'placed them at grave risk of conviction'. In addition, the judge ruled that Little had worked for at least 50% of her time as the candidate's campaign manager and agent (in all but name), but that these salary costs had not been ascribed to the candidate's expenses. He added that 'There appears to have been a belief that Central Headquarters staff salaries and accommodation of staff employed by Central Headquarters were a central party expense, even if those staff were living temporarily in a constituency for the duration of the election campaign'. He added that the official '. . .was not alone in that she worked in a culture which tolerated some of what she did' but '. . .that there is no evidence that anyone other than Marion Little was aware of the dishonest calculations and concealment of invoices'. Little's sentence was suspended for two years (on the grounds of the ill-health of her husband), but the judge concluded that: 'This case should operate as a warning to those involved in future elections that prison is the usual consequence of deliberately corrupt practice on a significant scale' (Courts and Tribunals Judiciary, 2019).

The implications of this ruling were significant because it was the national party official rather than the candidate or agent who was found guilty. Hitherto, it would have been more likely to be the candidate and agent who bore responsibility for the overspend. Additionally, it brought into sharp relief what expenses should be ascribed to candidates and which to national parties, especially in relation to leadership visits, the deployment of activists in particular constituencies and the associated staff time. Fisher (2018a, p. 176) suggested that the case might mean that 'all parties will seek to make absolutely sure that they are not vulnerable to accusations of mis-apportioning funds through effective self-policing'. This assertion proved to be broadly correct though parties differed in how they reacted.

For some parties, the ruling was a landmark; it introduced a new interpretation of the law, perhaps even changing the law. This was particularly apparent with visits by leadership figures to seats, such that costs of any visit were now potentially classified as candidate expenses. Parties' interpretations differed, however. One sought to keep such expenses as national ones by ensuring that the candidate was not seen with the visitor, going so far as to equipping the leadership tour buses with wholly party-spend compliant canvass materials and doorstep canvas scripts for door knocking. Other parties went further, apportioning leadership visits to candidate expenses, even if the candidate was not present. Leaflets, too, were affected. In target seats, for example, one party produced leaflets that featured information about the party and party leader on one side and information about the local candidate on the other. The costs of such leaflets were split evenly between candidate and party spend. Yet not all parties saw the ruling as being important. One described it as undoubtedly being a precedent case, 'but it might be a precedent case for not being stupid',[1] suggesting the law was already sufficiently clear. Whether or not this is a reasonable view is a moot point. But, it is clear that the ruling changed some aspects of behaviour—significantly for some parties—and suggested that there may now be sufficient clarity to not require the kinds of reforms that some had called for—at least in respect of visits to a constituency.

2. Trends in party income and expenditure

The normal pattern of party income is that it cycles with general elections—rising sharply in the year before an election and falling away again in the year after. This happened for all three parties, unlike the period after the 2015 election when Labour's post-election finances were buoyed significantly by the two leadership elections of 2015 and 2016 (Fisher, 2018*a*). That said, parties were affected to different degrees. While Conservative income declined after the 2017 election, the party still had a good financial year in 2018, securing a higher level of real terms income in the year after a general election than any of the previous three (2010, 2015 and 2017) and nearly doubling income from membership from £0.8 million to £1.5 million. This enabled the party to plan for any future election, spending nearly £2 million in staff costs expanding its campaign manager programme (Conservative Party, 2019, p. 6). Labour also generated a similar increase in revenue from membership—some £765,000—despite a decline of 8.1% (nearly

---

[1]The source of this and other non-published quotations in this article are interviews with national officials at the Conservative, Labour and Liberal Democrat parties

46,000) in membership. And, like the Conservatives, the party allocated increased resources for a future general election, noting the political uncertainty following the loss of the government's majority in 2017. Labour increased spending on staff costs by £2.7 million as an investment for future elections (Labour Party, 2019, p. 2). By way of contrast, the Liberal Democrats secured their lowest level of real terms central income since 2002, following a significant decline in donor income in the absence of a general election or referendum. Membership also fell by 3.9% (nearly 4,000), leaving the party to focus on 'restructuring initiatives' (Liberal Democrats, 2019, p. 5).

At the time of writing (April 2020), full accounts are only available up to the end of 2018. However, a review of annual central party income since 1989 (when the Liberal Democrats first filed accounts) shows a series of phases in respect of the Conservatives and Labour (see Figure 11.1). First, the phase of 'normal service', where the Conservatives were clearly the wealthier of the two main parties—a longer standing position that predates these graphs (Fisher, 2000, 2010). Secondly, there is the 'Blair revolution', where Labour became not only the party of government, but also the wealthiest party by some margin. Thirdly, the resumption of 'normal service', from soon after the 2005 election, with the

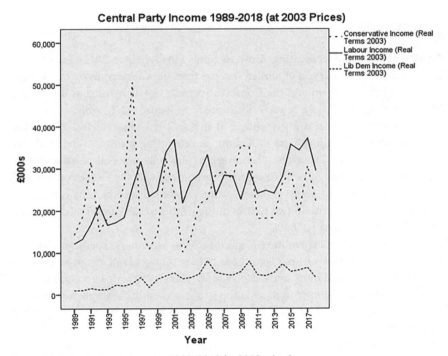

Figure 11.1 Central party income, 1989–2018 (at 2003 prices)

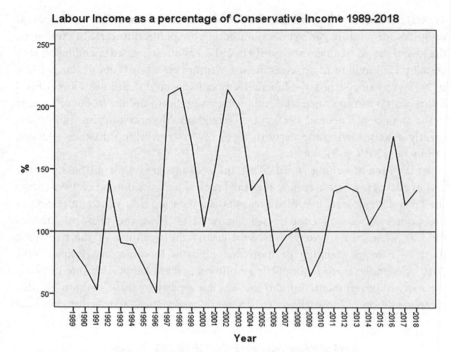

Figure 11.2 Labour income as a percentage of Conservative income, 1989–2018

Conservatives again generating most income. Finally, since 2011, Labour has again enjoyed higher levels of annual income than the Conservatives, though the difference between them and the Conservatives was not as marked as during the 'Blair revolution'. This is clearly illustrated in Figure 11.2, which calculates Labour annual income as a percentage of that of the Conservatives. Where the line rises above 100 on the graph, Labour is generating more income, and *vice versa*. For the Liberal Democrats, however, there is only one real phase through-out this period—that of relative poverty compared with the Conservatives and Labour. As Figure 11.1 shows, Liberal Democrat annual income only came close to that of either of the main two parties in the depths of the Conservative malaise in the late 1990s and early 2000s.

In terms of annual expenditure (Figure 11.3), as we might expect, similar pat-terns are evident. Not surprisingly, those parties that generate more income on an annual basis, spend more and the periods of Conservative or Labour annual fi-nancial advantage are mirrored, as is the gap in expenditure levels between the Liberal Democrats and the main two parties. What has been an important change, however, is the parties' financial prudence since the late 2000s. Figure 11.4 shows annual central expenditure as a percentage of annual central

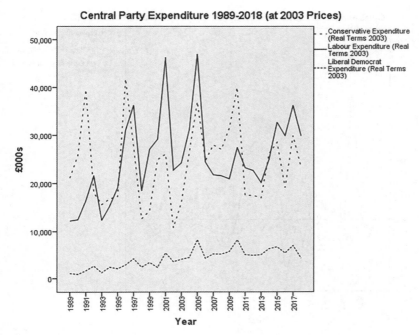

Figure 11.3 Central party expenditure, 1989–2018 (at 2003 prices)

income. Where the lines on the graph fall above 100, the parties are spending more than they earn in each year, and *vice versa*. In the period up until 2007 to 2008, parties regularly spent more in any year than they generated in income— considerably so in some years. This was for many reasons, not least that the income required for parties' annual operating costs were not well served by a cycle of income that reflected the timing of the general election. With parties fighting elections in every year and seeking to maintain their organisations, the flow of income was not matching their regular financial needs. Since 2007, however, the parties have clearly exercised significant levels of financial restraint. The Conservative and Labour parties have only rarely spent more in one year than they have earned. The picture for the Liberal Democrats has been slightly less positive. The party has continued to struggle to earn more than it needs to spend on an annual basis, though overspends have generally been rather lower than in the pre-2007 period. Overall, however, it shows that parties have become much more financially responsible. Indeed, in many ways, it would not be an exaggeration to think of them as models of efficiency—undertaking a great deal of activity with relatively little money.

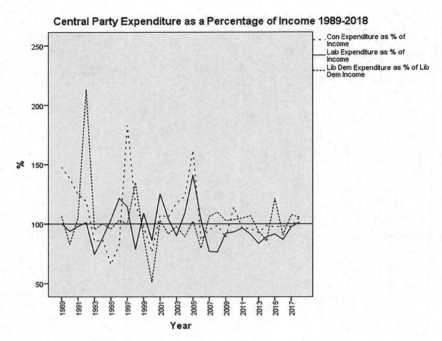

Figure 11.4 Central party expenditure as a percentage of income, 1989–2018

3. Donations 2010–2019

Figures 11.1–11.4 provide excellent context to the finances of the 2019 election, but of course, only go up to the end of 2018. So, to gain a fuller picture of central party income, we examine declared cash donations in each quarter from Quarter 3 in 2010 (the first quarter after the 2010 election) to Quarter 4 in 2019, which includes the 2019 election and the period up to 31 December (Figures 11.5 and 11.6). A description of some terminology is important. Declared donations are all donations of £7,500 or more made to the national party (rather than to a constituency one). The threshold of £7,500 is set for the reporting of donations to the Electoral Commission. The original threshold stipulated by the Political Parties, Elections and Referendums Act 2000 was £5,000, and was raised to £7,500 by the Political Parties and Elections Act 2009. Donations are reported every quarter by the Electoral Commission (and weekly from dissolution until polling day). Cash donations are distinct from non-cash donations, which are more commonly known as payments-in-kind. So, these data do not provide a complete picture of party income (as any donations below £7,500 are not captured), but they do reveal patterns in terms of sizable donations. As in 2017, this is particularly relevant in 2019 on account of the election cycle being truncated by the early poll.

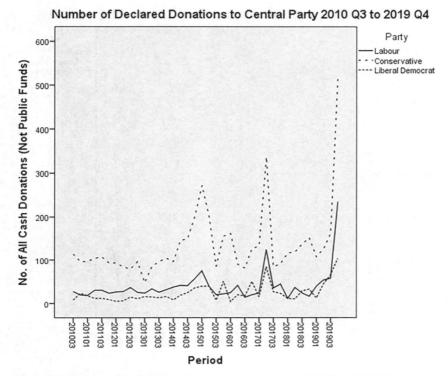

Number of Declared Donations to Central Party 2010 Q3 to 2019 Q4

Figure 11.5 Number of declared donations to the central party, 2010 Q3 to 2019 Q4

Figure 11.5 shows the number of declared cash donations. It reveals, first, that in all three elections in this period (2015, 2017 and 2019), the Conservatives experienced a significant boost in income in the run up to the election. This boost was more gradual in 2015 because the date of the election was known in advance as a result of the Fixed-term Parliaments Act. In both 2017 and 2019, however, the boost was rapid reflecting the sudden calling of the elections. Labour and the Liberal Democrats also benefited in similar ways, albeit with far fewer declared donations.

Secondly, while the Conservatives were able to attract 337 declared cash donations in the quarter that included the 2017 election, in 2019, they attracted some 523, with obvious financial benefits. Labour also received more declared donations in the final quarter of 2019 than in the two previous elections, at 235, but that was less than half of the number made to the Conservatives. The Liberal Democrats also received the most they had done over this period in Quarter 4 2019, with 103 declared donations.

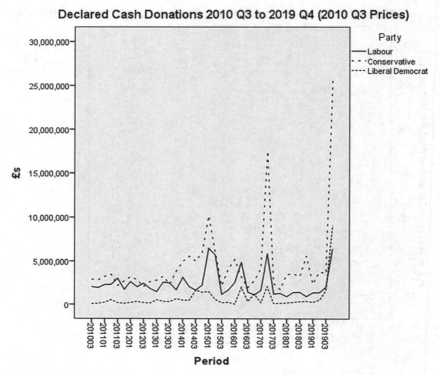

Figure 11.6 Declared cash donations, 2010 Q3 to 2019 Q4 (2010 Q3 prices)

Figure 11.6 illustrates how these donations were translated into income. Not surprisingly, the peaks and troughs in income from declared cash donations reflect the numbers of donations (indeed they correlate at 0.9), but what is intriguing about Figure 11.6 is how it reveals the scale of the Conservative advantage in 2019. In Quarter 4 2019, the Conservatives generated some £33.6 million in declared donations (the figure in the graph being lower as it is adjusted for prices over time). In the period up to and including polling day, this included 3 separate donations of £1 million (2 of which were from individuals and one from a company), 2 of £900,000, 2 of £750,000 and 12 of £500,000.

By way of contrast, Labour attracted £8.3 million in the same period, nearly £4.6 million of which came from Unite the Union. Indeed, the Liberal Democrats received more than Labour from declared cash donations in Q4 2019, some £11.8 million, though £8 million of this came in one single donation from Lord David Sainsbury. Even combined, the volume of declared donations received by Labour and the Liberal Democrats represented only 60% of the amount received by the Conservatives.

The Conservatives, then, had a significant financial advantage over their political opponents. In earlier elections, this might not have mattered so much in respect of the campaign as the lead time for many campaigning techniques such as direct mail and billboards meant that the more significant income for a party's campaign needed to be generated some months before polling day. That remains the case for campaigning techniques such as direct mail which endure. But the growth of digital campaigning is very significant in this respect as the lead time is considerably shorter, and therefore 'late money'—money that comes in during the campaign—can still be spent with the potential, at least, to be effective. Of course, there are national spending limits, set at £30,000 multiplied by the number of seats contested by a party. Thus, for a party that contested all 632 British seats (less that of the Speaker, making it 631), the limit for the 365 days before the election would be £18.93 million. The Conservative financial advantage in declared donations must be seen in that context. But regardless, the sizeable volume of donations meant that decisions would be guided much more by the expenditure limit than whether an activity could be afforded. Indeed, it is worth noting that the figure of £30,000 per seat contested has not been adjusted for inflation since its introduction in the 2000 Act. In real terms, the figure is now worth around 59% of what it was in the original legislation—approximately £17,690 (equating to a national limit of around £11.6 million based on 631 seats). Nonetheless, given the significant financial advantage enjoyed by one of the parties, it may have been beneficial that the figure had not been adjusted, else the spending disparity would have been even larger.

4. Campaign donations

A further illustration of the Conservatives' financial advantage in 2019 can be illustrated when examining donations made during the period between dissolution and polling day. The Political Parties, Elections and Referendums Act requires donations to be made weekly during this period. When the legislation was first introduced, what appeared like a well-intentioned provision in terms of transparency was of limited use because of the lead-time associated with major campaign initiatives. A good example of this was in the first general election under the regulations (2001) when the Conservatives received a donation of £5 million just before polling day and were required to declare it in their weekly reports, even though there was almost no opportunity to spend any of it on the election campaign (Fisher, 2001, p. 128). However, the growth of digital campaigning, with significantly shorter lead times means that this level of transparency is now much more informative.

Table 11.1 details all declared donations (cash and non-cash) and the category of cash donor over the period. All parties received more in this period in absolute

Table 11.1 Source of election period declared cash donations and levels of declared non-cash donations

	Conservative		Labour		Lib Dems	
	(£)	No.	(£)	No.	(£)	No.
Individual	13,246,521	193	159,442	13	1,004,998	32
Company	5,989,500	76	120,000	4	241,000	6
Trade union	–	–	5,039,754	28	–	–
Unincorporated associations	88,000	2	10,500	1	–	–
Limited liability partnership	20,000	1	–	–	–	–
Total cash donations	19,344,021	272	5,329,696	46	1,245,998	38
Total non-cash donations	26,887	3	81,600	2	–	–
Total all donations	19,370,908	275	5,411,296	48	1,245,998	38

Source: The Electoral Commission.

Table 11.2 Timing of weekly declared cash and non-cash donations

£s	Week 1	Week 2	Week 3	Week 4	Week 5	Week 6	Total
Conservative	5,673,646	2,967,000	3,590,500	3,201,965	2,545,500	1,392,297	19,370,908
Labour	218,500	3,488,000	521,909	1,017,417	165,471	0	5,411,296
Lib Dems	275,000	251,000	509,998	80,000	130,000	0	1,245,998

Source: The Electoral Commission.

terms than in 2017—the Conservatives received more than £6.6 million, Labour nearly £900,000 and the Liberal Democrats £30,000 (the party's large donation of £8 million coming in days before parliament was dissolved). Once again, the Conservatives had a significant financial advantage. Over 270 declared donations were made during the campaign period, totalling £19.3 million. This compared with Labour's 46, totalling up to £5.4 million and the Liberal Democrats' 38, totalling up to £1.2 million.

Table 11.2 details when the donations were received by the parties during the campaign. The Conservatives received a high volume of donations throughout. Indeed, the party received more in the first week (£5.7 million) than Labour did over the whole campaign (£5.4 million). And, although Week 6 lasted for only two days (11 and 12 December), the Conservatives received more in that period (£1.4 million) than the Liberal Democrats did over the whole period (£1.2 million). The Liberal Democrats actually got off to a better start in fundraising terms than Labour. In the first week of the campaign, the party received some £275,000 in declared cash donations compared with Labour's £218,500. By Week 2, however, Labour's large donations began to appear. £3,488,000 in declared cash donations was received, £3,008,000 of which came from Unite.

Coupled with that, trends noted in the 2017 election were again evident. The growing attractiveness of the Conservative Party to corporate donors continued. In 2010 and 2015, the party received 28 and 25 corporate cash donations, respectively, in the campaign period. In 2017, there were 48. The snap election in 2017 almost certainly inflated that figure, but the 2019 election was also called suddenly and the comparable number of corporate donations in this election was 76. Equally, corporate cash donations amounted to 25, 17 and 23% of the Conservatives' declared cash donations during 2010, 2015 and 2017 campaign periods. In 2019, that figure had risen to 31%. As in 2017, the likely implication was that companies were giving to the Conservatives in large numbers (and volume) in response to the growing perceived threat from the Labour Party—a perceived threat that had declined in the previous 30 years (Fisher, 1994, 2018a).

Trends also continued for Labour. Just as in 2017, the vast majority of declared cash donations in the campaign period came from trade unions—95%. In 2017, it was 96%. The comparable figures for 2015 and 2010 were 72 and 64%. Not only did the vast majority of the declared cash donations come from trade unions but a very large proportion, some 61%, came from just one: Unite. Relatedly, the proportion of declared cash donations from individuals was again very small at just 3%. In 2010, 2015 and 2017, the proportions were 24, 12 and 4%, respectively.

5. Election period expenditure

5.1 Conservatives

In the 2017 general election, despite being the party of government, the Conservative party machine was under-prepared (Fisher, 2018a). That was not the case in 2019. The national party was much better prepared for an early election, both organisationally, and as we have seen, financially. This meant, for example, that the party was far clearer about any campaign-related spending throughout 2019 to ensure that there was no danger of overspending on the national limit. Indeed, such was the party's relatively buoyant financial position that the 'late money' had relatively little impact on the digital advertising budget, the party having committed to a comparatively high level anyway. The Conservatives focussed most expenditure on digital advertising, direct mail and more generic print, there being rough parity between spend on digital and print.

The types of digital spending did change, however. In 2015 and 2017, Facebook had been the principal platform for digital campaigning. Facebook again dominated but was not quite as dominant as before. So, in addition to Facebook, there was digital advertising spend on Instagram (as part of Facebook), Google, YouTube and Snapchat. In addition, the party used advertising to 'take over' the websites of national newspapers such as the *Daily Express*. All of this contributed to digital advertising being more broadcast than narrowcast. Hitherto, much of the discussion around digital advertising had been in respect of micro-targeting. However, 2019 marked a shift. To an extent, this was due to Facebook itself making it more difficult for parties to use their own tools to segment the population, in part as a response to users coming off the platform if they received too much unsolicited advertising. It was also due to users changing their privacy settings. Instead, therefore, the party focussed its digital advertising on particular demographic groups rather than micro-targeted individuals within them.

Reflecting this broadcast approach, the party differentiated between digital advertising and social media. The former was designed to be shared and to spark discussion, the latter seen as a process of people communicating with each other. To that end, the spend on digital advertising was designed to give people 'something that they are going to talk about at the water cooler...even if they didn't agree with a word'. This change in emphasis reflected changes in staffing, the party bringing in people who 'weren't scarred by 1997, 2001 and 2010' and who were less concerned about any negative feedback to the party's advertising.

As in previous elections, while much of the election commentary focussed on digital campaigning, significant expenditure still occurred on printed matter, such that the budget matched that of digital campaigning. This was for two principal reasons. First, there was familiarity. The stakes in election campaigns are too high to simply shift strategies completely—especially if there is either evidence or perception that it is effective. As a Conservative official said: 'We tend to take an approach of, "What did we do before?" Unless we knew it didn't work, let's do quite a lot of that again, plus some extra stuff'. Secondly, direct mail allows for much more precise micro-targeting than digital for the reasons described above. Direct mail is much more expensive per person than digital but remains an important part of campaign spending.

Just as compliance issues shaped the focus of some of the digital expenditure, so they also impacted on telephone voter identification. The party continued to devote some expenditure to this approach, but its use was limited compared with previous elections as a result of existing telephone calling restrictions and the Information Commissioner's Office delivering more explicit guidance on the purchase of telephone numbers, such that parties can no longer purchase numbers unless the owners have expressly given consent for these to be shared with political parties.

A final significant area of expenditure was on polling. The party used a range of approaches, including their own multi-level regression poststratification (MRP) analysis to inform spending decisions (rather than predict the result). They also ran polling in representative areas (rather than regions) to help inform decisions. The principle of representative areas was, like digital advertising, based on demographic profiles. The party used these polls together with public polls and largely real-time feedback through canvassing (delivered through an app) to shift digital and direct mail expenditure during the campaign.

5.2 Labour

The 2017 Labour campaign was marked by a lack of coordination, with the leader's office and the central party effectively running two campaigns (Fisher, 2018a). In 2019, this was not an issue. But, just as in 2017, print continued to play an important role in campaign expenditure alongside the continuing growth of digital techniques. Indeed, overall spend was slightly more on print than on digital. This was in part because direct mail could be more finely targeted than digital and partly because a lot of direct mail was distributed in key seats before the election was called. However, changes in the make-up of the party made it slightly more difficult to capitalise on the distribution of mail. Typically, the party has sought to follow-up direct mail with contact on the doorstep. However, this has not always been possible, in part due to shifts in the geography of members. In the past, Labour's membership was distributed very 'efficiently' with large memberships in target seats (Fisher *et al.*, 2006). This, of course, was not by design, but gave the party an electoral advantage. Changes in the geographical distribution of the party's membership, however, have meant that the largest local parties are now found in London and the major English cities—not in the party's marginal seats, and those in the cities were often less willing to campaign elsewhere.

Labour spent nearly as much on digital advertising as it did on printed matter—predominantly on Facebook and Instagram (for younger voters), but also on Snapchat. In addition, there was some advertising on local media. The big advantages in terms of spending was that digital was much cheaper before the campaign proper started, but also that it was easier to shift emphasis as the campaign developed. This became necessary, for example, after the first YouGov MRP poll in *The Times*, which led to a changed strategy from offensive to defensive, with a focus on supporting the more defensive seats. Like the Conservatives, however, Labour found Facebook advertising to be less finely targeted than print. But the party also encountered issues with Facebook's 'incubation period' for adverts, where these are checked. This could be for up to 36 hours and meant that more planning was needed in digital advertising than in the past, and that rapid response advertising via Facebook was often not possible. Regulatory challenges also led to the party devoting little expenditure to telephone canvassing, and the timing of the election in the middle of winter also limited expenditure on items such as rallies. However, Labour did continue to conduct polling, running a poll of 20,000 voters and conducting MRP analysis in August (delaying the poll slightly as the party was confident an election was coming).

5.3 Liberal Democrats

Like the other parties, the principal items of campaign expenditure were digital and print, with the amount spent on digital increasing for the third consecutive election. Digital spend was principally on Facebook and Instagram, but unlike the other parties, the newer challenges in micro-targeting presented fewer problems. The reason was that the Liberal Democrats were principally targeting Remain-leaning voters. Such voters were much easier to reach on Facebook because they often shared similar demographic characteristics, such that Facebook could easily identify them. Coupled with that, the party had previously been running its Stop Brexit campaign, meaning the party could more easily target those voters who had previously supported that. All in all, it meant that voters in the party's target seats saw a lot of digital material, with adverts to Remainers focussing on Brexit and those who were less strongly Remain seeing adverts on the party's other policy areas, such as health and education. Like the other parties, however, the Liberal Democrats found telephone canvassing challenging, as a result of restrictions on obtaining numbers.

In addition to digital and print, the Liberal Democrats also devoted expenditure to wraparound adverts on large regional papers, including the *London Evening Standard*. In part, this advertising in the regional press was to support target seats. In London, for example, it was focussed on commuters from the party's targets in St Albans and Guildford as well as in some London seats. But of course, regional papers cover many seats so may not be so useful in targeting terms. For the Liberal Democrats, however, such advertising was also about building 'a background of presence'—reinforcing the idea that the party was in electoral contention in the region.

Like the other parties, the Liberal Democrats also conducted their own polling. They conducted an MRP analysis in the summer and conducted a range of constituency polls prior to the regulated period. Indeed, the party released details of these internal polls where they had moved into a competitive position. As with newspaper advertising, they needed to convince voters that they were now in a possible position to win seats. The party also used real-time feedback from canvassing from an app, but like Labour, had experienced a big shift in the distribution of its membership. Many had joined the party after the 2015 and 2017 elections, the EU referendum in 2016 and the 2019 European Elections. As result, the membership moved from being efficiently distributed in target seats (Fisher *et al.*, 2006) to being very heavily concentrated in Remain voting areas.

What really marked the Liberal Democrats' campaign out, though was its finances, despite the relatively poor financial year in 2018. As we have seen, a large donation came in just before the campaign, but the party also had an indication that several significant donations would be forthcoming as an election became more likely. As Figures 11.5 and 11.6 show, this uplift began in Quarter 2 2019. The party therefore planned an extensive campaign accordingly, and for the first time, had to be mindful of the national party spending limit, such that the party limited the use of party literature in non-target seats to ensure the limit was not breached. In the end, however, the party spent less than planned. As it became clear that the party's vote was getting squeezed, resource was progressively retrenched towards supporting a smaller pool of seats.

6. Conclusion

The 2019 election was characterised by a very significant financial advantage for the Conservatives. Large sums of money flooded into the party's coffers in 2019 and particularly in the run-up to the election. Neither Labour nor the Liberal Democrats were in financial poverty, but the Conservatives' election period income dwarfed theirs. Only the spending regulations introduced in 2000 kept the Conservatives' spending advantage from being even larger. Beyond that, some patterns continued from previous elections. Digital campaigning continued to grow in importance but, yet again, its importance (at least in terms of campaign expenditure) was arguably overstated. Spending on printed materials continued to be as important—the role of print is certainly not yet dead. And, because of changes in the behaviour of online platforms, print was the only means of micro-targeting. Digital advertising was critically important, but it was more broadcast than narrowcast compared with previous campaigns, meaning that the trend of the national campaign being subsumed into merely supporting constituency ones slowed a little. Digital advertising will undoubtedly continue to grow and become an even more important component of campaign spend. But just as in previous elections, there has been a tendency to assume that most spend is through this medium. That assumption remains incorrect. Coupled with that, campaigners on the ground still matter a great deal—knocking on doors, following up direct mail and sharing discussion about digital adverts. However, Labour and the Liberal Democrats are now in a position that has hitherto afflicted the Conservatives—their members are dispropor-tionately in seats in which they are already likely to do well. Overall, then 2019 was advantage Conservatives and in party finance terms, at least, 'normal ser-vice' appears to have been resumed.

Funding

Part of the research featured in this article was funded by the Economic & Social Research Council (ES/T015187/1).

References

Butler, D. E. and Kavanagh, D. (1974) *The British General Election of February 1974*, London, Macmillan.

Conservative Party (2019) *Annual Report and Financial Statements for the Year Ended 31 December 2018*, London, Conservative and Unionist Central Office.

Courts and Tribunal Judiciary (2019) 'R. V Mackinlay, Gray and Little', accessed at https://www.judiciary.uk/wp-content/uploads/2019/01/marion-little-sentencing-remarks.pdf on 25 March 2020.

Fisher, J. (1994) 'Why Do Companies Make Donations to Political Parties?', *Political Studies*, **42**, 690–699.

Fisher, J. (2000) 'Economic Evaluation or Electoral Necessity? Evaluating the System of Voluntary Income to Political Parties', *The British Journal of Politics and International Relations*, **2**, 179–204.

Fisher, J. (2001) 'Campaign Finance: Elections under New Rules', *Parliamentary Affairs*, **54**, 689–700.

Fisher, J. (2010) 'Party Finance – Normal Service Resumed', *Parliamentary Affairs*, **63**, 778–801.

Fisher, J. (2015) 'Party Finance: The Death of the National Campaign', *Parliamentary Affairs*, **68**, 133–153.

Fisher, J. (2018a) 'Party Finance', *Parliamentary Affairs*, **71**, 171–188.

Fisher, J. (2018b) 'Party Election Expenditure Election Effects: National *vs.* District Level and the Regulatory Challenges'. In Mendilow, J. and Phelippeau, E. (eds.), *Handbook of Political Party Funding*, Cheltenham, Edward Elgar, pp. 55–77.

Fisher, J., Denver, D. and Hands, G. (2006) 'The Relative Electoral Impact of Central Party Co-Ordination and Party Size at Constituency Level', *Electoral Studies*, **25**, 664–676.

Fisher, J., Denver, D., Fieldhouse, E., Cutts, D., and Russell, A. (2007) 'Constituency Campaigning in 2005: Ever More Centralization'. In Wring, D., Green, J., Mortimore,

R. and Atkinson, S. (eds.), *Political Communications: The British General Election of 2005*, Basingstoke, Palgrave, pp. 79–92.

Fisher, J. and Denver, D. (2008) 'From Foot-Slogging to Call Centres and Direct Mail: A Framework for Analysing the Development of District-Level Campaigning', *European Journal of Political Research*, **47**, 794–826.

Fisher, J., Cutts, D. and Fieldhouse, E. (2011) 'Constituency Campaigning in 2010'. In Wring, D., Mortimore, R. and Atkinson, S. (eds.), *Political Communication in Britain: The Leader Debates, the Campaign and Media in the 2010 General Election*, Basingstoke, Palgrave, pp.198–217.

Fisher, J., Fieldhouse, E., Johnston, R., Pattie, C. and Cutts, D. (2016) 'Is All Campaigning Equally Positive? The Impact of District Level Campaigning on Voter Turnout at the 2010 British General Election', *Party Politics*, **22**, 215–226.

Labour Party (2019) *Financial Statements for the Year Ended 31 December 2018*, London, Labour Party.

Liberal Democrats (2019) *The Liberal Democrats (Federal Party) Annual Report Year Ended 31 December 2018*, London, Liberal Democrats.

Trumm, S. and Sudulich, L. (2018) 'What Does It Take to Make It to the Polling Station? The Effects of Campaign Activities on Electoral Participation', *Party Politics*, **24**, 168–184.

Britain Votes (2019) 208–224

KATHARINE DOMMETT AND MEHMET EMIN BAKIR*

A Transparent Digital Election Campaign? The Insights and Significance of Political Advertising Archives for Debates on Electoral Regulation

Throughout the last decade, digital technology has become increasingly important in election campaigns. Each new election has seen growing coverage of the role played by websites, social media pages and online advertising in securing electoral victory. At the UK's 2019 general election, this narrative recurred, but while in the past digital technology has been a supplement to offline campaigning, digital was now an integral component of electoral activity. Whether measured in terms of spending on digital campaigning, activity on online platforms or media coverage of digital content, the online sphere was prominent as never before. While recognising the new status of digital campaigning it is, however, important to note that this activity is by no means uncontentious. Indeed, this election raised numerous questions about what is and is not permissible online and how problematic practices should be curtailed. We explore what we know about digital campaigning at the UK's 2019 general election, presenting the first academic analysis of newly available transparency data from the Facebook and Google advertising archives. Reviewing this data, we diagnose the need to revisit existing systems of electoral regulation and oversight with a view to questions of transparency.

1. Digital campaigning in 2019

A key lesson from the 2017 general election was the importance of digital campaigning tools. As Kreiss has argued, technology is often cited in accounting

*Katharine Dommett, Department of Politics, University of Sheffield; k.dommett@sheffield.ac.uk; Mehmet Emin Bakir, Department of Computer Science, University of Sheffield, m.e.bakir@sheffield.ac.uk

doi:10.1093/pa/gsaa029

for electoral outcomes (2016, p. 15) and for the Conservatives, electoral victory was at least partially attributed to the use of online advertising on Facebook. Labour also focused on technology as a key strength of their campaign, asserting that organic message dissemination and sharing helped to mobilise supporters and bypass traditional media outlets. As a result of these ideas, not only did Labour and the Conservatives internalise the importance of digital to future campaigns but so too did smaller parties and non-party campaign groups. Across the electoral landscape, therefore, consensus emerged around the importance of devoting resource and staffing to digital, resulting in significant investment in digital content. Indeed, levels of spending on paid-for digital advertising surpassed previous levels, with reports that political parties spent £4.3 million in 2017, and our analysis indicating that parties spent just under £9 million on Google and Facebook in 2019. In addition, campaigners invested in organic content and peer-to-peer message sharing strategies, with, for example, the Liberal Democrats recruiting 'Online Champions' to promote their messages (Liberal Democrats, 2019). This raft of digital activity was not only evident amongst party elites but was also initiated by local campaigns and non-party campaigners (Dommett *et al.*, 2020), resulting in a range of online activities.

The growing prominence of digital campaigning is of particular interest because, in the run up to the general election, it was widely argued that there was a need for urgent electoral reform. Indeed, the Electoral Reform Society has argued that electoral 'rules and laws have not always kept pace with the increasing use of digital campaigning' (2019, p. 17), while the Electoral Commission have suggested that digital campaigning raises concerns that 'our democracy may be under threat' (2018, p. 1). Given these trends, we review what we know about digital campaigning at the 2019 general election and discuss the significance of these insights for existing systems of regulatory oversight.

2. Transparency and the 2019 General Election campaign

The 2019 general election was different in many ways from previous elections, but, in particular, it marked a new high point for transparency in digital campaigning. For those interested in the study of online campaigning there have historically been few mechanisms by which it is possible to ascertain what is happening online. Although the Electoral Commission compels all parties and non-party campaigners (in the latter case spending above a certain threshold) to register with the Commission and complete spending returns, these requirements do not apply to all campaigners and do not result in detailed insight into digital campaigning activity (Dommett and Power, 2019).[1] This means there is little official data about who is conducting digital campaigning and what they are doing, with only patchy insights about paid-for content such as online advertising or sponsored content, and no official data on organic campaign material such as posts or memes made and shared by supporters or campaigns without payment (Fulgoni, 2015). Other means of monitoring campaign content have also been very limited, as the nature of social media means that content is often disseminated in closed groups or private messaging services (such as WhatsApp) and cannot be seen by those wishing to study a campaign. Targeted advertising, for example, is not visible to all users, but is only seen by those an advertiser wants to reach (Chester and Montgomery, 2017). This has meant that journalists, researchers and others have had few means by which to gather data about what is happening online—with only a small number of platforms providing access to data for researchers (Møller and Bechmann, 2019).

Ahead of the 2019 general election, however, researchers, journalists and users were given access to new forms of data. Following extensive criticism,[2] major companies, including Facebook and Google, took steps to increase transparency on their platforms (Leerssen *et al.*, 2019, p. 2). These changes were designed to shine 'a bright light on all ads, as well as the Pages that run them' making 'it easier to root out abuse – helping to ensure that bad actors are held accountable for the ads they run' (Facebook, 2018). In the context of election campaigns, this led to more information being disclosed to users, civil society and government through (amongst other measures) the creation of online advertising archives. These resources provide more information about the *advertising* content that appears in elections and can be used to highlight trends in digital campaigning activities. However, these are voluntary initiatives and so have not been provided by all online platforms, meaning there are many areas of the web where we have no understanding of how advertising is being used. Nevertheless, these innovations by Facebook and Google provide a window into two major sites of online advertising and hence provide a valuable resource for those seeking to understand this practice at elections. Accordingly, in the analysis below, we present the first detailed academic analysis of UK political advertising data released by Facebook and Google's advertising archives.

In offering this overview, it is important to state that these archives are varied in form (CITA, 2020) and have been criticised for deficiencies in scope and functionality (Boyd, 2019; Edelson *et al.*, 2019). Indeed, researchers and journalists

---

[1]The threshold for registering as a non-party campaigner are high—with only those spending over £20,000 in England and £10,000 in the rest of the UK needing to register. Spending returns also do not currently disaggregate spending about online campaign activities.

[2]Criticisms have been particularly prominent since 2016 and the Cambridge Analytica scandal.

have highlighted concerns including technical issues that led adverts to disappear from the archives (Scott, 2019), evidence of advert spend under-reporting (Hern and McIntyre, 2019) and a lack of precision in the data provided (such as lack of data on electoral constituencies and targeting parameters) (Leerssen *et al.*, 2019, p. 12). These archives therefore represent a significant advance in transparency around digital election campaigning, but they are by no means perfect.

It is also important to acknowledge that these archives focus upon only one kind of digital campaigning content, namely paid-for advertising. Campaigns also use other kinds of paid content beyond advertising (such as paying influencers or to boost organic posts) and they also rely on public posts and organic content to disseminate their messages and ideas. While some tools exist to provide insights into this kind of content (for example, CrowdTangle, a tool that collects data on social media sharing on Facebook, Instagram and Reddit) there is no way to systematically gather data about activity in closed or private spaces such as Facebook Messenger or WhatsApp groups. This means a significant realm of online activity is not being scrutinised, so we know little about whether campaigning occurs in these spaces, and whether it accords with electoral rules. While some scholars and journalists have made attempts to study private groups (for example, van Duyn, 2018), resource issues mean that scope is often limited, and ethical concerns limit the ability to gather data covertly (meaning that the dynamics of a group can change when a researcher is present). For these reasons, there are significant areas of digital campaign activity that we know little about, and many others where our insights are limited or imprecise. Acknowledging these limitations, we turn to review what we are able to ascertain from the newly created advertising archives.

3.   Advertising archives: what do they reveal?

The data reported below was gathered from the Facebook and Google archives, using each platform's Application Programming Interface (API). It was collected between 6 November and 19 December 2019 as part of a collaborative project conducted at the University of Sheffield. In obtaining these data, it is important to note that the Facebook API does not provide information only about adverts directly related to the election, rather data are provided for all advertisers who are classified as placing a social and political advert between 6 November and 19 December. This makes it necessary to develop inclusion criteria to determine which adverts are most likely to be related to the election. To do this, we created a list of all advertisers who spent at least £1,000 and a second list that included advertisers whose name contains one of the keywords from (i) a party name or its abbreviated name, (ii) a candidate name, (iii) or one of keywords 'party, vote, candidate, election, Brexit'. We then merged the lists, resulting in a sample of 2,693. Reviewing these data, we identified 1,217 entries that did not spend over

Table 12.1 Facebook and Google political advertising and expenditure activity by party and non-party advertisers, 2019 general election campaign (beginning 6 November)

Platform	Number of advertisers[3]	Number of adverts	Minimum spend	Maximum spend	Average spend
Facebook	1476	79,729	£7,064,500	£16,024,771	£11,544,636
Google	12	681	£665,100	£5,245,650	£2,955,375
Total	1488	80,410	£7,729,600	£21,270,421	£14,500,011

the £1,000 threshold and did not contain one of our key words. This left 1,476 entries from the Facebook archive. These were then manually labelled to indicate whether an advertiser was affiliated with a party, or whether they were a non-party actor. This process allowed us to remove a number of false positives from the data, but it is important to note that some of the 1,217 advertisers we did not label may have placed adverts related to the election. The analysis we therefore offer reflects specific coding and exclusion choices and should be viewed accordingly. It should be noted that data from Google did not require such extensive filtering because of the scope of their archive, however we did apply these criteria and identified one entry that did not fit our criteria. Reviewing this data, we consider what we know about four aspects of the digital advertising campaign:

(1) Platform use

(2) Party spending

(3) Party advertisers

(4) Non-party advertisers

3.1 Platform use

Looking at the headline figures gathered from each archive (Table 12.1), it is clear that both platforms were extensively used during the general election and that significant resource was being spent on both Facebook and Google advertising. Table 12.1 shows that, in total £14.5 million was spent on Facebook and Google by a range of actors active in the election period. Whilst its not possible to easily compare this figure to previous elections (because of a lack of available data), the Electoral Commission did report that at the 2017 general election political parties spent £4.3 million on digital advertising, with about £3.16 million spent on Facebook (Dommett and Power, 2019). In contrast, our analysis (Table 12.2)

---

[3]See section 3 for explanation of inclusion criteria used to generate these figures.

suggests that at the 2019 general election, just under £9 million was spent by parties on Google and Facebook, with just over £6 million on Facebook alone. Although drawing comparisons is therefore challenging, there appears to have been a marked increase in funding devoted to digital advertising.

Looking at the spending figures reported in Table 12.1 it is clear that the figures available from each company's advertising archive are not precise. Instead of giving a specific figure, Facebook and Google provide information about advertising spending in brackets (i.e. <£100, £100–£199 etc.) with each company using different bracket ranges to present their data. This means that it is only possible to report minimum, maximum and average spend, with the latter referring to the median amount between the minimum and maximum provided for each individual advert. This approach is far from ideal, as the variance between minimum and maximum is significant (ranging from just over £665,000 for minimum spend and £5.2 million for maximum possible spend on Google), making it unclear precisely how much resource was devoted to advertising on these platforms.

It is also challenging to draw simple conclusions from this data about the focus of advertising activity online. It may initially appear that Facebook was the most popular advertising platform, as the amount reported there appears significantly higher than on Google. It may also appear that more people were running adverts on Facebook than Google (as 1,476 advertisers were active on Facebook, while just 12 were active on Google) and that more adverts were placed on the former platform. And yet, it is important to be cautious when inferring insights from these figures. Facebook and Google have different criteria for what counts as a political advert and these differences account for at least some of the variation seen in each archive report. Facebook has an expansive definition that includes adverts '[m]ade by, on behalf of or about a current or former candidate for public office, a political figure, a political party or advocates for the outcome of an election to public office', that are '[a]bout any election, referendum or ballot initiative, including "go out and vote" or election campaigns; or [a]bout social issues in any place where the ad is being placed; or [r]egulated as political advertising' (Facebook, no date, a). In contrast, Google limits its definition of 'political' to adverts that reference 'political organisations, political parties, political issue advocacy or fundraising, and individual candidates and politicians' (Google, no date). This means that fewer adverts and advertisers are captured by the Google archive and that data is accordingly not directly comparable. While it therefore appears that more money was expended on Facebook and that more advertisers and adverts were on this platform it may be that similar content was placed on Google that has simply not been reported in the archive. This makes it challenging to draw clear insights from the data about relative platform use, showing the difficulties that emerge when data is not reported in a consistent way.

Table 12.2 Facebook and Google political advertising and expenditure activity by parties, 2019 general election campaign (beginning 6 November)

Platform	Party affiliation	Number of advertisers	Number of adverts	Average impression	Average spend
Facebook	Labour	367	9018	144,213,503	£2,074,391
	Conservatives	300	13,759	89,813,123	£1,523,921
	Liberal Democrats	243	14,204	92,553,402	£1,356,298
	Brexit Party	77	4824	26,845,588	£681,138
	Green Party	75	1114	10,462,443	£142,943
	Scottish National Party	31	288	6,535,856	£51,956
	Independents	47	457	2,314,772	£34,622
	Plaid Cymru	19	139	2,243,931	£19,581
	UKIP	3	13	42,494	£744
	Other	57	2153	8,409,424	£140,174
	Total	**1219**	**45,969**	**383,434,533**	**£6,025,768**
Google	Conservatives	2	298	107,279,852	£1,766,075
	Labour	2	114	60,934,943	£739,675
	Liberal Democrats	3	185	16,684,908	£242,950
	Brexit Party	1	7	8,304,997	£188,525
	Independents	1	28	1,679,986	£14,675
	Other	2	22	2,489,989	£1,800
	Total	**11**	**654**	**197,374,674**	**£2,953,700**

3.2 Party spending

Turning to look in more detail at the spending on advertising, it is possible to draw some more illustrative conclusions. Digging further into the headline figures, we can look at the amounts being spent by different parties on each platform.[4] Shown in Table 12.2, we can see that Labour reported the largest spending on Facebook, reporting an average spend of just over £2 million. This was largely comparable with the Conservatives (at £1.5 million), but dwarfed the amount spent by smaller parties, with the Brexit Party spending £681,138, the Greens £142,943 and UKIP just £744. It is also interesting to note that the distribution of party spending across platforms varied. So, while Labour focused more on Facebook, the Conservatives concentrated equally on both platforms (spending around £1.5 million on both platforms). There accordingly appear to be interesting differences in which platforms were used by political parties, and how extensively.

This data can also be used to calculate the proportion of parties' total campaigning budget that is being spent on online adverts on these platforms. Whilst

---

[4]This data has been aggregated from multiple party accounts - for more see section 3.3.

the limits of spending are nuanced, and official returns have not yet been made, we know that the spending limit for a political party standing candidates in each of the 650 UK constituencies is £19.5 million (BBC, 2019). Whilst parties rarely meet this spending limit, we can use this figure to get an idea of what proportion of possible spend is going on digital advertising on these two platforms. Taking Labour figures, for example, if we sum average spend data from Google and Facebook, we can see that £2,814,066 was spent on online adverts. This constitutes 14% of the total *possible* spend. In comparison, the Conservatives' average spend amounts to £3,289,996, a figure that represents 17% of possible expenditure. These figures are far vaster than smaller parties, with the Brexit Party's £869,663 constituting 4% of their possible total budget. These are large proportions of party spending, especially given that these figures are likely to underestimate the total proportion spent as we know that few parties (and especially smaller parties) meet imposed spending limits.

We can also use these data to gain an impression of how much was being spent by parties on individual adverts. By dividing the total average spend figure by the number of adverts, we can see how advert spending varied. Beginning with the figures for all parties , we can see that the average expenditure totalled £131 for a Facebook advert, while for Google it was £4,516. This explanation for this difference is unclear, but it may reflect the lack of small, low spending advertisers (such as local candidates or parties) on Google (with spend on this platform made by national party accounts aiming to reach larger audiences). Looking in more detail at how the spend of specific parties varied, we can see that Labour spent on average £230 for each advert on Facebook, the Conservatives spent £110, the Liberal Democrats £95 and the Brexit Party £141. On Google, in contrast, Labour's average spend was £6,488, the Conservatives £5,926, the Liberal Democrats £1,313 and the Brexit Party £26,932. As such, it appears that spending on each Google advert was on average far higher than for a Facebook advert.[5]

This data therefore indicates that parties were using online advertising differently. Whilst in general more was being spent online than in the past, it appears that Labour used Facebook more extensively than Google, at an average lower advert cost, and that the Conservatives spent similar amounts on the platforms but paid significantly more per advert on Google. Interestingly, despite being a much smaller party, the Liberal Democrats invested heavily in Facebook, spending over a million pounds on the platform, whilst the newly created Brexit Party spent over £680,000. The amounts spent by other parties reflect their focus (i.e. Scotland or Wales) or smaller infrastructure. Only a tiny amount was spent by UKIP—with just £744 spent on Facebook. It is therefore clear that parties are using online advertising platforms to different degrees.

---

[5]It should be noted that this data could be skewed by a particularly large spend on one or two adverts.

3.3 Party advertisers

In addition to insights on party spending, the data provided by Facebook (which reports data from different types of advertisers to Google) reveals two interesting things about *who* is campaigning. The first relates to the architecture of the *parties'* digital campaigns, while the second reveals something about the presence of *non-party campaigners*. Each issue is discussed separately in this section and the next.

First, Facebook data show that it is not only national parties who are placing adverts. In addition to national parties and party leaders, local candidates, parties and groups also create content and advertise online. In the Facebook archive, the data from these different actors is not aggregated, but by hand-coding data to identify party affiliations, we determined how many advertisers were affiliated to each party (it is this aggregated data that is reported above).

Table 12.2 shows that each party has different numbers of advertisers. These differences reflect what we know about parties' non-digital infrastructure. The Labour and Conservative parties have a history of local party organisation which is reflected in the presence of 367 advertisers for Labour and 300 Conservative advertisers (many of whom are local candidates, parties or even groups). In contrast, the Brexit Party, who as a new party had no established grassroots organisation, had only 77 advertisers. These figures are interesting as in a truly digital campaign we might expect each of the 650 parliamentary seats contested at the election to exhibit local party or candidate accounts, meaning that each party would have over 650 separate advertisers, but this is not the case. Indeed, even in Labour, the party with most advertisers, only around half of constituencies have local advertising presence (when removing national figures and other groups). As such there is significant potential for the local use of digital advertising to expand.

Looking in more detail at the differences, it is interesting to look at the four parties spending most on Facebook advertising. Distinguishing between the national party, party leader, candidates, regional parties (i.e. Scottish and Welsh branches of a national party), local parties, party groups and party media, it is possible to see the number of different actors placing adverts in each party. Figure 12.1 shows the number of adverts being placed by each type of actor within each party. This shows that the national party was responsible for the vast majority of adverts in the Liberal Democrat and Conservative cases but this was not the case for Labour, where candidates were dominant. What is also interesting is the role played by party leaders. Boris Johnson's account was the most prominent of the party leaders', placing 1,254 adverts. In contrast, Jeremy Corbyn's and Nigel Farage's accounts were used to field just under 800 adverts. What is particularly notable, however, is that Jo Swinson's account

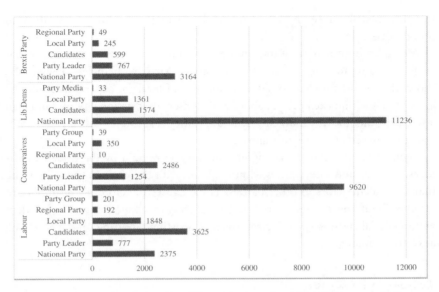

Figure 12.1 Advertisements placed by different sections of parties, 2019 general election campaign (beginning 6 November)

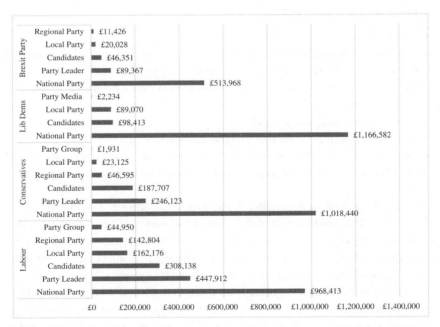

Figure 12.2 Advertising expenditure by advertisers within parties, 2019 general election campaign (beginning 6 November)

was not used to place any adverts, showing a markedly different strategy to other parties.

A detailed examination of the amounts spent by each party shows large variations according to amounts and tier within the party. Nonetheless, Figure 12.2 shows that whilst numbers of advertisements and levels of expenditure differed across levels within each party, Labour and Conservative national party campaign advertising did not vary markedly. Labour's national spend fell just shy of £1 million; the Conservatives' slightly above.

Figure 12.2 also shows that significant sums were paid by the leader, candidates, regional and local parties within Labour, with these actors spending more than equivalent actors in other parties. These figures therefore reveal important insights about how parties use political advertising that were hitherto not evident within official election spending returns or in existing reporting on the Facebook advertising archive.

3.4 Non-party advertisers

So far analysis has focused on parties, but it is also possible to identify a number of other actors who were placing adverts during the election campaign. We coded seven types of non-party actor:

- Companies
- Charities or non-governmental organisations that did not have an explicit electoral focus (such as Greenpeace or Amnesty International)
- Non-party, electorally focused campaign groups (such as Britain's Future or 3rd Party Ltd)
- Trade unions (such as the GMB)
- Media or news outlets (such as *The Independent*)
- Governmental accounts (such as the Mayor of London's official account), and
- Other accounts (such as universities or international political parties).

To get a sense of scale, looking at the data on advertisers from Facebook we identified 1,219 connected to political parties and coded 257 as belonging to one of the seven types of organisation listed above. While party accounts show a cumulative spend of £6,025,766 on Facebook, these other groups spent £5,518,870,[6] suggesting that these actors play a significant role in campaigns.

Looking at Table 12.3 it appears that there were several non-party campaign groups placing adverts at the election. These are groups that promote an explicit electoral message or candidate but which may or may not be affiliated to

---

[6]Reporting average spend data.

Table 12.3 Types of non-party advertiser on Facebook and Google, 2019 general election campaign (beginning 6 November)

Type of advertiser	Number of advertisers	Number of adverts	Average spend
Non-party campaign group	88	13,197	£2,711,452
Charity	52	14,331	£1,744,735
Company	52	2508	£429,646
Cause	19	2238	£227,981
Media	17	443	£135,828
Government	12	186	£128,457
Other	9	180	£13,610
Trade Unions	8	677	£127,161

parties. Specific examples here include 'Led by Donkeys', '3rd Party Ltd', 'Campaign Together' and 'Rage against the Brexit Machine'. As evident from these examples, many non-party campaign groups were focused on Brexit, with a number of local or regional groups explicitly focused on campaigning to promote candidates with favoured Brexit views. Other advertisers classified under this heading focused on providing voter advice. For example, 'Vote Smart' and 'Vote for Policies' offered information on candidate positions and tactical voting.

Some journalistic coverage highlighted examples of non-party groups that could mislead voters about the identity of the advertiser. Investigating the activities of 3rd Party Ltd, for example, Gian Volpicelli (2019), a journalist at *Wired*, reported that the group was created by an ex-Vote Leave staffer and was '"pretending" to be the Green Party by buying Facebook ads encouraging people to vote for the Greens'. Elsewhere Rory Cellan-Jones (2019) at the BBC reported that the 'Fair Tax Campaign' was started by a former Boris Johnson aide, and that 'Parents' Choice' was the creation of a former Conservative Minister. These examples suggest that non-party campaign groups were being used at the election to promote partisan messages without explicit party branding. While examples of this behaviour were not extensive, the presence of such groups raises questions about the activity of non-party campaign groups and has led to calls (discussed further below) for increased transparency.

These calls have been particularly prominent because of the amounts being spent by these groups. As shown in Table 12.3, non-party campaign groups spent just over £2.7 million during this period, suggesting that these organisations are an important medium for electoral activity.

Looking beyond non-party campaign groups, different kinds of advertiser can be identified, including charities and companies. However, it is important to be cautious about drawing conclusions from this data. Because Facebook's advertising archive includes non-political adverts as well as political content, it is necessary for researchers to determine frameworks for identifying political content (see footnote 3). For our analysis, we used inclusion criteria to identify advertisers whose name contained references to parties, candidates or a list of keywords such as 'vote', 'election', 'Brexit'. This allowed us to identify those adverts placed in this period most likely to be related to the election. Taking this approach our analysis highlighted examples of companies including 'The Radical Tea Towel Company', 'Brexit: The Board Game of Second Chances', 'Brexit Bear' and 'Brexit Cereals' that were selling products related to the election and its themes. However, as with any coding framework, this approach led us to include some false positives within our data set. Our list therefore included 'Ben and Jerry's', 'Unilever', 'Coca-Cola' and 'Patagonia'. Rather than excluding these cases from our analysis, we have retained these within our database in order to show the challenges of defining (and studying) political advertising.

4.   Implications for existing regulation

Online advertising archives represent a significant advance in our ability to understand digital campaigning activity. Whilst, as suggested at the outset, this source captures only a fraction of the campaign (as archives do not cover organic campaign material or other forms of paid content), they do highlight certain practices and dynamics that are of interest to observers of electoral politics. At the most basic level, they reveal important differences in campaign strategy and capacity amongst different actors. Whilst headline figures show a general increase in spending, this analysis reveals that different actors were placing different numbers of adverts at different costs during the election. In addition, it shows that parties are not the only actors using advertising, with non-party campaigners, charities, cause groups and companies also creating advertising content in the election period. These insights are extremely valuable for our understanding of digital campaigning, especially given the lack of data that researchers and journalists have historically obtained. Yet, in outlining the insights to be gained from these advertising archives, this analysis also raises questions about existing systems of regulation and oversight, specifically with regards to transparency. This point is significant in light of growing calls for increased regulation of digital campaign activity (All Party Parliamentary Group (APPG) for Electoral Campaigning Transparency, 2020; Electoral Reform Society, 2019) and suggests that there is an urgent case to revisit existing systems and laws.

When it comes to transparency, the two archives have offered a range of new insights, and yet it is also clear that the data provided by these two companies is far from perfect. Not only are there issues with the imprecision of spend data, there are also concerns about data quality and reliability that make it difficult to know whether these archives are providing an accurate picture of campaigning activity. Indeed, within our own analysis, we found instances of adverts being removed from the archive with no explanation, making it unclear to what extent this data provides an accurate and consistent overview of which adverts were fielded in the campaign. Moreover, our analysis has focused just on Facebook and Google but there are many other platforms on which political adverts can be placed. While some platforms have also provided information (often not in forms consistent with Facebook or Google) many others do not, resulting in significant gaps in our understanding of the extent of political advertising around elections.

This point is particularly important given recent calls for more standardised and extensive provision of online advertising archives (Electoral Commission, 2018). The Centre for Data Ethics has contended that archives should be more widely available and should contain standardised data about the 'content', 'financial transparency', 'intended audience' and 'impact' of an advert in ways that 'should be easy to analyse' (2020, p. 109). Our analysis supports the case for such regulation, but it also suggests that official election returns could also be supplemented to provide addition data against which to verify information provided by platforms. The Electoral Commission has already called for campaigners to 'subdivide their spending returns into different types of spending. . .[to] give more information about the money spent on digital campaigns' and asserted that '[c]ampaigners should be required to provide more detailed and meaningful invoices from their digital suppliers to improve transparency' (2018, p. 3). These changes would provide valuable means by which to gain further insight into political advertising, but also other forms of online activity—expanding our understanding beyond this specific form of online activity. As such, the new levels of transparency provided by Facebook and Google's archives illustrate how much we still do not know, suggesting the need for regulatory oversight systems that provide more information about digital campaigning activities.

5. Conclusion

This chapter has explored what we know about the digital election campaign at the 2019 general election by looking at online advertising archives provided by Facebook and Google. It has shown that digital campaigning has become an integral part of election campaigning and revealed a significant increase in spending on these platforms. Delving into data on who is campaigning, we have shown that parties deployed different strategies that reflected a preference for different platforms, and the existence of different organisational structures.

It has also shown that non-party campaigners are playing an important role in campaigns.

Reflecting on what this data reveals, we argue that there is an urgent need to think about the regulatory implications of these insights. In particular, this analysis reveals the need for more transparency, and for greater consistency in the data that is made available for analysis. Whilst these archives provide new information, there is much that we still do not know. We have data from just two advertising companies. Moreover, advertising represents only a fraction of the digital campaigning picture, revealing the need to gather new insights on other forms of paid content and organic campaigning activity. This suggests the need to pursue regulatory changes that provide more information about the digital campaign, both from platforms and systems of government oversight.

This analysis has therefore cast greater light on the activity of digital campaigning at the UK's 2019 general election, but it has also shown significant areas of ambiguity in our understanding of what is happening. Our findings therefore suggest the need for increased transparency and urgent regulatory reform, ensuring that we are better placed to monitor digital campaigning at forthcoming elections.

References

All Party Parliamentary Group (APPG) for Electoral Campaigning Transparency. (2020) 'Defending Our Democracy in the Digital Age', accessed at https://1u5lpf242yx l2669iu2mp449-wpengine.netdna-ssl.com/wp-content/uploads/2020/01/Defending -our-Democracy-in-the-Digital-Age-APPG-ECT-Report-Jan-2020.pdf on 20 February 2020.

BBC. (2019, 4 November) 'General Election 2019: How much can Parties Spend?', accessed at https://www.bbc.co.uk/news/election-2019-50170067 on 10 March 2020.

Boyd, A. (2019, 31 October) 'Facebook is Still Failing at Ad Transparency (No Matter What They Claim)', The Mozilla Blog, accessed at https://blog.mozilla.org/blog/2019/ 10/31/facebook-is-still-failing-at-ad-transparency-no-matter-what-they-claim/ on 12 February 2020.

Cellan-Jones, R. (2019, 18 November) 'The Obscure Groups buying up Facebook Election Ads', accessed at https://www.bbc.co.uk/news/technology-50458111 on 22 April 2020.

Centre for Data Ethics. (2020) *Review of Online Targeting*, London, Centre for Data Ethics.

Chester, J. and Montgomery, K. (2017) 'The Role of Digital Marketing in Political Campaigns', *Internet Policy Review*, **6**, 1–20. [online]

CITA (2020) 'Comparison of Platforms' Political Advertising Policies', accessed at https:// citapdigitalpolitics.com/wp-content/uploads/2020/02/Platform-Tables_AdPolicies_Feb 12020.pdf on 12 February 2020.

Dommett, K. and Power, S. (2019) 'The Political Economy of Facebook Advertising: Election Spending', *The Political Quarterly*, **90**, 257–265.

Dommett, K., Temple, L. and Seyd, P. (2020) 'Dynamics of Intra-Party Organisation in the Digital Age: A Grassroots Analysis of Digital Adoption', *Parliamentary Affairs*,

Digital, Culture, Media and Sport Select Committee. (2019) *Disinformation and 'fake news': Final Report:* Fifth Report of Session 2017–19. London, Stationery Office.

Edelseon, L., Sakhuja, S., Dey, D. and McCoy, D. (2019) 'An Analysis of United States Online Political Advertising Transparency', arXiv:1902.04385, accessed 5 February 2020.

Electoral Commission. (no date) 'Register of Non-Party Campaigners', accessed at http:// search.electoralcommission.org.uk/Search/Registrations? currentPage=1&rows=30& sort=RegulatedEntityName&order=asc&open=filter&et=tp&register=none&regStat us=registered&optCols=EntityStatusName on 22 April 2020.

Electoral Commission. (2018) *Digital Campaigning: Increasing Transparency for Voters*, London, Electoral Commission.

Electoral Reform Society. (2019) *Reining in the Political 'Wild West': Campaign Rules for the 21st Century*, London, Electoral Reform Society.

Facebook. (no date, a) 'About Ads about Social Issues, Elections or Politics', accessed at https://www.facebook.com/business/help/167836590566506? id=288762101909005, on 13 February 2020.

Facebook. (no date, b) 'About the Ad Library', accessed at https://www.facebook.com/ business/help/2405092116183307? id=288762101909005 on 13 February 2020.

Facebook. (2018) 'A New Level of Transparency for Ads and Pages', accessed at https:// about.fb.com/news/2018/06/transparency-for-ads-and-pages/ on 10 March 2020.

Fulgoni, G. (2015) 'How Brands Using Social Media Ignite Marketing and Drive Growth', *Journal of Advertising Research*, **55**, 232–236.

Google. (no date), 'Political Content', accessed at https://support.google.com/adspolicy/ answer/6014595? hl=en-GB on 13 February 2020.

Hern, A. and McIntyre, N. (2019) 'Google Admits Major Underreporting of Election Ad Spend', *The Guardian*, 19 November, accessed at https://www.theguardian.com/technol ogy/2019/nov/19/google-admits-major-underreporting-of-election-ad-spend on 19 February 2020.

Kreiss, D. (2016) *Prototype Politics*, Oxford, Oxford University Press.

Leerssen, P., Ausloos, J., Zarouali, B., Helberger, N. and de Vreese, C. (2019) 'Platform Ad Archives: Promises and Pitfalls', *Internet Policy Review*, **8**, 1–21.

Liberal Democrats (2019) 'We're Recruiting for Online Champions!', accessed at https:// www.libdems.org.uk/online-champions-2019 on 12 February 2020.

Møller, L. and Bechmann, A. (2019) 'Research Data Exchange Solution', accessed at https://www.disinfobservatory.org/download/26541 on 20 February 2020.

Scott, M. (2019) 'Political Ads on Facebook Disappeared Ahead of UK Election', *Politico*, accessed at https://www.politico.eu/article/facebook-political-ads-general-election-united-kingdom/ on 12 February 2020.

Van Duyn, E. (2018) 'Hidden Democracy: Political Dissent in Rural America', *Journal of Communication*, **68**, 965–987.

Volpicelli, G. (2019) 'An ex-Vote Leave Staffer is Running Facebook Ads Pushing the Greens', *Wired*, accessed at https://www.wired.co.uk/article/vote-leave-3rd-party-green-party on 22 April 2020.

MATTHEW FLINDERS*

Not a Brexit Election? Pessimism, Promises and Populism 'UK-Style'

The Nobel prize winning economist Elinor Ostrom (2000, p. 33) once warned against 'the danger of self-evident truths' and suggested that 'the fact that something is widely believed does not make it correct'. The role of the social and political scientist was, for Ostrom, not simply to examine and explore a specific topic, event or theme but also to be constantly aware of the need to step back and question, challenge and disrupt the dominant lens through which the object of analysis is generally conceived. This article injects Ostrom's provocative plea into the sphere of British politics to question the 'self-evident truth' that the 2019 general election was 'a Brexit election'. The 'danger' of accepting this interpretation is that it is arguably too obvious. It risks *over*-emphasising the visible machinations of recent events while *under*-emphasising the deeper socio-political factors that manifested themselves in the election. To accept the 2019 contest as a Brexit election is to focus on the tip of the iceberg and the aim of this contribution is to look beneath the (political) waterline. Its central argument is that the general election was less *a Brexit election* and more *a disaffection election*.

This argument demands some unpacking. To some extent the 2019 general election was clearly 'a Brexit election' for the simple reason that '[f]or most voters, how they cast their ballot in 2019 reflected where they stood in the Brexit debate' (Curtice, 2020, p. 12). As such, the election proved effective in breaking the legislative deadlock that had emerged at Westminster and the contextual relevance of Brexit cannot be overlooked (see Curtice in this volume). And yet, stepping-back (*qua.* Ostrom), this 'self-evident truth' can be questioned from at least two perspectives. First, as Cutts *et al.* (2020) have demonstrated, the outcome of general election 2019 was also shaped by a variety of long-term shifts in support for the main parties, most of which pre-date Brexit. Viewed from a historical perspective, Boris Johnson's desire to attract working class voters in northern English towns was hardly a new challenge for the party, even if the Brexit

---

*Matthew Flinders, Department of Politics and International Relations, University of Sheffield, m.flinders@sheffield.ac.uk

doi:10.1093/pa/gsaa030

context was new (Gamble, 2019). Second, it is vital to consider the underpinning social attitudes that led people to support Brexit. In this regard the evidence is relatively clear: the 'Brexistential angst and the paradoxes of populism' that Hay (2020) has highlighted are rooted in political apathy, democratic disappointment and anti-political sentiment (see, for example, Evans and Menon, 2017; Clarke and Newman, 2017; Jennings and Lodge, 2019). This was not *just* a Brexit election and a bolder thesis would suggest that the UK's relationship with the EU served as little more than the lightning-rod through which a far broader range of sociopolitical tensions were, once again, played out. The twist in this argument is that 'getting Brexit done' may not address, but may well amplify, many of these tensions.

The benefit of interpreting the 2019 general election primarily as a disaffection election is that it opens up new possibilities for understanding *how* and *why* the Conservative Party was able to win an 80-seat majority, its largest since 1987. It also offers new insights into the link between individual personality, political psychology and populism as a carefully calibrated statecraft strategy. This, in turn, can be used to demarcate a distinction between 'Brexit' and 'Brexit*ism*' that is crucial to understanding contemporary British political history, in general, and, specifically, the 2019 election. In developing this core argument, this article is divided into three sections. The first focuses on the build-up to the election and underlines the existence of high levels of both democratic disillusionment and Brexit fatigue. The second section focuses on the election campaign and the degree to which the main party leaders were able to funnel this frustration into support for their parties. In particular, it draws on a very specific sub-strand of the literature on populism to explain how Boris Johnson's idiosyncratic and unconventional political leadership proved so effective. The calibration of the election as the 'people versus the politicians' responded to the deep pool of social frustration highlighted in the opening section. This 'UK-style' populism raises critical questions about the political theatre and symbolism of 'Boris*onian* buffoonery' but also regarding the long-term viability of the 'Boris bounce' into power. The final section explores this latter issue through a focus on the polarisation of trust and the management of post-election public expectations in a post-Brexit but COVID-crisis world.

1. Democratic disillusionment and Brexit fatigue

This section focuses on the build-up to the election and develops two main arguments: that public trust in politics plummeted in the run-up to the election and that democratic dissatisfaction was positively correlated with support for leaving the EU. The Hansard Society's (2019) *16th Audit of Political Engagement* provides a powerful evidence base for the first of these arguments, as captured in the report's headline findings:

> Opinions of the system of governing are at their lowest point in the 15-year Audit series – worse now than in the aftermath of the MPs' expenses scandal. People are pessimistic about the country's problems and their possible solution, with sizable numbers willing to entertain radical political changes. Core indicators of political engagement remain stable but, beneath the surface, the strongest feelings of powerlessness and disengagement are intensifying (Hansard Society, 2019, p. 3).

Drilling-down into each of these points, the Audit revealed that, of those surveyed: 72% said the system of governing needs 'quite a lot' or 'a great deal' of improvement; 50% believed the main parties and politicians did not care about people like them; 75% thought political parties were too internally divided to serve the best interests of the country; 63% thought Britain's system of government is rigged to advantage the rich and the powerful; and 18% 'strongly disagreed' that political involvement can change the way the UK is run and 47% felt they had no influence at all over national decision-making, both 15-year lows. Moreover, only 25% of the public had confidence in MPs' handling of Brexit (with the government faring only slightly better on 26%).

It is, of course, true that a range of public opinion surveys have for at least 40 years found worryingly high levels of disaffection (see, for example, Ipsos MORI, 2014) and it could be suggested that expressing negativity has come to assume an almost ritualistic quality amongst large sections of the British public. Nevertheless, it is possible to suggest that the pre-election disaffection was distinctive for three inter-linked reasons. The first relates to *intensity* and evidence that sections of society were beginning to consider radical (and arguably illiberal) reform suggestions. For example, in the Hansard Society's 2019 Audit over half of those surveyed (54%) agreed with the statement that 'Britain needs a strong leader willing to break the rules', and 42% thought that many of the country's problems could be dealt with more effectively if the government did not have to worry so much about votes in parliament. Similar findings emerged from the most recent 'Future of England' survey:

> This year's study confirmed a number of growing trends. We found that Remain and Leave voters are highly polarised around the likely consequences of staying in or leaving the EU. A majority on either side of the divide said that the break-up of the union, undermining faith in democracy, protests in which members of the public get badly injured and violence directed toward MPs were 'worth it' to achieve their desired Brexit outcome (Henderson, 2019, p. 8).

The second distinctive element of pre-election disaffection was its highly *polarised* social dynamic and the manner in which it reflected a range of social cleavages (economic, place-based, educational, generational, etc.). Public attitudes regarding trust in politics or views about whether political processes or institutions 'worked' were, to a greater or lesser extent, defined by the dynamics of Brexit. Ironically, the only issue that united the country in the run-up to the general election was antipathy towards the political omnishambles that seemed to have consumed Brexit. But this, in turn, flows into a third pre-election distinctive disaffection dimension—*fatigue*. By June 2019, a YouGov poll found that a third of the public were actively avoiding news about Brexit; the following month a Deltapoll survey found that 60% agreed with the following comment: 'Right now, I no longer care how or when we leave the European Union, I just want it over and done with'; and by October a further YouGov poll found 70% diagnosing themselves with Brexit fatigue. Three-and-a-half-years after the June 2016 referendum an increasing proportion of the public, on both sides of the debate, had become frustrated with the whole topic and just wanted it resolved one way or another.

It was this emphasis on *intensity, polarisation* and *fatigue* that arguably created a distinctive disaffection context and therefore a distinctive opportunity for a distinctive politician. Moreover, although Boris Johnson may have won the July 2019 leadership election on the basis that he would 'Get Brexit Done' by 31 October (or 'die in a ditch' as he would later add), even the most bullish Boris seemed unable to break the deadlock as he faced a series of major legislative defeats and his decision to prorogue parliament was found unlawful by the Supreme Court. During September 2019 several government attempts to trigger a general election were rejected by MPs who feared a 'no deal' departure from the EU and were constitutionally protected by the Fixed-term Parliaments Act 2011, which required a two-thirds majority vote for an early general election or a vote of no confidence on a simple majority. By mid-October a somewhat truculent Prime Minister was forced to request a further EU extension. However, this rather wretched phase in British political history also created clear opportunities for Boris Johnson, whose rise to the apex of British politics had always shown a receptiveness to the populist signal, not least over Brexit. A scathing and unanimous Supreme Court defeat that would in all likelihood have ended most political careers instead became another example of 'them' (that is, 'the establishment' that wields power without responsibility) against 'us' (the Great British public). Defined this way, the Supreme Court ruling and House of Commons defeats were discursively framed to chime with an emergent populist signal, and associated ideas about the need for a strong leader (Hansard Society, 2019).

With the benefit of hindsight, three distinctive features emerge from this brief account of the election build-up: first, political dissatisfaction was already as intense as it was socially polarised and fatigued; secondly, the rules of political engagement appeared to be altering, almost beyond recognition; and finally, unconventional times created a 'window of opportunity' for an avowedly unconventional politician who was willing to break the rules, flaunt convention and flirt with populism. The next section develops this point through a more specific focus on political leadership and varieties of populism within the campaign itself.

2. Funnelling frustration and populism 'UK-style'

In challenging the characterisation of the 2019 contest as 'a Brexit election', it is critical to delve into both the longer-run dynamics and the immediate contextual factors that shaped its outcome. Although Cutts *et al.* (2020) are correct to suggest that the general election should not be interpreted as a major 'realignment', since the results align with longer-term voting trends, it can be argued that a critical and unique feature of the election was the emergence of a clear brand of populism. In arguing that the poll should be seen primarily as a 'disaffection election' it is important to note that other recent general elections have also been characterised by a similar funnelling of frustration (Flinders, 2015, 2018). Nonetheless, general election 2019 was novel with respect to the interplay between political trust and populism.

One hallmark of British politics since the 2016 referendum is that it has become more tribal and increasingly aggressive as a result of the polarising effects of Brexit. The tenor of political debate has adopted a populist inflection with often nationalist undertones, resulting in individual politicians being publicly abused as 'traitors' or 'turncoats'. While a hybrid form of populism emerged in the 2017 election, its location was squarely within the opposition party as part of 'the Corbyn effect' (Flinders, 2018). Corbyn's populism was fairly placid: 'populism wearing a cardigan' (Flinders, 2019). A very different brand of populism came to the fore in the 2019 election. Its locus was the current prime minister and its articulation was arguably more aggressive, based upon on a portrayal of a strong leader who was willing to break the rules.

It is not enough to simply highlight the populist playfulness of Boris Johnson or his reputation for acting as a clown. Beneath the veneer of 'Boris' and his 'whiff-whaff' theatrics there is a deeper statecraft strategy, key to which is an explicit focus on fuelling and funnelling frustration amongst those sections of the public most disaffected with 'conventional' politics. It can be argued that Johnson and those around him recognised the *changing emotional landscape of British politics* and their ability to resonate with this was ultimately what led to Conservative Party success in Labour's traditional heartlands (see Flinders, 2020a). Indeed, this argument can be used to *politicise* the notion of 'clowning around' and to explain how a man associated with personal indiscretion, professional mishaps and generating outrage secured the most resounding Conservative election victory in over 30 years.

The concept of populism has become as ubiquitous as it is contested, with some even describing the term as meaningless (Serhan, 2020). Nonetheless, working at a high level of generality it can be argued that populism operates through a three-stage argumentative logic:

> Step 1. The world can be separated into two homogenous and antagonistic groups, *'us'* (that is, 'the public', 'the people', 'the pure', etc.) and *'them'* (that is, 'elites', 'immigrants', 'minorities', etc.);

> Step 2. 'They' enjoy a privileged, protected and unfair position within society that they have used to exploit 'us' which is almost locked-in through the existing political system;

> Step 3. To break this deadlock and change the system, the public must put their faith in a strong leader who is willing to break the rules and drive through far-reaching reforms.

Populism is therefore a divisive political strategy that simplifies messy political realities and promotes simple answers to complex questions. It also revolves around not only funnelling pre-existing social frustrations but also fuelling them in order to generate political support. One of the prime ideological features of populist politicians and their 'insurgent' parties is a brand of nativism, a xenophobic form of nationalism. But, as Benjamin Moffitt's *The Global Rise of Populism: Performance, Political Style and Representation* (2016) demonstrates, populism is also characterised by significant performative aspects. Moffitt (2016, p. 38) therefore departs from the mainstream literature by conceiving of populism as a political style which is defined (with typical academic aplomb) as 'the repertoires of embodied, symbolically mediated performance made to audiences that are used to navigate the fields of power that comprise the political, stretching from the domain of government through to everyday life'. This, in turn, provides a way of understanding how populist identities are crafted and constructed. What Moffitt brings to the discussion is a focus on the verbal and non-verbal forms of communication associated with populism (think tousled hair, unkempt appearance, hanging from zip-wires, casual rule-breaking, crude comments, brandishing smoked kippers, etc.).

What is particularly significant about Moffitt's 'populist style' is the emphasis it places on the demonstration of bad manners by populist leaders, as seen in the rejection of political conventions or even polite discourse. To Moffitt, populists do not simply rely on socially divisive rhetoric, such as narratives of crisis that seek to blame a designated 'other'; they also utilise a sophisticated repertoire of performative tools to underline their 'outsider' or 'radical status'. These might include aggressive rhetoric, spectacular acts, exaggeration, calculated provocations or the intended violation of political and socio-cultural norms. This is often reflected in the coarsening of political rhetoric, a disregard for both appropriate modes of acting in the political realm, willingness to resort to anecdotes as evidence, and displays of studied ignorance of that which does not interest them. This has occurred alongside shifts in media business models through which the dominant 'media logic' has become one that is itself often simplistic, personalised, entertainment-focused, polarising and prone to affective appeals which are themselves favourable to populism. As such, populist and media styles have developed in an almost parasitical relationship that revolves around dramatic composition. Consequently, Moffitt (2016, p. 37) suggests that populist style fuses 'matter and manner, message and package'.

A benefit of utilising Moffitt's work is that it defines populist style as a gradational phenomenon which can be pushed forward or rolled back by a politician or party to suit the strategic priorities of a specific context. For instance, Theresa May condemned her opponents for impeding the popular will and invoked the threat of their obstruction to justify the June 2017 snap election. Conversely, during the 2019 election the Labour Party appeared to adopt a form of 'fiscal populism' in which a giveaway manifesto was followed by wave-after-wave of further spending commitments. That neither of these approaches proved electorally successful usefully reminds us that populism is not always popular, not least in the context of widespread public disaffection. Indeed, a clear element of recent elections is that none of the main party leaders has been popular (see Table 13.1).

If Table 13.1 illustrates how it is not unusual for party leaders to attract negative ratings, the 2019 election was distinctive for the scale of negativity. Boris Johnson's advantage was that he was the *least unpopular* leader. A YouGov poll at the beginning of the election campaign found 45% of the public believing that 'the party leaders are worse than *any* of their predecessors in history' (see Powell, 2019). The 2019 Ipsos MORI Veracity Index—published just days before the election—highlighted that public trust in politicians had fallen to just 14%, a five-

Table 13.1 Party leader public satisfaction ratings, 2015–2019 general elections

	GE2015	GE2017	GE2019
Conservative	David Cameron -2	Theresa May -7	Boris Johnson -20
Labour	Ed Miliband -19	Jeremy Corbyn -11	Jeremy Corbyn -44
Liberal Democrats	Nick Clegg -21	Tim Farron -19	Jo Swinson -22

Source: IPSOS Mori (2020) Political Monitor Satisfaction Ratings 1997–2020.
Note: Ratings are those at the survey closest to the general election.

point fall from 2018. General election 2019 was dominated as much by concerns regarding a lack of trust in politicians, in general, as it was about Brexit, in particular. From the outset, trust was a running theme of the campaign, whether in relation to Jeremy Corbyn's announcement that he would remain neutral if a second EU referendum were to take place or Boris Johnson's dismissal of criticism of his decision to delay the report from the Intelligence and Security Committee into Russian interference in elections.

That Johnson refused to apologise for using homophobic and racist language in his newspaper columns, or that polls found that more than twice as many felt Corbyn was 'more in touch with ordinary people', did not prevent him leading the Conservative Party to victory. In part, the explanation for this rests with the weakness of the Labour Party and the inability of the Liberal Democrats to break through as a viable centrist third party. But such interpretations risk overlooking the strategic and highly personalised campaigning approach which Johnson had been cultivating for some time. Indeed, drawing on Moffit's emphasis on the distinctive performative style of populism, framed for a socio-political context defined by anti-political sentiment, Johnson's buffoonery and pantomime antics appear not as the behaviour of a political clown but as the carefully calibrated statecraft of a sophisticated politician. Five inter-related themes help to substantiate this argument and differentiate the localised qualities of 'Boris*onian*' populism during the 2019 general election. These are outlined in Table 13.2 and discussed in the remainder of this section.

Table 13.2 Component elements of 'Borisonian' populism in the 2019 general election

ELEMENT	ESSENCE
Breaking the Rules	A constant willingness to court controversy in order to underline his 'unconventional' and 'outsider' status.
Distracting Dramaturgy	The capacity to dominate the headlines in ways that play to the media, entertain the public and ensure substantive policy issues are rarely discussed.
Territorial Targeting	Clarity of a 'politicians versus the public' message carefully targeted to 'England-beyond-London' and promises of a 'levelling-up' economic agenda.
Brexit and Brexit*ism*	A strategy of consciously expanding Brexit's specific and technical focus to encompass a broader range of social challenges and concerns (i.e., Brexit*ism*).
'Upper Crust' Populism	The capacity to promote a populist style that resonate with dominant cultural expectations while refracting his highly elitist and establishment-based background.

2.1   *Breaking the rules*

A key insight from Moffitt's comparative analysis is that populists not only engage in sophisticated forms of 'othering' to instigate simplistic blame-games but also seek to emphasise their 'outsider' status (and disruptive potential) by refusing to abide by pre-existing rules and conventions. A particular challenge arises for populist politicians who evolve from mainstream parties, requiring them to work harder to convince the public that they really are willing to 'do' politics differently. Their 'style' must designate difference and often becomes associated with a disregard for established modes of acting in the political realm, an intolerance of opposition or a willingness to use disrespectful or even obscene language in order to cultivate debate. In a context of political frustration and fatigue, a willingness to break rules and conventions can be interpreted by sections of society as a breath of fresh air and evidence of a commitment to change the *status quo*. From this perspective, being 'bad' can actually be 'good' in promoting popularity. Johnson responded to signals that the public appeared increasingly frustrated and open to a strong leader willing to break the rules. The prorogation of parliament is one obvious example but equally instructive was Johnson's September 2019 decision to expel 21 MPs from the parliamentary Conservative Party after they rebelled against him over Europe. That these MPs included two ex-chancellors of the exchequer, several former senior ministers and even Winston Churchill's grandson simply underlined his willingness to reject existing constitutional mores. 'I don't recognise this. It's the Brexit Party, rebadged', the former chancellor, Father of the House of Commons and MP for over half a century, Kenneth Clarke, told BBC2's *Newsnight* on 3 September.

Other examples might include the refusal of the Prime Minister's chief adviser, Dominic Cummings, to appear before a select committee (see HC1115, 2018), or the government's decision to withhold ministers from appearing on the BBC's flagship Radio 4 *Today* programme. The Conservative manifesto's references to 'getting away from the idea that Whitehall knows best' (p. 26) and 'MPs devoting themselves to thwarting the democratic decision of the British people' (pp. 47–48) similarly indicated a willingness to break and then redefine the rules as part of a 'people versus the politicians' election (Conservative Party, 2019). Countless examples highlight how a central element of Boris Johnson's populist style revolves around a consistent and strategically groomed willingness to flaunt the rules, break conventions and engage in offensive behaviour. Censured by colleagues for describing the European Union (Withdrawal) (No. 2) Act as the 'surrender act' and under pressure to apologise he simply hardened his tone to call it 'the capitulation act'. Likewise, he dismissed concerns about increasing public aggression towards MPs as 'humbug' and then raised the possibility that his government may refuse to comply with the Act if it were passed. That Johnson's past journalism revealed a penchant for provocation, describing gay men as 'tank-topped bumboys' or veiled Muslim women as looking like 'letter boxes' only served to solidify this distinctive populist style. Provocation is something that is *done* by politicians and political actors not as an ideology but as a way of *being*, 'a way of speaking, acting, and presenting oneself' (*qua.* Moffitt, 2016).

2.2 Distracting dramaturgy

The populist style associated with Boris Johnson's leadership in the run-up to the election has significance for the UK because of the way in which the country's constitutional configuration is founded on the self-restraint of those who hold power. 'In the UK, we have trusted politicians to behave themselves', Blick and Hennessy (2020, p. 3) note, adding 'We have long assumed that those who rise to high office will be "good chaps", knowing what the unwritten rules are and wanting to adhere to them. Recent events suggest it is worth considering the implications of a decline in the viability of the "good chap" system in this country'. Yet, levels of anti-political sentiment may well have created a political environment that has nurtured 'chaps' who are less inclined to be 'good'. Here, a second element of populist style seems particularly apt in relation to understanding the election strategy: adopting a distracting dramaturgy.

This distracting dramaturgy occurs in the context of a double dynamic of public disenchantment with 'normal' politics alongside the existence of a 24/7 sensationalised new media operating largely through snippets and pictures. In this context, a distinctive politician emerges who is more than willing to serve up a constant flow of mishaps, horseplay and tomfoolery in a manner that chimes with demands of 'disaffected democrats' for rule-breakers while also feeding a voracious news industry. To dismiss this populist style as 'clowning around' misses the point that such behaviour fulfils a highly political role by attracting attention while simultaneously distracting attention from substantive issues. An eccentric appearance or use of exaggerated gestures or outlandish props are all parts of a performative act intended to connect with the media's insatiable appetite for personalised, entertainment-focused and polarising stories which are themselves favourable to populism. This *distracting dramaturgy* proved incredibly effective during the election as 'Boris' remained 'the story' irrespective of whether it focused on describing the leader of the opposition as 'Stalin', his plans to move his girlfriend into No. 10 while still being married or even his 'submarine strategy' of not being interviewed. The constant swirl of drama surrounding Boris Johnson arguably prevented the discussion of deeper policy-related issues, hence Moffitt's (2016, p. 37) observation that populist style fuses 'matter and manner, message and package'.

2.3   *Territorial targeting*

One of the few areas where the distracting dramaturgy arguably did give way to the promotion of a clear policy was in relation to territorial targeting, in which the Conservative Party was able to win seats in Labour's traditional northern heartlands (often captured as the collapse of the 'red wall'). While this was undoubtedly a key feature of the election, a striking feature of this success was that it was not based upon the standard nativism and nationalism that is generally a hallmark of populist politics but on a more sophisticated form of subnationalism and territorial targeting. In recent years, it has been possible to identify a powerful new socio-political cleavage within *English* politics characterised by an increasingly stark divergence between the worldviews and wants of those who live in major cities and those who live in provincial or coastal towns (see Jennings and Stoker, 2016). As Jennings and Stoker (2016) stress, this polarisation is not simply a Brexit realignment. Rather, the symptoms of *long-term trends* connected to global growth patterns and the changing nature of work have become more acute and these have impacted differently on citizens residing in different geographical locations.

This leads to a second argument concerning the link between populism 'UK-style' and territorial targeting. To define Boris Johnson's statecraft during the election simply as nationalist nativism would be to miss an underlying subtlety. There was, of course, an element of nostalgic jingoism. There was also a generic and effective appeal to 'Get Brexit Done'. But there was also a much *sharper strategy of territorial targeting* that helps explain the collapse of the 'red wall'. The Conservative Party under Boris Johnson toned down the talk of 'Global Britain' and instead focused on a much tighter constituency: 'England-beyond-London.' This was a strategy that dovetailed not just with those sections of the public that had lost faith in politics but also with those that had increasingly identified as English, rather than British. These were the traditional working class communities for whom the Labour Party seemed to offer no coherent vision. In this context, Johnson was able to offer an effective twin-track narrative which combined dealing with the past (that is, 'Get Brexit Done') and defining the future (that is, 'addressing domestic structural inequalities by "levelling-up"'). An added dimension to this strategy is that to some extent Johnson served as the saviour of Englishness. For some time seen as almost a 'forbidden' identity with racist or tarnished associations, the dismissal of Englishness by a generally detached cosmopolitan elite served to fuel frustration in 'backwater' areas of England. This frustration was fuelled and funnelled through the strategy of territorial targeting.

The first results on election night quickly made clear that this strategy had worked. In terms of territorial representation an argument could be made that the strategy worked *too well*. The Conservative Party is now almost completely a party of England with 345 of 365 (95%) of its MPs holding English seats. The intra-party dynamics of this situation will be discussed in the final part of this article.

2.4 Demarcating Brexit from Brexitism

The final element of this discussion of populism 'UK-style' involves teasing apart Brexit from Brexit*ism* and exploring how a man with a background (or should I say 'pedigree') like Boris Johnson can engage in populist politics. In many ways, the explanation is that the specific topic of Brexit was cloaked in a far broader strategic narrative which, in turn, underpinned a distinct populist style. It is in this sense that Brexit from can be distinguished from Brexit*ism*. The inspiration for this argument comes from Finlayson's (2017: 1) belief:

> [T]hat this political philosophy—call it Brexit*ism*—has congealed into something about so much more and yet so much less than Brexit. It is now a central feature of our landscape: an anti-political politics organised around resentment at past losses and scepticism about promised futures.

Boris Johnson's success in promoting a brand of Brexit*ism* rather than a simple focus on Brexit was pivotal to how his strategy sought to focus on those who felt 'left behind' and had become democratically disaffected. Rather than a 'Brexit election' in the simple sense, it was an election defined by 'Brexit*ism*' in a far broader sense. During the election, there was a discernible shift in Brexit*ism*, which distinguishes it from Finlayson's initial diagnosis. Critically, Johnson's Brexitism *did* include an emphasis on 'promised futures'. Finlayson was correct to highlight an almost nihilistic turn amongst many Brexit enthusiasts in the sense that the future was viewed as being inevitably uncertain. The distinctive element of Johnson's Brexit*ism* is that it dismissed the previous conviction that there is no knowable future and sought to promote an imagined (and largely English) community through the notion of 'levelling-up'. Whether Johnson will be able to manage, let alone fulfil, the very significant public expectations created by this electoral strategy is considered in the final section.

2.5 Upper crust populism

Boris Johnson is not the most obvious candidate to adopt a populist style. A hugely paradoxical element of the election was that it featured a form of populism that was almost dripping in elitist trappings. Alexander Boris de Pfeffel Johnson can hardly claim to be a 'man of the people'. The son of a former Conservative Member of the European Parliament, Boris went to Eton before heading up to

Balliol College where he became President of the Oxford Union and a member of the male-only Bullingdon Club. His career proceeded, rarely without incident, through journalism, into parliament, the London Mayor's office into government and No. 10. The anti-politician, anti-establishment, anti-elite narratives that generally accompany a populist style therefore sit very oddly with someone who has been a professional politician for two decades, whose establishment credentials could hardly be stronger and who has circulated within and amongst elites all his life. Populism 'UK-style' seems to have taken the form of what might be labelled 'upper crust populism' in order to denote its particularly English class credentials. This provokes an obvious question: how was an establishment figure able to adopt a populist style, and why have large sections of the public apparently been willing to accept it?

Barr's (2009) work on political mavericks offers one way of engaging with this question. Mavericks are politicians who rise to prominence within an established, competitive party but then either launch a form of internal takeover in order to fundamentally reshape their party, or abandon it to compete independently within a new 'insurgent' party. The critical link to Moffitt's work is that mavericks often seek to distinguish themselves from the mainstream by adopting a performative strategy in which they are consistently seen to be breaking the rules (hence Blick and Hennessy's (2020) concerns regarding *Good Chaps No More?*). In this regard, it is important to note that it is Johnson's ill-discipline that actually encapsulates his populist appeal. Johnson's speeches and articles resonate not because of what he has to say but because of the way he says it, while critics respond in ways that simply heighten his visibility and populist appeal.

There is also a particularly English cultural dimension that needs to be teased out. In her influential anthropological analysis of the quirks, habits and foibles of the English people, Fox (2005) underlines the centrality of the importance of not being earnest as a dominant culture marker. Taking things too seriously is therefore something of a cultural taboo that could be seen as almost legitimating Johnson's frequent failure to master the detail. Populists adapt their content from their host culture. 'Boris Johnson's buffoonery' is therefore held out by Molyneux and Osborne (2017, p. 5) as 'an example of what we could call the idiocy of power in democratic societies', 'idiocy' here meaning a non-elitist simplicity or genuineness that resonates with those who have become disaffected with conventional politics. The genius of Johnson's carefully contrived performative act is that it leads opponents to make the mistake of dismissing him as a buffoon while large sections of the public appear to find him endearing. Whether this is a sustainable long-term approach to leadership in government, however, is another matter entirely.

3. The Boris 'bargain' and delivering promises

If general election 2019 was a 'disaffection election', it was also marked by the Conservative Party, under Boris Johnson, absorbing the populist tradition that had until that point resided in the UK Independence Party and then the Brexit Party. This shift in (populist) style signalled that a mainstream party was willing to transgress conventional boundaries and potentially even to break the rules. The implications of this shift are particularly stark in the context of Britain's (in)-famously uncodified 'political constitution' for the simple reason that it requires a sense of self-restraint on the part of the occupant of No. 10 Downing Street to make it work. Boris Johnson is well-known for possessing a range of personal qualities but 'self-restraint' is not one that is commonly mentioned. In this context, it is noteworthy that Levitsky and Ziblatt's *How Democracies Die* (2019) offers a set of 'key indicators of authoritarian behaviour' which starts by asking 'do they reject the constitution or express a willingness to violate it?' The answer to this question in the recent British context is arguably unsettling, which leads me to make three final points about pessimism, populism and promises in the context of the election.

The adoption of a populist style may well be effective in the short-term and as an electoral strategy but it is unlikely to form the basis of a 'strong and stable' government in the long-term. This is the first point. There are echoes here of Mario Cuomo's famous dictum, 'campaign in poetry, govern in prose', in that Johnson campaigned in a highly performative populist style but must now demonstrate that *being* Prime Minister is not a joke. This is particularly true in a post-Brexit context defined by social polarisation. Successfully 'facing the disillusioned in a new decade', to paraphrase the sub-title of a recent NatCen/ONS report (2020), is unlikely to occur with a populist style. As British Election Study data suggests, political trust has itself become more polarised, with Leave supporters now being significantly more trusting of MPs in general and more satisfied with UK democracy than Remainers (see Figure 13.1).

This more positive view from Leave voters is despite the fact that 'levels of political trust have typically tended to be higher among the educated, professional demographics that were more likely to vote Remain', Jennings *et al.* (2020, p. 1) 'Brexit identity seems to now condition trust in the UK's politicians and democracy. Confirming this, when asked how often the government in Westminster can be trusted to do the right thing, 23% of Leavers said "most of the time", more than double the number for Remainers (10%)' (Jennings *et al.*, 2020, p. 1). This flows into my second point: the 2019 general election was perhaps unique for the rather reluctant manner in which traditionally Labour voters and non-voters did vote Conservative. Those votes were often the product of frustration and fatigue rather than conviction and confidence. 'Your hand might have quivered over the

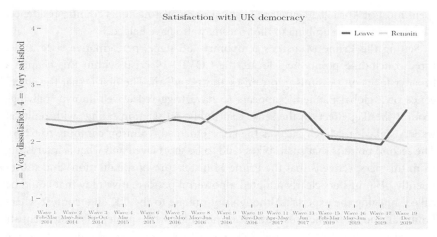

Figure 13.1 Satisfaction with UK democracy, February 2014–December 2019
Source: Jennings *et al.* (2020).

ballot paper as you put your cross in the Conservative box', Johnson conceded during his victory speech before acknowledging that a large number of people had 'lent him' their support. In a democracy, the consent of the citizens to allow an individual or group to govern is only ever given on a temporary basis but in the 2019 election, the extent of social fragmentation, the shift in social allegiances and the simple hatred and venom that defined debates has given what looks like a 'strong' majority a certain sense of fragility. The Boris 'bargain' was simple: vote for me and not only will I 'Get Brexit Done' but I'll also address long-term structural inequalities through a process of 'levelling-up' beyond London through massive economic investment. If public trust is not to fall and anti-political sentiment increase Johnson must now deliver on that bargain in a context where very high and often contradictory expectations have been generated around the sunlit uplands of a post-Brexit world (for a discussion see Hay, 2020).

The third and final point is that 'the trust terrain' of British politics has already shifted far beyond the socio-political landscape that shaped the election. The emergence of COVID-19 as a global pandemic has to a large extent swept Brexit off the agenda and put in its place a very different and yet closely related set of questions concerning public trust in politicians, political processes and political institutions (for a discussion see Flinders, 2020b). It has also raised questions about Boris Johnson's leadership skills, and his ability to absorb the detail and to keep his flippancy in check. Apart from his suggestion that the government's urgent search for medical ventilators should be called 'Operation Last Gasp', the Prime Minister has appeared suitably restrained and also aware of the existence of a serious trust-deficit amongst the public. (The fact that the Prime Minister spent most of April 2020 either in hospital or recovering at his country residence, Chequers, after succumbing to the virus may also have helped.)

Setting the Prime Minister's temporary 'off-stage' performative style aside, three concluding points help locate the COVID-19 crisis within this chapter's broader focus on pessimism, promises and populism. The first is that the emergence of a global pandemic appears to have triggered a well-known 'rallying-around-the-flag-effect' in the sense that public satisfaction ratings with political leaders spiked in March 2020 as the crisis emerged (Johnson climbing to 52%). The second point is that such spikes tend to be short-lived and what is interesting from this perspective is that the Prime Minister (pre-hospitalisation) and subsequently his ministers clearly adopted a powerful performative ploy that could be called 'hugging the experts'. Although not unique to the UK, in a context where politicians enjoy public trust ratings of just 14% while professors and scientists enjoyed trust-levels of 84% and 86% respectively (see Ipsos MORI, 2019), the stage has been set during the daily press briefings with 'the experts' (recently loathed vis-à-vis Brexit, now apparently loved in the context of COVID-19) standing very much shoulder-to-shoulder. With only the two-metre social distancing rule able to tease them apart on stage, the central element of any governmental script has been the constant cover of 'following the scientific evidence'. 'Blame-games' and 'blame-boomerangs' will undoubtedly emerge but the deeper implication of this performative element is that if public trust in politics has been heavily influenced in recent years by Brexit then there is little doubt that moving forward the future of British democracy is likely to be defined by the public's perception of how Boris Johnson's government was able to cope with the COVID-19 pandemic.

References

Barr, R. (2009) 'Populists, Outsiders and anti-Establishment Politics', *Party Politics*, **15**, 29–48.

Blick, A., and Hennessy, P. (2020) *Good Chaps No More?* London, Constitution Society.

Clarke, J., and Newman, J. (2017) 'People in This Country Have Had Enough of Experts: Brexit and the Paradoxes of Populism', *Critical Policy Studies*, **11**, 101–116.

Conservative Party (2019) *Get Brexit Done: Unleash Britain's Potential*, London, Conservative Party.

Curtice, J. (2020) 'Brave New World: Understanding the 2019 General Election', *Political Insight*, **11**, 8–12.

Cutts, D., Goodwin, M., Heath, O., and Surridge, P. (2020) 'Brexit, the 2019 General Election and the Realignment of British Politics', *The Political Quarterly*, **91**, 7–23.

Evans, G., and Menon, A. (2017). *Brexit and British Politics*, London, John Wiley & Sons.

Finlayson, A. (2017, 18 May) 'Brexitism', *London Review of Books*, **39**, accessed at https://www.lrb.co.uk/the-paper/v39/n10/alan-finlayson/brexitism on 20 April 2020.

Flinders, M. (2015) 'The General Rejection? Political Disengagement, Disaffected Democrats and 'Doing Politics' Differently'. In Tonge, J. and Geddes, A. (eds.) *Britain Votes 2015*, Oxford, Oxford University Press, pp. 241–254.

Flinders, M. (2018) 'Funneling Frustration: Anti-Politics as a Political Driver' In Tonge, J., Leston-Bandeira, C. and Wilks-Heeg, S. (eds.) *Britain Votes 2017*, Oxford, Oxford University Press, pp. 222–236.

Flinders, M. (2019, 12 November) 'UK Election 2019: This is What Populism Looks Like When Done by the British', *The Conversation*, accessed at https://theconversation.com/uk-election-2019-this-is-what-populism-looks-like-when-done-by-the-british-126733 on 11 May 2020.

Flinders, M. (2020a) 'Why Feelings Trump Facts: Anti-politics, Citizenship and Emotion', *Emotions and Society*, accessed at https://www.ingentaconnect.com/content/bup/eas/pre-prints/content-emsocd1900014r1 on 18 April 2020.

Flinders, M. (2020b) 'Democracy and the Politics of Coronavirus: Trust, Blame and Understanding', *Parliamentary Affairs*, on-line [forthcoming]

Fox, K. (2005) *Watching the English: The Hidden Rules of English Behaviour*, London, Hodder & Stoughton.

Gamble, A. (2019, 3 November) 'Adapt or Die: How the Conservative Party Keeps Power', *The Guardian*, accessed at https://www.theguardian.com/politics/2019/nov/03/how-conservative-party-changed-to-survive-brexit-purge on 18 April 2020.

Hansard Society (2019) *Audit of Political Engagement*, London, Hansard Society.

HC1115 (2018) 'Failure of a Witness to Answer an Order of the Committee', Third Special Report of the House of Commons Digital, Culture, Media and Sport Committee, Session 2017–2019.

Hay, C. (2020) 'Brexistential Angst and the Paradoxes of Populism', *Political Studies*, **68**, 187–206.

Henderson, A. (2019) 'Uncomfortable Answers', *Political Insight*, **10**, 8–11.

Ipsos MORI (2019, 26 November) 'Trust in Politicians Falls Sending Them Spiralling Back to the Bottom of the Ipsos MORI Veracity Index', accessed at https://www.ipsos.com/ipsos-mori/en-uk/trust-politicians-falls-sending-them-spiralling-back-bottom-ipsos-mori-veracity-index on 12 April 2020.

Ipsos MORI (2020) 'Political Monitor: Satisfaction Ratings 1997-2020', accessed at https://www.ipsos.com/ipsos-mori/en-uk/political-monitor-satisfaction-ratings-1997-present on 12 April 2020.

Jennings, W., and Stoker, G. (2016) 'The Bifurcation of Politics: Two Englands', *The Political Quarterly*, **87**, 372–382.

Jennings, W., and Lodge, M. (2019) 'Brexit, the Tides and Canute: The Fracturing Politics of the British State', *Journal of European Public Policy*, **26**, 772–789.

Jennings, W., Stoker, G., Gaskell, J., and Devine, D. (2020, 9 March) 'Political Trust Realigned after the General Election', *UK in a Changing Europe Blog*, accessed at https://ukandeu.ac.uk/political-trust-realigned-after-the-general-election/ on 10 April 2020.

Levitsky, S., and Ziblatt, D. (2019) *How Democracies Die*, London, Penguin.

Moffitt, B. (2016) *The Global Rise of Populism: Performance, Political Style and Representation*, Stanford, Stanford University Press.

Molyneux, M., and Osborne, T. (2017) 'Populism – a Deflationary View', *Economy and Society*, **46**, 1–19.

NatCen/ONS (2020) *Progress and Popularity: Facing the Disillusioned in a New Decade*, London, NatCen.

NatCen/ONS (2020) *Unresolved Public Policy Challenges*, London, NatCen.

Ostrom, E. (2000) 'The Danger of Self-Evident Truths', *PS: Political Science and Politics*, **33**, 33–44.

Powell, R. (2019, 24 November) 'Almost Half of Voters Think Leadership Worse Than in Previous Elections', *Sky News Blog*, accessed at https://news.sky.com/story/general-election-almost-half-of-voters-think-leadership-worse-than-in-previous-elections-11867871 on 10 April 2020.

Serhan, Y. (2020, 14 March) 'Populism is Meaningless', *The Atlantic*, accessed at https://www.theatlantic.com/international/archive/2020/03/what-is-populism/607600/ on 20 April 2020.

EMILY HARMER AND ROSALYND SOUTHERN[*]

'Girly Swots' and the Most Diverse Parliament Ever: Women's Representation, Voters and Issues in the 2019 Election Campaign

The 2019 election had felt inevitable for months once Theresa May had been replaced as Conservative leader and Prime Minister by Boris Johnson. The UK was back at the polls just two-and-a-half years after May's miscalculation that a snap election would produce a parliamentary majority large enough to pass the European Union (EU) withdrawal agreement. May's leadership had been dogged with the difficulties caused by her slim majority and subsequent confidence and supply arrangement with the Democratic Unionist Party. Once parliament asserted its right to approve the withdrawal agreement, her premiership became defined by her frustrated attempts to secure an agreement with the EU which her own Eurosceptic backbenchers, the more moderate members of her party and opposition parties would vote to approve. She fought on but her failure to pass a withdrawal agreement ultimately led to her resignation and Johnson's victory in the leadership election. As well as the Conservative Party dispensing with its female leader after only three years, the run-up to the campaign was marred by a number of high-profile women MPs taking the decision to stand down, citing threats and abuse they had received as partially responsible (Ross, 2019). Our analysis assesses the importance placed on women during the campaign by firstly discussing how women were portrayed. We then go on to discuss the parties' attempts to appeal to women voters through an analysis of their manifesto offerings, before discussing how women voted. Finally, we analyse the extent to which the representation of women in parliament was altered as a result of the election.

[*]Emily Harmer, Department of Communication and Media, University of Liverpool, E.Harmer@liverpool.ac.uk; Rosalynd Southern, Department of Communication and Media, University of Liverpool, R.Southern@liverpool.ac.uk

doi:10.1093/pa/gsaa031

1. The campaign

In 2017, many of the major political parties were led by women for the first time (as well as it being the first election contested by a female prime minister for 30 years). The landscape of female leadership changed dramatically in advance of the 2019 election. While Nicola Sturgeon and Arlene Foster remained in post and the Green Party retained the idea of gender-balanced co-leaders, Plaid Cymru and the Conservatives both elected male leaders and Jo Swinson was elected as the first female leader of the Liberal Democrats. These changes meant that the only viable candidates for prime minister were both men which led to women returning to the margins during this campaign.

In 2017, the Conservatives ran a highly personalised campaign centred around May's competence and leadership which proved risky (Harmer and Southern, 2018). Her disappointing election campaign should perhaps have served as a warning to any subsequent female party leader to avoid conducting a campaign that was focused around her own leadership credentials. Academic research has shown that personalised campaigns are particularly risky for women (Van Zoonen, 2006). The main problem is that they may inadvertently reinforce stereotypical assumptions about the incompatibility between traditional understandings of femininity and conventional ideals of political leadership. Political leadership is often associated with traditionally masculine traits and behaviours such as combativeness, strength and assertiveness (Campus, 2013; Conroy, 2015). Empirical evidence suggests that female politicians may generally be viewed as more compassionate, honest and warmer than male opponents by voters, while men are viewed as more competent, decisive and stronger leaders (Kahn 1996; Dolan and Lynch, 2014). Women, therefore, risk being perceived as 'compassionate' but lacking the necessary 'strength' expected of leaders. On the contrary, when they are portrayed as strong or assertive, they risk being perceived negatively because they are transgressing gendered behavioural norms (Murray, 2010). Jamieson (1995) describes this as a 'competence/femininity' double bind in which masculinity is associated with leadership, but negative consequences may await women who display masculine leadership qualities.

Despite these risks, the Liberal Democrats seemed content to emphasise Jo Swinson's leadership at every opportunity, even branding the party as Jo Swinson's Liberal Democrats on their campaign bus. This decision was perhaps particularly ill-advised given that her own parliamentary seat was very precarious. Much like May's attempt to own the pejorative title 'bloody difficult woman', Swinson attempted to capitalise on her position as the only woman leader of the Westminster parties by insisting that she ought to be included in the first Prime Ministerial debate to be broadcast. The Liberal Democrats set up an online petition calling for her inclusion in this televised debate, claiming Boris Johnson and

Jeremy Corbyn were running scared of debating the woman leader of the strongest party of Remain, arguing that the voters deserved to hear from Swinson, not just from two men who want to deliver Brexit. They also released campaign posters which simply said, 'Debate Her', alongside a photograph of Swinson.

At the same time as arguing that it was important for women's voices to be included, Swinson also attempted to portray herself as just as tough and competent as her male opponents by at times adopting masculinised campaign tactics. For example, she appeared in a boxing ring like her male opponents while wearing a T-shirt which read 'Girly Swot'—a reference to the revelation that Boris Johnson used this insult to describe a male rival. This attempt to reclaim a sexist put-down was only partially successful, however, as it has been argued that it seemed to support her framing by the press as a domineering 'head girl' figure (McKay, 2019). While a strategy of presenting women leaders as strong and combative can have advantages, there are also risks inherent in this approach. It may be desirable to be perceived as masculine in terms of leadership credentials, but it can also mean transgressing the expected norms of femininity which can have a negative impact on how voters perceive a candidate (Jamieson, 1995).

One particularly acute example of this phenomenon was when Swinson was asked in a television interview if she would consider using nuclear weapons. When she immediately responded in the affirmative without appearing to think about it, she was roundly criticised by political opponents and campaign groups alike (*The Independent*, 2019a). Nicola Sturgeon's response showed the inherent risk in Swinson's decision to embrace traditionally masculine politicking. She stated that 'it is sickening to hear this question asked and answered as if it's some kind of virility test and without any context' (*The Independent*, 2019b). With her use of the word 'virility' to describe effective leadership, Sturgeon disparages Swinson's willingness to engage in the masculinised rhetoric over an important issue. Sturgeon's remarks also served to undermine Swinson's efforts to present herself as a strong leader by drawing attention to the fact that as a woman she cannot be considered 'virile'. Sturgeon's comments also allowed some news organisations to stereotype these two women leaders as bitter rivals. This is perhaps best highlighted by the *Daily Mail* suggesting that Sturgeon celebrated her party's victory in unseating Swinson on election night too enthusiastically (*Mail Online*, 2019).

In previous elections, women voters have featured in marginal but distinct ways. A common trope since 1997 was to speculate about the voting intensions of target voters like Worcester Woman and 'mumsnetters' (Harmer and Wring, 2013). Much like the 2017 campaign, no female target group received attention. Even the one party that might be more interested in women voters and their political priorities, the Women's Equality Party, were marginal in the campaign despite fielding a handful of candidates. Some individual women gained prominence due to their robust questioning of politicians on the campaign trail, such as the junior doctor who confronted Boris Johnson about cuts to the National Health Service during a hospital visit (*The Independent*, 2019c).

News media are central to election campaigns as they offer a means for the electorate to gain information about the policies and values of political parties. Typically, women struggle to receive substantial representation in news coverage of elections (Ross *et al.*, 2013; Harmer and Southern, 2018). Election coverage also tends to focus on party leaders (Deacon and Harmer, 2019) so when the two most likely candidates for Prime Minister are male, this can mean women are even more marginalised in news coverage. Loughborough University's Centre for Research in Communication and Culture analysed the main print and broadcast output throughout the five weeks of the campaign. Their analysis showed that only five women appeared in the top 20 list of most prominent politicians in the coverage. Perhaps unsurprisingly, Jo Swinson was the most prominent woman and yet she was a distant fourth behind her Conservative and Labour counterparts and received less coverage than the Shadow Chancellor John McDonnell. Swinson was only just ahead of Brexit Party's Nigel Farage who, despite having no MPs in the previous parliament, was given more attention than Nicola Sturgeon (Deacon *et al.*, 2019). The other most reported women were Priti Patel, Angela Rayner and Diane Abbott, all prominent members of the cabinet or shadow cabinet. The Loughborough research also showed that at the end of the first week of the election, women accounted for just one-third of quotations on television and one-fifth of quotes in newspapers (Deacon *et al.*, 2019). The lack of women quoted in the campaign coverage demonstrates that once again women's voices were marginalised (Harmer and Southern, 2018).

The increased importance of digital media in election campaigns has led some scholars to suggest that by using social media, women are given an opportunity to counteract the fact that they are being ignored or reported stereotypically by mainstream print and broadcast media (Osei-Appiah, 2019). While this can be true, others have suggested that social media, particularly Twitter, tends to be full of gendered abuse and stereotypes, and that it reinforces the gendered coverage witnessed in print and broadcast (Southern and Harmer, 2019). An analysis of tweets sent to candidates in the last week of the campaign by Margetts *et al.* (2019) shows that well-known women like Diane Abbott received a high proportion of abusive tweets. Digital politics then appears to present the same gendered patterns as mainstream print and broadcast coverage.

2. Parties appeal to women voters: manifestos

One way of assessing the importance placed on women and their votes by political parties is to analyse their manifesto pledges for explicit or implicit references to gendered policy areas (Harmer and Southern, 2018). It is important to analyse the pledges made in manifestos as these are the most explicit means of targeting and representing women voters (Campbell and Childs, 2015). Women are obviously affected by all the policies that parties propose, but here we analyse the policies which explicitly invoke women in the manifestos. Here, we present a summary of the six main political party manifestos.

Just as in 2017, we see a lot of consensus around the kinds of policy areas where women are most visibly invoked in the manifestos. Many policy areas affecting women are devolved to the respective national governments of Scotland and Wales, meaning the manifesto commitments of the Scottish National Party and Plaid Cymru are aimed at a much smaller set of electors than the other parties discussed here. Nevertheless, including gendered proposals in their manifestos for the general election signals a set of clear priorities as far as women are concerned. Table 14.1 shows which issues were foregrounded by each party.

The following discussion will attempt to contextualise the policy positions of each party, since although there is a consensus on the range of issues associated with women, the approaches of each party can be very different. The policies which are included in the manifestos fall into seven main areas:

(1) Violence against women and girls

(2) Legal/Judicial

(3) Employment

(4) Social Security

(5) Lesbian, Gay, Bisexual, Transgender, Queer+

(6) Education

(7) Public life

All the major parties made some mention of specific gendered policy areas (although the Conservatives and Plaid Cymru had fewer mentions than most). The policy areas which directly referred to women followed a similar pattern to recent elections, with key policy areas revolving around women's caring responsibilities and work–life balance (Campbell and Childs, 2015; Harmer and Southern, 2018). All parties (except for the Conservatives) proposed a range of policies aimed at tackling structural inequalities. Labour, for example, proposed the creation of a new Department for Women and Equalities with a full-time Secretary of State to make sure all policies and laws are equality-impact assessed. Labour, Plaid Cymru, the SNP and Greens all made pledges to increase the representation of women in politics. Labour and the Green Party furthermore pledged to make it compulsory for parties to publish diversity data about their candidates. The SNP manifesto went the furthest in this respect by promising to push for further

Table 14.1 2019 general election manifesto issue coverage (X denotes manifesto mention)

	Con	Lab	LD	SNP	PC	Green
Violence against women						
Domestic violence	X	X	X	X	X	X
Sexual violence	X	X	X		X	X
Forced marriage/'Honour-based violence'/FGM	X					X
Ratify Istanbul Convention		X	X	X		
Legal/Judicial						
Women offenders			X		X	X
Family courts	X					
Misogyny as hate crime		X				X
Abortion		X	X			X
Employment						
Pay gap		X		X		X
Parental leave	X	X	X	X		
Maternity discrimination/pay	X	X				
Discrimination		X		X		
Menopause policy		X		X	X	
Flexible working	X	X	X			X
Social security						
Pensions equality	X	X	X	X	X	X
Rape clause		X		X		
Maternity/sexual health services		X	X		X	X
Child care	X	X	X	X	X	X
'Tampon Tax'	X			X		
Other gendered tax				X		
LGBT+						
Gender clinics					X	X
Gender Recognition Act			X		X	X
Education						
Sex and relationships			X			X
Public life						
Gender quotas				X		
Increase women's representation		X	X	X	X	X
Government department for women and equalities		X				
Gender audits		X	X	X		X

devolved power to acquire the option of imposing gender quotas for the Scottish Parliament. The Greens also promised to introduce job sharing at all levels of government to enable greater representation of women. Beyond political institutions, the Liberal Democrats and Greens both pledged to require 40% of company boards to be comprised of women and to carry out gender pay audits.

All six parties included policy proposals related to tackling gender-based violence. Some parties took a more detailed approach to these issues than others. The Conservatives included pledges to pass the domestic violence bill and to fight crime against women and girls, specifically citing female genital mutilation (FGM) and forced marriage. Many parties focused on addressing domestic abuse. Labour, the Liberal Democrats and SNP all promised to ratify the Istanbul Convention on preventing and combating violence against women and domestic violence. Labour, Plaid Cymru and the Liberal Democrats all pledged to address funding cuts to refuges and other services which have suffered under austerity. Plaid Cymru included policy proposals to register repeat offenders of domestic abuse and to improve police training around these issues. The Green Party offered the most comprehensive proposals for tackling violence against women, promising to develop and implement a UK-wide strategy to tackle violence against women and girls, including sexual violence, FGM and trafficking.

The area with perhaps the most policy proposals across the board was employment-related issues which recognise that women often experience the labour market differently. Labour, the Greens and SNP all promised to act to address the gender pay gap. All parties (except Plaid Cymru) made promises to make improvements to parental leave. Labour introduced plans to increase paid maternity leave from 9 to 12 months, double paternity leave to four weeks and increase provision for flexible working (where possible). The Conservatives' proposals were less definitive. They pledged to extend the entitlement to leave for unpaid carers (of whom women make up the majority) to one week, encourage flexible working (although it was unclear what they meant by 'encourage') and look at ways to make it easier for men to take paternity leave. The Conservatives (along with Plaid Cymru and the SNP) also pledged to reform the law to protect women from being discriminated against while pregnant or returning from maternity leave. The Liberal Democrats promised to increase statutory paternity leave and ensure that parents have the right to parental leave from day one of their employment. The SNP pledged to increase maternity pay, promote shared parental leave and increase paid leave for fathers to attend six antenatal appointments. While these policies are clearly aimed at younger women, the Labour and Green parties also targeted older voters by including proposals to encourage companies to implement menopause policies including menopausal leave.

Except for the SNP, all other parties proposed policies related to legal or criminal justice matters. Labour, the Liberal Democrats and Greens promised to ensure safe and legal abortions in all parts of the UK (including Northern Ireland). The Green Party pledged to make misogyny a specific hate crime and to improve press regulation to ensure complaints about discriminatory media coverage could be tackled. The Greens and Plaid Cymru proposed reducing the number of female prisoners by providing alternative punishments, in recognition of the poor outcomes for women in detention. Plaid Cymru also pledged to tackle the very low conviction rates for rape and provide more training for professionals working in the criminal justice system about sexual violence and its impacts on women.

The manifestos made a wide range of pledges relating to social security and taxation. All six parties addressed the provision of good quality childcare for working parents. Some of these policy proposals were vague, such as the SNP's pledge to increase childcare provision and the Conservative proposal to establish a £1 billion fund 'to help create more high quality, affordable childcare, including before and after school and during the school holidays' (Conservative Party, 2019, p. 17). The Labour Party, on the contrary, pledged to extend 30 hours of free childcare or preschool education for all two-, three- and four-year olds within the next five years. It also promised to increase childcare provision for one-year olds. The Liberal Democrats pledged free childcare from 9 to 24 months for working parents as well as extend free childcare for every child two to four years old. They additionally announced plans to invest £1 billion per year in children's centres. Plaid Cymru pledged free care and education for one to three-year olds. The Green Party promised the most by pledging to offer 35 hours free childcare from nine months. Other policy proposals aimed at parents included Labour and the SNP pledging to abolish the controversial 'rape clause' which requires women to disclose if their child was conceived as a result of sexual violence if they need to claim child benefit for more than two children. Plaid Cymru pledged a £35 a week payment for every child in low-income families in Wales. There were also pledges from the Conservatives and SNP to remove VAT on sanitary products.

Policies aimed at older women were mainly focused on correcting inequalities in the current pension regime. Labour, the Liberal Democrats, Plaid Cymru and the SNP all included proposals to support the so-called Women Against State Pension Inequality women, who were born in the 1950s and have been left disadvantaged by repeated changes to the pensions age. The Green Party proposed to assist these women first in the introduction of a universal basic income which would also help women of all ages.

Other policy areas included education and lesbian, gay and transgender rights. The Liberal Democrats and Green Party both pledged to improve sex and relationship education in schools. Labour, the Liberal Democrats, the Green Party and Plaid Cymru all pledged to reform the Gender Recognition Act to allow self-identification. The Greens and Plaid Cymru also pledged to provide further support for gender clinics.

3. Candidates

From the very beginning of the campaign, gender shaped the debate around candidates. Seventy-four MPs stood down, which was high compared to the 31 who stood down in 2017 but was slightly below the usual average of 86 between 1979 and 2010. There were also slightly fewer women than men who stood down with

9% of female MPs standing down compared to 13% of male MPs. What makes this particularly pertinent though is that several female MPs specifically cited on-line abuse and other malicious communications in their resignation statements in a way that few male MPs who were standing down did (Ross, 2019). Former Conservative Education Secretary, Nicky Morgan, spoke of the 'sacrifices involved in, and the abuse for, doing the job of a modern MP' in her resignation statement (*The Guardian*, 2019). She had earlier been subject to threats including from a man who rang her office to say her 'days were numbered'. The man was later jailed (*BBC News*, August 2019b). Former Conservative MP Heidi Allen, who defected to the Independent Group, which morphed into Change UK, left them to sit as an independent and later joined the Liberal Democrats, during the 2017–2019 parliament, made perhaps the strongest statement on the abuse she received when she announced she would not be standing for parliament again, saying: 'Nobody in any job should have to put up with threats, aggressive emails, being shouted at in the street, sworn at on social media, nor have to install panic alarms at home. Of course, public scrutiny is to be expected, but lines are all too often regularly crossed, and the effect is utterly dehumanising' (*BBC News*, October 2019c). Allen had also been subject to an abusive email campaign and her abuser also later jailed (*BBC News*, April 2019a). This led to a high-profile debate around the tone of political discourse often facilitated by the polarised Brexit debate and the disproportionate effect this may have on already under-represented groups.

Some parties had adopted new mechanisms for selecting candidates since the 2017 selection process. The number and proportion of candidates for each of the most prominent parties are shown in Table 14.2. Table 14.3 shows the number and proportion of women who were elected. In the lead up the last election, some had claimed that the snap election had led to processes not being properly followed when it came to gender balance. The Liberal Democrats seemed to learn this lesson, placing most of their new female candidates in their most winnable seats. This led to them now having 64% female MPs. Similarly, certain high-profile figures in the Labour Party had voiced disapproval over 2017s 'emergency' selections (Harmer and Southern, 2018), which some felt had side-lined female candidates in certain places. In light of this, Labour put in place extra mechanisms to ensure female representation did not slip back. This paid dehumanising dividends for them in terms of gender equality even despite their heavy losses on the night. It increased their number of female candidates dramatically compared to 2017, with 335 as opposed to 256, and meant that for the first time in their history, they now have more female MPs than male ones, at 51% female. However, the slight drop in terms of elected female MPs compared to selected female candidates potentially still raises questions about the placement of women into winnable seats.

Table 14.2 Candidate gender by party, 2017 and 2019 general elections

Party	2017[a] (Female[a])	Female (%)	2019[a] (Female[a])	Female (%)
Con	638 (184)	29	635 (194)	31
Lab	631 (256[b])	41	631[c] (335[d])	53
Lib Dem	630[e] (184[f])	29	611[c] (186[d])	30
UKIP	378 (49)	13	44 (8)	18
Green	476[g] (164[h])	35	497[i] (203[d])	41
SNP	59 (20)	34	59 (20)	34
PC	40 (11)	28	36 (9)	25
Sinn Féin	18 (7)	39	15 (4)	27
SDLP	18 (6)	33	15 (8)	53
DUP	17 (2)	12	17 (2)	12
WEP	7 (7)	100	3 (3)	100
Total		29		38

[a]Transgender and non-binary candidates are highlighted here simply to give visibility to them as representatives;
[b]including two trans women;
[c]including one non-binary candidate;
[d]including one trans woman;
[e]including one non-binary trans candidate;
[f]including two trans women;
[g]including two non-binary candidates and a trans man;
[h]including one trans woman;
[i]including four non-binary candidates.
Sources: House of Commons Library Briefing Paper (2017, p. 47); House of Commons Library Briefing Paper (2019, p. 41); Pink News (2019).

Table 14.3 Female MPs by party, 2017 and 2019 general elections

	2017	%	2019	%
	n		n	
Conservatives	67	21	87	24
Labour	119	45	104	51
Lib Dems	4	33	7	64
SNP	12	34	16	33
Green	1	100	1	100
Other	5	22	5	22
All	208	32	220	34

Source: House of Commons Library Briefing Paper (2019) 'Women in the House of Commons', p. 46.

In terms of the other parties, the Women's Equality Party predictably led the pack in terms of the percentage of female candidates, at 100%. The Labour Party and Social Democratic and Labour Party fielded a slate of candidates that were 53% female. The Green Party puts forward the next highest proportion of female candidates, at 41%—still below 50% but showing a marked improvement on female representation in their candidates at the last election, where only 35% were female. The SNP, the Conservative Party and the Liberal Democrats all selected women as around a third of their candidates and made no significant improvement, in terms of increasing female representation among their candidates, on the last election. Plaid Cymru and Sinn Féin both put forward a list of candidates that were around a quarter female, meaning both these parties had actually gone backward in terms of female candidates since the last election, Sinn Féin significantly so, falling from 39% in 2017 to 27% in 2019. Perhaps unsurprisingly, the two parties with the lowest proportion of female candidates were the UK Independence Party (UKIP) and the Democratic Unionist Party (DUP) with 18% and 12% female candidates, respectively. UKIP did make some improvements in the last election, moving up from 13%, but the DUP's female representation among their candidates remained stagnant. Overall, female candidates comprised 38% of all those who ran for parliament, showing that, except for a few parties, there is still long way to go before female representation in selections is equal.

Overall, 220 women were elected to parliament. This was 34% of the total and was the highest percentage in history, continuing a trend of continuously increasing female representation which started in 1979. Following the election, the Liberal Democrats now have 64% female MPs, Labour have 51%, the SNP have 33% and the Conservatives have 24%. This shows a steady but stubbornly glacial pace of improvement in female representatives elected to the House of Commons. It is welcome, however, that the Labour Party, the main opposition party and the Liberal Democrats now have female representation above (and in the case of the Liberal Democrats, way above) the long-touted 50% target for equal representation. At the very least, this shows that active initiatives, such as specifically selecting good female candidates to the most winnable seats, which the Liberal Democrats favoured, and all-women shortlists, which have long been used by Labour, do work in terms of increasing female representation. In terms of more intersectional female representation, the number of women of colour increased by 9 to 35 overall (Shendruk, 2019). These included Munira Wilson for the Liberal Democrats, meaning they doubled their black, Asian and minority ethnic women's representation, and Nadia Whitmore for Labour, who also became the baby of the House. Other notable 'firsts' were Labour's Kim Johnson becoming Liverpool's first black MP, Labour's Sarah Owen who became the UK's first female British-Chinese MP, and Labour's Apsana Begum, who became the first MP to wear hijab. The increase in new black female MPs furthermore led to a debate on racism after the *Evening Standard* and BBC repeatedly mislabelled photos of black female MPs, mixing their names up (*The Guardian*, 2020). The House of Commons is now more diverse than it has ever been.

4. Women voters

Earlier studies of gender and voting behaviour have largely concluded that there is little in the way of an aggregate gender gap in British voting patterns (Campbell, 2006). There is, however, a well-established pattern of a gender-generation gap (first identified by Norris, 1999), where older women voters are more likely to vote Conservative than older men, while younger women are more likely to vote for left-wing parties than their male counterparts. There was no focus on youth issues or a 'Youthquake' as there had been in the 2017 election, and what issues did emerge in the muddled campaign did not have the gendered and age implications of the highly prominent policies of the 2017 election, such as the so-called 'dementia tax'. In 2017, a gender gap in voting was present for each age group (Harmer and Southern, 2018) with women favouring Labour, and it is important to consider whether this gap endures even with the reduction in specific factors that may have accounted for this at the last election. We analysed Wave 19 of the British Election Study (BES) online survey, which was conducted in the ten days just after the 2019 general election. Here we present the findings from the question which asked voters to recall their actual vote. Figure 14.1 shows the recalled vote for the main parties by gender. Figure 14.2 shows the recalled vote of just the two main parties by gender and age. The data show that there was a small aggregate gender gap, with 42% of women voting Conservative compared to 44% of men, and 34% of women voting Labour compared to 31% of men. This is largely in keeping with the gender gap from the 2017 election, where there was also a three-point gender gap in votes for Labour.

A much more striking pattern emerges when age is considered alongside gender. Women aged 25 years and under voted overwhelmingly for Labour, with 58% of them doing so compared to 19% of them voting Conservative. There was still a large gap in favour of Labour for male voters aged under 25 years but not to the same degree as women. Here, 43% of men aged under 25 voted Labour compared to 28% who voted Conservative. For women between 26 and 35 years old, there is a still large but not as extensive gap in favour of Labour, with 43% voting for Labour compared to 30% for the Conservatives. In this age group, men still favour Labour, but the gap is narrow with 38% voting Labour compared to 34% voting Conservative. It is interesting to note that for the 56–65 years age group, slightly more women recalled voting Conservative than men in this age group (55.2% compared to 54.6%), but this stronger performance for the Conservatives among women than men then disappears for the oldest group (66+). This of course may reflect the results from 2015 (Wave 6 of the BES), where in all age groups above 46-year-old women voted Conservative at slightly higher rates, only now these voters have aged into an older cohort. However, the gap for women in favour of Labour in the very oldest group here suggests that

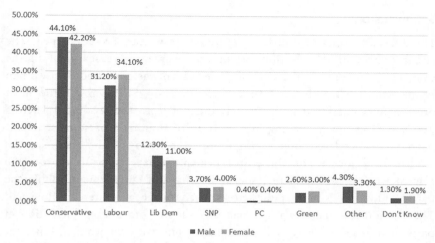

Figure 14.1 2019 general election recalled vote by gender
Source: BES Wave 19 (13–23 December 2019) n = 25,777, weighted.

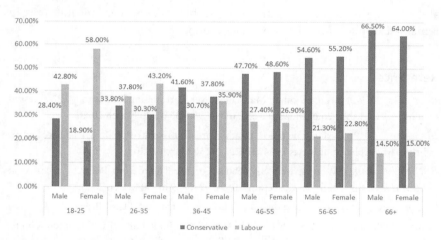

Figure 14.2 2019 general election recalled vote by gender and age
Source: BES Wave 19 (13–23 December 2019) n = 25,777, weighted.

policies such as the 'dementia tax' in the 2017 election, which was seemingly disproportionately targeted at older women, have not been so easily forgotten by these women. Overall, the generational gender hypothesis forwarded by Norris (1999) is supported here due to the overwhelming proportion of younger women who voted in favour of Labour compared to the Conservatives. The gap, however, is lower than it was in 2017, suggesting that even among a group that is seemingly inclined to vote for them, Labour did not offer enough to attract their votes compared to 2017. This might be something Labour wish to consider if they are serious about improving their performance at the next election.

5. Conclusion

The 2019 election was a mixed picture where women are concerned. The circumstances of the election meant that women were marginal in the campaign compared to the previous one, which was contested by a woman Prime Minister for the first time since 1987. Jo Swinson was the most prominent woman and unfortunately did not learn the lessons of Theresa May's 2017 campaign, falling into the trap of running a personalised campaign. The gendered policy proposals from each of the main parties tended to be focused on those areas which we have come to expect—the role of women in public life, social security and employment. While the parties addressed similar policy areas, their proposals differed somewhat. The election resulted in a very small increase in women's representation in parliament overall. There were some important gains for women, however, given that the Labour Party and Liberal Democrats have now both reached and surpassed the goal of 50% representation. Women's voting patterns altered slightly from the 2017 results, but the gender generation gap remained in place for all but one age group.

References

BBC News (2019a) 'Jarod Kirkman: Man Jailed over Threatening Emails to MPs', accessed at https://www.bbc.co.uk/news/uk-england-47982436 on 30 March 2020.

BBC News (2019b) 'Man Jailed for Death Threats to 'Anti-Brexit' MPs', accessed at https://www.bbc.co.uk/news/uk-49211222 on 30 March 2020.

BBC News (2019c) 'Women MPs Say Abuse Forcing Them from Politics', accessed at https://www.bbc.co.uk/news/election-2019-50246969 on 30 March 2020.

Campbell, R. (2006) *Gender and the Vote in Britain*, Colchester, ECPR Press.

Campbell, R. and Childs, S. (2015) 'All Aboard the Pink Battle Bus? Women Voters, Issues, Candidates and Party Leaders', *Parliamentary Affairs*, **68**, 206–223.

Campus, D. (2013) *Women Political Leaders and the Media*, New York, NY, Palgrave Macmillan.

Conroy, M. (2015) *Masculinity, Media and the American Presidency*, New York, NY, Palgrave Macmillan.

Conservative Party (2019) *Get Brexit Done. Unleash Britain's Potential*, General Election Manifesto, London, Conservative Party.

Deacon, D., and Harmer, E. (2019) 'The Present in Retrospect: Press Reporting of UK General Elections, 1918–2015', Journalism, **20**, 994–1013.

Deacon, D., Goode, J., Smith, D., Wring, D., Vaccari, C. and Downey, J. (2019) 'What Was All That about, Then? The Media Agenda in the 2019 General Election'. In

Jackson, D., Thorsen, E., Lilliker, D. and Weidhase, N. (eds.) *UK Election Analysis 2019: Media, Voters and the Campaign*, Bournemouth, Centre for Comparative Politics and Media Research, pp. 96–97.

Dolan, K. and Lynch, T. (2014) 'It Takes a Survey: Understanding Gender Stereotypes, Abstract Attitudes, and Voting for Women Candidates', *American Politics Research*, **42**, 656–676.

Harmer, E. and Southern, R. (2018) 'More Stable than Strong: Women's Representation, Voters and Issues'. In Tonge, J., Leston-Bandeira, C. and Wilks-Heeg, S. (eds.) *Britain Votes 2017*, Oxford, Oxford University Press, pp. 237–254.

Harmer, E. and Wring, D. (2013) 'Julie and the Cybermums: Marketing and Women Voters in the UK 2010 General Election', *Journal of Political Marketing*, **12**, 262–273.

House of Commons Library Briefing Paper (2017) *General Election 2017: Results and Analysis*, London, House of Commons.

House of Commons Library Briefing Paper (2019) *General Election 2019: Results and Analysis*, London, House of Commons.

Jamieson, K. H. (1995) *Beyond the Double Bind: Women and Leadership*, New York, Oxford University Press.

Kahn, K. F. (1996) *The Political Consequences of Being a Woman: How Stereotypes Influence the Conduct and Consequences of Political Campaigns*. New York, Colombia University Press,

Mail Online (2019) 'Nicola Sturgeon Admits She 'Got Overexcited' with Her Celebration of Jo Swinson Losing Her Seat amid Backlash Over 'Nasty' Response', accessed at https://www.dailymail.co.uk/news/article-7790265/Nicola-Sturgeon-admits-got-overexcited-celebrating-Jo-Swinson-lost-seat.html on 24 March 2020.

Margetts, H., Vidgen, B. and Hale, S. A. (2019) 'Online Hate and the Nasty Election'. In Jackson, D., Thorsen, E., Lilliker, D. and Weidhase, N. (eds.) *UK Election Analysis 2019: Media, Voters and the Campaign*, Bournemouth, Centre for Comparative Politics and Media Research, pp.16–17.

McKay, F. (2019) 'Gender Takes to the Shade in Scotland'. In Jackson, D., Thorsen, E., Lilliker, D. and Weidhase, N. (eds.) *UK Election Analysis 2019: Media, Voters and the Campaign*, Bournemouth, Centre for Comparative Politics and Media Research, p. 43.

Murray, R. (2010) *Cracking the Highest Glass Ceiling: A Global Comparison of Women's Campaigns for Executive Office*, Santa Barbara, CA, Praeger.

Norris, P. (1999) 'Gender: A Gender Generation Gap?'. In Evans, G. and Norris, P. (eds.) *Critical Elections: British Parties and Voters in Long Term Perspective*, London, Sage, pp. 148–163.

Osei-Appiah, S. (2019) 'Spot the Difference: How Nicola Sturgeon and Jo Swinson Self-Represented on Twitter'. In Jackson, D., Thorsen, E., Lilliker, D. and Weidhase, N. (eds.) *UK Election Analysis 2019: Media, Voters and the Campaign*, Bournemouth, Centre for Comparative Politics and Media Research, p. 84.

Pink News (2019, November 15) 'Meet the Trans and Non – Binary People Running for Parliament in the UK General Election', accessed at https://www.pinknews.co.uk/2019/11/15/uk-election-trans-non-binary-candidates-lib-dem-labour-greens/ on 15 March 2020.

Shendruk, A. (2019) 'The UK's New Parliament Is Its Most Diverse Ever', *Quartz*, accessed at https://qz.com/1769275/new-uk-parliament-has-record-number-of-female-non-white-and-lgbtq-mps/ on 30 March 2020.

Ross, K. (2019) 'Sorry, Not Sorry: Hubris, Hate and the Politics of Shame'. In Jackson, D., Thorsen, E., Lilliker, D. and Weidhase, N. (eds.) *UK Election Analysis 2019: Media, Voters and the Campaign*, Bournemouth, Centre for Comparative Politics and Media Research, p. 14.

Ross, K., Evans, E., Harrison, L., Shears, M. and Wadia, K. (2013) 'The Gender of News and News of Gender: A Study of Sex, Politics, and Press Coverage of the 2010 British General Election', *The International Journal of Press/Politics*, **18**, 3–19.

Southern, R. and Harmer, E. (2019) 'Twitter, Incivility and "Everyday" Gendered Othering: An Analysis of Tweets Sent to UK Members of Parliament', *Social Science Computer Review*, doi:10.1177/089443931986551.

The Independent (2019a, November 20) 'Yes! Jo Swinson Gives Short Answer to Idea of Using Nuclear Weapons during ITV Election Interview', accessed at https://inews.co.uk/news/politics/jo-swinson-interview-itv-general-election-nuclear-weapons-1312124 on 23 March 2020.

The Independent (2019b, November 20) 'Sickening': Jo Swinson Condemned for Unhesitatingly Saying She Would Use Nuclear Weapons', accessed at https://www.independent.co.uk/news/uk/politics/jo-swinson-nuclear-weapon-button-war-lib-dems-election-debate-a9210456.html on 24 March 2020.

The Independent (2019c, November 3) 'Boris Johnson Lambasted by Doctors over "Unprecedented" NHS Crisis', accessed at https://www.independent.co.uk/news/uk/politics/general-election-nhs-unprecedented-crisis-conservative-party-british-medical-association-a9182811.html on 28 March 2020.

The Guardian (2019, October 30) 'Amber Rudd to Step Down as MP', accessed at https://www.theguardian.com/politics/2019/oct/30/amber-rudd-to-step-down-as-mp on 30 March 2020.

The Guardian (2020, February 4) 'News Outlets in Racism Row over Mislabelled Photo of Black MPs', accessed at https://www.theguardian.com/media/2020/feb/04/news-outlets-in-racism-row-over-mislabelling-photos-of-black-mps on 29 March 2020.

Van Zoonen, L. (2006) 'The Personal, the P01olitical and the Popular: A Woman's Guide to Celebrity Politics', *European Journal of Cultural Studies*, **9**, 287–301.

SARAH HARRISON*

A Vote of Frustration? Young Voters in the UK General Election 2019

Scholars have long understood the importance of the elections that take place during the early years of adulthood. For instance, Butler and Stokes (1974) showed that the electoral choice of our early elections could shape our life-long partisan preferences. Moreover, Bruter and Harrison (2017, 2020) suggest that turnout in one of the first two elections when a citizen is eligible to vote will shape their political participation for years to come. At the same time, a lot of attention has been devoted to the extent to which young people converge with or depart from the electoral preferences of other generations. In the UK, that question has been particularly prominent since the referendum on the UK's membership of the European Union in 2016. This divisive political moment revealed the amplitude of the rift between younger and older generations and continues to linger in the British political debate. The UK general election of 2019 presented a test of whether such a rift still existed and what it entailed.

Two key models are usually presented to explain the so-called 'generational effects'. One suggests that preference gaps will not reduce over time. The other, the 'life-cycle effects', model indicates that young people will ultimately converge towards the attitudes and behaviours of their older counterparts when they reach the same age (Dalton, 1977; Henn *et al.*, 2002; Grasso, 2014, 2016; Jennings and Niemi, 2014; Neundorf and Niemi, 2014; Smets, 2016).

However, I argue that there may be another distinction worth exploring, that is, whether age differences can be perceived as experiential. To test this, I compare the attitudes and behaviours of first-time voters to other young voters in the context of the 2019 general election. The existing literature typically assumes that age effects, be they generational or life cycle, can be explained mostly by demographics.

The opportunity to explore this distinction between first-time voters and other young voters is unique because existing data sets do not encompass this scope. In

*Sarah Harrison, Department of Government, London School of Economics and Political Science, s.l.harrison@lse.ac.uk

doi:10.1093/pa/gsaa032

the vast majority of general population surveys where young people are compared to the rest of the population, only a few dozen cases of first-time voters, at most, may be present and those would not be representative of first-time voters in the country in general. This c subgroup of the population is often overlooked, mainly due to insufficiently large samples in most general population surveys.

To address those limitations, this article relies on data derived from two parallel panel studies collected for the Electoral Psychology Observatory (EPO) at the 2019 general election. The first study consisted of a survey of 2,000 respondents representative of the general population in December 2019 and January 2020 in which the answers of those aged 29 years and under were contrasted to those of citizens aged >30%, and a separate subsample of 500 who were eligible to participate in a general election for the first-time in that month. This subsample enables testing of experiential differences (first-time voters versus the rest) and separation of demographic differences (young people versus the rest).[1]

I thus approach the question of young people in the 2019 UK general election with several unique considerations in mind. To start with, I compare not only young voters (aged 18–29 years) to other generations but also distinguish between first-time voters specifically and the rest of the young cohort. Secondly, I am not only interested in the two standard dependent variables of the electoral literature—turnout and electoral choice—but also in understanding how young people's electoral psychology and notably phenomena such as democratic frustration and the perception of group dynamics (including questions of integration or marginalisation) were experienced and expressed by young voters in this fourth national vote in the space of four-and-a-half years. The EPO data facilitate the study of the electoral experience, emotions, attitudes, and behaviour of both the British population in general, using a representative sample of the country's general population and a specific subsample of first-time voters.

1.   From the psychological nature of frustration to the challenge of turnout estimations

Established and new democracies alike are increasingly confronted by a recurrent trend: citizens are disillusioned and disappointed by their democratic institutions. Insights derived from the psychology literature (Sorensen, 1982; Brooks, 1985; Kim, 2018) can help us to understand the increasingly fraught and frustrating nature of citizens' interaction with their democratic systems.

---

[1]Overall survey sample: 2004 respondents, including 130 respondents aged under 29 years, separate first-time voter sample: 501 respondents. Fieldwork main survey: 19–21 December 2019. Fieldwork first-time voter sample: 20 December 2019–24 January 2020. All fieldwork conducted online by Opinium.

Specifically, Harrison (2020) suggests that citizens become frustrated when a perceived democratic delivery deficit interacts with a strong democratic expectation or desire. In that sense, citizens' frustration (as distinct disengagement) will stem from necessarily strong democratic desire and expectations. Young people are often most vocal in their expression of democratic frustration, often criticising how democracy works and what it has to offer them but also the most idealistic in terms of expectations regarding delivery. This interactive nature means that those with higher expectations will care more about negatively perceived delivery, which in turn is more likely to compound the expression of frustration. In the lead up to the general election, a consequence of rising levels of frustration was noted by Bruter and Harrison (2020) as electoral hostility, that is, negative feelings towards regular citizens who vote (or are perceived to vote) differently from the hostile citizen. Unlike affective polarisation, this model does not even assume that it is strongly partisan people who start resenting others, but often those claiming that they do not even care about politics. Electoral hostility may emerge as negative feelings (frustration, anger, contempt, and disgust) held towards individuals or groups as a result of their effective or perceived electoral preferences. It may occur in the campaign, post-election, and reinforce into self-perpetuating cycles of hostility (Bruter and Harrison, 2020). Since the referendum on the UK's membership of the European Union, political divisions within society have largely been presented as a generational divide, with old people preferring to support Leave, whilst young citizens were described as overwhelmingly pro-Remain. Whilst this is a crude and oversimplified presentation of fracture lines, its repeated characterisation could easily infiltrate perceptions of who the electoral 'other' is. Thus, it is crucial to understand both the sources of frustration and electoral hostility in an increasingly divided society sent to the polls in the winter of 2019.

The study measures not only the level of hostility of young citizens and comparing it to that of older voters but also in understanding whether young citizens tend to primarily associate electoral others to different age groups or to other potentially relevant social, political, and demographic division lines such as urbanity, social categories, regional characteristics, and more. Methodologically, however, the study of young people in elections is fraught with difficulties. First, there is no consensus in the literature on what constitute the age boundaries of 'youth' in a study of elections. The most widely used age criteria focus on the 18–24 and 18–29 brackets (or sometimes 16–24 or 16–29 in countries where the electoral franchise starts at 16). In the context of this piece, we use the latter but also focus on the separate category of first-time voters who have never had an opportunity to vote in a first-order election before, typically 18–20 in this case. Additionally, a constant difficulty pertains to the estimation of youth turnout. The problem here is that most group turnout estimates rely on survey responses (including exit polls) but respondents routinely over-claim participation, so surveys use a weighting system to recreate a realistic model of turnout. However, as noted by Harrison (2018), one issue with that method is that surveys typically ask citizens if they participated in the election or not without controlling for registration, whilst turnout is calculated on the basis of registered voters only.[2] Young people aged 18–24 years are significantly less likely to be registered than other generations. Those many young people who are not registered (and therefore not part of formal turnout calculations) often risk being wrongly counted as abstentionists.[3] Because of the weighting process, this can disproportionately overestimate the abstention of young citizens vis-à-vis other categories, where non-registration is a more marginal problem. The EPO survey tackles this issue by controlling for registration, excluding citizens who are not electorally registered or who are ineligible to vote from turnout and electoral choice calculations.

2. The participation and electoral choice of young and first-time voters in the 2019 general election

Looking first at turnout, the fact that young people are less likely to vote than the rest of the population is well known and confirmed in the figures derived from the EPO survey. Table 15.1 shows that, after controlling for registration, whilst the population of over 30s report a turnout of 67%, that figure is down to 51% amongst young voters and 52% amongst first-time voters.

Crucially, however, a constant and critical difference between young people and the rest of the population is that young people are far less likely to choose to vote by post than in person. Amongst those aged 30 years and over, one-third of those who voted in the election did so by post. However, amongst those aged between 18 and 29 years, that proportion was down to 22% and 21% amongst first-time voters. These findings echo those of Cammaerts *et al.* (2016) as well as Bruter and Harrison (2020) who confirm that young people who vote are far keener than the rest of the population to fully experience the polling station atmosphere and less likely to choose remote voting options. This is notably true of first-time voters who see the election as a new experience, alongside many other coming-of-age moments of their teenage years. In that generation, the excitement of the experience is therefore a far stronger mobilising factor than the duty to vote, and it weighs disproportionately in favour of in-station voting whilst

[2]In July 2014, the Electoral Commission confirmed that 'younger people (under 35) are considerably less likely to be registered' with only 70.2% of 20–24 years old on electoral registers, against 95.5% of those over 65 years (LSE, 2017)

[3]One in three were not registered on the electoral roll in September 2019, compared to 17% of the general population that had not signed up to cast their ballot yet (BBC News, 2019).

Table 15.1 Turnout and mode of participation in the 2019 general election, across three age categories (%)

	First-time voters	29 years and under	30 years and over
In person	39 (36)	38 (34)	45 (42)
Postal	11 (10)	11 (10)	22 (20)
Proxy	2 (2)	2 (2)	0 (0)
Chose not to vote	40 (37)	40 (36)	29 (27)
Unable to vote	9 (8)	10 (9)	4 (4)
Total	100	100	100
Ineligible/unregistered (discounted from net)	(7)	(9)	(6)

Notes: Main figure represents the net percentages of voters from each age category having voted in person, postally, by proxy (those three add up to the 'total turnout estimate'), chosen not to vote, or unable to vote after ineligible/unregistered respondents have been discounted. Figures in brackets are percentages from gross figures including ineligible/unregistered. Each column totals 100 (±1 due to rounding).

Table 15.2 Party choice of voters in the 2019 general election, across three age categories (%)

	First-time voters	29 years and under	30 years and over
Labour	58	62	30
Conservative	20	14	46
Liberal Democrats	7	12	12
Greens	4	7	2
Brexit Party	2	0	2
Scottish National Party (SNP)	2	2	4
Independent	1	1	1
Other	1	1	0
Prefer not to say	5	0	0

Notes: The figures represent the percentages of people from each age category voting for each of the parties mentioned. Each column totals 100 (±1 due to rounding).

limiting the appeal of postal voting, whose experiential value is perceived as far less fulfilling.

In terms of electoral choice, Table 15.2 demonstrates that the tendency of young voters to support Labour more than other age groups remained true in 2019. The EPO data suggest that 58% of first-time voters and 62% of young voters cast a vote for Labour in the election, whilst only 30% of those aged 30 years and above made a similar choice. The Green vote was similarly higher than average amongst young voters (7%) with 4% of first-time voters and 2% of those aged ≥30 years supporting the party. The Conservative vote was only 20%

amongst first-time voters and 14% amongst young voters (aged 29 years and under), compared to 46% amongst the rest of the population (aged ≥30 years). First-time voters were less likely than average to vote for the Liberal Democrats (7%), but 12% of other young voters, below the age of 30 years but not voting for the first time, were just as likely to support Jo Swinson's party as were older voters aged 30 years and above.

It is worth noting that as in 2017, strategic backing of Labour or Liberal Democrat candidates could vary significantly across constituency profiles (Harrison, 2018). In 2019, there was also the possibility of a voter turning during the campaign to a party or candidate that was not their natural first choice, to prevent someone being elected that they disliked more. There was also the possibility that less experienced voters, with potentially less knowledge of a constituency and its electoral outcomes, might choose their preferred candidate or party late in the campaign. However, the EPO study indicates that the timing of the electoral decision of young voters, presented in Table 15.3, did not differ significantly from that of others.

On average, 22.4% of those aged 29 years and under made up their mind within a week of the election which is very similar to the proportion of over 30s who made a late decision (23.1%). However, first-time voters had a higher percentage of later deciders (28.6% within the last week). In terms of election day deciders, this represented 6.4% of respondents aged 30 years and above, 7.2% of those aged 29 years and under, and 8.5% of first-time voters.[4]

When it comes to how enthusiastic citizens were about their vote, however, the contrast was even more markedly between first-time voters and the rest, rather than between young voters and those aged 30 years and over, as shown in Table 15.4.

Only 14.4% of first-time voters felt some enthusiasm about their vote, well below the enthusiasm reported by other young voters (33%) and those aged over 30 years (26.2%). However, across all three age categories, roughly a third of the population felt that their electoral choice was limited to casting a preference for the 'lesser of some evils' (30.7% for those aged ≥30 years, 33.9% for those aged 29 years and under, and 34.3% for first-time voters). This suggests that, on balance, first-time voters felt particularly underwhelmed by the electoral choices offered to them.

3.   Frustrated youth?

Does the lack of enthusiasm of young and notably first-time voters translate into a greater sense of frustration amongst young people than older voters? Apathy amongst young voters would make frustration impossible, in that whilst the latter

---

[4]Survey data are not available to compare 2019 general election to other previous elections.

Table 15.3 Period of party choice in the 2019 general election, across three age categories (%)

	First-time voters	29 years and under	30 years and over
Before final week	71.4	77.7	76.9
Final week (except final day)	20.1	15.2	16.7
Final day	8.5	7.2	6.4

Notes: The figures represent the percentages of voters from each age category who claim to have made up or finally changed their minds before the last week, during the last week except election day, and on election day. Each column totals 100 ($\pm$1 due to rounding).

Table 15.4 Level of enthusiasm of electoral choice in the 2019 general election, across three age categories (%)

	First-time voters	29 years and under	30 years and over
Lesser of two evils	34.3	33.9	30.7
Quite happy	51.3	33.0	43.2
Enthusiastic	14.4	33.0	26.2

Note: Each column totals 100 ($\pm$1 due to rounding).

is characterised by irritation at a failure to deliver apathy would indicate a lack of caring for, or valuing of, democratic processes. The findings, shown in Table 15.5, suggest that the key difference is not to be found between young and older voters but rather between those who vote for the first time and in the rest of the population.

There are three dimensions which, whilst overlapping to some extent, underpin democratic frustration and expectation. The first is ideological—what set of ideas and aspirations—the worldview of an elector—might be satisfied by the act of voting. The second is institutional—what can the bodies to which representatives are elected deliver? The third is political, based upon the expectations of parties to deliver effective and relevant policies. On all three dimensions of democratic frustration, first-time voters score significantly lower than the rest of the population, even though a majority of them qualify as democratically frustrated. Levels of democratic frustration for first-time voters range from 4.84 (institutional dimension) to 9.25 (political dimension) on a scale ranging from −100 to +100 with 0 being the frustration neutrality point. The differences between young voters aged 29 years and under and the rest are minimal. Young people prove slightly less frustrated than older generations in terms of the political dimensions (24.39 versus 28.5 on the scale), whilst results are almost exactly

Table 15.5 Level of democratic frustration in the 2019 general election, across three age categories

	First-time voters	29 years and under	30 years and over
Ideological	6.45 (23.04)	19.30 (30.79)	18.58 (28.02)
Institutional	4.84 (22.93)	19.57 (29.16)	19.76 (29.02)
Political	9.25 (28.09)	24.39 (33.98)	28.50 (33.92)

Notes: Main figures are mean frustration levels on a −100 to +100 scale. Figures in brackets represent standard deviations.

similar on the institutional dimensions (19.57 versus 19.76). When it comes to the ideological dimension, the mean frustration score for young people (19.3) is slightly higher than for the rest of the population (18.58) but the difference is not statistically significant.

This suggests that on balance, with the possible exception of the political dimensions, age is not a significant factor in how democratically frustrated people feel. What the EPO survey finds, however, is that this frustration crystallises *after* young people have been given a chance to vote for the first time. In short, these data do not support the suggestion that young people were more frustrated than the rest of the population at the 2019 general election. Equally, however, the data do not suggest that young people were less frustrated than older groups, but there are signs that young people's democratic frustration might be shaped by different dimensions than the rest of the population (i.e. less focused on disillusion vis-à-vis political personnel as opposed to institutional and ideological qualities of democracy). As frustration is often built upon preconceptions and expectations of what electoral democracy can provide and deliver, experiential rather than demographic, a distinction can be seen between first-time voters and the rest of the population rather than between the young and the old.

4. From frustration to hostility

The literature suggests that an increasing proportion of citizens experiences feelings of electoral hostility towards those who vote differently from them (or who they perceive to vote differently) (Bruter and Harrison, 2020). Unlike theories of affective polarisation, hostility is not related to (and does not require) strength of partisanship. It is also not necessarily related to the actuality of a citizen's or group's vote but may instead be based on perceptions of group dynamics. The Brexit debate, for example, was consistently framed as a largely generational one. The survey data enable us to assess whether young citizens and first-time voters were electorally hostile to those of a different view and whether the basis of their

Table 15.6 Levels of perceived hostility to 'opposite' voters in the 2019 general election, across three age categories

	First-time voters	29 years and under	30 years and over
Anger	4.97 (3.11)	5.05 (3.23)	3.45 (3.55)
Frustration	5.29 (2.99)	6.08 (3.24)	4.68 (3.75)
Sympathy	3.82 (2.82)	3.45 (2.89)	2.20 (2.73)
Hostility	4.49 (2.98)	4.78 (3.21)	3.00 (3.33)
Solidarity	3.78 (2.89)	3.02 (3.00)	1.78 (2.57)
Disgust	4.62 (3.00)	4.99 (3.14)	3.53 (3.66)
Envy	3.71 (3.07)	2.90 (2.93)	1.29 (2.14)
Contempt	4.25 (2.95)	4.06 (3.00)	3.47 (3.55)
Distrust	5.03 (3.07)	5.65 (2.67)	4.15 (3.74)
Hatred	4.30 (3.02)	4.19 (3.21)	2.19 (2.94)
Animosity	4.21 (2.91)	4.55 (3.34)	3.21 (3.41)
Sense of ever-growing distance	4.92 (2.91)	5.86 (3.11)	4.49 (3.69)
Sense of resolution	3.77 (2.83)	3.05 (2.90)	2.05 (2.62)

Notes: Main figures are average levels for each qualification on a 0–10 scale. Figures in brackets represent standard deviations. 'Opposite' voters are those voting for other parties.

hostility was significantly focused on age differences as opposed to other potential fracture lines, such as region or social class.

Comparing average levels of hostility (i.e. negative feelings towards those who are perceived to vote differently from a respondent) across the three age categories, the results differ from those pertaining to democratic frustration and reflect an evolution which seems far more tightly related to demography than to experience.

Indeed, Table 15.6 illustrates that across categories of hostile feelings held towards 'opposite' voters (those who vote for other parties), young people in general (including first-time voters) tended to be significantly more hostile than their older counterparts. For young people in the context of the general election, the level of 'anger' towards voters of an opposite persuasion averages 5.05 on a scale from 0 to 10 (and 4.97 amongst first-time voters) in contrast to only 3.45 amongst the rest of the population. Self-declared 'frustration' stands at 6.08 amongst young voters aged under 29 years (5.29 amongst first-time voters) as compared to 4.68 amongst those aged 30 years and over, and 'contempt' at 4.06 (4.25 for first-time voters), whilst for the rest of the population that level is only 3.47.

The same differences are measured when it comes to more extreme negative feelings. For example, levels of 'disgust' amongst those aged 29 years and under average 4.99 on the same 0–10 scale (4.62 for first-time voters) compared to 3.53 for those aged 30 years and above. Self-declared 'hostility' amongst the young has an average score of 4.78 (4.49 for first-time voters) and only 3 amongst those aged 30 years and over. 'Hatred' towards opposite voters scores an average 4.3 amongst the young and 4.19 amongst first-time voters, whilst its average score is only 2.19, that is, more than two points lower, amongst the rest of the population.

Note that unlike the distribution of democratic frustration, there is no obvious pattern of difference between first-time voters and other young voters when it comes to feelings of hostility. First-time voters, for example, are even more negative than other young voters in terms of 'contempt' and 'hatred', but a little more moderate than other young voters when it comes to 'distrust', 'anger', 'frustration', 'hostility', 'disgust', and 'animosity'. In contrast, for all the above scales, first-time and young voters alike hold, on average, significantly more negative feelings towards 'opposite' voters than their older counterparts.

5.   An age fracture?

However, the difference in levels of hostility does not necessarily mean that hostility must necessarily be age-related. In recent years, much has been made of the stark differences in electoral preferences between the young and the old, notably with regards to Brexit. As electoral hostility is based on perceptions of electoral alterity ('otherness'), it is therefore important to know whether hostile young people are electorally opposed to others along age lines, rather than the other social and demographic dimensions that people have historically associated with electoral cleavages in the UK such as wealth, social status, and geographical splits.

To consider this in relation to the general election, the EPO survey asked citizens what adjectives best characterise people who they perceive to vote differently from themselves, including both evaluative characterisations (such as selfishness, intelligence, or naivety) but also presupposed social and demographic traits (such as old or young, rich or poor, urban or rural, etc.) which reflect respondents' perceptions of the social fractures underlying electoral divides in the country. Respondents were asked to pick the three characteristics which best described 'opposite' voters from a list of objective and evaluative categories. The results are shown in Table 15.7.

Whilst 27.7% of first-time voters feel that their electoral nemeses can be described as 'wealthy' (total wealth and poverty references: 36.7%), 26.5% characterise them as 'old' (total age references: 41.3%). In contrast, only 7.8% would refer to them as 'rural' (total geographical references: 14.8%).

In the view of voters aged under 30 years, age differences were the highest perceived source of electoral fracture in the 2019 general election. For those young voters, the age characterisation is even more predominant than for first-time voters. At 30.8%, 'old' was the single most used characterisation ahead of 'wealthy'

Table 15.7 Top three perceived characteristics of those who voted differently at the 2019 general election, across three age categories

	First-time voters	29 years and under	30 years and over
Old	26.5	30.8	10.8
Young	14.8	8.5	12.8
Wealthy	27.7	27.7	16.4
Poor	9.0	3.8	4.7
Stupid	19.4	13.8	22.9
Intelligent	13.0	9.2	4.0
Selfish	25.7	30.0	26.0
Selfless	9.0	6.9	3.9
Urban	7.0	6.2	8.3
Rural	7.8	3.1	3.9
Naïve	23.0	26.2	44.9
Realistic	10.8	3.8	4.4
Nice	12.2	3.8	3.4
Unpleasant	14.4	13.8	12.2
None of the above	14.8	23.8	28.9

Note: Figures represent the percentages of voters from each age category who used each of those descriptors as one of the three main ways to characterise 'opposite' voters.

(27.7%). In total, for those voters aged below 30 years, age-related characteristics, at 39.3%, were more prevalent than wealth-related (31.5%) and geographical ones (9.3%).

Age characterisation of electoral polarisation was far less prominent amongst older respondents. Only 23.6% of those aged 30 years and above characterised 'opposite' voters based on their age (old or young). However, this difference also affected other characterisations such as wealth (only 21.1% describe 'opposite' voters as likely to be either 'wealthy' or 'poor') and geography (12.1% see them as likely to be either 'urban' or 'rural'). In other words, differences in age reference are primarily due to older respondents being more likely to select evaluative characterisations of other voters, sometimes negative such as 'stupid', over social and demographic ones.

Overall, the results indicate that, when it comes to the way in which voters perceive the social, economic, and demographic divides which electorally split British society, all three groups of voters think that age is the single most important predictor of people holding opposite views, ahead of wealth and geography. Secondly, whilst young voters are more likely to express negative feelings towards 'opposite' voters, they are in fact less likely to hold a disparaging image of such voters and describe them based on their supposed naivety or claimed intellectual inferiority.

6. Conclusion

The specificity of young citizens when it comes to electoral behaviour has been the subject of academic and broader debate. Much of the analysis has accepted the premise that young people could be analysed as a unified age group but questioned whether the group's specificity in behaviour was related to generational differences or cyclical effects related to individuals' progression throughout the different stages of their lives. This vision has been partly constrained by methodological limitations related to what social scientists can infer from nationally representative samples in which young people typically represent small numbers. The EPO study instead focused upon another critical potential distinction in the nature of age specificities: the difference between demographic and experiential effects. In other words, whether some characteristics deemed to be specific to the young are in fact unique to first-time voters instead. This differentiates between elements of a generational divide and democratic learning. It makes sense to test for differences between those who have already voted and those who have not. After all, if voting made no difference to attitudes to politics or levels of democratic discontent, questions might reasonably be asked of its purpose.

This analysis of young people in the 2019 general election in the UK, the third election in addition to a major referendum in less than five years, confirms a tale of two stories beyond the documented differences in terms of party choice (young voters being more pro-Labour) than older voters. The first highlights an increasingly entrenched generational rift between young British citizens and the rest of a population with whom they feel they have little in common, with some older voters willing to define younger counterparts in negative terms. The second, however, indicates differences between voting novices, those casting their vote for the first time, compared to other young voters who nonetheless had already voted in the past. Whilst democratic frustrations are evident across a wide section of the electorate, what perhaps perturbs is that first-time participation in elections may be the onset of disenchantment rather than creating a sense of fulfilment.

Funding

Research Grants: Economic and Social Research Council (ESRC): First and Foremost (ES/S000100/1) and European Research Council (ERC) ELHO (no. 788304).

References

BBC News (2019, 27 November) 'Who Can Register to Vote in a General Election?', accessed at https://www.bbc.co.uk/news/uk-politics-49595260 on 30 March 2020.

Brooks, J. E. (1985) 'Democratic Frustration in the Anglo-American Polities: A Quantification of Inconsistency Between Mass Public Opinion and Public Policy', *The Western Political Quarterly*, **38**, 250–261.

Bruter, M. and Harrison, S. (2017) 'Understanding the Emotional Act of Voting', *Nature Human Behaviour*, **1**, 1–3.

Bruter, M. and Harrison, S. (2020) *Inside the Mind of a Voter: A New Approach to Electoral Psychology in Six Democracies*, Princeton, NJ, Princeton University Press.

Butler, D. and Stokes, D. (1974) *Political Change in Britain: Basis of Electoral Choice*, London, Springer.

Cammaerts, B., Bruter, M., Banaji, S., Harrison, S. and Anstead, N. (2016) *Youth Participation in Democratic Life: Stories of Hope and Disillusion.* New York, Springer.

Dalton, R. J. (1977) 'Was There a Revolution? A Note on Generational Versus Life Cycle Explanations of Value Differences', *Comparative Political Studies*, **9**, 459–474.

Grasso, M. T. (2014) 'Age, Period and Cohort Analysis in a Comparative Context: Political Generations and Political Participation Repertoires in Western Europe', *Electoral Studies*, **33**, 63–76.

Grasso, M. T. (2016) *Generations, Political Participation and Social Change in Western Europe*, London, Routledge.

Harrison, S. (2018) 'Young Voters', *Parliamentary Affairs*, **71**, 255–266.

Harrison, S. (2020) 'Democratic Frustration: Concept, Dimensions and Behavioural Consequences', *Societies*, **10**, 19–30.

Henn, M., Weinstein, M. and Wring, D. (2002) 'A Generation Apart? Youth and Political Participation in Britain', *The British Journal of Politics and International Relations*, **4**, 167–192.

Jennings, M. K. and Niemi, R. G. (2014) *Generations and Politics: A Panel Study of Young Adults and Their Parents*, Princeton, NJ, Princeton University Press.

Kim, J. (2018) 'On Frustration: Toward a Theory of a Democratic Politics of Perseverance', University of Pennsylvania, accessed at https://repository.upenn.edu/dissertations/AAI10845562/ on 31 March 2020.

LSE (2017) 'EU Referendum: Breaking Indifference - How Age Affected Voting', accessed at http://www.lse.ac.uk/about-lse/connect/connect-2017/eu-referendum-breaking-indifference on 31 March 2020.

Neundorf, A. and Niemi, R. G. (2014) 'Beyond Political Socialization: New Approaches to Age, Period, Cohort Analysis', *Electoral Studies*, **33**, 1, 1–6.

Smets, K. (2016) 'Revisiting the Political Life-cycle Model: Later Maturation and Turnout Decline among Young Adults', *European Political Science Review*, **8**, 225–249.

Sorensen, R. (1982) 'Democratic Frustration of Vast Majorities', *Political Studies*, **30**, 272–273.

Britain Votes (2019) 272–287

DOMINIC WRING AND STEPHEN WARD*

From Bad to Worse? The Media and the 2019 Election Campaign

From Twitter to the BBC, media platforms were perceived as having had 'a bad election'. The story of the 2019 media campaign focussed primarily on the negative. There were continual claims of misinformation and deliberate disinformation spread via social media and amplified by the so-called mainstream news. Accusations of bias were widespread and not just aimed at the highly partisan newspaper sector. Public service broadcasters were repeatedly accused of inaccurate and biased coverage by both main parties. In the case of social media platforms, they were criticised for polluting debate, heightening polarisation and generally responsible for sustaining high levels of incivility (and even abuse) in politics. The parties themselves were also accused of exploiting the supposedly toxic atmosphere by avoiding scrutiny, refusing to engage with difficult events, or by flooding the campaign with a barrage of dubious claims. Ultimately, the media stood accused of failing in the fundamental task of holding parties to account through properly scrutinising politicians' claims. Although none of this is new, 2019 might have set a new low and potentially accelerated the further erosion of trust in political information or discussion. Yet, how far any of this cut through to the average voter remains open to question. After months of endless Brexit coverage, the sense of wanting it to all to end was perhaps the overriding concern in the 2019 election. This piece reconsiders these issues. First, it analyses the way the media attempted to frame the campaign and particularly the newspaper hostility towards Corbyn's Labour. Secondly, it examines how rival parties, with an increased capacity to bypass established media, attempted to manufacture attention or distract voters, and what impact this had on the style and tone of the campaign.

*Dominic Wring, Centre for Research in Communication and Culture, Loughborough University, d.j.wring@lboro.ac.uk; Stephen Ward, Politics and Contemporary History, University of Salford, s.j.ward@salford.ac.uk

doi:10.1093/pa/gsaa033

Table 16.1 Main issues: press and television news, 2019 general election campaign (%)

Issue	TV	Press	All
Electoral process	31	32	31
Brexit/the EU	18	11	13
Business/economy/trade	6	9	8
Health/health care	7	7	7
Standards/scandals	6	7	7
Taxation	4	6	5
Minorities/religion	4	4	4
Defence/military/security/terrorism	3	4	4
Public services	4	3	3
Environment	4	2	3
All other issues	13	15	15

Source: Deacon *et al.* (2019).

1. Topics and personalities: what the news media reported (or did not)

Radio and television editors often emulate their print counterparts in terms of selecting and reporting similar stories including, critically, at election times (Cushion *et al.*, 2018). During the 2019 campaign, there were notable parallels in how the press and broadcasters covered the issues (Table 16.1).

Traditionally 'electoral process' is the leading category in campaign news terms. This coverage includes the so-called 'horse race' elements of the election, including voter profiling, party strategies, personalities and poll ratings. Here prominent narratives included the potential abandonment of Labour by the so-called 'Workington Man' and voters living in 'red wall' seats. Some of this speculation related to the EU, the single most prominent policy issue in the campaign. When Sky News labelled its coverage 'The Brexit Election', Labour complained (in vain) to regulator Ofcom arguing the phrase reinforced Conservative framing of the issues. Boris Johnson's single-minded focus on this controversy helped reinforce his core 'Get Brexit Done' message. Although Johnson's 'oven ready deal' and Labour's promise of a second referendum ensured that the EU was mentioned, much of the related coverage was dominated by sloganeering rather than analysis of the rival policy options (Deacon *et al.*, 2020).

The media campaign covered traditional electoral issues such as tax and the economy, a terrain strongly contested by politicians wanting to move on from austerity. Labour spokespeople were keen to highlight their commitment to greater spending and nowhere more so than on the National Health Service (NHS). Allegations of health underspending dramatically came to the fore when the *Yorkshire Evening Post* published the image of a child lying in a corridor of Leeds General Infirmary (Sheridan, 2019). The newspaper disclosed that the boy's mother had left her son there due to a shortage of available beds. Labour seized on the incident as compelling evidence of a systemic NHS funding crisis. The story continued to dominate the headlines following a false claim, amplified in a tweet by BBC political editor, Laura Kuenssberg, that a Conservative aide had been punched by a Labour supporter outside the Infirmary. Johnson guaranteed the controversy further airtime when he snatched and pocketed the phone of a reporter attempting to show him the boy's image. The Prime Minister's apparent desire to avoid scrutiny had already become a story, particularly when the BBC's Andrew Neil ridiculed him for declining to be interrogated in a televised interview. This criticism culminated with presenter Piers Morgan accusing Johnson of hiding in a walk-in fridge to avoid questioning from an ITV colleague.

Jeremy Corbyn came under renewed media scrutiny during the election. When Chief Rabbi Ephraim Mirvis wrote in *The Times* that Corbyn represented a threat to Britain's Jewish community, he reignited discussion of Labour's alleged anti-Semitism (Mirvis, 2019). Related interventions by *Jewish News* and the *Jewish Chronicle* ensured coverage of standards and minorities attracted considerable press and broadcast attention. Shadow Defence Secretary Nia Griffiths responded, telling Sky News anti-Semitism was 'a shame on us'. In his interview with Andrew Neil, Corbyn's replies intensified the controversy before he apologised over the matter on ITV's This Morning programme. Boris Johnson also faced renewed questioning about his character following the terrorist attack in London, which led to increased news interest in security-related matters. When Johnson linked the perpetrator's early release to the last Labour government's policy, the father of one victim accused him of exploiting the tragedy for electoral reasons.

Widespread flooding, together with a dedicated Channel 4 leaders' debate, helped foreground the environment as an issue. But the resulting media attention was not so great despite this and the reporting of climate change during the preceding months. In contrast, other potentially newsworthy issues such as education and housing struggled for coverage even though polling indicated their importance. These subjects also had to contend with Christmas-related events, the impeachment of President Trump and Prince Andrew's disastrous interview with BBC Newsnight. If certain issues struggled to generate interest, then so did some politicians in a campaign largely represented by both newspapers and (to a lesser extent) television as a binary choice between Labour and Conservative.

In media terms, the 2019 election was even more presidential than 2017. Unsurprisingly, Boris Johnson was his party's dominant representative in terms of media coverage (Table 16.2).The coverage was varied, straddling: policy issues; photo-opportunities, most notably, including him driving a JCB digger

Table 16.2 Politicians' share of press and television appearances, 2019 general election campaign (%)

Rank	Name	Party	Role	%
1	Boris Johnson	Conservative	Leader/PM	30.2
2	Jeremy Corbyn	Labour	Leader	25.9
3	John McDonnell	Labour	Shadow Chancellor	7.5
4	Jo Swinson	LibDem	Leader	6.0
5	Nigel Farage	Brexit	Leader/MEP	5.9
6	Jonathan Ashworth	Labour	Shadow Health	4.0
7	Nicola Sturgeon	SNP	Leader/MSP	3.8
8	Sajid Javid	Conservative	Chancellor	3.2
9	Matt Hancock	Conservative	Health	2.1
10	Priti Patel	Conservative	Home Secretary	2.0

Source: Deacon *et al.* (2019).

emblazoned with 'Get Brexit Done' through a huge 'Gridlock' sign; alleged misconduct as Mayor of London involving the entrepreneur Jennifer Arcuri; and material he had written as a journalist, with Johnson apologising, for instance, on LBC radio for having called single mothers 'irresponsible' (LBC, 2019).

Jeremy Corbyn was by some margin the second most high-profile politician. His and Johnson's prominence were reinforced by the first ever face-to-face televised debates restricted to the two major leaders. Although the Prime Minister had better personal ratings than his opponent, they virtually tied in snap polls taken on who performed best in their opening encounter. If the response to Corbyn was better than anticipated, this encounter did not prove the game changer his supporters had hoped. The Liberal Democrats and the Scottish National Party (SNP) felt so aggrieved over their exclusion from every leader debate, they launched (unsuccessful) legal challenges against the broadcasters. Having declared her aim to become Prime Minister, Jo Swinson attracted a fraction of the news interest afforded her two major rivals. Unfortunately for Swinson, YouGov polling suggested that the more voters saw the Liberal Democrat leader, the less they liked her (Smith, 2019).

Nigel Farage received almost the same amount of media attention as Swinson, although most of this was before the Brexit Party stood down many of its candidates. They and their SNP, Green and Plaid Cymru counterparts also participated in some leader debates but the significance of these televised encounters was diminished by their Labour and Conservative rivals preferring to send colleagues, including Rishi Sunak and Rebecca Long-Bailey to represent them. Their inclusion reflected the prominence afforded economics, personified by both John McDonnell and Sajid Javid during the campaign.

Jon Ashworth and Matt Hancock had similarly significant roles due to media interest in health, although Ashworth's higher profile resulted from the leaking of a recorded private phone conversation in which he said his party was facing defeat.

2. Questions of bias: broadcast as well as print

The period before the election was marked by tensions between politicians and media with Dorothy Byrne, Channel 4's Head of Current Affairs, describing the Prime Minister as 'a known liar'. Relations further deteriorated when Michael Gove was excluded from representing Johnson in the broadcaster's environmentally themed leaders' debate. With Gove refused entry, Channel 4 further incensed the Conservatives by situating a melting ice statue in Johnson's place. A complaint to Ofcom about the 'stunt' was accompanied by stories that the party would review the broadcaster's licence if re-elected. In another tense exchange, Channel 4's Ciaran Jenkins challenged Gove over a Conservative Twitter account renamed 'FactCheck UK' during the opening leaders' debate. But it was the BBC that faced most scrutiny during the election. When Andrew Neil criticised the Prime Minister for being the only leader to avoid his flagship interview programme, the former's comments went viral. The Conservatives dismissed the charge with Johnson later raising the possibility of abolishing the BBC licence fee. Labour regarded this failure to interrogate the Prime Minister as evidence of the Corporation's unwillingness to hold the government to account. Journalist Peter Oborne argued this reflected an institutional bias against Corbyn, pointing to accusations that the BBC had edited appearances of Johnson to make him appear more statesmanlike whilst laying a wreath and also during a leader debate where he was ridiculed by some audience members (Oborne, 2019). If the major parties complained of mistreatment, the others were more likely to berate the BBC and other broadcasters for ignoring them and their policies.

Traditionally newspapers are regarded as the primary source of partisan coverage during elections. Although campaign stories now go viral through digital sharing, many still originate from print (Chadwick *et al.*, 2018). This continues to happen despite a steep decline in paper sales: between the elections of 2017 and 2019, the combined hard copy circulations of the 10 paid-for national dailies fell by 25%. It inevitably means that newspapers are diminished compared with their 'tabloid' heyday of the 1970s and 1980s. Nonetheless, the contemporary press is, in a qualitative sense, similar because most titles have (re)embraced the kind of partisanship familiar in the Thatcher era but abandoned during the Blair years (Deacon and Wring, 2002). Despite the marked decline in overall circulation, editorialising in the press was as polemical as it had been a generation ago. Six of the 10 dailies adopted strong editorial positions in 2019, the same number as in the

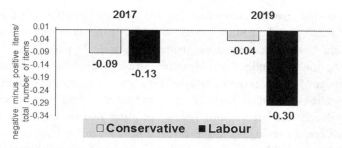

Figure 16.1 Press evaluations of the main parties: 2017 and 2019 general elections
Source: Deacon *et al.* (2019).

Table 16.3 Newspaper partisanship: editorial declarations in the 2019 general election

Title	Endorsement	Circulation (in 000s)
Daily Mirror	Very Strong Labour	455
Daily Express	Very Strong Conservative	298
Daily Star	None	289
The Sun	Very Strong Conservative	1217
Daily Mail	Very Strong Conservative	1133
The Daily Telegraph	Very Strong Conservative	309
The Guardian	Weak Labour	129
The Times	Strong Conservative	365
The i	None	220
Financial Times	Very Weak Liberal Democrat	163
Total		4578
Share of endorsements by circulation	Con 72.5%; Lab 12.8%; LD 3.6%; none 11.1%	

Source: Wring and Deacon (2019).

1987 general election. In 2001, only two had done so. And if this reporting had been decidedly anti-Labour in 2017, it was even more so this time (Figure 16.1).

Although the Conservatives received negative press over issues like health, they were the only party to enjoy positive newspaper coverage throughout the election (Deacon *et al.*, 2019). Anybody purchasing a hard copy daily would have been nearly three times more likely to be reading a Johnson supporting title than any other kind of (non-)partisan newspaper. This three-million circulation provided the party with helpful support in a fragmented media landscape. The best-selling *The Sun* and *Daily Mail* accounted for half of all sales and helped amplify Boris Johnson's Brexit message (Table 16.3). Simultaneously, they attacked Labour and Jeremy Corbyn as threats to Britain's future. In his 2017 party conference speech, Corbyn had criticised the *Daily Mail* over its coverage of that year's election, stating that the paper had devoted 14 pages to attacking the Labour Party on the eve of the contest (Press Gazette, 2017). Given that Labour's vote had grown, Corbyn challenged the paper to dedicate 28 pages next time. The newspaper duly responded with blistering articles that denounced the Labour leadership as Marxists, terrorist sympathising anti-Semites, and levelled similar charges against a so-called 'Dirty Dozen' candidates. Strong content was reproduced by likeminded papers, with *The Sun* berating 'Red Jez' as unfit to lead and the *Daily Express* warning readers 'Brexit and Britain (are) in your hands'. Whilst acknowledging the dilemma facing 'Remain minded liberal Conservatives', even *The Times* managed a fulsome editorial endorsement of Johnson.

Half of the paid-for dailies were non-Conservative but accounted for approximately only a quarter of circulations. Unlike the 'Tory press', their opinions were far more heterogeneous. The *Daily Mirror*, Labour's only reliable print ally, enthusiastically denounced Boris Johnson as a liar. The party's other press sympathiser, *The Guardian*, was markedly less enthusiastic, having been previously highly critical of Corbyn. But it did endorse the party as 'not perfect but progressive' whilst excoriating the Conservatives. The *Financial Times* was critical of both main parties, labelling them 'populist', and offered highly qualified support to the Liberal Democrats despite their 'poor campaign'. In market terms, *The i* and *Daily Star* are polar opposites, but both made a virtue of being non-partisan.

3. Social media: Labour's phoney advantage?

In 2017, Labour dominated social media in nearly all the main metrics, and the expectation was that they would continue to maintain that advantage in 2019. This was, in part, due to the organic focus of their campaign—utilising their large online support base, activist groups and partisan digital news network. On the eve of polling, Labour was confident they had repeated their prior success, going as far as to say it was 'the most successful social media campaign this country has ever seen', with the party chairman, Ian Lavery, suggesting that it was an effective counter against 'Tory dominated media' (Labour Party, 2019). On some levels, Labour outdid other parties with their digital campaigning, in terms of followers and reach across social media platforms (Walsh, 2019*a*). Whilst some reports found that the Conservatives successfully closed the gap in this election (Sharma 2019), especially in terms of their social media output, this claim is more a reflection of starting from the low base of their poor performance in 2017. Both main parties and leaders increased their followers throughout the campaign with Corbyn even managing to extend his lead across a range of platforms. Even on newer platforms, such as TikTok, it seemed Labour and Corbyn had sizeable leads in terms of support; somewhat surprisingly, given their profile, only the Brexit Party posted any content there.

Whilst the number of followers gives a broad indication of potential audience, it is a relatively crude metric. Campaigners tend to be more interested in engagement, click-rates and shareability. The hiring of two young New Zealanders, Sean Topham and Ben Guerin, by the Conservatives, attracted much media comment in terms of their digital strategy. Earlier in 2019, they had worked on the Australian Liberal Party's campaign, delivering a surprise victory, with their communication style heavily associated with the promotion of so-called 'boomer memes' aimed at older audiences and 'shitposting' to promote attention, but also acting as a distraction device. Essentially, their tactics were to promote quantity over quality, producing lots of amateurish looking memes often associated with popular culture to tap into basic voter emotions: fear, anger, pride and excitement (Waterson, 2019). Within days of their arrival, the Conservatives were trialling online adverts crudely portraying Corbyn as a chicken and promoting a Brexit advert in the widely derided Comic Sans font. Several commentators suggested that the digital content was deliberately bad to attract attention and maximise sharing but, crucially, not simply amongst their own sympathisers (Stokel-Walker, 2019).

Social media engagement metrics indicate that the Conservatives performed significantly better in 2019 partly by increasing the volume of material, especially on Facebook. The data on sharing, and particularly reaction, to social media posts are less clear, but there are some indications that they were gaining more favourable responses than other parties (Owen, 2019). However, Labour were still regarded as maintaining a clear advantage, especially in terms of shares on most other platforms, notably on Twitter. Labour further led the way in relation to engagement with viral video content helped by Momentum's grassroots activism and YouTube shares (Charles, 2019). Whilst engagement with content is important, what voters share or discuss is arguably even more so. Data suggest that the main issues in terms of online discussion during the campaign were, not surprisingly, Brexit and the NHS; racism also cut through—linked to claims of anti-Semitism and Islamophobia. Although this aligns somewhat to what politicians were talking about, there were clear differences between the parties. Whilst the Conservative and Liberal Democrat core messages were about Brexit, Labour highlighted the NHS, pensions, housing and nationalisation (Scott, 2019).

Overall, aside from Labour's apparent online dominance, there are two other standout features in the metrics debate. The first was the clear advantage of the two main parties, with little evidence of equalisation of campaign competition online . For instance, despite their social media success in the EU elections, the Brexit Party had minimal impact this time (Ramley *et al.*, 2019). Lacking direction, the party appeared to spend nothing in the first week on digital adverts, then attacked Johnson's Brexit, before stepping down in Conservative-held constituencies (Duncan *et al.*, 2019). Its failure to cut through was further highlighted when its head of digital strategy resigned half-way through the campaign. The second standout feature was (as with legacy media) the growing importance of party leaders in terms of presence and driving traffic towards campaign content. Corbyn, Johnson, Swinson, Sturgeon and Farage all had sizeable social media followings, bigger than their parties' official sites. Leaders have become central to the content and focus in digital campaigning. Whilst this kind of personalisation has been noted for several decades, the fan-based, celebrity-style, nature of social media is further accelerating and deepening this process.

In the wake of Labour's defeat, commentators suggested that their social media advantage was a mirage or, rather more crudely, it did not matter in electoral politics. Critics emphasised the unrepresentative nature of the platforms, accusing Labour supporters of living in a detached bubble. This sentiment was summed up by Piers Morgan: 'Twitter loses yet another election' (Morgan, 2019). More nuanced scrutiny questioned whether social metrics missed some of the Conservatives' successful Facebook tactics of targeting key voters with the issues that mattered. Others queried who Labour was really reaching. Despite its sizeable online audience, there was a strong suspicion that the party talked to itself and its sympathisers online, rather than the key swing voters. As noted, Labour's digital campaign barely engaged with Brexit—the central issue for many voters, especially in Labour Leave seats—instead promoting a leadership that had also alienated some in Remain areas (Bridge and Kenber, 2019). Nevertheless, writing social media off is misguided. It needs to be assessed in the context of the wider campaign. Moreover, it can be a multipurpose tool, fulfilling different functions for different parties. Arguably, for the Conservatives, it allowed them to reach areas where they had little or no ground operation, whilst for Labour, it enabled them to remobilise grassroots supporters and activists.

4. The tone of the online campaign—nasty, brutish and misleading?

Assessing the benefits of Internet campaigning and looking for mobilisation effects have been consistent themes of election reporting over the past 20 years. However, increasingly, since 2016, there have been growing concerns about the supposed detrimental impact of social media in the political sphere (Chadwick and Vaccari, 2019). Leading platforms have repeatedly been accused of coarsening, destabilising and polarising debate, through allowing the proliferation of personalised abuse, disinformation and even facilitating foreign interference in democratic elections (Howard and Bradshaw, 2018). Hence, given the stalemate around Brexit, there were considerable fears of this kind going into the 2019 campaign.

4.1 Social media abuse

Since 2015, several studies have charted the apparent growth of abuse of MPs via social media and the targeting of individual representatives primarily on gender and race grounds (Southern and Harmer, 2019; Ward and McLoughlin, 2020). In the immediate run-up to the election, several prominent politicians (mainly women) highlighted abuse as influencing their decision to stand down, citing Jo Cox's murder as an example of what could happen. During the campaign, the level of abusive tweets aimed at candidates ranged from 2% to as high as 4.5% of all the material they received. Although slightly higher than the 2017 election, it was comparable with previous studies of abusive tweets sent to MPs (Gorrell *et al.*, 2020; Margetts *et al.*, 2019). The targets for such attacks were widespread, with around 36% of the candidates in one study receiving abuse (Margetts *et al.*, 2019). A smaller number of higher-profile figures, especially leaders, seem to have accounted for a significant volume of this abuse. Whilst male candidates received a slightly higher percentage of vitriol, female counterparts were targeted with a different kind of often sexist abuse (Southern and Harmer, 2019).

Conservative candidates received more abuse during the campaign, but in the immediate aftermath of the result, abuse of defeated Labour candidates peaked (Gorrell *et al.*, 2020). Indeed, overall abuse seems to have peaked on election day itself, where beforehand spikes in such behaviour were closely linked to mainstream media events: the televised leaders' debates fuelled the most vitriolic comments (Margetts *et al.*, 2019). Nearly all the trends identified in 2019 are a continuation of patterns witnessed over the previous parliamentary term. It is difficult to know whether social media abuse spills over into offline abuse or attacks as information is sparse. One small study indicated that candidates were reporting widespread trolling and even violent threats. A significant majority thought that the situation had become nastier in 2019 than during previous campaigns (Singh, 2020). However, the National Police Chiefs' Council has indicated that no physical assaults on candidates were reported. Whilst most reports of threatening behaviour towards candidates came via malicious (on and offline) communications, very few met the threshold for prosecution (NPCC, 2019).

4.2 Disinformation and misinformation

Social media has often been held responsible for rising levels of political misinformation. Concerns centre on the lax regulatory climate where the so-called 'dark ads' can be targeted at voters without scrutiny and transparency about who produces and pays for them (see Dommett and Bekir chapter, this volume); fears of manipulation involving foreign states intent on destabilising Western democracies; and the creation of sophisticated so-called 'deep-fakes' and the spread of malicious information via so-called bots (Kaminska *et al.*, 2017). Whilst plenty of misinformation circulated throughout the election, the extent, source and impact of this misinformation have been contested.

Most independent fact check studies found that it was parties themselves, rather than foreign states, who were the main source of online misinformation circulating during the campaign (Hollowood and D'Ancona, 2019; Skopeliti and Morrish, 2019). These ranged from blatant attention-grabbing tactics to the manipulation of local newspaper sources or data. The former included the crude rebranding of the Conservative Twitter feed as a supposedly neutral FactCheck UK site during the first leaders' debate and the video manipulation of an interview with Keir Starmer about Labour's Brexit policy. Both were not only heavily lambasted but also widely shared.

Although various parties provided misleading information, the Conservatives were often seen as the main offenders. One startling headline had the Party responsible for 88% of misleading online content and Labour none. Somewhat ironically this claim, which went viral, was also misleading. The figure was based on only one week from the campaign, rather than the entire election, and corresponded with an upsurge in Conservative Facebook campaigning (Lee, 2019). Moreover, the report was subsequently revised to show a small number of Labour adverts that were also misleading. Aside from parties, other online groups and websites created several false political stories that attracted mainstream media attention. One of the most bizarre to go viral was related to Jo Swinson's supposed predilection for attacking squirrels that appeared to originate from the *Daily Mirror* before spreading rapidly on social media (Kwan, 2019). Despite its ludicrous nature, Swinson had to repeatedly deny the story.

Whilst social media sources were blamed for purveying misleading information, traditional party literature (leaflets, posters and manifestos) was similarly culpable with television not far behind according to one study (Hollowood and D'Ancona, 2019). Indeed, in some instances, online platforms fact-checked mainstream media claims. When Robert Peston and Laura Kuenssberg both reported that Health Secretary Matt Hancock's aide had been punched by a Labour activist outside Leeds General Infirmary, video footage circulated online clearly showed that the alleged incident was accidental. Hancock had been visiting because a child had been pictured lying on the hospital's floor due to a reported bed shortage, with this story becoming the focus of further controversy when 'a friend' of a nurse suggested that the photograph was a set-up. The claim, which widely shared on social media, was refuted by the *Yorkshire Post* as fake news. Away from this most fears about deep-fakes and foreign interference appear misplaced. That said, documents from the Reddit platform used by Labour to highlight a potential future NHS deal with the Trump administration were later shown to have had a Russian source (Satariano and Tsang, 2019).

Whether misleading information made much direct impression on voters is questionable. However, the examples above are illustrative of the wider issue: first, they underscore the hybrid nature of the media ecosystem and relationship between social media and mainstream media (Chadwick and Vaccari, 2019); secondly, they highlight the difficulties of containing false information once it has gone viral; moreover, how this can impact on the campaign agenda even if the story is subsequently discredited; and finally, even if individual stories make a little impact themselves, there may be a longer-term consequence through a corrosion of trust across all media sources.

5. The impact of media in the campaign: two electorates?

Assessing the impact of campaigning on voters is increasingly difficult in a highly fragmented media environment, despite the myriad of metrics and big data. As already noted, digital material is now integral to mainstream campaigning and heavily intertwined with other news sources. At the time of writing, there is little specific data on the impact of the media on voters in 2019. Nevertheless, one study of news consumption during the campaign, by the Reuters Institute, offers some useful insights (Fletcher *et al.*, 2020). Whilst online media were the most popular platforms, voters' largest sources of news are still the BBC and then sites related to traditional newspapers (*Daily Mail, The Sun* and *The Guardian*). In general, non-partisan broadcast sites are still the most popular. Perhaps more strikingly, in terms of digital engagement, voters spent just 16 minutes a week or 3% of their total Internet time on online news. Moreover, news consumption decreased over the campaign. The consumption spiked at the outset and again after voting closed to access results and analysis. During this time, the most popular online news stories were not primarily election-related. They included Prince Andrew, flooding and the terrorist attack in London that resulted in the deaths of two young people. Whilst voters did not ignore the election, there was perhaps unsurprisingly diminished enthusiasm for it given months of Brexit coverage. Nor was there much evidence of online echo-chambers or selective exposure, given the limited engagement primarily spent on non-partisan media sites or on a mix of sources (Fletcher *et al.*, 2020).

The Reuters study highlighted an increasing age divide, whereby older voters (aged 35–65 years) spend more time with television, particularly the BBC, and legacy media sites. Younger voters still use these sources but to a considerably lesser degree. Again, lack of engagement is perhaps the most notable result: those aged 18–34 years spent just eight minutes per week accessing online news source, around a third of the time spent by older voters. However, as the study acknowledges, voters over 65 years are not included, and the division in usage by age is likely to be even greater (Fletcher *et al.*, 2020). Overall, therefore, the focus on misinformation, interference and polarisation may be misplaced. Perhaps more attention needs to be placed on information and engagement gaps, and the potentially accelerating divides between the minority of politically attentive citizens and the wider electorate. Whilst these divides are not necessarily new, the social media era risks them being accelerated and further entrenched.

6. Conclusion

The increasingly digitalised media landscape has impacted on politics as it has on all aspects of public life. Elections are now self-evidently conducted online and offline with broadcasters and newspapers continuing to have reach in terms of their healthy, if declining, audiences. Despite the fragmented information environment, legacy media still matter because older people—more likely to vote than their younger counterparts—consume traditional forms of news. Digital platforms continue to grow and are now as integral to campaigning as they are to journalism. The notion of a distinct so-called 'internet election' is redundant; the 2019 campaign experienced flows of information between online, social and traditional news media, and vice-versa. Hard copy sales of national newspapers may have declined by a quarter since 2017's election but they continue to influence the wider news agenda. This is self-evident in the way major news broadcasters' routinely incorporate press reviews in their formats, and in turn this reflects how print continues to shape debate editorially as well as on air.

In 2019, partisan newspapers were more single-minded in supporting the Conservatives and aggressively denouncing Labour than they had been in any election for over a generation. Leaving the EU also provided the ideal topic on which they could proselytise, and here sloganeering tended to substitute for analysis. Labour did well to promote health as a campaigning issue. But non-electoral news, as well as Brexit, crowded out earnest debate of other subjects that might have potentially given Jeremy Corbyn the kind of impetus he experienced campaigning against Theresa May in 2017. Boris Johnson proved a more resilient opponent, with the Conservatives' promotional strategy remorselessly championing his 'Get Brexit Done' mantra. Even though Labour succumbed to a fourth electoral defeat, its digital campaign may ultimately have been most successful in ensuring that it, and it alone, remains the major alternative party of government. From a media perspective, however, the 2024 election remains quite a long time away and much may change before then.

References

Bridge, M. and Kenber, B. (2019, 14 December) 'How Social Media Gave Labour False Hope', *The Times*, accessed at https://www.thetimes.co.uk/article/election-2019-result-how-social-media-gave-labour-false-hope-5whzhnt3s on 30 March 2020.

Chadwick, A., Vaccari, C. and O'Loughlin, B. (2018) 'Do Tabloids Poison the Well of Social Media? Explaining Democratically Dysfunctional News Sharing', *New Media & Society*, **20**, 4255–4274.

Chadwick, A. and Vaccari, C. (2019) *News Sharing on UK Social Media: Misinformation, Disinformation, and Correction*, Loughborough, Loughborough University.

Charles, A. (2019, 14 November) 'When It Comes to Social Media, Might the Tories Beat Labour at their own Game?', *The Conversation*, accessed at http://theconversation.com/uk-election-2019-when-it-comes-to-social-media-might-the-tories-beat-labour-at-their-own-game-127037 on 30 March 2020.

Cushion, S., Kilby, A., Thomas, R., Morani, M. and Sambrook, R. (2018) 'Newspapers, Impartiality and Television News', *Journalism Studies*, **19**, 162–181.

Deacon, D., Smith, D., Wring, D., Goode, J., Vaccari, C. and Downey, J. (2019) 'News Media Coverage of the 2019 General Election', Report 5, Loughborough, Centre for Research in Communication and Culture, accessed at https://www.lboro.ac.uk/news-events/general-election/report-5/ on 24 April 2020.

Deacon, D. and Wring, D. (2002) 'Partisan Dealignment and the British Press'. In Bartle, J., Crewe, I. and Gosschalk, B. (eds.) *Political Communications: The British General Election of 2001*, London, Frank Cass, pp. 197–211.

Deacon, D., Wring, D., Smith, D. and Vaccari, C. (2020) 'Here, There, and Everywhere? Brexit and Mainstream News Coverage during the 2019 General Election'. In Mair, J., Clark, T., Fowler, N., Snoddy, R. and Tair, R. (eds.) *Boris, Brexit and the Media*, Suffolk, Abramis, pp.27–35.

Duncan, P., Pegg, D. and McIntyre, N. (2019, 12 November) 'UK Election: Which Parties Are Winning the Online War for Cash, Ads and Votes', *The Guardian*, accessed at https://www.theguardian.com/politics/2019/nov/12/uk-election-parties-winning-online-war-ads-cash-votes-digital-dashboard on 29 March 2020.

Fletcher, R., Newman, N. and Schulz, A. (2020) *A Mile Wide, Inch Deep: Online News and Media Use in the 2019 General Election*, Oxford, Reuters Institute.

Gorrell, G., Bakir, M. E., Roberts, I., Greenwood, M. A. and Bontcheva, K. (2020) 'Online Abuse Toward Candidates During the UK General Election 2019', arXiv preprint arXiv: 2001.08686.

Hollowood, E. and D'Ancona, M. (2019, 11 December) 'Big little lies', *Tortoise Media*, accessed at https://members.tortoisemedia.com/2019/12/11/lies-191211/content.html on 30 March 2020.

Howard, P. N. and Bradshaw, S. (2018) 'The Global Organization of Social Media Disinformation Campaigns', *Journal of International Affairs*, **71**, 23–32.

Kaminska, M., Gallagher, J., Kollanyi, B. and Howard, P. N. (2017, 31 May) 'Junk News and Bots During the 2017 UK General Election: What Are UK Voters Sharing over Twitter?', Oxford Internet Institute, accessed at https://blogs.oii.ox.ac.uk/wp-content/uploads/sites/89/2017/06/Junk-News-and-Bots-during-the-2017-UK-General-Election.pdf on 31 March 2020.

Kwan, V. (2019, 3 December) 'Responsible Reporting on Disinformation: Lessons from the UK Election So Far', *First Draft*, accessed at https://firstdraftnews.org/latest/responsible-reporting-on-disinformation-lessons-from-crosscheck-uk/ on 31 March 2020.

Labour Party (2019, 11 December) 'Labour Runs the Most Successful Social Media Campaign Ever Seen', accessed at https://labour.org.uk/press/labour-runs-most-successful-election-social-media-campaign-ever-seen/ on 31 March 2020.

LBC (2019, 29 November) 'Boris Johnson Grilled by a Single Mother and a Nurse During LBC Phone-in', accessed at https://www.lbc.co.uk/radio/presenters/nick-ferrari/boris-johnson-grilled-single-mother-nurse/ on 2 May 2020.

Lee, G. (2019, 17 December) 'Did a Report Really Find 0% of Labour Ads Misleading?', accessed at https://www.channel4.com/news/factcheck/factcheck-did-a-report-really-find-0-of-labour-ads-misleading on 28 March 2020.

Margetts, H., Vidgen, B. and Hale, S. (2019) 'Online Hate and the "Nasty" Election'. In Jackson, D., Thorsen E., Lilleker, D. and Wiedhase, N. (eds.) *UK Election Analysis 2019: Media, Voters and the Campaign*, Bournemouth, Centre for Comparative Politics and Media Research, pp. 16–17.

Mirvis, E. (2019, 25 November) 'What Will Become of Jews in Britain Is Labour form the Next Government?', *The Times*, accessed at https://www.thetimes.co.uk/article/ephraim-mirvis-what-will-become-of-jews-in-britain-if-labour-forms-the-next-government-ghpsdbljk on 10 April 2020.

Morgan, P. (2019, 12 December) @piers.morgan, accessed at https://twitter.com/piersmorgan/status/1205247925753913345? lang=en on 31 March 2020.

National Police Chiefs Council (NPCC) (2019, 11 December) 'General Election: Police Forces Have Had Direct Contact with 70 Per cent of Election Candidates about Their Security', accessed at https://news.npcc.police.uk/releases/general-election-police-receive-198-reports-related-to-candidate-safety on 31 March 2020.

Oborne, P. (2019, 3 December) 'In Its Election Coverage, the BBC Has Let Down the People Who Believe in It', *The Guardian*, accessed at https://www.theguardian.com/commentisfree/2019/dec/03/election-coverage-bbc-tories on 10 April 2020.

Owen, J. (2019, 5 December) 'Tories Winning the Social Media Battle for Hearts and Minds', *PR Week*, accessed at https://www.prweek.com/article/1667859/exclusive-tories-winning-social-media-battle-hearts-minds on 30 March 2020.

Press Gazette (2017, 27 September) 'Jeremy Corbyn Goads Daily Mail Editor Paul Dacre Saying British People Saw Through Paper's 14-Page Attack on Labour', accessed at https://www.pressgazette.co.uk/jeremy-corbyn-goads-daily-mail-editor-paul-dacre-saying-british-people-saw-through-papers-14-page-attack-on-labour/ on 11 May 2020.

Ramley, Z., Rossiter, L. and Harris, M. (2019) *EU Elections: How the Brexit Party Won the Online Battle in the UK*, London, 89Up.org.

Satariano, A. and Tsang, A., (2019, 10 December) 'Who's Spreading Disinformation in U.K. Election? You Might Be Surprised', *The New York Times*, accessed at https://www.

nytimes.com/2019/12/10/world/europe/elections-disinformation-social-media.html on 30 March 2020.

Scott, K. (2019, 5 December) 'Corbyn's Winning the Social Media General Election', *Vuelio Blog*, accessed at https://www.vuelio.com/uk/blog/corbyns-winning-the-social-media-general-election/ on 30 March 2020.

Sharma, R. (2019, 22 November) 'Labour Is Winning the Social Media War This Election – But It's Much Closer Than in 2017', *The i* accessed at. https://inews.co.uk/news/general-election-2019-labour-campaign-social-media-tories-last-vote-1320368 on 29 March 2020.

Sheridan, D. (2019, 9 December) '"It Was Chaos": Shocking Photo Shows Leeds Four-year-old with Suspected Pneumonia Forced to Sleep on Floor of LGI due to Lack of Beds', *Yorkshire Evening Post*, accessed at https://www.yorkshireeveningpost.co.uk/news/people/it-was-chaos-shocking-photo-shows-leeds-four-year-old-suspected-pneumonia-forced-sleep-floor-lgi-due-lack-beds-1334909 on 10 April 2020.

Singh, A. (2020, 2 February) 'Politicians Report "Nastier" Election Including Death Threats, Street Harassment and Abuse', *Huffington Post*, accessed at https://www.huffingtonpost.co.uk/entry/election-candidates-abuse-survey-racism-threats_uk_5e39a3aec5b6ed0033ad5aa9 on 30 March 2020.

Skopeliti, C. and Morrish, L. (2019, 14 December) 'High-level Disinformation and False Polling Reports in the Final Week', *First Draft*, accessed at https://firstdraftnews.org/latest/uk-general-election-2019-round-up-voting-day/ on 29 March 2020.

Smith, M. (2019, 20 November) 'Has Familiarity with Jo Swinson Bred Contempt?', YouGov, https://yougov.co.uk/topics/politics/articles-reports/2019/11/20/has-familiarity-jo-swinson-bred-contempt on 10 April 2020.

Southern, R. and Harmer, E. (2019) 'Twitter, Incivility and "Everyday" Gendered Othering: An Analysis of Tweets Sent to UK Members of Parliament', *Social Science Computer Review*, **35**, 1–17.

Stokel-Walker, C. (2019, 23 October) '"They're Doing This Badly on Purpose": Why the Tories' Latest Online Ads Look So Ugly. Welcome to the Era of Political Shitposting', *New Statesman*.

Walsh, M. (2019a, 5 November) 'UK Election 2019: Here's How the Parties' Social Media Campaigns Have Fared So Far', *The Conversation*, accessed at https://theconversation.com/uk-election-2019-heres-how-the-parties-social-media-campaigns-have-fared-so-far-126444 on 29 March 2020.

Ward, S. and McLoughlin, L. (2020) 'Turds, Traitors and Tossers: The Abuse of UK MPs via Twitter', *The Journal of Legislative Studies*, **26**, 47–73.

Waterson, J. (2019, 23 October) 'Tories Hire Facebook Propaganda Pair to Run Online Election Campaign', *The Guardian*.

Wring, D. and Deacon, D. (2019) 'The Final Verdict: Patterns of Press Partisanship'. In Jackson D., Thorsen E., Lilleker, D. and Weidhase, N. (eds.) *UK Election Analysis 2019: Media, Voters and the Campaign*, Bournemouth, Centre for Comparative Politics and Media Research, pp. 104–105.

JONATHAN TONGE, STUART WILKS-HEEG AND LOUISE THOMPSON*

Conclusion: The BBC and the Election: Boris, Brexit and Corbyn

The decisive victory for the Conservatives at the 2019 general election had three core explanations. First, the election of Boris Johnson as party leader instantly improved the Conservatives' prospects. Secondly and strongly related, decisiveness on Brexit delivered seats for the party in places previously unimaginable, as Labour's so-called 'red wall' of previously solid seats in northern England, the Midlands, and north Wales tumbled apace. Thirdly, Labour's inability to ditch a leader who some within the party and many beyond viewed as unelectable presented the prospect of victory to any semi-competent Conservative campaign.

1. The 'Boris bounce'

The Conservatives' 'Get Brexit Done' slogan was a thing of genius for a public exasperated by three-and-a-half years of wrangling since June 2016. Whatever its glibness, the appeal to bring an end to seemingly interminable political turmoil resonated with an aggravated electorate. Johnson was chosen as leader by his party in the summer of 2019 on the grounds he was a winner with charisma—the antithesis of his predecessor. Two wins in London mayoral contests indicated his status as an electoral asset and, even allowing for the unusual circumstances of the 2019 contest, his achievement in securing an 80-seat majority was impressive. No government holding office for so long had ever put on seats at an election. Johnson assisted the Conservative 'feel-good' factor. Most (72%) said they were voting positively in favour of their party, its leader and policies than negatively (23%) against what the 'other side' was offering (Ashcroft, 2020, p. 10).

Johnson recognised the need for clarity on the delivery of Brexit. As James Dennison's contribution has shown, the message from the 2019 European Parliament elections, at the denouement of Theresa May's unfortunate leadership

*Jonathan Tonge, Department of Politics, University of Liverpool; j.tonge@liverpool.ac.uk; Stuart Wilks-Heeg, Department of Politics, University of Liverpool, swilks@liverpool.ac.uk; Louise Thompson, Politics, School of Social Sciences, University of Manchester, louise.thompson-4@manchester.ac.uk

doi:10.1093/pa/gsaa034

of the Conservatives, could hardly have been starker. Nigel Farage's Brexit Party swept to victory with 30.5% of the vote, almost 11% more than the second-placed Liberal Democrats, winning 29 seats in a parliament of which it wanted no part. Significantly, the Brexit Party won the most seats in every constituency in England and Wales except London and obtained the support of 75% of Leave identifiers—compared to only 9% backing the Conservatives (Fieldhouse *et al.*, 2020). The Conservatives' overall performance, obtaining only 8.8% of the UK vote, was the party's worst in any national election, ever. With the Brexit Party threatening to become the major force of Leave, the Conservatives' natural territory, there were obvious risks for the governing party. Whilst European elections had long been notoriously unrepresentative of what happened at a subsequent general election, failure to resolve the Brexit issue posed an obvious danger for the Conservatives, even allowing for the inadequacies of Corbyn's Labour.

With Theresa May departing as Prime Minister after the European election debacle, Boris Johnson looked to break the Brexit deadlock in the autumn. He was determined to end the parliamentary—'no Brexit option is acceptable'—stalemate. The first move was to quickly reach an arrangement with the Taoiseach, Leo Varadkar, to keep the border in Ireland seamless. This involved Johnson unceremoniously dumping the Conservatives' parliamentary allies, the Democratic Unionist Party (DUP), who Johnson had wooed only the previous year but now found surplus to requirements. The short-term difficulty was that the DUP, fearing that Johnson's Brexit marginalised Northern Ireland's place in the UK by aligning it uniquely close to the European Union (EU), now joined the vast ranks of MPs prepared to vote against Brexit in the Commons, accentuating the stalemate. To break the impasse, a winter election became inevitable.

2. Brexit

'Getting Brexit Done' meant 'Getting Leave Voters' for the Conservatives. Johnson's emphasis upon Brexit delivery staunched the flow of Leave votes to the Brexit Party and marginalised Farage. The huge lead for the Conservatives amongst 2016 Leave voters—more than four times as likely to vote for Boris Johnson's party compared to Jeremy Corbyn's—made an enormous contribution to their 2019 triumph. Labour's lead amongst 2016 Remain voters was substantial, but the Conservatives had a much bigger lead in a slightly bigger pool of voters, those who had voted Leave in the Brexit referendum. A more modest lead for Labour amongst a minority of 2016 voters was not going to suffice.

Labour was, of course, hampered in that there were more parties fishing in the Remain waters but the party's failure to achieve even an overall majority of Remain voters (47%) was a damning indictment of the party's obfuscations (Ashcroft, 2020). Only just over half (52%) of those who voted Leave in 2016 and

Labour in 2017 stayed Labour in 2019, whereas the Conservatives retained 92% of their 2017 voters who had opted for Leave in 2016 (YouGov, 2019b). Labour also struggled to hold the votes of those on the other side of the Brexit divide, 16% of its Remain voters deserting the party between the two subsequent elections (Kellner, 2019).

The regular portrayal of 'Labour Leave' seats, full of Brexiteers feeling betrayed by a Remain-leaning Labour Party needs some nuance. That type of Labour Leave voter was most certainly present, particularly in the constituencies which fell to the Conservatives in 2019 (the Conservatives gained 28 seats with a Leave vote of more than 60%) but within those seats, Labour voters were more likely to have voted Remain than Conservative voters. Nonetheless, as John Curtice noted in this volume, there were particularly large swings from Labour to the Conservatives in strongly Leave-voting seats, those where more than 60% opted in 2016 to quit the EU. There was an average 9.3% swing from Labour to Conservative in such Labour-held seats and 7.5% in Conservative-held constituencies. These were swings way above the average Labour to Conservative swing of 4.7 points. Such extensively Leave seats were not rare either, amounting to 26% of the ones Labour was trying (often vainly) to defend and 29% of those the Conservatives were (comfortably) holding. Large parts of the electoral map turned blue and the existing blue deepened. Moreover, the Brexit damage for Labour in Leave seats was not confined to England. As Jonathan Bradbury observed, all of Labour's six losses in Wales came in pro-Brexit constituencies.

Labour's obfuscations and implausibility on Brexit made it impossible for the party to seize the initiative on the issue. The Conservatives were equally divided in some respects—a Cabinet split, a parliamentary party that was pro-EU, and a membership pro-Brexit. Those divisions were, eventually, cast asunder by a new leader with a decisive policy of at least achieving EU withdrawal, even if the post-EU trading terms were anything but apparent. Action first, details later, played well with a bored and frustrated electorate. Meanwhile, Labour, having opposed a variety of options in parliament, had developed a policy which stretched credulity. The party would miraculously negotiate a better withdrawal deal with the EU and put this to the people in a second referendum. Voters would be offered a choice between a 'credible Leave' option versus Remain. The obvious question begged was whether Labour would campaign against the decent Leave deal it had just negotiated. Given the pro-Remain sentiments of the bulk of Labour MPs and members that seemed likely, so the scenario would be a referendum with the leadership likely to oppose the fruits of its negotiating efforts.

Corbyn and his supporters might complain legitimately that the problem for Labour on Brexit was created internally mainly by those in the centre and on the right of the party, whose anti-Brexit sentiments prevented acceptance of the 2016 verdict. Corbyn might personally have accepted the referendum result without much demur. Given his status as a lifelong EU sceptic, Corbyn's assertion that he voted Remain had always been an eyebrow-raiser. In the aftermath of the result, he called for Article 50 to be triggered immediately, to commence the withdrawal process. Left to his own devices, there seems little doubt that Corbyn would have readily acquiesced in the people's verdict and backed a 'Lexit' based upon workers' rights and socialism within an independent United Kingdom. Given his commitment to internal Labour democracy, however, Corbyn could not simply ignore the many party voices wanting a second referendum. When Keir Starmer added to the text of his pre-circulated party conference address in Liverpool in 2018, to call for a second referendum in which 'nobody is ruling out Remain as an option', he won a standing ovation from many of those assembled. Labour's course was effectively set: a slow retreat from acceptance of the Leave vote. The constructive ambiguities associated with that retreat were to prove expensive as Labour's 'red wall' of pro-Brexit seats fell in big numbers to the Conservatives in 2019. Blyth Valley, Leigh, Sedgefield, and Workington had been Labour-held for more than 80 years. Whatever the electoral damage wrought by the creep from Brexit, Starmer's alignment with much of his party was personally rewarded. His election as Labour leader in April 2020 was convincing, as he achieved overall majority backing within each section of the party.

3. The Corbyn factor

According to Ashcroft's (2020, p. 7) survey of more than 10,000 voters, Jeremy Corbyn's status as 'not an appealing leader' was an even bigger explanation (just) of the election result than Brexit. The unappealing prospect of a Corbyn-led Labour government made a comfortable election victory possible for any Conservative leader capable of running a competent campaign. More than half of Labour defectors gave not wanting Corbyn as Prime Minister as their primary reason for desertion (Ashcroft, 2020, p. 8).

The 2019 election outcome thus truly exposed the haplessness of Theresa May's 2017 campaign and it is plausible, if obviously speculative, to contend that her continuation as Conservative leader might have again denied her party an overall majority. May's resignation on 7 June 2019, after the nadir of the European elections, marked the beginning of the end for Corbyn. Her inability to deliver for the Conservatives had succeeded in partially masking Corbyn's unpopularity. As Sam Power, Tim Bale, and Paul Webb noted in their contribution, remarkably, the rating gap between May and Corbyn even disappeared entirely for a short time. Johnson's elevation left the Labour leader far more exposed. Whilst aspects of Corbynism remained popular, such as state ownership of the railways, few saw the Labour leader as a credible future Prime Minister. As David Denver highlighted in the opening results section, Corbyn's net rating for the first half of the election year was abysmal, at −57 but this dreadful score perhaps looked a little less hideous when the −37 average for Mrs May was considered. Come autumn and the advent of Johnson's premiership, Corbyn fell to a −60 negative rating, the worst in British political history. Whilst Johnson's honeymoon period was hardly marked by polling glories as he pursued the election campaign with a −20 negative rating, it was at least a sizeable improvement upon May. Corbyn's figure remained worse than that endured by May, at −44. Put simply, Corbyn was the most unpopular leader of a major party ever. The fears of swathes of Labour's parliamentary party that Corbyn was unelectable proved entirely justified. Most stayed put nonetheless to await their fate, which in most cases was at least a happier one than those who defected to the short-lived Change UK. As James Dennison showed, this was little more than an ill-conceived, leaking holding company for a disparate and increasingly desperate assortment of MPs, all decisively rejected at the election.

Corbyn was up against it, given the damning press verdicts upon him, which as Dominic Wring and Stephen Ward note, were as partisan as anything previously experienced in what is often brutal election coverage. As those two contributors observe, Labour more broadly had a tough task in selling Corbyn's message. Only the *Daily Mirror* offered the party wholehearted support, with the Conservatives backed by 72% of the press, based upon circulation, compared to Labour's 13%. This begs the age-old question of whether newspapers mainly lead or reflect public opinion. There is also the issue of whether newspapers still matter. The parties seem to think so. Justin Fisher's analysis of campaign expenditure indicated that they spent slightly more on print than digital advertising, with the big two parties, according to the analysis of Katharine Dommett and Mehmet Emin Bakir, spending similar amounts on Facebook and Google advertising. As Fisher notes, Facebook's 'incubation period' for adverts, to allow checking, diminished its capacity for rapid rebuttal. He also notes how Corbyn and Labour were also confronted by the much bigger financial firepower provided for the Conservatives, which no election expenditure regulatory framework can entirely ameliorate or equalise. During the campaign, the Conservatives raised over £19 million and Labour £5.4 million.

Corbyn's aspiration was to turn Labour into a transformative social movement. Yet many of its members and certainly the outriders on the left, in Momentum, were incapable of connecting with the population beyond the 500,000 strong party membership, to deliver any such prospect (Fielding, 2019). Far from developing a movement-based alternative, factionalism and an inability to operate as a credible potential alternative government—the key task of opposition—meant that Labour struggled to function as a political party. Rather than building a strong movement, Labour struggled to retain its supporters between elections far more than the Conservatives. Whilst northern cities remained loyal to Labour, this effectively meant the party was 'wasting' many more votes than the Conservatives in piling up huge majorities. Exit the cities for the towns and suburbs and it was soon possible to leave 'Labourland'.

Whilst there were other issues of more pervasive salience, Corbyn's apparent incapacity to root out anti-Semitism bedevilled his leadership, as shown by Eunice Goes. It demonstrated an inability to decisively address awkward issues requiring authoritative action. To Brexit and anti-Semitism might be added Scotland, where Scottish Labour and the Corbyn–McDonnell London Labour leadership were not always at ease. In Scotland, Labour struggled to locate itself on a political axis shaped by nationalism versus unionism. This was perhaps understandable and was a problem which preceded Corbyn. However, the difficulties appeared to be exacerbated when the Shadow Chancellor, John McDonnell, astonished Labour's Scottish leader, Richard Leonard, in announcing, in August 2019, that Labour should allow a second independence referendum if the Scottish Parliament voted for one (*The Guardian*, 2019). McDonnell's concession was in direct contravention of Labour Party policy. Although Labour is obviously 'small u' unionist, it is not defined by it to anywhere near the extent of the Conservatives. The result was that the party of nationalism, the Scottish National Party (SNP) won 48 of the 59 seats and the party of unionism, the Conservatives, came second, albeit distantly and with losses, with six. Labour managed to hold a solitary seat. Nine years previously, the party held 41.

The extent of Labour's problems under Corbyn was highlighted by Ashcroft's (2020) finding that 85% of voters said they would have voted the same way had Brexit not been an issue. Most Leave voters had already decided they disliked the Labour leader anyway (Sandvoss, 2019). That had been priced in ever since the 2017 contest. Of course, it could be observed that the 15% who might have changed their vote *sans* Brexit was the difference between election victory and defeat. Believers in the Corbyn project might argue that, without Brexit as the dominant election issue, Labour would have at least gone close. Such a narrative might also point to Labour's better-than-expected performance at the 2017 election, which deprived the Conservatives of a majority. Yet these arguments appear thin given how Labour trailed the Conservatives by 55 seats in 2017 despite the haplessness of Theresa May's campaign.

As Eunice Goes has highlighted, Labour's 2019 campaign pledged even more money than the 2017 offering. The 'Advent calendar' approach unveiled expensive spending pledges daily, at a time when Labour's capacity for fiscal responsibility remained unproven amongst the electorate. Labour's extensive 107-page manifesto contained expensive spending pledges on the majority of the first 80 pages, before it turned to constitutional issues, Brexit and internationalism (Labour Party, 2019). Yet the party began the campaign with only 15% of voters thinking its spending plans affordable (Smith, 2019). The manifesto was more explicitly socialist than the 2017 version. In addition to increased taxation of individual high earners, the plans indicated that the UK would raise more in corporation tax than any other G7 country (Institute for Fiscal Studies, 2019). Corbyn's UK would be the land of the free. Free broadband, university tuition, prescriptions, and TV licences for the elderly were all part of the prospectus.

The Conservatives' own manifesto offering, at a mere 64 pages, was more minimalist but did contain expensive promises on the NHS, to diminish Labour's seemingly permanent advantage on this territory and see off the ritual allegations of being pro-privatisation. The Conservatives' proposals almost matched those offered by Corbyn's party, the pledge of a 3.4% NHS spending increase bettering even the 3% extra offered by Labour in its fabled 'longest suicide note in history' 1983 manifesto. Johnson declared the NHS as his number one priority, in the immediate aftermath of the election. The veracity of this claim was tested within three months, as the nation was engulfed by a pandemic and the government struggled to cope. Schools and infrastructure accounted for other planned expenditure increases, framed by Johnson as core elements of his 'levelling-up' agenda, but were accompanied by promises not to raise the rates of income tax or VAT (Conservative Party, 2019). Asked 'which political party would be the best at handling the economy?', voters consistently preferred the Conservatives throughout the campaign, the lead never less than 15%, with Labour favoured by only one-in-four respondents (YouGov, 2020).

Yet many economic aspects of Corbynism involving a greater role for the state were popular. YouGov (2019*a*) reported majority support for the following policies: increasing income tax for those earning more than £80,000 per year (60%); nationalising the railways (56%); and wealth taxes (53%) whilst far more electors favoured nationalising the water, gas, and electricity companies than opposed the idea. Whilst Corbyn's post-assertion claim that Labour had 'won the arguments' was understandably widely derided amid the party's crushing defeat, the contention was perhaps not as absurd as it first appeared. The Conservatives had clearly learnt lessons from the 2017 election, when Labour's promise to end austerity had helped it win over voters who no longer wanted to be told there was 'no magic money tree'. By 2019, the Conservatives had declared that austerity was over and promises of higher spending on the NHS, schools, infrastructure, and policing were central to Johnson's promise to 'unleash Britain's potential'. Nonetheless, the sharp contrast between how the electorate responded to the 2017 and 2019 Labour manifestos is telling. The inescapable conclusion is that, whilst the electorate stood to the left of Johnson's Conservatives economically, there was an abject lack of faith in the capability or competence of a Corbyn administration to deliver its promised mixture of effective state control and redistribution.

4. The future

The Conservative Party won its biggest overall majority since the 102-seat one enjoyed by Margaret Thatcher in 1987. The party won a higher share of the vote than did Tony Blair in the fabled 1997 Labour landslide. Given that 2019 saw the Conservatives increase their share of the vote for the sixth consecutive election, to the highest level since 1983, in securing an overall majority of 80 seats, it amounted to a remarkable victory even allowing for the obvious weaknesses of the opposition. Whilst Labour's bastions in the largest English and Welsh cities remained intact (a metropolitan left more socially liberal, less concerned with immigration, and slightly pro-Remain), there was scant comfort beyond. Every English region and Wales saw a sizeable swing from Labour to the Conservatives.

The Conservatives won a fourth consecutive term with little promise of the fiscal discipline that had characterised their return to power nearly a decade earlier. The new government intended to invest—aka borrow—'£100 billion for infrastructure projects' (Conservative Party, 2019, p. 27). There was much talk of increased spending to reward those poorer northern areas which had eschewed Corbyn's Labour and lent their support to Boris Johnson's party. What to do about these newly Conservative constituencies exercised the initial thoughts of the government before any lingering financial reserve evaporated amid the stringencies of the COVID-19 virus emergency.

Even if the biggest peacetime crisis in anyone's memory subsides at some point—and there is absolutely no guarantee at the time of writing—the Conservative government will evidently no longer have the fiscal room for manoeuvre that might have allowed the financial targeting of northern areas with transport and connectivity infrastructure projects. Concurrently, there will be little money to address perhaps the biggest issue avoided by successive governments, that of social care. The 'dementia tax' criticism aimed at Theresa May, when she (briefly) tried to tackle the issue at the 2017 election, warned her successor off the territory. The lack of financial scope for investment may yet prove problematic because the essence of support for the Conservatives was conditional and based on push and pull factors. It was partly a reward for Conservative clarity on Brexit allied to respect for the Leave vote and also amounted to a clear repudiation of Corbyn as Labour leader but was not necessarily an outright rejection of all economic aspects of Corbynism. The new Conservative voters may desire economic redistribution in their favour. They were also concerned with cultural 'security'. A Conservative programme fusing Brexit and greater control of immigration with the promise of economic rewards appealed to some voters in northern towns for whom the process of detachment from support for Labour had been a long-term event. As Matthew Flinders noted in his contribution, the

2019 election result was partly the outworking of long-term political trends. Brexit may have been the catalyst but did not commence such patterns.

Retention of the 2019 'new Conservatives' is far from assured. It is worth re-membering that only 5,000 votes separate the Conservatives from Labour in the 10 most marginal seats. With Keir Starmer elected as a more feasible Prime Minister-in-waiting, Labour's prospects are far less bleak than the Corbyn years. Four consecutive defeats may concentrate Labour minds, as they did after the 1979–1992 wilderness years. The formation of a shadow cabinet which looks like a potential government, allied to fiscal responsibility, should see a competitive Labour Party. Given the repudiation of Corbyn was not a rejection of many of the economic aspects of Corbynite socialism, there is scope for Starmer to remain radical. The money ploughed into the Conservative government's furlough scheme to protect workers during the COVID-19 crisis made Corbyn's economic proposals look models of fiscal rectitude in comparison. The age of fiscal rules has passed. The future impact of Brexit is uncertain. It is perhaps less a case of Starmer having to force his party to compromise with the electorate and more a need to present to voters a credible team that appears capable of achieving gov-erning competence. That said, it may be difficult to conceive how Starmer—pro-EU, pro-free movement of labour, socially liberal and southern—might handle aspects of the cultural conservatism that characterises sections of Labour's north-ern working-class support. The permanence of the desertion of Labour is now conditional primarily upon Conservative performance. Labour's support amongst the middle-class is now of sufficiently long-standing that it is unlikely to disappear. The recovery of a section of working-class voters provides the key to election victory. Those voters have peeled away over several elections, ever since the heyday of the Blairite cross-class coalition. Some had already deserted Labour for the UK Independence Party in 2015 before supporting the Conservatives.

It is folly to overthink along class lines these days given that, as a modern vot-ing variable, it is the mere embellishment and detail that was once Pulzer's (1967) everything. It is finally, belatedly, time to give the Alford Index[1]—on death row for so long—a quiet burial. It is also time to stop thinking of the working-class as comprising mainly traditional male manual workers, given that a much larger section comprises service employees, many of them women working in low-security delivery, call centre, or cleaning jobs (as examples). This working-class,

---

[1]The Alford Index was commonly used to measure social class when class was the dominant explana-tion of how Britain voted. It was a crude measure by which the proportion of Labour's support amongst the middle-class was deducted from the proportion of the middle-class voting Labour. There were large differentials from the 1940s until the 1970s, when Labour regularly attracted two-thirds of the working-class vote but only around one-fifth of that of the middle-class. The measure has long been criticised for its limited methodological and practical utility, a relic of a long-departed era of two-party class-based politics.

which is also ethnically diverse, may be bereft of the fixed party loyalties of old. Whilst working-class conservatism is hardly new, the age when it was regarded as somehow deviant has long passed. The Conservatives led comfortably in 2019 amongst the working- and middle-class but the advantage is not secured.

In terms of modern variables, age is what matters most. Labour's best hope is to avert the generational effect where voters flip to the Conservatives as they mature in years. Sarah Harrison's contribution shows that 58% of first-time voters and 62% of young (18–24 years old) voters supported Labour in the election but only 30% of those aged 30 years and over made a similar choice. Even that stark age variable brought less comfort for Labour than at the previous contest. Whereas in 2017 the crossover age at which a voter was more likely to vote Conservative than Labour was 47, this fell sharply to 39 in 2019, with almost two-thirds of those aged >65 years voting Conservative (YouGov, 2019*b*). It appeared that the 'young middle-aged', aged 35–54, were most prepared to switch from Labour to the Conservatives (Ipsos MORI, 2019).

If the bark of social class has been quietening for a long while, it is not the only variable on mute. Gender as a voting determinant seems perpetually so. As Emily Harmer and Rosalynd Southern noted, there was (again) only a small aggregate gender gap, with 42% of women voting Conservative compared to 44% of men and 34% of women voting Labour compared to 31% of men. The significance of the 2019 election lay in other gendered aspects. For the first time, a majority of Labour MPs are female but the party's post-election change of leader made it 21 from 21 successes for a male candidate.

Some of the Conservative government's problems lie north of their new unlikely heartlands. Assuming replication in the Scottish Parliament elections, the SNP's advancement of its position will maintain pressure from the First Minister, Nicola Sturgeon, upon Boris Johnson for a Section 30 order, transferring the power for a second independence referendum to Holyrood, ending its reserved status under the Scotland Act. Such a transfer will be resisted and conceivably never conceded, but this will be tricky politics if the SNP tide refuses to go out. The disjuncture between Conservative and SNP positions—and, naturally, their supporters—on defining questions is obviously acute. The Scottish Election Study data cited by James Mitchell and Ailsa Henderson showed this starkly. The Conservatives polled at a mere 1% amongst those electors who support Scottish independence and EU membership (remarkably, the SNP managed to win support from almost one in 10 of those opposed to both independence and EU membership). Whilst the Conservatives can seek solace in the far more abject performance of Scottish Labour, that alone does not resolve anything. Meanwhile, an older constitutional question has not disappeared. In Northern Ireland, the power to call a border poll lies with its Secretary of State, required to hold one under the terms of the Good Friday Agreement if a majority for a united Ireland appears likely. Although constitutional issues will always be to the fore, it seems most unlikely that the current government would initiate such a poll.

In closing, for Labour to win an overall majority at the next election would be remarkable but not impossible. A 100-seat Conservative majority in 1959 was overturned by Labour, under a new leader of a reinvigorated party, by 1964. Starmer needs to emulate Harold Wilson. There is much uncertainty over the political fallout from the COVID-19 virus crisis, with normal political rules suspended—although that was also largely the case during the Brexit saga. A hung parliament, with Labour cutting a deal with other parties, is the minimum Labour aspiration and an indecisive result is highly possible, based on John Curtice's analysis in this volume. As he notes, despite the changes in the geography of party support in 2019, there are still too few seats that are marginal between Labour and the Conservatives for the system to exaggerate the lead of the largest party over the second party to the extent once seen. This, plus the sizeable chunk of other parties in the House of Commons (the SNP will not disappear anytime soon; ditto the Northern Ireland parties), means that a hung parliament is a live prospect. Given that editions of *Britain Votes* have appeared at two-year intervals in recent years, our self-indulgent- and entirely apolitical editorial aspiration—may be that the next dramatic contest might not come until 2024.

References

Ashcroft, L. (2020) 'Diagnosis of Defeat: Labour's Turn to the Smell the Coffee', Lord Ashcroft Polls, accessed at https://lordashcroftpolls.com/wp-content/uploads/2020/02/DIAGNOSIS-OF-DEFEAT-LORD-ASHCROFT-POLLS-1.pdf on 7 April 2020.

Conservative Party (2019) *Get Brexit Done: Unleash Britain's Potential*, London, Conservative Party.

Fieldhouse, E., Green, J., Evans, G., Mellon, J. and Prosser, C. (2020) 'British Election Study Internet Panel Waves 1-19', accessed at https://www.britishelectionstudy.com/data-object/british-election-study-combined-wave-1-19-internet-panel/ on 13 May 2020.

Fielding, S. (2019, 31 July) 'The Myth Behind Corbyn's Plan to Transform Britain', *The Spectator*, accessed at https://www.spectator.co.uk/article/the-myth-behind-corbyn-s-plan-to-transform-britain on 7 April 2020.

Institute for Fiscal Studies (2019, 21 November) 'Labour Manifesto: An Initial Reaction from IFS Researchers', accessed at https://www.ifs.org.uk/election/2019/article/labour-manifesto-an-initial-reaction-from-ifs-researchers on 9 April 2020.

Ipsos MORI (2019, 20 December) 'How Britain Voted in the 2019 Election', accessed at https://www.ipsos.com/ipsos-mori/en-uk/how-britain-voted-2019-election on 25 April 2020.

Kellner, P. (2019, 16 December) 'Five Crucially Important But Frequently Ignored Facts about the 2019 Election', *Prospect*, accessed at https://www.prospectmagazine.co.uk/pol itics/five-crucially-important-but-frequently-ignored-facts-about-the-2019-election-la bour-conservatives-brexit-corbyn-johnson on 8 April 2020.

Labour Party (2019) *It's Time for Real Change: For the Many Not the Few*, Election Manifesto, London, Labour Party.

Pulzer, P. G. J. (1967) *Political Representation and Elections in Britain*, London, Allen & Unwin.

Sandvoss, C. (2019) 'Last Fan Standing: Jeremy Corbyn Supporters in the 2019 General Election'. In Jackson, D., Thorsen, E., Lilleker, D. and Weidhase, N. (eds.) *UK Election Analysis 2019: Media, Voters and the Campaign*, Bournemouth, Centre for Comparative Politics and Media Research, p. 112.

Smith, D. (2019, 10 November) 'Labour Turns on Spending Taps But Voters Fear a New Recession', *The Sunday Times.*

The Guardian (2019, 6 August) 'John McDonnell Open to Second Scottish Independence Vote', accessed at https://www.theguardian.com/politics/2019/aug/06/john-mcdon nell-open-to-second-scottish-independence-vote on 6 April 2020.

YouGov (2019a, 12 November) 'Labour Economic Policies Are Popular, So Why Aren't Labour', accessed at https://yougov.co.uk/topics/politics/articles-reports/2019/11/12/la bour-economic-policies-are-popular-so-why-arent- on 7 April 2020.

YouGov (2019b, 17 December) 'How Britain voted in the 2019 general election', accessed at www.yougov.co.uk/topics/politics/articles-reports/2019/12/17/how-britain-voted-2019-general-election on 14 April 2020.

YouGov (2020, 2 April) 'Which Political Party Would Be the Best at Handling the Economy?', accessed at https://yougov.co.uk/topics/politics/trackers/which-political-party-would-be-the-best-at-handling-the-economy on 8 April 2020.

INDEX